Encyclopedia of Electronic HRM

Encyclopedia of Electronic HRM

Edited by
Tanya Bondarouk and Sandra Fisher

DE GRUYTER

ISBN 978-3-11-099166-6
e-ISBN (PDF) 978-3-11-063370-2
e-ISBN (EPUB) 978-3-11-062998-9

Library of Congress Control Number: 2020939277

Bibliographic information published by the Deutsche Nationalbibliothek
The Deutsche Nationalbibliothek lists this publication in the Deutsche Nationalbibliografie;
detailed bibliographic data are available on the Internet at http://dnb.dnb.de.

Cover image: slavemotion/E+/gettyimages.de
Typesetting: Integra Software Services Pvt. Ltd.
Printing and Binding: CPI books GmbH, Leck

www.degruyter.com

Contents

Part 7: **Serving Different Audiences**

Part 8: **Technical Issues in e-HRM**

Sandra L. Fisher and Tanya Bondarouk

Introduction

We have been working on this project for almost three years, and we are proud to offer the Encyclopedia – a unique book about electronic Human Resource Management. The world does not lack for HRM and technology books, podcasts, videos, and articles. Hundreds of researchers and business leaders produce thousands of knowledge-items about HRM and technology each year. But few dare to build bridges from the past history towards the future. That is the idea of this encyclopedia – with respect for history, grounded in research, connected with practice, but built for questions to guide future inquiries.

The field of electronic human resource management, or e-HRM, has become an important interface between people and technology in organizations. As the importance of digital technologies in the management of people has increased, so has the volume of information available about tools, processes, and theories for doing this more effectively. Our concept for this encyclopedia was to offer a valuable companion for HR researchers, HR executives, PhD candidates and students wanting to find concise definitions, summaries and debates about a plethora of terms within the e-HRM field in one place. This volume includes state-of-the art contributions from leading experts in the field, who also offer their views on the future research directions. You will find here more than one hundred research questions, that each on its own can inspire a new PhD project! While there has been much discussion about the definition of e-HRM and how it differs from related concepts such as human resource information systems (HRIS) and virtual HR (Florkowski, 2018), we treat e-HRM inclusively in this encyclopedia, including a wide range of topics that touch on this use of digital tools to manage people both now and in the future. An earlier encyclopedia (Torres-Corronas & Arias-Olivas, 2008) explicitly tied together HRIS and e-HRM, and this volume strives to provide an updated viewpoint on many of those topics.

Brief History of e-HRM

The field of e-HRM has developed significantly over the past 20 years, becoming a legitimate area of study and practice within broader human resource management. One artifact of this development is the Sierra-Cedar industry survey, now in its 22nd year of tracking organisational-level adoption of HR technologies. Started in 1997 by the Hunter Group as a survey on HR self-service technologies, the survey has grown substantially in both breadth of coverage and number of respondents and has provided researchers and practitioners with an effective gauge of changes in the field.

https://doi.org/10.1515/9783110633702-202

The presence of the international conference on e-HRM is another indication of growth and development in the field. International researchers in e-HRM started a biannual conference series in 2006, allowing researchers to gather in a venue promoting the exchange of the latest research findings in the field, mixing with business leaders and consultants to ensure the connection with practice. Conference locations have included the Netherlands, the United Kingdom, France, Germany, the United States, Italy, and Denmark. The conference started expanding beyond a tight definition of e-HRM to include concepts of digital HRM in 2016, Industry 4.0 in 2018, and digitalized organizations and ecosystems in 2020. We also see many sessions on e-HRM topics at mainstream international conferences in management and I/O psychology, such as the Academy of Management Meetings, the Society for Industrial/Organizational Psychology, and the European Association of Work and Organizational Psychology.

There have been no fewer than ten special issues of peer reviewed journals focusing on e-HRM research in the past 15 years (Bondarouk, Ruël & Parry, 2017), starting with a special issue of *Human Resource Management* on e-HR in 2004. These special issues have addressed topics such as value creation, workforce management, e-HRM in a multinational or cross-national context, and the transformation of the HR function. These special issues have helped to promote the development of an emerging field, placing special attention on publication opportunities for authors in related areas. Similarly, a number of edited books examining e-HRM have been published throughout the years, some as an outgrowth of the international e-HRM conferences (e.g., Bissola & Imperatori, 2019; Bondarouk, Ruël & Parry, 2017) and others as part of a professional book series (e.g., Bondarouk, Ruël, & Looise, 2011; Gueutal & Stone, 2005). These books have helped move the field forward by publishing accessible volumes of recent research, providing detailed information on selected topics. We have also seen publication of textbooks on e-HRM, with Kavanaugh, Thite and Johnson (2012) as an example of an early text blending HRIS and HR practices, and Thite (2018) specifically addressing e-HRM. There has also been development of academic study programs at multiple universities allowing students to focus their studies on this intersection of HRM and technology. And, by 2020, there have been more than twenty PhD projects dedicated to a topic within e-HRM.

With all of these developments, we believed it was time to assemble this encyclopedia to recognize and further promote formalization and institutionalization of the academic field of e-HRM. Many of the contributors to this encyclopedia noted that the science behind application of technology to HRM is lagging behind the practice. This offers great opportunity to researchers to conduct research that will test and evaluate the many ways in which e-HRM is already in use, making recommendations for the effective and ethical application of technology to managing people in organisations.

Interdisciplinary and Diverse

One of our goals with this encyclopedia was to integrate contributions about e-HRM from different disciplines like Information Systems, Computer Sciences, Design Sciences, Decision Science, Organizational Behavior, Human Resource Management, and Industrial/Organizational (Work) Psychology, demonstrating the interdisciplinary nature of the research. This is reflected in the wide range of theories applied, published works cited, and perspectives taken. The 42 different authors of the entries are diverse in other respects as well. Given the practical nature of the topic we have a mix of academic researchers and practitioners represented. The academic researchers are working in schools of business or management, and departments of psychology, economics, industrial engineering, social and political science, management information systems, and business development and technology. The practitioners include both consultants and industry representatives. The authors also represent the global nature of the e-HRM field, with authors from 14 different countries.

Overview of the Entries

There are 47 entries in the encyclopedia. Many of them represent specific systems with which HR professionals or employees might interact, such as recruiting, selection, performance management, talent management, socialization, mentoring, and e-learning. These systems have formed the backbone of e-HRM research and application. Entries in this section address the foundational components of such functional areas and look forward to how such systems are changing to leverage new technologies and support emerging HR needs.

Other entries focus on specific theories underpinning some of the research. These theoretical approaches include institutional theory, resource-based view of the firm, and human computer interaction. Other key theories used in e-HRM research, such as those related to trust, communication, person-organisation fit, and leadership, are described in entries found in other sections of the encyclopedia.

The next section examines organizational level issues in the implementation of e-HRM. Here authors consider the strategic nature of e-HRM and various organizational goals for the use of e-HRM systems. One common framework looks at operational, relational, and transformational outcomes of e-HRM systems, with transformational outcomes generally defined as those of a strategic nature. This has been a key debate in the e-HRM literature since Marler and Fisher (2013) noted there was little empirical evidence that e-HRM makes the HR function more strategic. Factors related to this debate and the overall contribution of e-HRM to organizational functioning are discussed further in this section and will doubtless continue to be an important point of discussion moving forward.

Another group of entries addresses various contexts within which e-HRM is used. This section includes entries on generational differences, emerging economies, the gig economy, and Industry 4.0. These entries examine ways in which the specific context in which the technology is used offers both opportunities and limitations for the application of e-HRM. For example, developments in the online gig economy require development of new ways to manage workers through technology, while Industry 4.0 challenges HRM to increase digitalization and support new characteristics of work.

Entries in the next section address how e-HRM affects work that is performed within the HR function, both what kind of work is performed and how it is accomplished. These entries address shared service centers, the role of employees in HR work and how e-HRM facilitates co-creation, the use of HR metrics in driving and assessing HR practices, and the role of HR analytics in the modern HR function. Without a doubt, the role of HR professionals has changed significantly due to e-HRM. These entries explore some of these changes and how the HR function can continue to have a positive impact on organisations. For example, the use of data and analytics is often viewed as one route to more strategic application of e-HRM, and the authors in this section help identify key issues in this effort.

The next section focuses on underlying technological, structural and organizational issues with any e-HRM system such as trust, ethics, risk management, cybersecurity, organizational change, and legal constraints. Many of the individual entries in other sections of the volume also mention ethical concerns. Rapidly changing law regarding the use and management of employee data creates challenges for employers and consultants alike. Europe has had the strongest data protection regulations with the GDPR but other countries are enhancing legal protections for employees in ways that will likely impact use of HR data in coming years. Indeed, the 2020 implementation of new data privacy regulations in the California Consumer Protection Act also governs the use of some employee data, requiring disclosure of how data will be used. Other regulations govern the use of algorithms for employment decision making. Issues of trust, risk management, and organizational change are intertwined as employees decide how they feel about new technologies as part of their work lives and act accordingly.

Another group of entries details how foundational technology concepts originating in other disciplines are applied to emerging e-HRM practices. Here authors describe and debate how data science, big data, algorithms, gamification, robots, social media, blockchain and other concepts apply to e-HRM. HR researchers and practitioners often see these concepts in the media and may draw some intuitive but inaccurate conclusions about their application to HR practices. The entries in this section clarify, for example, what data science entails and how it is related to HRM, and if we really have Big Data in HR. Similarly, the entry on gamification clarifies how this technique is different from games, and how it can be applied to recruiting, selection, training, and performance management. The entry on digitalization technologies describes five core technologies (social, mobile, analytics, cloud, and internet of things) and explains how all five, known as SMACIT, are included in the study of e-HRM. All five of these technologies are also addressed in other entries.

One core challenge of developing a volume such as this is keeping up with the rapid developments in technology, even between submission of the entries in 2019 and the actual publication of the book in 2020. Many of the entries specifically address the evolution (and in some cases, revolution) of technologies in their area. For example, the entry on applicant tracking systems (ATS) describes the gradual evolution of these systems from a recruiting database system to a full-service recruiting platform. Developments in augmented and virtual reality technologies affect opportunities to develop new methods for e-learning and trainee assessment, and advances in artificial intelligence are rapidly changing recruiting and selection practices. We are pleased that authors were able to offer general principles and frameworks underlying these technologies to assist the reader in better understanding the current state but also to help accommodate further developments. In the spirit of continuous development, each entry offers future research directions to provide guidance for the field. The authors have also provided their recommendations for the most important readings for learning more about each topic. We hope that all readers find the volume useful, whether you have been a part of the e-HRM community for many years or are just now joining in the journey.

References

Bissola, R. & Imperatori, B. (Eds.) (2019), *HRM 4.0 For Human-Centered Organizations* (Advanced Series in Management, Vol. 23), Emerald Publishing Limited

Bondarouk, T., Parry, E., & Furtmueller, E. (2017). Electronic HRM: four decades of research on adoption and consequences. *The International Journal of Human Resource Management, 28*(1), 98–131.

Bondarouk,T., Ruël, H. J. M. & Looise, J. C. (Eds.) (2011), *Electronic HRM in Theory and Practice (Advanced Series in Management, Vol 8)*

Florkowski, G.W. (2018). HR Technology Systems: An evidence-based approach to construct measurement. *Research in Personnel and Human Resources Management, 36*, 197–239.

Gueutal, H., Stone, D. L., & Salas, E. (2005). *The Brave New World of eHR: Human Resources in the Digital Age*: Wiley

Kavanagh, M.J., Thite, M. & Johnson, R. D. (Eds.) *Human Resource Information Systems: Basics, Applications & Directions*. Thousand Oaks, CA: Sage.

Marler, J., & Fisher, S.L. (2013). An evidence based review of e-HRM and strategic human resource management. *Human Resource Management Review, 23*, 18–36.

Thite, M. (2018). *E-HRM: Digital Approaches, Directions, and Applications*. Routledge.

Torres-Corronas, T. & Arias-Olivas, M. (Eds.) (2008). *Encyclopedia of Human Resources Information Systems: Challenges in e-HRM*. Hershey: IGI.

Part 1: **Basics of e-HRM**

Julio Canedo
Strategic Electronic Human Resource Management

The field of Strategic Human Resource Management (SHRM) is developing compared to other well-established areas of management research (e.g., organizational strategy, organizational behavior, information systems). The idea of human resource management (HRM) as a potential source of competitive advantage and, as a consequence, a strategic organizational player was introduced to scholarly research in the 1990s (see, for example, Wright & Snell, 1991; Wright & McMahan, 1992; Snell, Youndt, & Wright, 1996). The study of electronic forms of HRM (e-HRM) is an even more recent development (see Bondarouk, Parry, & Furtmueller, 2017; Stone, Deadrick, Lukaszewski, & Johnson, 2015), and includes e-recruiting, e-selection, e-training, e-learning, and e-performance management. Given Strategic e-HRM (SeHRM) is in its infancy, it has received limited attention from scholars and even more limited empirical evidence (e.g., Marler & Fisher, 2013). This entry (1) defines SeHRM, (2) examines relevant findings in the topic, and (3) discusses its future.

Definitions

Electronic Human Resource Management (e-HRM): "an umbrella term covering all possible integration mechanisms and contents between HRM and Information Technologies aiming at creating value within and across organizations for targeted employees and management." (Bondarouk & Ruël, 2009, p. 507).

Human Resource Information Systems (HRIS): information systems "used to acquire, store, manipulate, analyze, retrieve, and distribute information regarding an organization's human resources to support HRM and managerial decisions" (Kavanagh, Thite, & Johnson, 2015, p. 17).

Strategic Electronic Human Resource Management (SeHRM): synergic e-HRM and HRIS intended to align the contributions of all incumbents to organizational strategies.

Conceptualization

The idea of e-HRM as a potential strategic organizational contributor has been in the literature for about a decade. Marler (2009) argued that e-HRM has the capability to be strategic, but that very rarely is it to create competitive advantage.

https://doi.org/10.1515/9783110633702-001

She proposed a model in which e-HRM can deliver three different outcomes by playing three different roles:

1. Cost savings, if the HR function is not considered strategic. Role: Administrative expert.
2. Strategic alignment, if the HR function is considered strategic, but not a source of competitive advantage. Role: Strategic partner.
3. The development of human capital and dynamic capabilities, if the HR function is considered strategic and a source of competitive advantage. Role: Capability builder.

One problem with SHRM lies in its own conception. This entry includes a definition, but the term is so slippery that many others can be found. This elusiveness is, in part, due to the wide scope, levels, variables, and lenses that can be used in analyzing the phenomenon. In a recent publication, Lengnick-Hall, Lengnick-Hall, and McIver (2019) highlighted two characteristics of SHRM that set it apart from traditional HRM. They argue that HRM practices are strategic when they are aligned with the strategic intent and interrelated with one another as opposed to isolated. A number of factors determine the meaning of SHRM; each of these factors can take on a number attributes (Lengnick-Hall et al., 2019):

1. Focus: Corporate or business unit.
2. Level: HR philosophy, HR policies, HR programs, HR practices, or HR climate.
3. Fit and flexibility: External/vertical fit, internal/horizontal fit, resource flexibility, or coordination flexibility.
4. International scope.
5. Theoretical foundation: Resource-based view (Barney, 1991), human capital theory (Becker, 1964), or social exchange theory (Emerson, 1976).

What We Have Learned

Marler and Fisher (2013) reviewed 40 studies published from 1999 to 2011 to assess the relations between e-HRM and SHRM. They found no empirical evidence that e-HRM predicts strategic outcomes and concluded that there is a need for theoretical and empirical research in this area. Later, these researchers stated that the value that e-HRM adds to organizations continues to be unclear, not meaning that e-HRM does not add value, but recognizing that we have not produced evidence-based research to support this assertion (Marler & Fisher, 2016).

After reviewing four decades of empirical research in e-HRM, Bondarouk et al. (2017), identified three factors affecting the adoption of e-HRM: Technology, organization, and people. In addition, they classified consequences as operational, relational, and transformational. In this review, Bondarouk et al. (2017) found that the goals of e-HRM have changed from efficiency to strategy and that research has shifted its focus from operational to relational and transformational. Before we move to produce empirical research, they argue, we need more theory development. In particular, they recommend a multi-functional, multi-level approach.

The ultimate goal of SeHRM is to align individual contributions to the organization's strategic intent. In practice, this can be most easily thought of as the implementation of comprehensive e-HRM systems (i.e., HRIS solutions similar to SAP Successfactors or BambooHR). Very limited empirical research supports a positive relation between the adoption of HRIS and organizational performance (e.g., Qaisar, Shahzad, & Arif, 2018). We know implementation of e-HRM systems can lead to outcomes that many organizations would consider strategic: reduction in costs, improved communication, information and knowledge sharing, efficiency, flexibility, employee participation, enhancement of decision making, increases in organizational citizenship behaviors, trust, readiness, alignment, attainment of strategic organizational goals, retention, performance, etc. (Bondarouk & Brewster, 2016; Burbach, 2019). There are, however, a number of potentially negative consequences of poor implementations: work stress, disappointment with technological properties, frustration, lack of trust, isolation, loss of intellectual capital (due to people being let go), resistance to change, privacy concerns, financial losses, etc. (Bondarouk & Brewster, 2016; Burbach, 2019).

The absence of business drivers in the decision making process, of course, prevents strategic impact and causes e-HRM initiatives to focus on preventing dissatisfaction (Schalk, Timmerman, & van den Heuvel, 2012). The phenomenon is so complex that characteristics that, in other circumstances, would be considered superfluous, like aesthetics (interface design) can cause undesired results in the implementation of e-HRM systems (Johnson, Lukaszewski, & Stone, 2017). In addition, some factors affecting the adoption of e-HRM are beyond organizational control. For example, global, legal, political, and economic forces, regulations, headquarters' influence, availability of resources, the presence of unions, and demands from the community (Bondarouk & Brewster, 2016; Bondarouk, Schilling, & Ruël, 2016).

The Future

In an increasingly online working environment where automation, artificial intelligence, alternative work arrangements, the internet of things, big data, and other technological trends, the digital employee experience will only continue to grow (Canedo, Graen, Grace, & Johnson, 2017; Lengnick-Hall et al., 2019). This warrants a growing use of HRIS and e-HRM experiences. Organizations will continue to adopt and adapt technologies to give their incumbents online services and allow them to use these technologies to deliver their work. Researchers and practitioners need to engage in studying and understanding these phenomena to disentangle their strategic contribution. The main questions remain:

1. Do e-HRM services contribute to the organization's strategic intent?
2. Are there some e-HRM services that have greater strategic contribution compared to others?
3. How can organizations ensure they will have strategic achievements by implementing e-HRM initiatives?
4. Can e-HRM be the source of competitive advantage?

As usual, differences exist in the interests and motivators between researchers and practitioners (academia and organizations). Having in front of us a topic as elusive and novel as the strategic impact of e-HRM, we can anticipate researchers will continue to study the phenomenon to gain understanding, while practitioners will continue their search for new practices that add to the organization's bottom line: financial results, competitive advantage, and long-term survival.

Further Readings

All references listed below provide good insight and ideas about future research in the topic. Start by reading Bondarouk et al. (2017); Lengnick-Hall et al. (2019); Marler and Fisher (2013); and Wright and Snell (1991).

References

Barney, J. (1991). Firm resources and sustained competitive advantage. *Journal of Management, 17,* 99–120.

Becker, G. (1964). *Human Capital.* New York, NY: Columbia University Press.

Bondarouk, T., & Brewster, C. (2016). Conceptualising the future of HRM and technology research. *The International Journal of Human Resource Management, 27,* 2652–2671.

Bondarouk, T., Parry, E., & Furtmueller, E. (2017). Electronic HRM: four decades of research on adoption and consequences. *The International Journal of Human Resource Management, 28,* 98–131.

Bondarouk, T. V., & Ruël, H. J. M. (2009). Electronic human resource management: Challenges in the digital era. *The International Journal of Human Resource Management, 20,* 505–514.

Bondarouk, T., Schilling, D., & Ruël, H. (2016). eHRM adoption in emerging economies: The case of subsidiaries of multinational corporations in Indonesia. *Canadian Journal of Administrative Sciences, 33,* 124–137.

Burbach, R. (2019). Strategic evaluation of e-HRM. In M. Thite (Ed.), *E-HRM: digital approaches, directions & applications* (pp. 235–249). New York, NY: Routledge.

Canedo, J. C., Graen. G., Grace, M., & Johnson, R. D. (2017). Navigating the new workplace: Technology, millennials, and accelerating HR innovation. *Transactions on Human – Computer Interaction*, *9*, 243–260.

Emerson, R. M. (1976). Social exchange theory. *Annual Review of Sociology*, *2*, 335–362.

Johnson, R. D., Lukaszewski, K. M., & Stone, D. L. (2017). The importance of the interface between humans and computers on the effectiveness of eHRM. *Transactions on Human-Computer Interaction*, *9*, 23–33.

Kavanagh, M. J., Thite, M., & Johnson, R. D. (2015). *Human resource information systems: Basics, applications, and future directions* (3rd Ed.). Thousand Oaks, CA: Sage.

Lengnick-Hall, M. L., Lengnick-Hall, C. A., & McIver, D. (2019). Strategic management approach to technology-enabled HRM. In M. Thite (Ed.), *E-HRM: digital approaches, directions & applications* (pp. 25–41). New York, NY: Routledge.

Marler, J. H. (2009). Making human resources strategic by going to the Net: reality or myth? *International Journal of Human Resource Management*, *20*, 515–527.

Marler, J. H., & Fisher, S. L. (2013). An evidence-based review of e-HRM and strategic human resource management. *Human Resource Management Review*, *23*, 18–36.

Marler, J. H., & Fisher, S. L. (2016). The eHRM value propostion: Introduction to the special edition. *Canadian Journal of Administrative Sciences*, *33*, 91–94.

Qaisar, N., Shahzad, K., & Arif, M. (2018). Extent of HRIS adoption and its impact on organization's performance: Moderating role of HR staff expertise. *Abasyn Journal of Social Sciences*, *18*, 1–11.

Schalk, R., Timmerman, V., & van den Heuvel, S. (2012). How strategic considerations influence decision making on e-HRM applications. *Human Resource Management Review*, *23*, 84–92.

Snell, A. A., Youndt, M. A., & Wright, P. M. (1996). Establishing a framework for research in strategic human resource management: Managing resource theory and organizational learning. *Research in Personnel and Human Resources Management*, *14*, 61–90.

Stone, D. L, Deadrick, D. L., Lukaszewsky, K. M., & Johnson, R. (2015). The influence of technology on the future of human resource management. *Human Resource Management Review*, *25*, 216–231.

Wright, P. M., & McMahan, G. C. (1992). Theoretical perspectives for strategic human resource management. *Journal of Management*, *18*, 295–320.

Wright, P. M., & Snell, S. A. (1991). Toward an integrative view of strategic human resource management. *Human Resource Management Review*, *1*, 203–225.

Richard D. Johnson
Human Computer Interaction and HRIS

From the earliest systems supporting payroll to today's integrated cloud based systems with artificial intelligence, it is clear that the use of human resource information systems (HRIS) has fundamentally changed the practice of human resources (HR). An HRIS is "used to acquire, store, manipulate, analyze, retrieve, and distribute information regarding an organization's human resources to support HRM and managerial decisions" (Kavanagh & Johnson, 2018, p. 8). Research has shown that an HRIS can affect a variety of important applicant, employee, and organizational outcomes (Bondarouk, Harms, & Lepak, 2017; Stone, Deadrick, Lukaszewski, & Johnson, 2015). In fact, an HRIS can "impact the types of individuals who apply for open positions, how they are selected, how employees are evaluated, how compensation and benefits decisions are made, how employees react to HR policies, how employees are managed" (Johnson, Lukaszewski, & Stone, 2016, p. 151).

Core to how these decisions are made is the design of the interface and how employees and managers interact with the system, e.g. human-computer interaction (HCI). The field of HCI focuses on the relationship between a user and a computer. The goal of HCI design is to maximize the effectiveness of the interactions between humans and computers through more effective hardware, software, and interface designs. HCI research is broad, focusing on topics such as objective system usability, interface design, user-centered design, social computing, technology trust, augmented reality, mobile versus desktop platforms, ubiquitous computing, and psychological and social responses to computers. Types of outcomes of interest to HCI researchers and designers include usability, adoption intentions, user attitudes and behavior, psychological responses to computers, and design quality (Galletta & Zhang, 2009; Zhang, Li, Scialdone, & Carey, 2009).

It is also important to note that in today's HRIS environment, where HR data are accessed over the cloud, where employees and applicants use kiosks and smartphones to interact with the system, the term computer in HCI can refer to a variety of devices such as desktop computers, tablets, smartphones, kiosks, GPS, etc. In addition, it is important to note that the interface design of HRIS can also be affected by the rich and complex relationship between humans and computers, that often mirrors human-human relationships (Marakas, Johnson, & Palmer, 2000; Nass & Moon, 2000). For this reason, those interested in studying HRIS must be aware of how interface design and interaction methods can affect key HR outcomes. We focus on three of the major issues below.

https://doi.org/10.1515/9783110633702-002

Adoption and Use of HRIS

Early design scholars emphasized the importance of objective usability when designing software, arguing software that is not usable will see low rates of utilization and effectiveness. However, researchers have argued that objective usability is simply one of a myriad of factors, such as fit with employees' preferred work style, perceived usefulness, and ease of use that can affect the adoption rate of these systems (Davis, 1989; Rogers, 2003). Research has found that these design characteristics can affect an individual's decision to adopt an HRIS (Marler, Fisher, & Ke, 2009). In addition, research has found that the design of the recruitment website can affect how prospective candidates perceive the organization and the likelihood that they will apply for a position with the firm. Specifically, factors such as aesthetic appeal, navigability, ease of use, and customizable experience can affect often organizational attractiveness and intention to apply for jobs with the firm. (Cober, Brown, Levy, & Cober, 2003). Further, research has found that customizing user experiences can actually reduce the likelihood that a poor-fitting applicant will apply for a position (Dineen & Noe, 2009).

Decision-Making

One of the major goals of computer-based decision aids is to help individuals make better decisions. However, the extent to which these tools can improve performance is dependent upon how information is displayed. For example, research has found that summarized data (e.g. graphical output) can lead to more efficient and effective decisions than viewing raw or chart form data (Dickson, Senn, & Chervany, 1977). The reason for this is that the summarized and graphical data helps individuals find trends and see patterns. However, care must be taken when providing employees with the ability to interactively work with data and display in different formats, because it may enhance individuals' confidence in decisions without a related increase in performance. In other words, the more interactive a system is, the higher the risk is that employees or managers think they are making more effective decisions, when they may not be. In addition, the display of information may lead individuals to underestimate the complexity of the problem or to assume that the only data relevant to the problem are those captured by the system. Finally, a number of studies have looked at how the display of tabular or raw data can affect decision-making. The results suggest that rather than improving decision-making, computer based decision aids are often used to reduce decision-making time and effort (Vessey, 2006).

Together, this research suggests that the design decisions made by the developers of an HRIS in regards to the guidance provided to employees, may restrict how the data are accessed, displayed, and summarized. In turn, this may affect applicant, employee, and managerial decisions. These differences are particularly critical for those implementing an HRIS because decisions regarding employment, promotions, compensation, and perforrmance are often made with data from the system. If organizations do not understand the design implications of the tools supporting HR decisions, then decisions may be made that are based upon system related characteristics rather than the criteria ostensibly used.

HCI Considerations for ESS and MSS

HCI is particularly important for employee self-service (ESS) and managerial self-service (MSS) capabilities of an HRIS. ESS allows employees to access and manage their personal information and HR services such as benefits enrollment, time off requests, etc. MSS allows managers to directly access to subordinate information and make decisions using that information. For example, a manager can approve an employee's time off request, or can access the information needed to evaluate performance or recommend a raise.

Although similar in nature, different HCI considerations are important for ESS compared to MSS. With ESS, designers should utilize HCI principles that encourage quick, clear access to the information that employees need to manage. On the other hand, HCI considerations for MSS revolve around the decisions managers make. Designers should consider not only what type of decision is made, but also how the display of information might affect that decision. In addition, there is some scientific evidence that the design of these systems may benefit from the customization of the layout and format to the managers' preferences (Pankaj et al., 2006).

Responding Socially to a Robot

The final area of HCI to discuss revolves broadly around the tendency of individuals to anthropomorphize their relationships with computing technology and robotics. Some might wonder what robotics has to do with HRIS and that is an appropriate question. The major reason why robotics is becoming more important to HRIS is that the use of human – robot teams in industry is becoming more and more common. In some cases, robots are even beginning to fill the role of supervisor (Robert, 2018), and the ability of firms to integrate robots into teams of the future will becoming increasingly important to their success (Robert, 2018). Thus, in situations where robots manage employees, robots will need to access employee data and use artificial intelligence algorithms to make decisions, about employees. For this reason, robots will both rely on, and become part of the HRIS.

How humans will interact with robots will depend upon how they are designed. For example, research has found that employees prefer receiving feedback from a computer, because it is viewed as more neutral to that provided by a manager (Earley, 1988). However, research has also found that people are responding to robots and computers in the same way they would a human (Nass & Moon, 2000). Thus, how individuals respond to feedback from robots depends upon design characteristics that may induce people to respond to the robot as they would another human

In addition, interface design characteristics (e.g. the use of human voice, the language of the machine, the identification of the computer as a teammate, etc.) can encourage individuals to react to them as if they were human (Johnson, Marakas, & Palmer, 2006; You & Robert, 2018). Further, the interface can affect how employees trust data from a robot and how employees interpret and use that data. Because HRIS designers are not often closely involved in the HR decision-making process, they may make design decisions that are sub-optimal for HR decision-making, and organizations will need to understand how this may affect managers' decisions regarding hiring, performance management, compensation, and more.

Conclusion

In this chapter, the role of HCI in HRIS design was briefly discussed, along with examples of how HCI design considerations may affect HR decisions in different functional areas. However, given the continued revolution in design tools available to HR staff and employees, the growth in rich data analytic tools, and the variety of tools through which data are accessed, we have just begun to scratch the surface in our understanding of how HCI can inform HRIS design and its impact on the different functions of human resources. Moving forward, the richest and most effective systems will incorporate key HCI design principles to allow organizations to best recruit, support, and manage the workforce of the future.

Further Readings

Nass, C. & Yen, C. (2012) *The Man who Lied to his Laptop: What we can learn about Ourselves from our Machines*, New York: Penguin Group.

Shneiderman, B & Plaisant, C. (2009). *Designing the User Interface: Strategies for Effective Human-Computer Interaction* (5th Ed.), Reading, MA: Addison-Wesley Publishing Co.

Smith, G. (2018) *The AI Delusion*, Oxford, UK: Oxford University Press.

Zhang, P. & Galletta, D. (2006) *Human-computer interaction and management information systems: Foundations: Advances in Management Information Systems* (Vol. 5). Armonk NY: ME Sharpe.

References

Bondarouk, T., Harms, R., & Lepak, D. (2017). Does e-HRM lead to better HRM service? *International Journal of Human Resource Management, 28*(9), 1332–1362.

Cober, R. T., Brown, D. J., Levy, P. E., & Cober, A. B. (2003). Organizational Web Sites: Web Site Content and Style as Determinants of Organizational Attraction. *International Journal of Selection and Assessment, 11*(2–3), 158–169.

Davis, F. D., Bagozzi, R. P., & Warshaw, P. R. (1989). User acceptance of computer technology: A comparison of two theoretical models. *Management Science, 35*(8), 982–1003.

Dickson, G. W., Senn, J. A., & Chervany, N. L. (1977). Research in management information systems: The Minnesota experiments. *Management Science, 23*(9), 913–934.

Dineen, B. R., & Noe, R. A. (2009). Effects of Customization on Application Decisions and Applicant Pool Characteristics in a Web-Based Recruitment Context. *Journal of Applied Psychology, 94*(1), 224–234.

Earley, P. C. (1988). Computer-generated performance feedback in the magazine-subscription industry. *Organizational Behavior and Human Decision Processes, 41*(1), 50–64.

Galletta, D., & Zhang, P. (2009). Introducing AIS Transactions on Human-Computer Interaction. *AIS Transactions on Human-Computer Interaction, 1*(1), 7–12.

Johnson, R. D., Lukaszewski, K. M., & Stone, D. L. (2016). Introduction to the special issue on human resource information systems and human computer interaction. *AIS Transactions on Human-Computer Interaction, 8*(4), 149–159.

Johnson, R. D., Marakas, G. M., & Palmer, J. W. (2006). Differential social attributions toward computing technology: An empirical investigation. *International Journal of Human-Computer Studies, 64*(5), 446–460.

Kavanagh, M. J., & Johnson, R. D. (2018). *Human Resource Information Systems: Basics, Applications, and Future Directions* (Vol. 4). Sage Publications.

Marakas, G. M., Johnson, R. D., & Palmer, J. W. (2000). A theoretical model of differential social attributions toward computing technology: when the metaphor becomes the model. *International Journal of Human-Computer Studies, 52*(4), 719–750.

Marler, J. H., Fisher, S. L., & Ke, W. (2009). Employee Self-Service Technology Acceptance: A Comparison of Pre-Implementation and Post-Implementation Relationships. *Personnel Psychology, 62*(2), 327–358.

Nass, C., & Moon, Y. (2000). Machines and Mindlessness: Social Responses to Computers. *Journal of Social Issues, 56*(1), 81–103.

Pankaj, P., Hyde, M., Rodger, J. (2006). Business Dashboards- Challenges and Recommendations. AMCIS 2006 Proceedings. Paper 184.

Robert, L. P. (2018). Motivational theory of human robot teamwork. *International Robotics & Automation Journal, 4*(4), 248–251.

Rogers, E. M. (2003). *Diffusion of innovations* (5th ed.). New York: Free Press.

Stone, D. L., Deadrick, D. L., Lukaszewski, K. M., & Johnson, R. D. (2015). The influence of technology on the future of human resource management. *Human Resource Management Review, 25*(2), 216–231.

Vessey, I. (2006). The theory of cognitive fit. In P. Zhang & D. Galletta (Eds) *Human-computer interaction and management information systems: Foundations.* 141–183.

You, S., & Robert, L. P. (2018). Emotional Attachment, Performance, and Viability in Teams Collaborating with Embodied Physical Action (EPA) Robots. *Journal of the Association for Information Systems*, *19*(5), 377–407.

Zhang, P., Li, N., Scialdone, M. J., & Carey, J. (2009). The Intellectual Advancement of Human-Computer Interaction Research: A Critical Assessment of the MIS Literature (1990–2008). *AIS Transactions on Human-Computer Interaction*, *1*(3), 55–107.

Stefan Strohmeier
HR Digitalisation Technologies

Technologies as Enabler of HR Digitalisation

It is a truism that the available technologies constitute the enabler of digitalizing HRM. From the early punch card technologies that emerged more than half a century ago to artificial intelligence algorithms that are currently emerging, available base technologies determine the possibilities to realize digital HRM. Punch card technology, for instance, allowed for an early automation of payroll processing while artificial intelligence technologies at present allow for an algorithmic applicant selection. Given this fundamental importance of technologies, this entry portrays current core technologies relevant for the current and future digitalisation of HRM. The current discussion on the general digitalisation of organizations frequently employs the concept of *SMAC* and later of *SMACIT* (Social-, Mobile-, Analytics-, Cloud- and Internet of Things [IoT])-Technologies to identify four and later five core technological developments as a driving force behind the digital transformation of organizations (e.g., Cornelius, 2013; Dewan & Jena, 2014; Sebastian et al., 2017). SMACIT-technologies emerged over the last two decades with social technologies as the oldest and the IoT as the newest technological development. The potentials for deep organizational transformations are expected from a synergetic interaction of the five technologies, rather than from the isolated technologies (e.g. Dewan & Jena, 2014). SMACIT-technologies show also broad potentials for the future HR digitalisation and, thus, are relevant for HRM.

Research on HR Digitalisation Technologies

So far, the SMACIT-concept is unfamiliar in HR research. However, all five SMACIT-categories are researched, and there are contributions regarding social technologies (e.g. Bondarouk & Olivas-Lujan, 2013), mobile technologies (e.g. Böhm & Niklas, 2012), analytical technologies (e.g. Angrave et al., 2016), cloud technologies (e.g. Gosh & Tripathi, 2018), and IoT-technologies (e.g. Strohmeier, 2018) in HRM. These contributions explore the potentials of the respective technology in HRM and initially confirm their relevance (also) in HRM. Firstly, however, research on the five SMACIT-technologies clearly differs in scope and intensity. While, for instance, research on the development of social technologies in HRM is broad, multifaceted, and already summarized in reviews (Kluemper, Mitra & Wang, 2016), research on the latest development of IoT-technologies in HRM is scarce and restricted to very few studies that estimate possible future applications rather than examine the existing ones (e.g. Strohmeier,

https://doi.org/10.1515/9783110633702-003

2018). Secondly, research typically deals with SMACIT-technologies in an isolated manner, i.e. it regularly ignores the crucial synergy between the five technologies. At best, synergies are taken into account implicitly. For example, contributions on analytic technologies in HRM (see the review of Marler & Boudreau, 2017) also deal with social technologies and IoT-technologies as "data providers". In sum, there is research on SMACIT-technologies in HRM, which, however, mostly deals with one isolated technology and shows clearly differing intensities.

Framework of HR Digitalisation Technologies

For a better understanding of the single technological categories and their interactions a simple framework is employed in the following. With a view to the core logical functions of a digital technology (Zachmann, 1987), base, application and presentation technologies can be distinguished. Base technologies offer basic technological functions to HRM, such as providing processing power or storage capacities. Application technologies provide domain-specific functions to HRM to automate or support HR tasks and processes. Finally, presentation technologies provide interaction functions that allow human end users to make inputs in application technologies and get outputs back from them. Assigning the different SMACIT-technologies to the functional categories allows a better understanding of their functional interaction and potentials (see Figure 3.1).

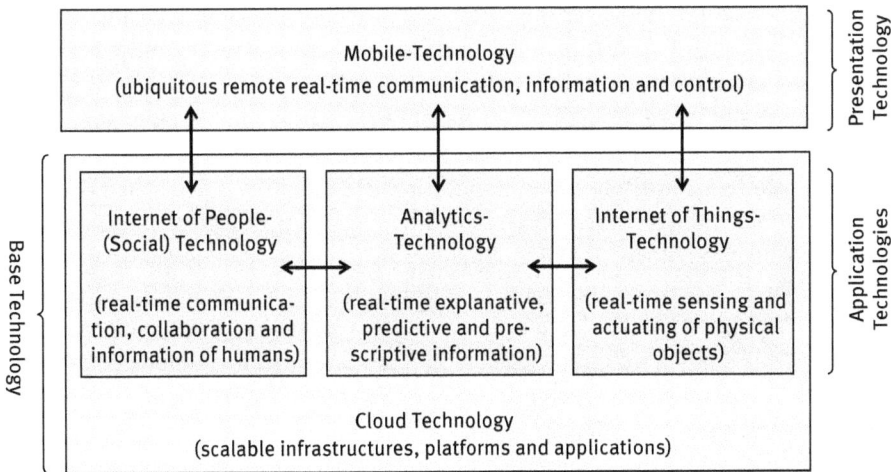

Figure 3.1: Framework of Core HR Digitalisation Technologies.

Categories of Core HR Digitalisation Technologies

In the above-mentioned framework *cloud technologies* offer different digital services via the Internet. Regularly three different cloud service models are distinguished (e.g. Gosh & Tripathi, 2018): Infrastructure as a service (IaaS) allows HRM the access to and the usage of hardware such as servers, networks and storage capacities. Thus, all hardware necessary for digitalizing HRM can be provided. Platform as a service (PaaS) allows HRM the access to and the usage of runtime and/or development environments. Thus, individual applications of digital HRM can be developed and operated. Software as a service (SaaS) allows HRM the access to and the usage of existing software applications. Thus, HRM can apply prefabricated applications of digital HRM quickly and easily. In sum, cloud technologies provide HRM with all services necessary for digitalisation of HRM. Compared to a conventional internal provision clouds entails advantages regarding comfort, scalability and costs of services. Potential disadvantages regarding security and privacy of services in public clouds can be countered with a private cloud approach, which offers services by a trusted external party via secured networks (e.g. Gosh & Tripathi, 2018). Cloud technologies thus constitute the technological backbone for realizing application technologies in HRM. Further SMACIT-technologies, in particular social-, analytics- and IoT-applications can be advantageously realized based on cloud services. Thus, cloud technologies constitute a base technology that provides HRM with the technical performance necessary for digitalisation. While systematic empirical insights are missing, cloud technologies seem to be increasingly used in HRM, in particular for providing HR software.

Social (media) technologies offer HRM the possibility to communicate, collaborate, and exchange information with all its stakeholders independently from time and place (e.g. Bondarouk & Olivas-Lujan, 2013). After an initial phase of passive receiving roles of users, in the interim social technologies imply highly active user roles in creating user generated content and building online communities. Social technologies thus constitute a first application technology. As depicted above, social technologies are powered and enabled by cloud technologies. Mobile devices are increasingly employed for ubiquitous access to social technologies, therewith linking them to mobile technologies. In addition, the content generated by users of social technologies constitutes an abundant data reservoir, often understood as "big data" for analytics technologies (see Figure 3.1). Social technologies provide HRM with a comprehensive potential to organize all types of human interactions necessary and useful in HRM in an efficient and innovative way. Following the prominent concept of the IoT (see below), social applications thus can be also designated as Internet of People (IoP). As it plays an important role in HRM, the IoP will maintain and expand this position in the future digitalisation of HRM. By now, a broad set of useful applications of social technologies is discussed and practiced in HRM. These range from communication with external stakeholders in employer branding to information of and a collaboration with internal stakeholders in employee training (see e.g. the overview in Kluemper et al. 2012).

As the newest SMACIT-technology in HRM, the *IoT* refers to connecting physical objects to the Internet and thus equiping them with the unprecedented functionality of an autonomous context-adequate behaviour (e.g. Strohmeier, 2018). In order to obtain information about the state of a physical object (and its surroundings), one or more sensors are placed on the object. Sensors ascertain relevant variables in very short time distances and send the resulting data to the Internet. For getting physical control over an object, one or more actuators can be placed at the object. Actuators move and control the object based on remote manual or digital instructions. Based on sensing and actuating, things can be remote monitored and controlled (e.g. Strohmeier, 2018). This allows for a broad range of future HR applications that are so far not fully elaborated and developed. An obvious potential refers to a massive improvement of HR information provision based on multiple sensors placed at tools employees use or wearables that employees wear (Strohmeier, 2018). Moreover, "smart" objects such as tools, workpieces or vehicles could be used for automating HR tasks such as training, instruction or appraisal of employees (Strohmeier, 2018). Thus, IoT technologies constitute a second application technology with broad potentials for the future digitalisation and transformation of HRM. As depicted above, IoT-technologies are also "powered" and enabled by cloud technologies. Again, mobile technologies allow for connecting HR IoT-applications with humans such as employees in training or HR professionals in gaining employee performance information. Moreover, it is evident that particularly the IoT (concretely, the sensing enabled by the IoT) offers abundant, highly detailed real-time data as input for analytical technologies in HRM (Strohmeier, 2018). While systematic empirical research is missing, the current application of IoT-technology in HRM seems quite nascent and mainly refers to the first attempts of using sensors to gain information.

Analytical technologies offer HRM the possibility to improve the information provision and decision support distinctly (e.g. Marler & Boudreau, 2017). Based on increasing data stocks in HRM, advanced analyses, in particular from the machine learning area, allow for the provision of advanced information. While conventional approaches so far offer mainly descriptive HR information (describe what has happened), it is expected that advanced approaches offer explanative (explain why something has happened), predictive (predict what will happen), and prescriptive (prescribe what to do) HR information. Based on these types of information, it is evident to expect substantial improvements in HR decision quality and thus in HR success (e.g. Marler & Boudreau, 2017). Analytics technologies constitute a third application technology in the future digitalisation of HRM. Again, analytics technology rest on cloud technology as base technology that offers the storage capacity for large data volumes and the processing power for advanced analysis methods. As indicated before, analytics technology depends massively on data generation from both the IoP and the IoT. Content data generated by numerous IoP-users and measurement data generated by numerous IoT-sensors show the joint potential to produce "big data" also in HRM. As manifested in the prominent concept of "HR analytics" (see the review of Marler & Bodreau, 2017), the broad potentials of analytic technologies (also) in HRM are recognized and broadly discussed. While systematic empirical insights are missing, there seems to be at least first realization attempts in practice.

Finally, *mobile technologies* offer HR end users access to application technologies at any time and from any place (e.g. Mülder, 2016). Technically mobile applications are based on wireless networks and mobile devices. While smart phones and tablets constitute core mobile devices, further devices such as smart glasses or headmounted displays open up further application potentials. Mobile technologies thus allow for a connection of all HR stakeholders with further SMACIT-technologies and thus constitute the core presentation technology for the further digitalisation of HRM. Based on the ubiquitous access, the general advantages of mobile technologies are as follows: time saving, efficiency gains, and improvement of process flows. Regarding the application in HRM, there are well-established application scenarios such as mobile recruiting, mobile learning or mobile HR administration (e.g. Mülder, 2016).

Future Directions in Core Digitalisation Technologies

While SMACIT-technologies are not unresearched or unpractised in HRM, their systematic consideration and exploitation constitutes a core challenge for a successful future digitalisation of HRM. Rather than applying (and researching) isolated technologies for isolated tasks and problems of HRM, the major challenge for future (design) research is the elaboration of an integrated view and exploitation approach of the SMACIT-potentials for the future digitalisation of HRM. This entails the research tasks to examine the individual potentials of different SMACIT-technologies and their interactions systematically, formulate digital HR strategies, which concretize the value to be offered to an organisation based on SMACIT-technologies, the design realization of integrated SMACIT-applications and the empirical evaluation of such applications.

Further Readings

Cornelius, D. A. (2013). SMAC and transforming innovation. Paper presented at PMI® Global Congress 2013 – North America, New Orleans, LA. Newtown Square, PA: Project Management Institute.

Sebastian, I., Ross, J., Beath, C., Mocker, M., Moloney, K., & Fonstad, N. (2017). How big old companies navigate digital transformation. *Management Information Systems Executive*, *16*(3), 197–213.

References

Angrave, D., Charlwood, A., Kirkpatrick, I., Lawrence, M., & Stuart, M. (2016). HR and analytics: why HR is set to fail the big data challenge. *Human Resource Management Journal, 26*(1), 1–11.

Böhm, S., & Niklas, S. J. (2012). Mobile recruiting: Insights from a survey among German HR managers. In M. Adya, & R. Norton (Eds.), *SIGMIS-CPR'12* (pp. 117–122). New-York, NY: ACM.

Bondarouk, T., & Olivas-Lujan, M. R. (2013). Social Media and Human Resource Management: It Takes Two to Tango. In Social Media and Human Resource Management (pp. XI-XV). Bingley: Emerald Group Publishing Limited.

Cornelius, D. A. (2013). SMAC and transforming innovation. Paper presented at PMI® Global Congress 2013 – North America, New Orleans, LA. Newtown Square, PA: Project Management Institute.

Dewan, B., & Jena, S. R. (2014). The state-of-the-art of Social, Mobility, Analytics and Cloud Computing an empirical analysis. In *2014 International Conference on High Performance Computing and Applications (ICHPCA)* (pp. 1–6). IEEE

Ghosh, V., & Tripathi, N. (2018). Cloud computing and e-HRM. In M. Thite (Ed.), *e-HRM: Digital Approaches, Directions & Applications* (pp. 106–122). New York, NY: Routledge Publications.

Kluemper, D. H., Mitra, A., & Wang, S. (2016). Social media use in HRM. In M. Ronald Buckley, Jonathon R. B. Halbesleben, & Anthony R. Wheeler (Eds.), *Research in Personnel and Human Resources Management* (pp. 153–207). Emerald Group Publishing Limited.

Marler, J. H., & Boudreau, J. W. (2017). An evidence-based review of HR Analytics. *The International Journal of Human Resource Management, 28*(1), 3–26.

Mülder, W. (2016). Mobile Human Resource Management. In T. Barton, C. Müller, & C. Seel (Hrsg.), *Mobile Anwendungen in Unternehmen* (pp. 51–64). Wiesbaden: Springer Fachmedien.

Sebastian, I., Ross, J., Beath, C., Mocker, M., Moloney, K., & Fonstad, N. (2017). How big old companies navigate digital transformation. *Management Information Systems Executive, 16*(3), 197–213.

Strohmeier, S. (2018). Smart HRM–a Delphi study on the application and consequences of the Internet of Things in Human Resource Management. *The International Journal of Human Resource Management*, 1–30.

Zachman, J. A. (1987). A framework for information systems architecture. *IBM Systems Journal, 26*(3), 276–292.

Sebastian Marin and Richard Landers

Gamification in e-HRM

Gamification is the process of adding game mechanics, features, and elements to non-game systems to alter the user experience (Arthur Jr, Doverspike, Kinney, & O'Connell, 2017; Deterding, Dixon, Khaled & Nacke, 2011; Landers et al., 2018b). The most common game elements employed are points, badges, leaderboards, and levels, although any game element, like narrative or fantasy, could be used to differing effects. A common goal of gamification is to elicit a *gameful experience*, which is the psychological state targeted in the design of analog and digital entertainment games (Landers et al., 2018b). Gamification has become popular within the last decade due to its ease of implementation at a reduced cost relative to game development. Some researchers advocate for the potential of gamification to improve organizational outcomes, whereas critics argue that gamification is inherently manipulative and exploitative (Bogost, 2011; Gabrielle, 2018). Empirical research on the effectiveness of gamifying existing e-HRM systems is sparse, and high-quality empirical studies on gamification more broadly are also uncommon (Koivisto & Hamari, 2019). Despite this, existing research suggests potential for improving organizational outcomes using gamification.

Games are different from gamification. Although researchers do not uniformly agree on its definition, a *game* generally refers to a set of voluntary activities that absorbs all attentional resources and creates an "imaginary world that that may or may not have any relation to life" in which rules for play are established (Michael & Chen, 2005, p. 8). Games are systems of game elements, whereas game elements are systems of specific features (Deterding et al., 2011). For example, a leaderboard game element will be associated with its own subsystems of rules and processes that dictate how the leaderboard changes, reacts to other game elements, and reacts to the player based on a scoring and ranking system. Although points, badges, leaderboards, and levels are common in gamification, the game elements seen in digital games are much broader, encompassing complex sound and graphical systems, action languages that translate player behaviors into in-game actions, and so on. Such game elements could be used in gamification but are atypical. One common type of game in e-HRM, *serious games* or *games for learning*, are games in which learning is the primary design objective rather than entertainment (Michael & Chen, 2005). Another type of e-HRM game increasing in popularity is the game-based assessment, which is used for assessment in hiring, promotion, training, and development. Games, serious games, and game-based assessments are all standalone activities that are designed and developed to achieve organizational goals through gameplay (Landers, Auer, Helms, Marin, & Armstrong, 2019).

Thus, gamification is complementary to the idea of games. Where games are standalone activities, gamification is a design process that relies upon game design

https://doi.org/10.1515/9783110633702-004

principles to add game elements to non-games, typically targeting specific behavioral and psychological outcomes (Landers, Auer, Collmus, & Armstrong 2018a). As a design process, gamification involves the integration and application of game elements to an existing organizational system to improve said system. Gamification may or may not result in a game depending upon the game elements used and, more critically, whether the final product of gamification creates a playful rulebound activity in which players can immerse themselves. In e-HRM, there are several specific application domains where gamification is now observed and researched.

Gamifying Recruitment

Organizations typically recruit through several avenues, such as job fairs, online postings, and referral systems, to seek and attract talent (Nikolaou, Georgiou, Bauer, & Truxillo, 2019). Recruiting in HRM has shifted online due to organizational changes triggered by globalization and the introduction of the internet (Nikolaou et al., 2019). These shifts have not only changed the recruitment process for organizations but have changed job-seeking behaviors as well (e.g., Catalano & Doucet, 2013; Laumer, Eckhardt, & Weitzel, 2012). Recruiters are now searching for talent online because they can reach a wider range of candidates at a reduced cost, increasing the need for recruiters to identify, attract, and retain top talent.

Gamification of recruitment processes has been proposed as a potential tool for this purpose. For example, gamifying referral systems by awarding points to employees who recruit new applicants can widen the applicant pool (Armstrong, Landers, Collmus, 2016). Gamified apps can be used to help job candidates evaluate their own knowledge about the work while simultaneously experiencing a realistic job preview online (Armstrong et al., 2016). Although research is limited, organizations that have started to gamify parts of recruitment have reported positive results (Chow & Chapman, 2013).

Gamifying Selection

Researchers have suggested that gamifying selection assessments can bring many potential benefits, although empirical data are limited. For example, it has been proposed that gamified selection assessments reduce test anxiety and improve measurement validity (Mavridis & Tsiatsos, 2017), as well as increase intrinsic motivation (Dickey, 2007). This in turn might allow for longer, more in-depth tests with improved reliability compared to traditional tests. Researchers generally agree, however, that gamification is not risk-free. As some researchers call for additional validation studies (Nikolaou et al., 2019), others highlight risks associated with game elements that games research suggests might affect performance differentially by gender (see Albuquerque, Bittencourr, Coehlo, & Silva, 2017).

Most current empirical work on the validity of gamified assessments surrounds gamified situational judgment tests (SJTs). Georgiou, Gouras, and Nikolaou (2019) argued that gamified SJTs improve applicant reactions and potentially increase the prediction of job performance. After creating a gamified SJT, they tested its measurement equivalence versus a traditional SJT, finding that the gamified SJT performed just as well as the traditional SJT, although criterion-related validity evidence was absent. Another example of gamifying assessments for selection is the addition of progress bars (Weidner & Short, 2019), which are associated with increased satisfaction and completion rates (Conrad et al., 2010; Cheema, & Bagchi, 2011), an effect that depends upon consistency with expectations of progress (Weidner & Short, 2019).

Gamifying Training

Among all its application domains, the effects of gamification on learning is one of the most extensively researched (Koivisto & Hamari, 2019; Landers et al., 2019). Although most of this research focuses upon education, much also has applications in the context of employee learning. As a theoretical foundation, the theory of gamified learning (Landers, 2014) can help explain how game elements impact learning outcomes. Game elements are posited to mediate and moderate learning outcomes depending on their implementation, and the causal mechanisms by which game elements can be designed to enhance learning outcomes can be understood via major learning theories, such as self-determination theory (Ryan & Deci, 2000). Within this theoretical frame, game elements are seen as intrinsic or extrinsic motivators depending upon their design and implementation, and these motivators can target learning-relevant behaviors. For example, a recent meta-analysis has shown increases in cognitive, motivational, and behavioral learning outcomes within gamified environments over traditional ones depending on the type and quantity of games elements used (Sailer & Homner, 2019).

There are many empirical examples of gamified training. In one, an existing PowerPoint-based training program was modified by converting slides into narratives to make the experience more game-like. Results showed that trainees in the fictional game training were more satisfied in their training than the original training, although knowledge retention was slightly worse (Landers & Armstrong, 2017). Another example is Alcivar and Abad (2016) who implemented an online training system that incorporated a host of game elements and game mechanics to improve learning and satisfaction. Results showed trainees in the gamified condition had increased gains in knowledge and satisfaction compared to the non-gamified, control group.

Gamifying Job Performance

Research on gamifying organizational performance processes generally supports that gamification can be used to enhance motivation, but specific theoretical mechanisms are still being explored (Weidner & Short, 2019). In one exploration founded in goal-setting theory (Locke & Latham, 2002), Landers, Bauer, and Callan (2017) found that the scores on a leaderboard, a game element commonly found in gamification, functioned similarly to traditional goal-setting in a brainstorming task. In another example, based on the job characteristic model, Liu, Huang, and Zhang (2018) targeted job motivation, satisfaction, and performance at a manufacturing plant via smartphone-based gamified job design. Results indicate improvements in motivation, satisfaction, and operators' performance, measured by time of completion of manufacturing and percentage of end-of-day qualified products, compared to control groups. Workers were compared across two different manufacturing plants.

Future Directions

Although it is tempting to try to draw broad conclusions about gamification in general, the specific design considerations in any implementation of gamification suggest more nuanced study. For example, there has recently been growing evidence that including leaderboards is an effective way to alter outcomes across multiple domains, especially for learning and training (Dominguez et al. 2013; Landers et al., 2017; Mekler et al., 2017). However, the specific design of "leaderboards" is often taken for granted in terms of goal selection, aesthetic approach, ranking approach, scoring frequency, and time of interaction with the leaderboard. Does the leaderboard's ranking approach, such as relative ranking or top-five ranking, affect motivation differentially? To what degree does the frequency of scoring and ranking players impact training motivation? Does the amount of time exposed to a leaderboard alter its effect on motivation and behavior in the long-term? More specific questions like these are necessary to understand the motivational potential of leaderboards alone, and future research should be similarly nuanced regarding other game elements as well. For example, what is the effect of storylines and narratives on motivational outcomes compared to more common game elements, and how does this vary based upon the writing approach used to develop those storylines and narratives? What specific narrative elements, such as conflict or perspective-taking, are most important to the success of narrativization as a gamification strategy?

Further Readings

Deterding, S., Sicart, M., Nacke, L., O'Hara, K., & Dixon, D. (2011, May). Gamification: Using game-design elements in non-gaming contexts. In *CHI'11 extended abstracts on human factors in computing systems* (pp. 2425–2428). ACM.

Landers, R. N., Auer, E. M., Collmus, A. B., & Armstrong, M. B. (2018). Gamification science, its history and future: Definitions and a research agenda. *Simulation & Gaming, 49*(3), 315–337.

Kapp, K. M. (2012). *The gamification of learning and instruction: Game-based methods and strategies for training and education.* San Francisco, CA: Wiley.

Koivisto, J. & Hamari, J. (2019). The rise of motivational information systems: A review of gamification research. *International Journal of Information Management, 45*, 191–210.

Armstrong, M. B., Landers, R. N., & Collmus, A. B. (2016). Gamifying recruitment, selection, training, and performance management: Game-thinking in human resource management. In *Emerging research and trends in gamification* (pp. 140–165). IGI Global.

References

Albuquerque, J., Bittencourt, I. I., Coelho, J. A., & Silva, A. P. (2017). Does gender stereotype threat in gamified educational environments cause anxiety?: An experimental study. *Computers & Education, 115*, 161–170.

Alcivar, I., & Abad, A. G. (2016). Design and evaluation of a gamified system for ERP training. *Computers in Human Behavior, 58*, 109–118. doi:10.1016/j.chb.2015.12.018

Armstrong, M. B., Landers, R. N., & Collmus, A. B. (2016). Gamifying recruitment, selection, training, and performance management: Game-thinking in human resource management. In *Emerging research and trends in gamification* (pp. 140–165). IGI Global.

Arthur Jr, W., Doverspike, D., Kinney, T. B., & O'Connell, M. (2017). The impact of emerging technologies on selection models and research: Mobile devices and gamification as exemplars. *Handbook of Employee Selection*, 967–986.

Bogost, I. (2011, May 3). Persuasive games: Exploitationware. *Gamasutra*. Retrieved from http://www.gamasutra.com/view/feature/6366/persuasive_games_exploitationware.php

Catalano, F., & Doucet, K. J. (2013). Digital 'badges' emerge as part of credentialing's future. Institute for Credentialing Excellence.

Cheema, A., & Bagchi, R. (2011). The effect of goal visualization on goal pursuit: Implications for consumers and managers. *Journal of Marketing, 75*(2), 109–123.

Chow, S., & Chapman, D. (2013, October). Gamifying the employee recruitment process. In Proceedings of the *First International Conference on Gameful Design, Research, and Applications* (pp. 91–94). ACM.

Conrad, F. G., Couper, M. P., Tourangeau, R., & Peytchev, A. (2010). The impact of progress indicators on task completion. *Interacting with computers, 22*(5), 417–427.

Deterding, S., Sicart, M., Nacke, L., O'Hara, K., & Dixon, D. (2011, May). Gamification: Using game-design elements in non-gaming contexts. In *CHI'11 extended abstracts on human factors in computing systems* (pp. 2425–2428). ACM.

Dickey, M. D. (2007). Game design and learning: A conjectural analysis of how massively multiple online role-playing games (MMORPGs) foster intrinsic motivation. *Educational Technology Research and Development, 55*(3), 253–273.

Domínguez, A., Saenz-De-Navarrete, J., De-Marcos, L., FernáNdez-Sanz, L., PagéS, C., & MartíNez-Herrálz, J. J. (2013). Gamifying learning experiences: Practical implications and outcomes. *Computers & Education, 63*, 380–392.

Gabrielle, V. (2018, October 10). How employers have gamified work for maximum profit. *Aeon Magazine*. Retrieved from https://medium.com/aeon-magazine/how-employers-have-gamified-work-for-maximum-profit-9be506c07afc

Georgiou, K., Gouras, A., & Nikolaou, I. (2019). Gamification in employee selection: The development of a gamified assessment. *International Journal of Selection and Assessment*. doi:10.1111/ijsa.12240

Koivisto, J., & Hamari, J. (2019). The rise of motivational information systems: A review of gamification research. *International Journal of Information Management, 45*, 191–210.

Landers, R. N. (2014). Developing a theory of gamified learning: Linking serious games and gamification of learning. *Simulation & Gaming, 45*(6), 752–768.

Landers, R. N., & Armstrong, M. B. (2017). Enhancing instructional outcomes with gamification: An empirical test of the Technology-Enhanced Training Effectiveness Model. *Computers in Human Behavior, 71*, 499–507.

Landers, R. N., Auer, E. M., Collmus, A. B., & Armstrong, M. B. (2018a). Gamification science, its history and future: Definitions and a research agenda. *Simulation & Gaming, 49*(3), 315–337.

Landers, R. N., Auer, E. M., Helms, A. B., Marin, S., & Armstrong, M. B. (2019). Gamification of Adult Learning: Gamifying Employee Training and Development. *The Cambridge Handbook of Technology and Employee Behavior*, 271–295.

Landers, R. N., Bauer, K. N., & Callan, R. C. (2017). Gamification of task performance with leaderboards: A goal setting experiment. *Computers in Human Behavior, 71*, 508–515.

Landers, R. N., Tondello, G. F., Kappen, D. L., Collmus, A. B., Mekler, E. D., & Nacke, L. E. (2018b). Defining gameful experience as a psychological state caused by gameplay: Replacing the term "gamefulness" with three distinct constructs. *International Journal of Human-Computer Studies*. doi:10.1016/j.ijhcs.2018.08.003

Laumer, S., Eckhardt, A., & Weitzel, T. (2012). Online gaming to find a new job–examining job seekers' intention to use serious games as a self-assessment tool. *German Journal of Human Resource Management, 26*(3), 218–240.

Liu, M., Huang, Y., & Zhang, D. (2018). Gamification's impact on manufacturing: Enhancing job motivation, satisfaction and operational performance with smartphone-based gamified job design. *Human Factors and Ergonomics in Manufacturing & Service Industries, 28*(1), 38–51.

Locke, E. A., & Latham, G. P. (2002). Building a practically useful theory of goal setting and task motivation: A 35-year odyssey. *American Psychologist, 57*(9), 705–717.

Mavridis, A., & Tsiatsos, T. (2017). Game-based assessment: Investigating the impact on test anxiety and exam performance. *Journal of Computer Assisted Learning, 33*(2), 137–150.

Mekler, E. D., Brühlmann, F., Tuch, A. N., & Opwis, K. (2017). Towards understanding the effects of individual gamification elements on intrinsic motivation and performance. *Computers in Human Behavior, 71*, 525–534.

Michael, D., & Chen, S. (2005). *Serious games: Games that education, train, and information*. Boston, MA: Thomson Course Technology.

Nikolaou, I., Georgiou, K., Bauer, T. N., & Truxillo, D. (2019). Applicant reactions in employee recruitment and selection: The role of technology. *The Cambridge Handbook of Technology and Employee Behavior*, 100–130.

Ryan, R. M., & Deci, E. L. (2000). Self-determination theory and the facilitation of intrinsic motivation, social development, and well-being. *American Psychologist, 55*(1), 68–78.

Sailer, M., & Homner, L. (2019). The gamification of learning: A meta-analysis. *Educational Psychology Review*, 1–36. doi: 10.1007/s10648-019-09498-w

Weidner, N., & Short, E. (2019). Playing with a purpose: The role of games and gamification in modern assessment practices. *The Cambridge Handbook of Technology and Employee Behavior*, 151–178.

Valentina Battista and Emma Parry
Social Media and Human Resource Management

The use of social media by the Human Resource Management (HRM) function within the organisation to attract, engage and communicate with existing and potential employees is a growing phenomenon within the workplace. Here we define social media as "a group of Internet-based applications that build on the ideological and technological foundations of Web 2.0, and that allow the creation and exchange of user-generated content" (Kaplan & Haenlein, 2010).

Over the last few years, organisations have increased their presence on social media such as LinkedIn, Facebook, Twitter, and Instagram. For example, data suggest that in 2015 over 50 million organisations worldwide had a Facebook business page, compared to only 700,000 in 2010 (Maiorescu, 2017). Research suggests that online digital platforms offer organisations the opportunity of communicating with both existing and potential employees in an informal and friendly way in order to contribute, in some cases, to enhanced employee engagement (Martin, Parry & Flowers, 2015; Parry, Martin & Dromey, 2019). This entry will explore the potential of using social media to encourage communication and collaboration in the workplace and to engage with both existing and potential employees. It will also examine extant evidence regarding the challenges and factors that employers need to consider when using social media.

Social Media for Recruitment

Social media is perhaps most commonly used in HRM as a means to engage with future potential employees as part of the recruitment process (Nikolaou, 2014). This process has been described as "e-recruitment 2.0" (Girard & Fallery, 2010) and allows companies to make contact with both active and passive job seekers and to build a (albeit superficial) relationship with them (Parry & Solidoro, 2013). The evidence suggests that social media allows companies to directly contact a large number of potential employees quickly and simultaneously (Parry & Solidoro, 2013) and to promote both their employer brand (Miller-Merrell, 2012; Carrillat, d'Astous & Gregoire, 2014) and organisational brand via the provision of content that relates to the organisation. In addition, some organisations use social networking sites as a means to screen and select applicants by verifying information provided by candidates (Smith & Kidder, 2010). In particular, digital platforms such as LinkedIn, Facebook, and Twitter are increasingly used by organisations to gather information about potential employees and, in most cases, these digital platforms offer HR with

https://doi.org/10.1515/9783110633702-005

relevant and additional information to support the traditional recruiting process (e.g. resume screening, interview, etc.) allowing them "to make better, more holistic decisions" (Zide, Elman & Shahani-Denning, 2014, p. 584) (Kluemper, 2013; McDonald, Thompson & O'Connor, 2016). In addition to offering support to the recruitment stage, research on the use of social media within the HRM function has found that these digital platforms can be successfully employed by organisations to enhance employee voice in the workplace (Holland, Cooper & Hecker, 2016; Parry, Martin, & Dromey, 2019) and thus promoting communication, collaboration, and engagement among the members of the organisation.

Social Media for Promoting Employee Communication, Collaboration and Engagement

The use of social media by the HRM function to attract, engage and communicate with potential employees has increased over the past few years. Research suggests that social media platforms can serve different organisational purposes such as (a) enhancing collaboration and engagement among the members of the organisation, (b) promoting organisational learning via the use of tools for knowledge sharing, (c) connecting organisations with a new digital-generation of employees, and (d) encouraging individuals to raise their own voice rather than using the collective voice of unions (Martin, Parry & Flowers, 2015; Parry, Martin & Dromey, 2019).

A stream of research has focused its attention on understanding the potential of social media to enhance workplace engagement by giving voice to employees (e.g. Holland, Cooper & Hecker, 2016; Martin, Parry & Flowers, 2015; Parry, Martin & Dromey, 2019; Parry & Solidoro, 2013). These studies suggest that by enhancing employee engagement, organisations are more likely to achieve high levels of performance as they can rely on individuals who are attentive, emotionally connected, integrated, focused on their performance, more willing to contribute to the organisation by taking initiatives and seeking opportunities, and who work harder to meet clients' expectations (Parry & Solidoro, 2013).

In order to enhance the level of employee engagement, it is paramount for managers to promote employee participation in the decision-making processes of the organisation by, for example, encouraging them to take part in bottom-up discussions (Denyer, Parry & Flowers, 2011; Sievert & Scholz, 2017). Due to their collaborative and interactive nature, social media technologies offer organisations a tool for facilitating this process by 'reducing the distance' between the members of the organisation (Parry & Solidoro, 2013). For example, online forums such as chatrooms, can be created to connect people with similar responsibilities or expertise across the organisation so that people can share experiences, ask for and receive support from their peers. Moreover, by promoting dialogue across the different levels of the organisation, digital networking can facilitate the integration of employees into the organisation, thus supporting the development of a sense of community and strengthening the organisational culture (Parry, 2013). This will ultimately increase collaboration and knowledge sharing within the workplace contributing to higher levels of job satisfaction and, indeed, enhanced engagement (Behringer, Sassenberg & Scholl, 2017; Holland, Cooper & Hecker, 2016). Some research also suggests that social media networking represents an effective channel for listening and understanding employees' needs, contributing to improve HRM processes and practices (Parry, 2013). Finally, social media represent a powerful tool also for promoting communication with external stakeholders (Opgenhaffen & Claeys, 2017). Some companies, indeed, encourage employees to contribute on social media by, for example, sharing or retweeting the organisation's campaigns or specific vacancies, in order to disseminate company information through their own network (Carim & Warwick, 2013).

Realizing the Benefits of Social Media in HRM

The evidence does provide examples of organisations using social media successfully to foster employee engagement in the workplace and to improve communication and collaboration particularly between dispersed employees (Parry, Martin & Dromey, 2019). However, research also suggests that the adoption of this type of technology by organisations is not uniform and the results vary across the adopters (Martin, Parry & Flowers, 2015). In this regard, research suggests that the effectiveness of using social media at work may depend on a number of factors. For example, research suggests that some technologies can highly engage only certain groups of employees, while disengaging others (Parry, Martin & Dromey, 2019). Therefore, organisations that want to introduce social media at work should consider the technological engagement of individuals in relation to the specific form of social media they are considering introducing. On this matter, Holland, Cooper and Hecker (2016) found that younger employees (Generation Y, born between 1981–1996) are more likely to use social media as a form of employee voice in the workplace, compared to their older colleagues. These results suggest that the age of employees might play a critical role when considering the effectiveness of using social media at work (Holland, Cooper & Hecker, 2016).

Also important is the issue of trust, which has been found to be fundamental for the effectiveness of using social networking to foster employee engagement (Holland et al., 2012; Opgenhaffen & Claeys, 2017; Sievert & Scholz, 2017). Employees perceiving high level of trust and autonomy from managers, will be more willing to use technologies to express their voice (Parry, Martin & Dromey, 2019). This is also related to the perceived "honesty of signals sent out by senior leaders and middle managers on respectful dialogue" (Martin, Parry & Flowers, 2015, p. 559) which has been found to affect the extent to which employees will share their ideas, freely. To this end, an additional factor seems to merit attention as employee engagement to use social media in the workplace also depends on the perceived usefulness of the tool adopted by the organisation and the individual consideration of the importance of contributing to the organisational knowledge (Behringer, Sassenberg & Scholl, 2017).

Indeed, the existing organisational culture together with the leadership style plays a crucial role for employees to express their voice. In particular, the way that an organisation's leadership is perceived by employees has been found to directly affect employee engagement as it provides the context for communication to happen (Men, 2015). As Parry and Solidoro (2013) suggest "organisations must ask themselves whether they are truly ready for collaborate, create and exploit knowledge and whether existing social interactions are open or closed" (p. 128). In line with this, Poba-Nzaou et al. (2016) found that a conservative attitude of managers in relation to the use of social media at work represents a challenge for HRM to promote employee participation in using social media. Finally, the majority of studies also agree that an existing "blended employee engagement" (Sievert & Scholz, 2017, p. 902) is a prerequisite for fostering engagement in the workplace through social media (Martin, Parry & Flowers, 2015; Parry & Solidoro, 2013).

Future Research Directions

This entry has highlighted that research on the use of social media within the HRM function has found that organisations are mainly using social media for supporting the recruitment process (e.g. Kluemper, 2013; McDonald et al., 2016) and to enhance employee voice in the workplace (Holland, Cooper & Hecker, 2016; Parry, 2013). However, organisations should consider the full potential of these digital platforms which can not only support the recruitment process, but also allow the management to be aware of potential workplace issues in 'real-time' (Holland, Cooper & Hecker, 2016; Parry, Martin & Dromey, 2019). Therefore, future research may further explore ways of fostering engagement in the workplace by means of new technologies. Potential research questions may be (but are not limited to):

- What are the new technologies (in addition to social media) which could be adopted by organisations to promote engagement in the workplace?
- What is the role of the HRM function in promoting communication in the workplace? is there any policy in practice?

Further Readings

Holland, P., Cooper, B. K., & Hecker, R. (2016). Use of social media at work: a new form of employee voice?. *The International Journal of Human Resource Management*, 27(21), 2621–2634.

Parry, E., Martin, G., & Dromey, J. (2019). Scenarios and Strategies for Social Media in Engaging and Giving Voice to Employees. In *Employee Voice at Work*, P. Holland et al. (eds), Springer Nature Singapore Pte Ltd.

Parry, E., & Solidoro, A. (2013). Social media as a mechanism for engagement?. In T. Bondarouk and M.K. Olivas-Luján (eds), *Social media in Human Resource Management (Advanced Series in Management, Volume 12)*, Bingley: Emerald Group, 121–141.

References

Behringer, N., Sassenberg, K., & Scholl, A. (2017). Knowledge contribution in organizations via social media. *Journal of Personnel Psychology*, 16(1),12–24.

Carim, L., & Warwick, C. (2013). Use of social media for corporate communication by research-funding organizations in the UK. *Public Relations Review*, 35(3),317–319.

Carrillat, F. A., d'Astous A., & Gregoire E. M. (2014). Leveraging social media to enhance recruitment effectiveness. *Internet Research*, 24(4),474–495.

Denyer, D., Parry, E., & Flowers, P. (2011). "Social", "Open" and "Participative"? Exploring Personal Experiences and Organisational Effects of Enterprise 2.0 Use. *Long Range Planning*, 44, 375–396.

Girard A., & Fallery, B. (2010). Human resource management on the internet: new perspectives. *Journal of Contemporary Management Research*, 4(2),1–14.

Holland, P., Cooper, B. K., & Hecker, R. (2016). Use of social media at work: a new form of employee voice?. *The International Journal of Human Resource Management*, 27(21), 2621–2634.

Holland, P., Pyman, A., Teicher, J., & Cooper, B. (2012). Trust in management: The role of employee voice arrangements and perceived managerial opposition to unions. *Human Resource Management Journal*, 22, 377–391.

Kaplan, A. M., & Haenlein, M. (2010). Users of the world unite! The challenges and opportunities of social media. *Business Horizons*, 53(1),59–68.

Kluemper, D. (2013). Social network screening: pitfalls, possibilities, and parallels in employment selection, in T. Bondarouk and M.K. Olivas-Luján (eds), *Social media in Human Resource Management (Advanced Series in Management, Volume 12)*, Bingley: Emerald Group, 1–21.

Martin, G., Parry, E., & Flowers, P. (2015). Do social media enhance constructive employee voice all of the time or just some of the time?. *Human Resource Management Journal*, 25(4), 541–562.

Maioresco, M. D. (2017). Using online platforms to engage employees in unionism. The case of IBM. *Public Relations Review*, 43, 963–968.

McDonald, P., Thompson, P., & O'Connor, P. (2016). Profiling employees online: shifting public-private boundaries in organisational life. *Human Resource Management Journal*, 26(4), 541–556.

Men, L. R. (2015). The internal communication role of the chief executive officer: Communication channels, style, and effectiveness. *Public Relations Review*, 41, 461–471.

Miller-Merrell, J. (2012). The workplace engagement economy where HR, social, mobile and tech collide. *Employee Relations Today*, 39(2),1–9.

Nikolaou, I. (2014). Social networking web sites in job search and employee recruitment. *International Journal of Selection and Assessment*, 22(2),179–189.

Opgenhaffen, M., & Claeys, A. (2017). Between hope and fear: developing social media guidelines, *Employee Relations*, 39(2),130–144.

Parry, E., & Solidoro, A. (2013). Social media as a mechanism for engagement?. In T. Bondarouk and M.K. Olivas-Luján (eds), *Social media in Human Resource Management (Advanced Series in Management, Volume 12)*, Bingley: Emerald Group, 121–141.

Parry, E., Martin, G., & Dromey, J. (2019). Scenarios and Strategies for Social Media in Engaging and Giving Voice to Employees. In *Employees Voice at Work*, P. Holland et al. (eds), Springer Nature Singapore Pte Ltd.

Parry, E. (2013). Engaging employees using Social Media. *HR Zone*. 222. www.HRzone.com.

Poba-Nzaou, P., Lemieux, N., Beaupré, D., & Uwizeyemungu, S. (2016). Critical challenges associated with the adoption of social media: A Delphi of a panel of Canadian human resources managers. *Journal of Business Research*, 69, 4011–4019.

Sievert, H., & Scholz, C. (2017). Engaging employees in (at least partly) disengaged companies. Results of an interview survey within about 500 German corporations on the growing importance of digital engagement via internal social media. *Public Relations Review*, 43, 894–903.

Smith W., & Kidder D. L. (2010). You've been tagged! (then again maybe not): employers and Facebook. *Business Horizons*, 53(5),491–499.

Zide, J., Elman, B., & Shahani-Denning, C. (2014). LinkedIn and recruitment: how profiles differ across occupations, *Employee Relations*, 36(5),583–604.

Part 2: **Context of e-HRM**

Emma Parry and Hilla Peretz
Organizational Outcomes and e-HRM

This entry will focus on the impact of e-HRM on outcomes at the organizational level. We will define e-HRM as a set of "configurations of computer hardware, software and electronic networking resources that enable intended or actual HRM activities (e.g. policies, practices and services) through coordinating and controlling individual and group-level data capture and information creation and communication within and across organizational boundaries" (Marler & Parry, 2016, p. 2).

Marler & Fisher (2013, p. 33) noted that "no studies directly examined the relationship between e-HRM adoption and any kind of organizational performance measures such as competitive advantage, organizational performance, reduced costs or improved HR outcomes such as increased human capital, reduced turnover or increased organizational commitment or job satisfaction". This is still the case. However, scholars have suggested that organizations can improve their performance and increase competitive advantage via the use of e-HRM to achieve administrative and strategic benefits (Bondarouk, Harms, & Lepak, 2015; Bondarouk, Parry, & Furtmueller, 2017). Typically, e-HRM has been suggested to have three types of benefits: first, those that focus on operational outcomes, efficiency or cost effectiveness; second, those that improve the effectiveness of the HR function, either by improving HR service delivery or by promoting relationships between HR and managers; and third, those that allow the HR function to become more strategic (Lepak & Snell, 1998; Parry & Tyson, 2011; Ruël, Bondarouk, & Looise, 2004). This entry will therefore focus on these three areas in our analysis of the outcomes of e-HRM.

Impact of e-HRM on Efficiency

The literature suggests that e-HRM can improve the efficiency of HR activities by both reducing costs and by increasing the speed of transactions (Marler, 2009; Martin, Reddington, & Alexander, 2008; Parry & Tyson 2011). Early research into e-HRM provided evidence of these outcomes. For example, several authors found that e-HRM allowed the HR function to operate more efficiently by reducing the ratio of HR practitioners to employees, increasing the speed of processes, reducing costs and taking on administrative work (Ruël et al., 2004; Ruta, 2005; Strohmeier, 2007). However, other analyses have disputed this suggestion, failing to find support for cost savings due to e-HRM (Reddick, 2009). Parry (2011), for example, found that companies using e-HRM did not have a lower HR headcount than those that do not use e-HRM, therefore casting doubt on the idea that e-HRM can allow the HR function to make such efficiencies.

https://doi.org/10.1515/9783110633702-006

Impact on Effectiveness

Ruël et al. (2004) suggested that the use of technology could help to improve the service that the HR function provides to its employees. This notion is supported by evidence that e-HRM is related to positive perceptions of the HR function (see for example Bondarouk, Ruel, & van der Heijden, 2009; Lukaszewski, Stone, & Stone-Romero, 2008; Voermans & Van Veldhoven, 2007) and also through evidence that e-HRM can lead to increased accuracy in data entry (Gardner et al 2003; Parry & Tyson, 2011). Lepak & Snell's (1998) suggestion that e-HRM can have positive relational consequences has been supported by evidence pertaining to improved communication, cooperation and relationships (Bondarouk et al., 2017; Reddick, 2009).

Impact on the Strategic Role of the HR Function

Whereas interest in the impact of e-HRM on efficiency and effectiveness has waned in recent years, a more significant amount of research has been undertaken regarding the possible influence of e-HRM on the role of the HR function (Marler, 2009). Early literature regarding e-HRM suggested that the use of such technologies could support the HR function in transforming itself into a function that is more strategic or spends more time on delivering the business strategy rather than on transactional or administrative activities (see for example Lepak & Snell, 1998; Hendrickson, 2003; Lawler & Mohrman, 2003; Shrivastiva & Shaw, 2004). However, this notion was much debated with other authors suggesting that the HR function was not actually achieving this outcome (see for example Tansley, Newell, & Williams, 2001; Burbach & Dundon, 2005).

It is because of this debate perhaps that much of the recent work on e-HRM has been devoted to addressing the question of whether e-HRM can really help the HR function to become a more strategic function. For example, Parry (2011) used survey data to examine this question and found a positive relationship between the use of e-HRM and HR's strategic involvement.

Marler & Fisher (2013) examined the extant evidence regarding the impact of e-HRM on the role of the HR function and concluded that, taking a deterministic perspective, there was little scientific evidence to support the claim that e-HRM makes the HR function more strategic. In particular, they noted that, despite the existence of six studies that tested the relationship between e-HRM and how strategic the HR role was, none of the studies were able to establish causality. Rather, Marler and Fisher's findings supported an organizational imperative perspective, in which e-HRM is an outcome of strategic decision-making by HR managers rather than a driver of this strategic orientation. Marler & Parry (2016) built upon this research, finding that e-HRM and the strategic role of the HR function were in fact reciprocally related, suggesting that managers could deploy e-HRM when making strategic decisions but that e-HRM could also have a significant influence on the strategic role of HRM in organizations. This is an area that still requires significant research (Marler & Parry, 2016; Bondarouk et al., 2017).

Factors Affecting the Outcomes of e-HRM

It might be that the mixed research findings with regard to the operational, relational and transformational outcomes of e-HRM are because these are contingent on other factors. There is some research that examined the factors that might affect these outcomes, although more is needed. For example, scholars have suggested that the nature of the HR function is a key determinant of the outcomes of e-HRM, in relation to whether it is strategically oriented (Voermans & Van Veldhoven, 2007; Marler, 2009). Ruël et al. (2007) found that the success of e-HRM adoption was affected by the amount of information employees were provided about the system. Parry and Tyson (2011) found that efficiency and effectiveness outcomes of e-HRM were to some extent dependent on the design and implementation of the e-HRM system, on training of users and on engagement of users with the technology; whereas the achievement of transformational outcomes was influenced by whether HR practitioners developed the new skills needed for a more strategic role.

In addition, several scholars (e.g Lazazzara & Galanaki, 2018; Ruël & Van der Kaap, 2012, Florkowski & Olivas-Lujan, 2006) have recently argued that institutional factors may affect e-HRM adoption and outcomes. Weerakkody, Dwivedi and Irani (2009) suggested that organizations in different political, socioeconomic and cultural contexts often react differently to similar internal and external challenges, particularly those that involve IT-induced change resulting from limitations imposed by the environment in which they operate. Accordingly, e-HRM adoption and usage will vary on a cross-national basis due to country-specific factors, resulting in different effects on outcomes.

Summary

This entry has provided an overview of the evidence regarding the impact of e-HRM on organizational outcomes. While there is not yet any research that looks at the direct effect of e-HRM on organizational performance or competitive advantage, the literature suggests that e-HRM might have an impact on the efficiency and effectiveness of the HR function as well as on its role in relation to strategic involvement. The evidence regarding these impacts is somewhat mixed, particularly in relation to the role of e-HRM in allowing HR to become more strategic. A number of factors that might affect the impact of e-HRM – including design and implementation issues, HR skills and institutions – have also been highlighted.

Further Readings

Bondarouk, T.V, Parry, E., & Furtmueller, E. (2017). Electronic HRM: four decades of research on adoption and consequences. *International Journal of Human Resource Management, 28*(1), 98–131.
Bondarouk, T.V., Ruel, H., & Parry, E. (2017). *Electronic HRM in the smart era*. UK: Emerald Group Publishing Ltd.

References

Bondarouk, T.V, Parry, E., & Furtmueller, E. (2017). Electronic HRM: four decades of research on adoption and consequences. *International Journal of Human Resource Management, 28*(1), 98–131.
Bondarouk, T.V., Harms, R., & Lepak, D.P. (2015). Does e-HRM lead to better HRM service? *International Journal of Human Resource Management, 28*(9), 1332–1362.
Bondarouk, T.V., Ruel, H.J.M., & van der Heijden, B. (2009). E-HRM effectiveness in a public sector organisation: a multi-stakeholder perspective. *International Journal of Human Resource Management, 20*(3), 578–590.
Burbach, R., & Dundon, T. (2005). The strategic potential of human resource information systems: evidence from the Republic of Ireland. *International Employment Relations Review, 11*(1/2), 97–117.
Gardner S.D., Lepak D.P. & Bartol K.M. (2003). Virtual HR: the impact of information technology on the human resource professional. *Journal of Vocational Behavior, 63*, 159–179.
Florkowski, G., & Olivas-Lujan, M. (2006). The diffusion of human resource information technology innovations in US and non-US firms. *Personnel Review, 35*, 684–710.
Hendrickson, A. (2003). Human resource information systems: backbone technology for contemporary human resources. *Journal of Labor Research, 24*(3), 381–394.
Lawler, E., & Mohrman, S. (2003). HR as a strategic partner: what does it take to make it happen? *Human Resource Planning, 20*(2), 365–379.
Lazazzara, A., & Galanaki, E. (2018). E-HRM adoption and usage: a cross-national analysis of enabling factors. In *Digital Technology and Organizational Change* (pp. 125–140). Switzerland, Cham: Springer.
Lepak, D.P., & Snell, S.A. (1998). Virtual HR: strategic human resource management in the 21st century. *Human Resource Management Review, 8*, 215–234.
Lukaszewki, K.M., Stone, D.L., & Stone-Romero, E.F. (2008). The effects of the ability to choose the type of human resources system on perceptions of invasion of privacy and system satisfaction. *Journal of Business and Psychology, 23*, 73–86.
Marler, J. (2009). Making human resources strategic by going to the net: reality or myth. *International Journal of Human Resource Management, 20*(3), 515–527.
Marler, J., & Fisher, S.L. (2013). An evidence based review of e-HRM and strategic human resource management. *Human Resource Management Review, 23*, 18–36.

Marler, J.H., & Parry, E. (2016). Human resource management, strategic involvement and e-HRM technology. *International Journal of Human Resource Management, 27*(19), 2233–2253.

Martin, G., Reddington, M., & Alexander, H. (2008). *Technology, outsourcing and transforming HR.* Oxford: Elsevier.

Parry, E. (2011). An examination of e-HRM as a means to increase the value of the HR function. *International Journal of Human Resource Management, 22*(5), 1146–1162.

Parry, E., & Tyson, S. (2011). Desired goals and actual outcomes of e-HRM. *Human Resource Management Journal, 21*(3), 354–335

Reddick, C.G. (2009). Human resource information systems in Texas city governments: scope and perception of its effectiveness. *Public Personnel Management, 38*, 19–34.

Ruël, H., Bondarouk, V.T., & Looise, J.K. (2004). E-HRM: innovation or irritation – an explorative empirical study in five large companies on web-based HRM. *Management Revue, 15*, 364–381.

Ruël, H., Bondarouk, V.T., & Van der Velde M. (2007). The contribution of e-HRM to HR effectiveness. *Employee Relations, 29*, 280–291.

Ruël, H., & Van der Kaap, H. (2012). E-HRM usage and value creation. Does a facilitating context matter? *German Journal of Human Resource Management, 26*(3), 260–281.

Ruta, C. (2005). The application of change management theory to HR portal implementation in subsidiaries of multinational corporations. *Human Resource Management, 44*(1), 35–53.

Shrivastiva, S., & Shaw, J. (2004). Liberating HR through technology. *Human Resource Management, 42*(3), 201–222,

Strohmeier, S. (2007). Research in e-HRM: review and implications. *Human Resource Management Review, 17*, 19–37.

Tansley, C., Newell, S., & Williams, H. (2001). Effecting HRM-style practices through an integrated human resource information system. *Personnel Review, 30*(3), 351–370.

Voermans, M., & Van Veldhoven, M. (2007). Attitude towards e-HRM: an empirical study at Phillips'. *Human Resource Management Digest, 36*(6), 887–902.

Weerakkody, V., Dwivedi, Y.K., & Irani, Z. (2009). The diffusion and use of institutional theory: A cross-disciplinary longitudinal literature survey. *Journal of Information Technology, 24*, 354–368

Rita Bissola
Industry 4.0 and e-HRM

Nowadays industrial production is undergoing a deep and lasting challenge. The global competition and the ever-changing customer requests lead to reduced time-to-market, shorter product lifecycles, and the need to cut costs in order to stay competitive. In such an environment, Industry 4.0, also known with other terms such as Smart manufacturing or Integrated industry, offers new possibilities for companies to streamline their innovation processes, to cope with customers asking for more customization and flexibility, and to update their business model to a higher level of efficiency and service orientation (Hecklau, Galeitzke, Flachs, & Kohl, 2016; Rojko, 2017).

The neologism originates from considering the ongoing transformation as the fourth industrial revolution (Hecklau et al., 2016; Schneider, 2018). The industrial revolution historically started with the adoption of mechanized production plants driven by water and steam power, which represents the first stage of the process. The second industrialization wave came with electrification, which enabled mass production and brought about the division of labor. The digitalization of industrial manufacturing by means of programmable logic controllers opened the third phase characterized by microelectronics and flexible production lines, which allowed for the manufacture of a variety of products. The smart automation of cyber-physical systems enabled by the Internet of Things (IoT) and other technologies triggered the current digitalization era. The self-organizing cyber physical production systems facilitate flexible production in terms of product specifications, volumes, and timing, thus achieving the goal of meeting the customers' needs (Habracken & Bondarouk, 2017; Rojko, 2017).

Definition and Origin of the Term

Industry 4.0 focuses on manufacturing. A thorough definition describes industry 4.0 as: *"the increasing digitization of the entire value chain and the resulting interconnection of people, objects and systems through real time data exchange. As a result of that interconnection, products, machines and processes are equipped with artificial intelligence and get enabled to adapt to spontaneous changes of the environment independently. Furthermore, smart objects become embedded in broader systems, which enhance the creation of flexible, self-controlling production systems"* (Hecklau et al., 2016, p. 2).

Even though scholars do not converge on a well-established and widely accepted definition, they all agree on the main components of Industry 4.0: a network-centric approach, smart objects that enable flexible self-controlling production techniques,

https://doi.org/10.1515/9783110633702-007

the integration of people, products, manufacturing systems and processes within and across companies, thus connecting the entire supply chain for value creation (Habraken & Bondarouk, 2017; Lasi, Fettke, Feld, & Hoffmann, 2014).

The Organizational Impact of Industry 4.0

Three elements distinguish Industry 4.0 from the previous generations of highly automated manufacturing systems (e.g. computer-integrated manufacturing): a human-centered perspective, far-reaching networking, and decentralization of decisions and control (Schneider, 2018). While the previous visions in automated manufacturing aimed at reaching a completely automated factory that operates without humans, industry 4.0 intends to promote an improved human-machine interaction, the adaptation of manufacturing systems to human needs, and more flexible and friendlier environmental conditions (Lasi et al., 2014; Rojko, 2017; Schneider, 2018).

The main impact of advanced connectivity far beyond the company's boundaries, from a micro-organizational point of view, is the transformation of work (Hecklau et al. 2016). The digital content of job tasks also increases in the production field (Annunziata & Biller, 2015). Easy and repetitive tasks are being automated, while workers are requested to contribute to more complex activities, which often require new forms of human-robot collaboration (Hecklau et al. 2016; Schneider, 2018). Employees in charge of production planning and control of manufacturing systems can perform their activities remotely, therefore increasing the virtual part of their job and decreasing the importance of their location.

Besides the digitalization of activities, the decentralization of decision-making, control and coordination functions, which will partly be automatically carried out by CPS and smart objects, industry 4.0 will mainly affect the job of employees in charge of supervising the production process. As a consequence, these managers will have to deal with more complex, flexible, and partially invisible manufacturing processes, which require a broader comprehension of the overall production journey, while taking into consideration possible cross-companies collaborations and interdependencies (Schneider, 2018).

Human Resource Management 4.0

The above described characteristics of Industry 4.0, together with the integration of advanced technologies, offer a tremendous opportunity to HR to increase its strategic contribution, transform and upgrade the efficacy of HR practices, and promote an individually diverse employee-organization relationship (Bondarouk & Brewster, 2016). In the following part of the paragraph, more details on each of these aspects are clarified.

Part of the strategic role of HR is to assure the effective employment of qualified cohorts of employees, support their commitment, and develop future possible substitutes to allow the achievement of the company's objectives (Lewis & Heckman, 2006). In the deeply changing work environment of Industry 4.0, one of the main challenges that companies are facing is employing a competent workforce. On the labor market, there is a lack of the technical knowledge and skills requested by the new jobs in the smart enterprises, therefore companies need to develop specific strategies to cope with this situation (Kane, Palmer, Phillips, & Kiron, 2017). HR's effectiveness in attracting, committing to support, and retaining highly qualified employees can make the difference in driving the change to the Industry 4.0 standard. Consequently, HR should also focus on the development process of the required competencies, which is a long-term, but fundamental oriented action. This activity implies identifying required competences, detecting critical gaps with respect to workforce skills, and designing training activities to develop the lacking knowledge of resources and therefore close the gap (Hecklau et al. 2016; Quint, Sebastian, & Gorecky, 2015). Although this is a crucial HR contribution for the competitiveness of the company, HR professionals still need to offer effective solutions to quickly develop digital capabilities in the short term (Schneider, 2018). Centralization of the existing expertise and participation to teaching or demonstration factories are among the very few suggestions that emerge from the literature (Agarwal & Brem, 2015; Rentzos, Mavrikios, & Chryssolouris, 2015; Schuh, Gartzen, & Rodenhauser, 2015).

The interconnection of people, objects and systems through real time data exchange, together with the paramount power of obtaining analytics typical of Industry 4.0, let HR obtain a bulk of new information on employees and their performance. This allows HR to add objectivity to their practices, such as performance and career management (Bondarouk & Brewster, 2016). People analytics also allow for the prediction of employees' behaviors and decisions, such as intention to quit or organizational commitment thus supporting a more informed workforce strategy.

Similarly, the application of smart technologies to HR management systems further widens the HR possibilities. Adopting them in recruitment and selection allows for the increasing efficiency of these activities, while obtaining a better person-job fit (Bissola & Imperatori, 2014a). In particular, social media and artificial intelligence enable a relevant progression in résumé screening, as well as the employment of intelligent machines to perform part of the selection process (van Esch, Black, & Ferolie, 2019). Advanced technologies apply effectively to HR development systems as well. Augmented reality or sensors seem to enhance learning processes of highly requested competences (e.g. complex problem solving), while blogs, wikis and social media logic shift learning on a virtual dimension, thus making it more efficient and independent from working time and place (Yanson & Johnson, 2016).

Lastly, the availability of real-time data and the high capacity to process them enables HR to obtain individual information about single employees. Moreover, web-based relational e-HRM functionalities enhance an individual dialogue between employees and the HR department (Bissola & Imperatori, 2014b). On this basis, the HR department holds the capacity to customize some HR practices in order to meet the employees' needs, thus supporting their motivation. This is the case of rewards composition (e.g. benefit choice), welfare initiatives, work time scheduling, or steering training or career development (Bondarouk & Brewster, 2016).

HRM in Industry 4.0: The Role of e-HRM

Industry 4.0 is challenging HRM and the changes that it is experiencing go in the direction of an increased digitalization of HR. E-HRM systems are a useful basis for the journey towards HRM 4.0. Companies which already adopt e-HR tools can shift more easily to more technologically advanced people management practices. Similarly, the ability to use digital HRM can be of aid in learning how Industry 4.0 enabled HR systems work. In this case, the employment of e-HRM and their ease of use, a component of e-HRM's strength, can be valuable measures to test the organizational familiarity with digital HR (Bondarouk, Harms, & Lepak, 2017).

A great challenge for HR, coming from Industry 4.0, is the provision of HRM services aligned with the new characteristics of work. Human-machine integration, as requested for example when working with cobots, the surpassing of time and space standards, and the decentralization of decision-making require adequate HR practices to manage employees in the new working conditions. They also call for support to the managers in renewing their leadership and developing different managerial competences.

Transformational e-HRM systems devoted to enabling communication and knowledge exchange among people can usefully contribute to supporting dispersed organizations and decentralized decision making (Ruel, Bondarouk, & Looise, 2004; Parry & Tyson, 2011). However, they need to evolve and enable the processing of large amount of data (Big Data), as well as supporting people-machine communication. Likewise, important functionalities of future transformational e-HRM systems are the selection and aggregation of information bulks and their presentation in forms that can be understandable and significant for employees.

To promote an empowering human-machine interaction, training will be crucial. As a result of e-HRM systems' flexibility and cutting-cost opportunity, e-learning and advanced digital tools will be useful for the necessary broad and intensive training program. However, learning to effectively cooperate with machines and humanoid robotics will surely require further investments to innovate training systems. Specifically, programs will include new contents and tools for the training in human-machine interaction, whereas spaces will purposefully be designed to enable the performance of new training activities.

Another main mission of HR stemming from the fourth industrial revolution concerns the monitoring of the authentic human-centered vocation of Industry 4.0. Since the organization unit is devoted to developing and sustaining the human capital, the HR department is expected to reject the idea of completely automated organizations where human work is no longer needed. Instead, it should uphold digitalization initiatives and human-machine collaborations aimed at empowering employees, thus allowing them to perform activities beyond their own ability and enhance their competences.

This can be considered a novel strategic task of the HR department directly connected to Industry 4.0. Transformational e-HRM systems aimed at supporting knowledge sharing and relational ones adopting a social network technology promote spontaneous communication and an efficient information exchange. This can assist employees in sharing remarks directly coming from their experiences, thus promoting knowledge sharing and making the human contribution to Industry 4.0 always up-to-date and more valuable. Nevertheless, this task transcends the adoption of HR practices, e-HRM tools included, as it mainly involves the HR department in the role of change agent. Indeed, it concerns the cultural challenge of Industry 4.0 that HR should take on in order to maintain the original human-centered character of Industry 4.0, avoid the decline in human work and the consequent arising social problems.

Beyond the specificity of each of the issues that Industry 4.0 posits to e-HRM, the common thread that resides at the base of all of them is the centrality of training. Some jobs will soon disappear and new ones will emerge. Companies will not be able to meet the needs for new competences by simply turning to the external job market; therefore, employees should attend training activities to convert their competences. Similarly, the HR department cannot postpone approaching technological competences anymore, as it truly risks not to be able to support managers and employees of 4.0 organizations.

However, taking into consideration the technological revolution entailed by Industry 4.0, it is reasonable to expect that significant differences between diverse organizational contexts will persist similarly to what Bondarouk and Brewster (2016) observed in the case of smart technologies.

Future research should particularly focus on relational e-HRM to find out the new and more effective e-learning solutions, also enabled by smart technologies, to support continuous development of competences aligned with the different essence of work. A further research avenue is talent management. Digital tools could offer opportunities to increase attractiveness and efficiency of this HR practice, that will be crucial in the next decades.

Further Readings

Ghobakhloo, M. (2018). The future of manufacturing industry: a strategic roadmap toward Industry 4.0. *Journal of Manufacturing Technology Management, 29*(6), 910–936.

Porter, M. E., & Heppelmann, J. E. (2015). How smart, connected products are transforming companies. *Harvard business review, 93*(10), 96–114.

Sivathanu, B., & Pillai, R. (2018). Smart HR 4.0–how industry 4.0 is disrupting HR. *Human Resource Management International Digest, 26*(4), 7–11.

Wilkesmann, M., & Wilkesmann, U. (2018). Industry 4.0–organizing routines or innovations? *VINE Journal of Information and Knowledge Management Systems, 48*(2), 238–254.

References

Agarwal, N. & Brem, A. (2015). Strategic business transformation through technology convergence: implications from General Electric's industrial internet initiative. *International Journal of Technology Management, 67*(2-4), 196–214.

Annunziata, M. & Biller, S. (2015). The industrial Internet and the future of work. *Mechanical Engineering Magazine Select Articles, 137*(09), 30–35.

Bissola, R. & Imperatori, B. (2014a). Recruiting Gen Yers Through Social Media: Insights from the Italian Labor Market. In *Social media in human resources management* (pp. 59–81). Bingley, UK, Emerald Group Publishing Limited.

Bissola, R. & Imperatori, B. (2014b). The unexpected side of relational e-HRM: Developing trust in the HR department. *Employee Relations, 36*(4), 376–397.

Bondarouk, T. & Brewster, C. (2016). Conceptualising the future of HRM and technology research. *The International Journal of Human Resource Management, 27*(21), 2652–2671.

Bondarouk, Harms, & Lepak, (2017). Does e-HRM lead to better HRM service? *The International Journal of Human Resource Management, 28*(9), 1332–1362.

Habraken, M., & Bondarouk, T. (2017). Smart Industry Research in the Field of HRM: Resetting Job Design as an Example of Upcoming Challenges. In Tanya Bondarouk, Huub J.M. Ruël, Emma Parry (eds.) *Electronic HRM in the Smart Era*, pp. 221–259. Bingley, UK, Emerald Publishing Limited.

Hecklau, F., Galeitzke, M., Flachs, S., & Kohl, H. (2016). Holistic approach for human resource management in Industry 4.0. *Procedia Cirp, 54*, 1–6.

Kane, G. C., Palmer, D., Phillips, A. N., & Kiron, D. (2017). Winning the digital war for talent. *MIT Sloan Management Review, 58*(2), 17.

Lasi, H., Fettke, P., Kemper, H. G., Feld, T., & Hoffmann, M. (2014). Industry 4.0. *Business & information systems engineering, 6*(4), 239–242.

Lewis, R. E., & Heckman, R. J. (2006). Talent management: A critical review. *Human resource management review, 16*(2), 139–154.

Parry, E., & Tyson, S. (2011). Desired goals and actual outcomes of e-HRM. Human Resource Management Journal, 21(3), 335–354.

Quint, F., Sebastian, K., & Gorecky, D. (2015). A mixed-reality learning environment. *Procedia Computer Science, 75*, 43–48.

Rentzos, L., Mavrikios, D., & Chryssolouris, G. (2015). A two-way knowledge interaction in manufacturing education: The teaching factory. *Procedia CIRP, 32*, 31–35.

Rojko, A. (2017). Industry 4.0 concept: background and overview. *International Journal of Interactive Mobile Technologies (iJIM), 11*(5), 77–90.

Ruël, H., Bondarouk, T., & Looise, J. K. (2004). E-HRM: Innovation or irritation. An explorative empirical study in five large companies on web-based HRM. *Management Revue, 15*(3), 364–380.

Schneider, P. (2018). Managerial challenges of Industry 4.0: an empirically backed research agenda for a nascent field. *Review of Managerial Science, 12*(3), 803–848.

Schuh, G., Gartzen, T., Rodenhauser, T., & Marks, A. (2015). Promoting work-based learning through industry 4.0. *Procedia CIRP, 32*, 82–87.

van Esch, P., Black, J. S., & Ferolie, J. (2019). Marketing AI recruitment: the next phase in job application and selection. *Computers in Human Behavior, 90*, 215–222.

Yanson, R., & Johnson, R. D. (2016). An empirical examination of e-learning design: The role of trainee socialization and complexity in short term training. *Computers & Education, 101*, 43–54.

Huub Ruël

e-HRM goals, Types and Outcomes in e-HRM Innovation

E-HRM innovations are triggered by ongoing societal, economic and technological developments. New societal trends, ageing population, environmental awareness, work-life balance, labor market shortages, circular economy – all of these directly or indirectly influence HRM decision-makers to change, adjust and advance e-HRM goals and types, leading towards targeted outcomes. Since this is a continuous and dynamic process, e-HRM innovation is a continuous and dynamic process as well. But every organization is unique in a sense and therefore there is no "one size fits all" approach to e-HRM innovations.

E-HRM, considered as an integration of digital technology and human resource management strategy and practices, requires oversight. In this entry I perceive technology as both technical and social, and both dimensions require guidance from the organization to achieve meaningful and optimal value creation. Without conscious and targeted oversight, this is virtually impossible. I present a model (see Figure 8.1) which describes how e-HRM can help organizations successfully from HRM strategy, to e-HRM goals, types and e-HRM outcomes.

The e-HRM model consists of four components: HRM strategy development, e-HRM goals, e-HRM types and e-HRM outcomes which we will discuss successively in this section.

e-HRM Strategy

E-HRM innovation in organizations requires guidance, or even stronger, it requires an e-HRM strategy. Without a clear strategy, it is almost certain that e-HRM applications do not function adequately in conjunction with each other, that overlap between applications is created and that users do not clearly know what the organization expects. This leads to suboptimal results. Already in the beginning of this century, Ruël and colleagues (2004) found that an e-HRM strategy and then the specific goals of new e-HRM innovations should be linked to the HRM strategy and practices. An HRM strategy should clarify how the HRM services are delivered to employees and management and what the role of them is in realizing the HRM strategy. So the e-HRM strategy should be part of the organization-wide HRM strategy, policies and practices.

These HRM strategy and practices differ, of course, by organisation. However, based on research and insights from Harvard researchers Michael Beer and colleagues (1984), it has been found that three types of HRM are distinguishable. They call these

https://doi.org/10.1515/9783110633702-008

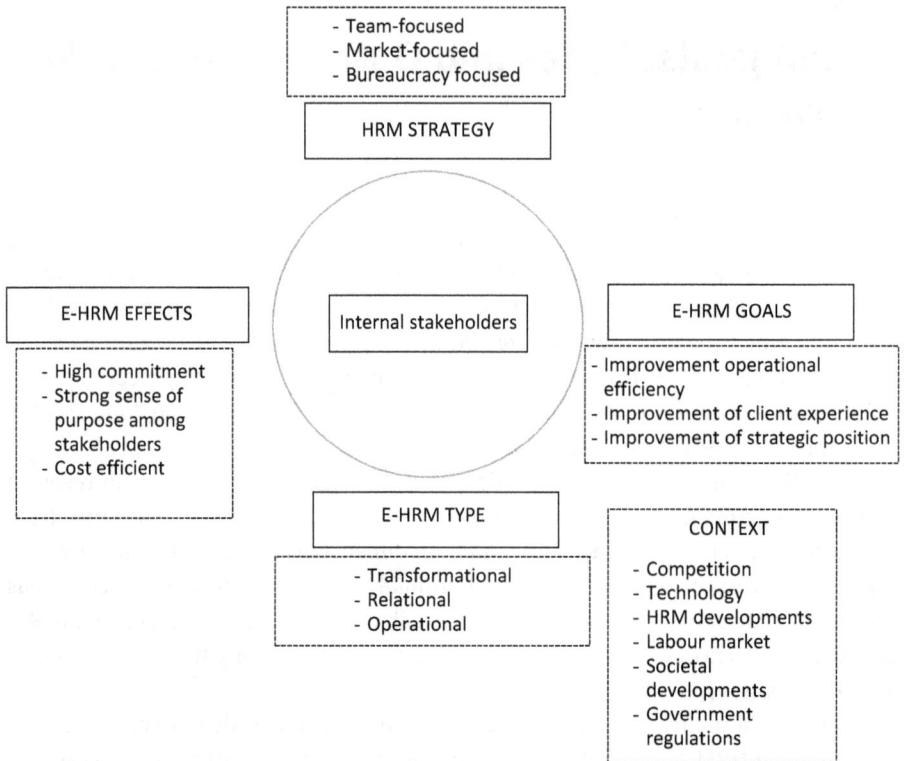

Figure 8.1: The E-HRM model (Ruël et al., 2004).

HRM policy choices: oriented on the 'bureaucracy', on the market, and on the group ('Clan'). Organizations that want to implement e-HRM innovations do not start from scratch with HRM, they have already made implicit or explicit strategic HRM policy choices in the four core areas of HRM that Beer and colleagues distinguish: Employee participation, staff through flow, remuneration and organization of labor and organisation. The three HRM policy choices differ from each other in the following four core areas.

e-HRM Goals

The e-HRM strategy aims to determine the specific goals that an organisation wants to achieve with e-HRM innovations. Here too, the influence of e-HRM providers on organisations is clearly visible, after all, they promise to be able to fulfil more than e-HRM innovations. The risk is that by lack of knowledge of e-HRM, both on the technical side and on the organisational side, organizations are not optimally able to make the right choices for e-HRM innovations.

Research on e-HRM in recent decades has made it clear that there are three types of goals for e-HRM to distinguish (Bondarouk & Furtmueller-Ettinger, 2012): Improving the strategic orientation and position of HUMAN resources (HRM as strategic Business partner), cost savings and improving the efficiency of HRM processes, and improving the quality of service to HRM clients e-HRM innovations aimed at improving the strategic role of HR mainly means investing in applications that can provide HR data analyses (HR Analytics) for strategic staffing planning and future scenarios and that provide key figures that are important for strategic decision-making.

E-HRM innovations to achieve cost savings – for example, reducing HRM employees – and improving HRM processes – for example accelerating the recruitment, selection and commissioning of new staff – mainly means investing in applications and applications that reduce the role of paper forms and the role of people in handling HRM processes. E-HRM employee and management self-service applications where HRM-actions are directly placed in the hands of employees and management are the most suitable.

Improving the quality of HRM services mainly means investing in e-HRM applications that are very well aligned with the wishes, needs and behaviour of clients of HRM. Quality of service is especially an experience. Applications and applications must be intuitive to use. A lot of research has been done on the design of IT applications and also e-HRM applications. A study by Ruël and Bondarouk in 2005 pointed out that especially a good design of e-HRM applications for employees is the most important factor to actually start using those applications.

The Technology Acceptance Model by Fred Davis of Texas Tech University (Venkatesh & Davis, 2000) is probably the most widely used and strongest explanatory model for the acceptance of new technology applications by end users. Without going into this model now, this demonstrates that perceived usability and experienced user-friendliness are decisive for actual use of applications.

These three goals can also be pursued in combination in e-HRM innovation projects, but research shows that ambitions are often not realised. An important explanation for this lies in the 'mismatch' between the technical design of applications and perceived usability and experienced user convenience, simply put between the technical system and the social system (Bondarouk and Ruel, 2009).

Another interesting fact is that the goal of achieving cost savings and efficiency improvement is very difficult to achieve in e-HRM innovation projects. In many cases, the costs – or in other words the necessary investments – appear much higher than estimated. But also the parts where savings are realised are often unrealistic, so late research of Bondarouk and Ruël (2004, 2007, 2013). Organizations often forget that by transferring HRM tasks to employees and managers through all sorts of beautiful self-service concepts the demand for HRM-services is no less. New and higher expectations of HRM are emerging, and questions and the call for support are also shifted to people and organizational components outside the HRM department. Also, for managers, the HRM-job package expands and many managers need to get used to it – or they are not well trained.

Research also confirms that e-HRM applications alone are not sufficient to reinforce the strategic role of HRM (Marler & Fisher, 2013). It also calls for a strategic HRM and a process of organisational renewal in which technology is at the most facilitating. The importance of this process of change is sometimes underestimated.

Does this mean that e-HRM innovations are actually pointless? On the contrary, e-HRM innovations are no longer reminiscent of organisations, but they demand a clear e-HRM strategy and realistic objectives. In order to achieve this, an e-HRM innovation project should be considered as an organisational process and not an IT project. One reason why e-HRM innovations are no longer to be thought of is that employees implicitly assume that many things can easily be arranged or selected via a mobile device. After all, in everyday life, the smartphone or other smart devices are also a support and commitment to communication, shopping and arranging financial matters.

A movement has also been underway for over a decade in which young people who start a career expect to be at the wheel of their careers. Above all, highly educated are expecting more and more to be able to give direction to their career development instead of expecting organisations to 'regulate' it. This development also requires e-HRM innovations.

e-HRM Types

E-HRM innovation calls for a strategy and for clear and realistic objectives that follow from the strategy. From the objectives, organizations can then choose types of e-HRM, more sharply formulated, for the nature of the constellation of e-HRM applications. Ruël et al. (2004) distinguish three types of e-HRM: Transformational e-HRM, relational e-HRM and operational e-HRM. Transformational e-HRM means the implementation and use of e-HRM innovations that facilitate strategic decision-making and strategic change processes. Relational e-HRM is the implementation and use of e-HRM applications that support HRM service processes. Operational e-HRM includes e-HRM applications that aim to facilitate employees by making personal HR information easily available and through competency development, performance management and reward.

The e-HRM types described here are suitable for professionals and consultants as lens to look at e-HRM in organizations. In practice, organizations will use e-HRM applications that have characteristics of all three types. And also not all parts will be equally well integrated and widely used. There are many anecdotes about managers who need to approve employee leave requests in an e-HRM application, but in daily practice 'outsource' this to their management assistants. They often do not have the formal power to do so, and it can also prevent them from actually being able to access data that should remain confidential.

Also, the e-HRM types can help organizations to 'align' their e-HRM strategy, objectives and types themselves, i.e. to ensure that strategy, objectives and types form a coherent whole. This is quite difficult for organizational practice to realise and also a source for failures or disappointing results in E-HRM innovations.

e-HRM Outcomes

E-HRM should deliver results, create value for organizations. If that is not the case, organizations will not want to invest in e-HRM innovations. The result that e-HRM should start delivering, the 'outcome', differs from the e-HRM targets as described above. E-HRM is a way in which HRM-strategy and practices are delivered to HRM clients, namely digitally facilitated. The content of this facilitation is a matter of HRM strategy and policy choices, as explained earlier: E-HRM strategy follows from the HRM strategy. The e-HRM objectives cannot stand alone: after all, an objective to save costs or to improve the quality of HRM services is to create value for the organization and more specifically for its human resources. Michael Beer and his colleagues from Harvard Business School distinguish in their book from 1984 four outcomes of HRM policy choices:
1. high commitment of all employees (high commitment)
2. competent human resources (high competence)
3. cost effective human resources (cost effectiveness)
4. better relations between different internal stakeholders, between management and employees and good balance in the rewards for various staff groupings (higher congruence)

Highly engaged employees mean that they are motivated and set up the organizational importance. It also means that there is a good dialogue between management and staff who makes it possible to constantly discuss changes that are needed to remain successful from a collaborative organization. The role that HRM should be able to play for this is that of change agent, to speak in terms of Ulrich et al., (2008). Competent human resources refers to the capacity of employees to continue to develop to ensure that knowledge and skills are up-to-date and remain. For HRM itself this means that it must be able to fulfil the role of employee champion by stimulating and facilitating the development orientation of employees (Ruel et al., 2007).

Cost-effective human resources refers to the pursuit of a reward system that promotes maximum productivity at the lowest possible wage costs (taking into account labour market conditions), to healthy staff outflows and to acceptable costs due to loss of productivity, for example strikes or other personnel actions. In this case, it is important for HRM to be able to fulfil the role of 'administrative expert'.

Better relationships between different groupings within the organization, say a balanced organization contributes to organizational performance. E-HRM can facilitate this. Good e-HRM analytics applications, applications that promote transparency on reward structures, which improve industrial relations in organizations, facilitate communication and interaction, and applications that self-evaluate and develop support are suitable for this purpose.

e-HRM and the HRM Function

In the previous section, I discussed the four components that form the core of successful e-HRM innovations in organizations: a clear HRM strategy and policy choices, e-HRM objectives, e-HRM types and finally e-HRM outcomes. E-HRM innovations cannot be left to pieces of technology, but require an integrated approach in which the "social system", the organization, controls the "technical system", the design and content of E-HRM applications. The four components stem from each other and the outcomes again provide input to adjust the HRM strategy and policy choices. E-HRM innovations are therefore not static, but are dynamic. The context (environment) is outside the e-HRM circle, but is an important source of influence on the design of e-HRM.

Technology only "comes to life" in human use. Technology is not neutral, but designed by people. And it must remain that way. If technology is no longer understood by people or is not under the control of people, then undesirable situations threaten. This may sound science-fiction-like and futuristic, but with the rapid developments in, for example, artificial intelligence, there are risks of technological developments getting out of hand. That is why the e-HRM model (Figure 8.1) focuses on internal stakeholders, management and employees. They must give direction and give substance to e-HRM innovations.

HRM and technology are inextricably linked. HRM naturally revolves around people and helping them move forward in their role, way of working together, wellbeing, development and performance in organizations, but technological applications are needed to make this possible in organizations now and in the future.

Research Questions

E-HRM innovation is a continuous and dynamic process. Society, economy, organizations and technology keep on developing and changing, which require e-HRM to adapt, adjust and in particular to renew, advance and innovate. Future research on the link between e-HRM strategy, goals, types and outcomes needs to address questions such as to what extent organizations actively try to link e-HRM strategy, goals, types and outcomes? How do the dynamics among internal stakeholders influence e-HRM innovation trajectories? And how does the link between e-HRM strategy, goals, types and outcomes differ per type of organization, for example profit vs. not-for-profit and small and medium size organizations vs large corporations?

Further Readings

Bondarouk, T., Ruël, H.J.M., & Parry, E. (2017). *Electronic HRM in the Smart Era*. Emerald Group Publishing Limited: WA, UK.

Bondarouk, T., Ruël, H.J.M., Oiry, E., & Guiderdoni-Jourdan, K. (2009). (Eds.), *Handbook of Research on E-Transformation and Human Resources Management Technologies*, Information Science Reference, Hershey: New York.

References

Beer, M., Spector, B., Lawrence, P., Mills, D. Q., & Walton, R. (1985). Human resource management: A general manager's perspective.

Bondarouk, T., & Furtmueller, E. (2012, July). Electronic human resource management: Four decades of empirical evidence. In *Academy of Management Proceedings* (Vol. 2012, No. 1, p. 15668). Briarcliff Manor, NY 10510: Academy of Management.

Bondarouk, T. V., & Ruël, H. J. (2009). Electronic Human Resource Management: challenges in the digital era. *The International Journal of Human Resource Management*, 20(3), 505–514.

Bondarouk, T. V., & Ruël, H. J. (2007, March). Human Resource Management Via the Web: Opportunities and Threats. In *WEBIST (3)* (pp. 179–187).

Bondarouk, T., & Ruël, H. (2013). The strategic value of e-HRM: results from an exploratory study in a governmental organization. *The International Journal of Human Resource Management*, 24(2), 391–414.

Marler, J. H., & Fisher, S. L. (2013). An evidence-based review of e-HRM and strategic human resource management. *Human Resource Management Review*, 23(1), 18–36.

Ruël, H., Bondarouk, T., & Looise, J. K. (2004). E-HRM: Innovation or irritation. An explorative empirical study in five large companies on web-based HRM. *Management revue*, 364–380.

Ruël, H. J., Bondarouk, T. V., & Van der Velde, M. (2007). The contribution of e-HRM to HRM effectiveness. *Employee Relations*.

Venkatesh, V., & Davis, F. D. (2000). A theoretical extension of the technology acceptance model: Four longitudinal field studies. *Management Science*, 46(2), 186–204.

Ulrich, D., Younger, J., & Brockbank, W. (2008). The twenty-first-century HR organization. *Human Resource Management*, 47(4), 829–850.

Stefan Strohmeier
Algorithmic Decision Making in HRM

Definition of Algorithmic Decision Making in HRM

An HR decision refers to the choice between different alternatives under uncertainty. The selection of a suitable applicant constitutes a classic example. It is evident that HR decisions show significant influences on success, and that improvements of decision quality directly improve the success of HRM. An HR algorithm refers to an unambiguous set of instructions to solve an HR problem based on a finite number of well-defined individual steps. For reasons of convenience and feasibility, HR algorithms in the interim are regularly designed for and performed by computers. HR decision algorithms thus constitute a subset of HR algorithms that solve HR decision problems. Based on this, *algorithmic decision-making (ADM) in HRM* is defined as *employing computer-based HR decision algorithms for drawing or supporting HR decisions*.

Practice of Algorithmic Decision Making in HRM

Due to the lack of empirical research on ADM in HRM (see below), only a few general estimates can be made of the current practice. Using algorithms to support decisions undoubtedly has a tradition in HRM, as, for instance, in employee scheduling algorithmic decision support has been practiced for decades (e.g. van den Bergh et al., 2013). However, a broader usage of decision algorithms in HRM has only recently become possible based on developments in artificial intelligence (AI) combined with growing data volumes (e.g. Strohmeier & Piazza, 2013 and 2015). In the interim, first commercial applications of AI-based ADM in HRM are available and applied mainly in recruiting and selection. Here decisions are supported by predicting characteristics of the personality, the suitability for a certain position or the future success of applicants, and the like (e.g. Campion, Campion & Campion, 2018).

Algorithms of Algorithmic Decision Making in HRM

Depending on the understanding of "decision algorithms" a broader variety of procedures might be subsumed as an algorithm. A simple automated comparison of job requirement profiles with applicant qualification profiles and a subsequent automated selection of the best qualified applicant might already be seen as a simple variety of ADM. Due to the particular importance of machine learning algorithms for ADM, this

https://doi.org/10.1515/9783110633702-009

category is exemplarily presented in the following (Campion et al., 2018; Gandomi & Haider, 2015).

Machine learning algorithms use historical data to predict decision-relevant future developments (e.g. Strohmeier & Piazza, 2013). Classification algorithms, such as classification trees or neural networks, constitute a core category in this respect (e.g., Strohmeier & Pizza, 2013). For instance, if a long-term retention of employees is intended, classification algorithms can be used to predict whether an applicant will stay or leave quickly after hiring. For this purpose, historical applicant data with leaving and staying employees are used to classify applicants into the classes of "long-term employee" and "quickly leaving employee". Such patterns can be used to predict the class of a current applicant to be used for hiring decisions. Classification patterns can be transparent. Classification trees, for instance, formulate explicit prediction rules based on predictors. Classification patterns, however, can also stay opaque. Artificial neural networks, for instance, do not directly uncover the classification solution found. For a proper classification, input data need to show general quality and specific relevance. General data quality refers to the question whether input data are correct, complete and current, among others. Specific data relevance refers to the question whether input data comprise of valid predictor data fields that are able to predict a decision-relevant outcome. Based on machine-learning algorithms, more and more decision-relevant developments can be predicted.

Requirements of Algorithmic Decision Making in HRM

For an applicability in practice, ADM in HRM must meet basic requirements. While *success of ADM* doubtlessly constitutes the main requirement, the *transparency*, *equality*, *privacy*, and *acceptancy* of ADM constitute further, interrelated secondary requirements.

Firstly, ADM must warrant decision *success*, while this refers to quality and efficiency of ADM (Strohmeier & Piazza, 2013). Quality refers to the question whether ADM is able to improve decision quality as compared to human decision-making (HDM). Efficiency refers to the question whether ADM is able to reduce the human and financial effort as compared to HDM. It is obvious that ADM should be applied only if it is of higher quality and/or efficiency. Regarding the success of ADM there are general meta-studies on ADM quality that include some studies referring to HR decisions, in particular, hiring decisions (Meehl 1996; Grove et al., 2000). Interestingly, these meta-studies uncover a slight superiority of ADM compared to HDM. While this superiority in quality is not huge, it is expected that algorithmic decisions are of superior efficiency since they can be drawn in an automated and thus fast and cheap manner (e.g. Grove et al. 2000). Even though these results need a systematic re-examination against the background of HR decisions, they pose the question of who/what should decide in HRM, man or machine, with a new impetus.

Secondly, ADM needs to be *transparent*. Transparency shows the sub-dimensions of explainability and accountability. Explainability refers to the question whether the procedure and result of an algorithmic decision can be communicated to and is understandable by affected persons. Accountability refers to the question whether responsibility for decisions is diffused and unclear or can be assigned to known persons or institutions. Transparency is necessary due to the latent opacity of ADM. Opacity can emerge due to the protection of an intellectual property of algorithm inventors ("intentional opacity"), the algorithmic illiteracy of affected persons ("illiterate opacity"), and due to the obscuring characteristics of some algorithms such as artificial neural networks ("intrinsic opacity") (Burell, 2016). While only transparent ADM can be monitored, controlled and improved (Zerili et al., 2018), there is doubt whether a complete uncovering of algorithms (detailed input data and source code) is actually necessary and useful. Uncovering input data might cause privacy problems. Uncovering source code might not contribute to understanding of technically illiterate persons. Moreover, a full disclosure offers algorithmically literate persons a possibility to manipulate their own data to influence the decision outcome ("gaming the system"). Therefore, a "practical justification" (uncovering which factors with which weight have led to which decision) is often regarded as meaningful (Zerilli et al., 2108).

Thirdly, ADM needs to care for *equality* of treatment. Since learning from historic data, ADM can "learn" and perpetuate existing discriminations relating to age, gender, ethnicity etc. of affected persons. Developers and users of algorithms thus should be aware of discriminating biases and avoid them. A useful and comprehensive variety refers to "equality by design". This initially refers to not employing potentially discriminative data fields such as age, gender, race, etc., as input data in order to avoid an explicit discrimination by algorithms. Moreover, it should be additionally checked whether predictors of (un-)desired future developments, also predict certain age, gender or ethnicity categories, and if so, exclude them. If, for instance, the "number of previous job transitions" predicts "employee leave" as undesired future development, but additionally also predicts the age category "applicants > 50 years", this predictor should not be applied in order to avoid age discrimination.

Fourthly, ADM needs to preserve *privacy* of input data (needed for training the algorithm) and decision data (needed for applying the algorithm). Privacy refers to the prevention of information on natural persons from being read, used and/or disseminated without knowledge and consent of this person (e.g. Strohmeier & Piazza, 2013). In ADM there are two major approaches of realizing privacy (e.g. Strohmeier & Piazza, 2013): The permission-approach aims at gaining written permission of employees regarding ADM. This represents the risk that employees do not give the consent, and is feasible for input and decision data. The depersonalization-approach aims at an anonymization of personal data. This approach is only feasible for input data, yet not for decision data, which need to stay un-anonymized.

Fifthly, ADM needs *acceptancy* of the persons affected by ADM. Humans need to accept that decisions with positive and negative implications for them are drawn or at least supported by algorithms. Regarding this, the concept of *algorithm aversion* denotes a deep scepticism of humans against algorithmic decision-making (e.g. Dietvorst, Simmons & Massey, 2015). Empirical results show that human decisions were preferred even in the situations where they were considerably worse than machine decisions. In the interim, however, there are also divergent results, which portray a more positive attitude towards ADM. The concept of *algorithm appreciation* thus denotes the explicit appreciation of the advantages of ADM (e.g. Logg, Minson & Moore, 2019).

Legal Regulations of Algorithmic Decision Making in HRM

Depending on national contexts, ADM is subject to regulations of different kinds and intensities. In the European Union, for instance, there are different laws regarding data protection, equality and codetermination, which are directly relevant for ADM in HRM. Since a comprehensive discussion is far beyond the scope of this entry, *Art. 22* of the *European Data Protection Regulation (GDPR)* is briefly presented in the following, as the norm that directly regulates automated decisions on natural persons and thus represents a core regulation for ADM (e.g. Goodman & Flaxman, 2017). Art. 22 GDPR regulates, that a "decision based solely on automated processing, including profiling", which "produces legal effects" or "significantly affects" a natural person, is prohibited. This means that a fully automated ADM without a subsequent human verification is not permitted. It is, however, possible to use ADM to support a human decision-maker, who evaluates the suggestion of ADM and draws his or her own decisions. Moreover, Art. 22 entails three exceptions that allow fully automated decisions: a) if a decision "is necessary for entering into, or performance of, a contract", b) if an EU or EU member state law authorises ADM, c) if there is explicit consent of the person that is subject to ADM. Regarding ADM in HRM the first and the third exception might be relevant. The first exception allows for decisions that are necessary for entering and performing of an employment contract, while "necessary", however, constitutes an indeterminate legal term that needs an interpretation. The third exception allows for an explicit consent of the affected person, while this consent must be voluntary and not compulsory, for example, as a pre-condition for offering an employment contract.

Research on Algorithmic Decision Making in HRM

Research on ADM in HRM is so far mostly method- and very infrequently domain-oriented. This means that contributions stem mainly from methodical and technical disciplines, and mainly focus on the development of decision algorithms for HRM. Domain-oriented research, for instance, regarding research questions, such as the success, transparency, equality, privacy and acceptancy of ADM, is, however, very infrequent. Beside a couple of initial contributions that deal with ADM as the main topic (e.g., Cheng & Hackett, 2019; Leicht-Deobald et al., 2019) there are currently few contributions in the still emerging HR analytics research that occasionally deal with ADM as a side issue (see the review of Marler & Boudreau, 2017). In sum, current insights on ADM in HRM are in a very nascent state while there is particularly a lack of HR-specific research.

Future Directions in Algorithmic Decision Making in HRM

Based on the current practical developments, research on ADM in HRM is both necessary and promising (Campion et al., 2018). This refers to two major research approaches. Firstly, *design research* should contribute to the development of ADM in HRM. Artefacts such as ADM concepts, algorithms, use cases or software should be systematically developed in order to contribute to a useful and responsible future development of the field. Secondly, *empirical research* should contribute to the assessment of ADM in HRM by means of a systematic evaluation of already existing and applied concepts, algorithms, use cases and software for ADM. Both research streams should consider the above-introduced criteria of success, transparency, equality, privacy and acceptancy of ADM in order to contribute to an appropriate future development of ADM.

Further Readings

Cheng, M. M., & Hackett, R. D. (2019). A critical review of algorithms in HRM: Definition, theory, and practice. *Human Resource Management Review, in press.*
Strohmeier, S., & Piazza, F. (2013). Domain driven data mining in human resource management: A review of current research. *Expert Systems with Applications, 40*(7), 2410–2420.

References

Burrell, J. (2016). How the machine thinks: Understanding opacity in machine learning algorithms. *Big Data & Society*, *3*(1), 1–12.

Campion, M. C., Campion, M. A., & Campion, E. D. (2018). Big data techniques and talent management: Recommendations for organizations and a research agenda for IO Psychologists. *Industrial and Organizational Psychology*, *11*(2), 250–257.

Cheng, M. M., & Hackett, R. D. (2019). A critical review of algorithms in HRM: Definition, theory, and practice. *Human Resource Management Review*, *in press*.

Dietvorst, B. J., Simmons, J. P., & Massey, C. (2015). Algorithm aversion: People erroneously avoid algorithms after seeing them err. *Journal of Experimental Psychology: General*, *144*(1), 114.

Gandomi, A., & Haider, M. (2015). Beyond the hype: Big data concepts, methods, and analytics. *International Journal of Information Management*, *35*(2), 137–144.

Goodman, B., & Flaxman, S. (2017). European Union regulations on algorithmic decision-making and a "right to explanation". *AI Magazine*, *38*(3), 50–57.

Grove, W. M., Zald, D. H., Lebow, B. S., Snitz, B. E., & Nelson, C. (2000). Clinical versus mechanical prediction: A meta-analysis. *Psychological Assessment*, *12*(1), 19–30.

Leicht-Deobald, U., Busch, T., Schank, C., Weibel, A., Schafheitle, S., Wildhaber, I., & Kasper, G. (2019). The Challenges of Algorithm-Based HR Decision-Making for Personal Integrity. *Journal of Business Ethics*, 1–16.

Logg, J. M., Minson, J. A., & Moore, D. A. (2019). Algorithm appreciation: People prefer algorithmic to human judgment. *Organizational Behavior and Human Decision Processes*, *151*, 90–103.

Marler, J. H., & Boudreau, J. W. (2017). An evidence-based review of HR Analytics. *The International Journal of Human Resource Management*, *28*(1), 3–26.

Meehl, P. E. (1996). *Clinical versus statistical prediction: A theoretical analysis and a review of the evidence*. Northvale, NJ: Jason Aronson. (Original work published 1954)

Strohmeier, S., & Piazza, F. (2013). Domain driven data mining in human resource management: A review of current research. *Expert Systems with Applications*, *40*(7), 2410–2420.

Strohmeier, S., & Piazza, F. (2015). Artificial intelligence techniques in human resource management – A conceptual exploration. In C. Kahraman & S. Ç. Onar (Eds.), *Intelligent Techniques in Engineering Management* (pp. 149–172). Cham: Springer International Publishing.

Van den Bergh, J., Beliën, J., De Bruecker, P., Demeulemeester, E., & De Boeck, L. (2013). Personnel scheduling: A literature review. *European Journal of Operational Research*, *226*(3), 367–385.

Zerilli, J., Knott, A., Maclaurin, J., & Gavaghan, C. (2018). Transparency in Algorithmic and Human Decision-Making: Is There a Double Standard?. *Philosophy & Technology*, 1–23.

Part 3: **Organizational Issues in e-HRM**

Tanya Bondarouk

Implementation of e-HRM: Definitions and Theoretical Approaches

There has been much research and many follow-up recommendations on how to introduce e-HRM systems to minimize troubles during its implementation. However, despite a long history of research and practice of e-HRM implementations, such projects are still known to be time consuming, indirect, and sometimes impulsive developments, leading to a mismatch between the initial ideas behind information technologies and the use in practice, the employees' perceptions and their experience. This entry explores lessons from information technology (IT) studies that e-HRM researchers can learn and apply to better understand the complexity of e-HRM implementation projects.

After many years of dramatic technological changes, the implementation issues are still as relevant today as they were in the past. How can one ensure e-HRM project completion within budget and on time? When rolling out a new e-HRM system, why do users complain? Why does the espoused use of e-HRM differ from the actual one, and why do projects fail? Which vendor to choose out of hundreds available on the software market, including major players such as PeopleSoft/Oracle, SAP, Workday, ADP, AFAS, Lumesse, Exact, Kronos, Lawson, TalentSoft, or develop it in-house?

Different Views on e-HRM Implementation

Broadly defined, the use of a new IT system is the result of an implementation process. The word *process* is crucial. As a process, e-HRM implementation has at least two interrelated characteristics which I call: 1) process boundaries and 2) the progression curve. Concerning the process boundaries, I distinguish three blocks of processes (Figure 10.1). The beginning stage is usually easier defined. The e-HRM implementation ideally starts with the strategic call for a new system, which requires the presence of a strong HRM system with the distinctive content and future orientation. Having a well-established strategy and content of HRM or (some of its) functional domains is a necessary condition to start the implementation process of a new e-HRM application. It is ideally followed by a preparation block for the introduction of e-HRM to targeted users. This preparation block has several steps, each of its own vital importance, for example: needs assessment, requirements analysis, establishment of criteria to choose a vendor's/in-house solution, developing and presenting a business case, training of future targeted users, piloting of (one of) applications, integration with existing systems, data conversion, and introducing it to the users (rolling out). The final block in the implementation process is more

https://doi.org/10.1515/9783110633702-010

Strategic call for a new e-HRM application

Setting the stage: identifying goals for a new e-HRM package. goals HRM strategy is well-defined; HR practices are clearly designed and aligned.
There is a strong HRM system with the distinctive content and future orientation.

Preparation for the introduction of e-HRM to targeted users

User needs assessment, requirements analysis, choice of a vendor / in-house solution, developing a business case, piloting of training future users, piloting of applications, planning to integrate new applications within the existing IT infrastructure, data conversion, roll-out.

Introduction of e-HRM to the targeted users

Introduction of new e-HRM applications to all targeted users.
Incorporating e-HRM into a daily life of users and organisational routines.

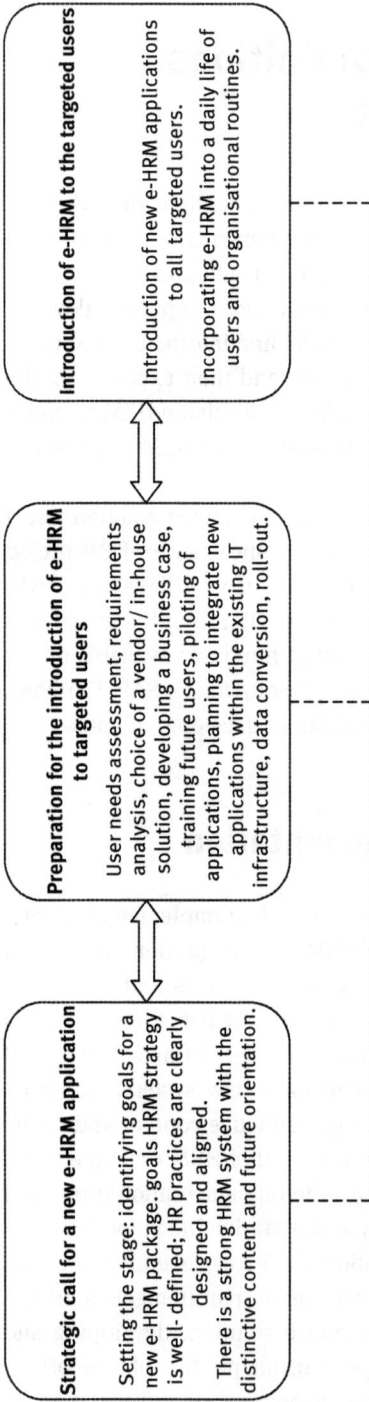

Figure 10.1: Process boundaries of e-HRM implementations.

difficult to define. Various authors have different views, and these are mostly implicit. Indeed, how to define when is the implementation completed? When it is accepted by the users, objectives are met, installation is finalized, or when targeted users are happy to work with it? But then, how do they really interact with e-HRM? It becomes obvious that it is not an easy task to choose the implementation completion point. For IT designers, e-HRM will be implemented upon its technical installation, while for HR professionals and (line) managers the introduction of e-HRM will mark the beginning of the implementation. These sometimes polar differences are rooted in different theoretical approaches to e-HRM implementations.

Related to the theoretical approaches, I turn to the second characteristic of e-HRM implementations, its progression curve. Enough research has been done in IT studies to inspire and to warn scholars and practitioners to stop seeing the implementation process as a linear development and accept its dynamic, fluid, difficult, and contradictory nature; and to make a shift from the deterministic (technology- or human-driven) towards a situational, context-bounded socio-material and boundary-less process (Strohmeier, 2009; Bondarouk, 2011).

Theoretical Approaches to e-HRM Implementations

Over time, various research theories on IT implementation have been developed as a result of combining a range of theoretical perspectives on technology and organisations. It is not my purpose to describe them all, and elaborate overviews are available in the literature and elsewhere in this volume. Just as examples I mention: Media Richness Theory, User Interface Design, Socio-Technical Systems Theory, Technology Acceptance Model, Contingency Theory translated to IT research, Coordination Theory, Activity Theory, Network Analysis, Affordances Theory, Agency Theory, Actor-Network Theory, Improvisation Theory, and Structurational models.

I argue that there is a lot that can be learnt from the IT studies to better understand implementations of e-HRM. To help e-HRM researchers find their way in the forest of IT implementation concepts, I propose to categorize them by classifying implementation approaches along two theoretical dimensions. The first dimension tackles the relative importance of a prescriptive versus an enacted e-HRM implementation. The second dimension concerns the extent to which an e-HRM application is understood as a 'tangible' physical system versus a mental framework. These two dimensions shape two opposing approaches to e-HRM implementation: linear and fluid dynamic.

The Linear Approach to e-HRM Implementations

In reviewing the literature, it would appear that the early (pre-1990) work was dominated by this approach to the implementation of IT, concentrating on the role of the technology and the technical aspects of its implementation. This approach offered concrete, linear-based solutions for IT-related problems (systems design, user resistance issues, etc.). Due to its long history, it still has a strong influence on e-HRM research. Those adopting this approach view technology as a given material substance with 'tangible' technical properties and services that have to be used by the targeted employees. Thus, in-line with this thinking, the e-HRM implementation will be well defined as a step-based development, directed at achieving organisational goals and user satisfaction. The linear approach to IT implementation tends to offer a panacea to organisations that are striving to implement a new technology. Examples of practical solutions will include special tactics for e-HRM project management, alignment with the organisational strategy and culture, and human-computer interaction aspects.

This approach partly clarifies what really constitutes the implementation process since it does not pay sufficient attention to the dynamic interactional reality of the *process* of implementation. However, I would attribute to these studies the awareness of different technical, organisational, social, and human 'issues' and their importance for IT and e-HRM implementation success (Bondarouk, Parry, & Furtmueller, 2017): organisational (alignment of e-HRM strategies with organisational strategies, structure, power distribution, and politics and culture); managerial (leading e-HRM projects: end-user participation, education and training, availability of support resources); 'human' (psychological aspects, appropriation, acceptance, behavioural intention). Looking at what these studies have found, I note that this dominant stream of work has been devoted to discovering factors and processes, i.e. 'issues', associated with the failure or success of IT, and, thus, can be transferred to e-HRM studies.

Overall, management is supposed to rationally implement e-HRM changes. End-users (employees and line managers) are supposed to work happily with the new technology towards a promised growth in HRM and organisational performance. If the users are resistant, or less happy than expected, it is because of mistakes made in the design process, the lack of shared beliefs, 'wrong' age and 'wrong' subjective norms, insufficient software experience, or lack of support in training. Disgruntled human interactions with the HR technology can be improved by better rewards, with technical assistance, or by redesigning job tasks.

Next, there is also a tendency in the linear IT studies to view the context as a static and stable entity, and assume that it can be measured in cross-case studies of e-HRM implementation in organisations. As a result, they fail to investigate the reciprocal interaction between context and use of e-HRM technology, wherein social context affects and is affected by the use of IT.

The Fluid Dynamic Approach to e-HRM Implementations

As I wrote in earlier works (e.g., Bondarouk, 2011), in contrast to the linear approach, the dynamic one considers the e-HRM-related problems as ill-defined: the technology is perceived as part of a wider social and political system. The implementation is seen as an interactive, on-going process between the human, organisational and technological features. These studies address the dynamic nature of the implementation process and tackle many criticisms levelled at the more traditional IT research.

The e-HRM technology itself is perceived as a social construct rather than as a physical entity, and therefore it is seen as subject to change during the implementation process. The goal of a researcher is to understand the implementation process instead of prescribing factors of success.

The context in which an e-HRM is designed and used also has both technical and social components. In the case of payroll technology, the organisation will provide a rich context including individuals, groups, and divisions. Their interactional practices, culture, and norms will shape the technology. The question is how to distinguish the content and context of e-HRM technology if, traditionally defined, both include technical and social components. In other words, technology design involves decisions about the allocation of roles between technology and its environment. The definition of e-HRM technology becomes the definition of its sociotechnical context. The proponents of this stream argue that an understanding of the process by which technological projects are conducted can be gained by "following the actors": socio-material combinations in their interactions as they construct and elaborate the technology, the context, themselves and each other. Thus, the goals of e-HRM research, following this tradition, are likely to explore technical and social aspects of the content and context of the e-HRM applications.

The dynamic models show the effective use of social construction ideas by seeing implementation as an enacted, dynamic, changeable, and situated process. In contrast to the linear approach, these studies view people as active enablers of the technology implementation, and therefore, different human agents can use the same e-HRM technology differently, which may result in different implementation outcomes (Bondarouk, 2011).

The main limitation of this approach concerns its practical applicability. For example, it is an often-mentioned shortcoming of the actor-network theory that it discusses technology implementation at a very abstract level and lacks the 'instrumental' part with respect to analysis of the actors and their networks. The dynamic IT studies, in their attempts to echo the dynamic reality of IT implementations, might be a step 'too far' from the practice of e-HRM projects. They may give an understanding of the process of e-HRM implementation, but this may prove rather abstract for practitioners in terms of results and recommendations.

Conclusion: What is e-HRM Implementation?

Now I return to an earlier question: when does the implementation of e-HRM end – when are the prescribed issues complete? When does an e-HRM system achieve sta-bilisation – or should we accept the fundamental "open-endedness" of technology implementation?

Having accepted that human interpretive schemes can endlessly change the on-going use of technology, it would be easy to conclude that the use of technology can never be stabilised, that every engagement with the system is contextual and temporal (Orlikowski, 2000). However, starting from the users' point of view, I con-sider that implementation is complete when users contentedly work with an e-HRM application, having acquired the necessary skills to master the program, fully un-derstand the e-HRM, and are ready to enact the rules and norms. This means that although an e-HRM system may still require changes after some time in use, the im-plementation is complete because employees, line managers, and HR professionals feel comfortable working with it, are not afraid of any technological modifications, and appreciate performing their job tasks through the system.

This calls for looking at the *stable use* of e-HRM technology by different users, rather than looking for the stabilisation of technology. Therefore, the indicator of successful e-HRM implementation will be skilful and task-consistent operating with the e-HRM application by the targeted users (Bondarouk, 2011).

I conclude this entry by defining the implementation of e-HRM as the translation process in which the usage of new e-HRM application is incorporated into daily organ-isational life by targeted users, through its skilful, motivated and task-consistent use by employees, line managers, and HR professionals.

Therefore, future research questions are:
- How to develop multi-level organisational capabilities to secure success of dynamic implementation of e-HRM?
- Which multi-disciplinary multi-theory competences are required for HR profes-sionals to lead e-HRM implementations?

Further Readings

Cascio, W. F., & Montealegre, R. (2016). How Technology Is Changing Work and Organizations. *Annual Review of Organizational Psychology and Organizational Behavior, 3*(1): 349–375.
Leonardi, P. M. (2013). Theoretical foundations for the study of sociomateriality. *Information and organization, 23*(2): 59–76.
Verbeek, P.-P. (2006). Materializing Morality: Design Ethics and Technological Mediation. *Science, Technology, & Human Values, 31*(3): 361–380

References

Bondarouk, T. (2011). Theoretical approaches to e-HRM implementations. In: T. Bondarouk, H. Ruël, & J.C. Looise (Eds.). *Electronic HRM in Theory and Practice, Advanced Series in Management.* Emerald Group Publishing Limited: WA, UK, pp. 1–20.

Bondarouk, T., Parry, E., & Furtmueller, E. (2017). Electronic HRM: four decades of research on adoption and consequences. *The International Journal of Human Resource Management, 28*(1),98–131.

Orlikowski, W.J. (2000). Using technology and constituting structures: a practice lens for studying technology in organisations. *Organization Science, 11*(4), 404–428.

Strohmeier, S. (2009). Concepts of e-HRM consequences: a categorisation, review and suggestion. *The International Journal of Human Resource Management, 20*(3), 528–543.

Sandra L. Fisher
Organisational Change in the Context of e-HRM

Implementation of human resource management technology in organisations requires change on many levels. Roles and responsibilities for employees, managers,
IT staff, and HR professionals may all change with the introduction of new technological systems for HR processes (Marler & Fisher, 2016). Employees in all of these
user groups may not welcome the changes for a variety of reasons, with HR professionals having simultaneously the greatest potential for gain and the greatest risk
with e-HRM. Further, it appears that organisations often underestimate the complexity and importance of organisational change related to new information technology systems such as e-HRM, leading to the failure or reduced effectiveness of
many technology implementation projects (Dorsey, 2002). This entry reviews issues
germane to organisational change resulting from adoption of e-HRM and describes
different approaches found to be effective in helping organisations adopt new HR
technology throughout the implementation process.

The organisational change literature offers many models that can be applied to
implementation of e-HRM, although it is interesting to note that the e-HRM research
literature has not clearly applied or tested these models, relying more on models of
technology adoption instead of organisational change. Kotter's classic organisational change model helps organisations decide who should be involved and how
information should be communicated before, during and after a change project
(Kotter, 1995). Organisations implementing new e-HRM systems would benefit from
motivating organisational members through a sense of urgency and vision for the
new technology. Reasons for adopting a new system may range from influence from
a multi-national parent firm (Bondarouk, Schilling & Ruël, 2016) to competitive or
supply chain partner pressures. Regardless of the organisational level motivation, a
statement about vision should specifically address how employees will benefit from
the new technology, especially if there might be fears that the technology could be
used for exploitative purposes (Nishii, Lepak & Schneider, 2008). Kotter's model
also strongly advocates identifying a powerful guiding coalition to lead the project,
which would include a project champion, suggested by Dorsey (2002) as the most
important role on a technology implementation team.

The DICE equation developed by Boston Consulting Group (Sirkin, Keenan &
Jackson, 2005) helps organisations plan organisational change projects with a guided
assessment. Change leaders evaluate five key factors of the project: the duration of the
project or time between planned milestone reviews, the integrity of the team as defined
by project team members' skill levels, commitment of both senior management and the
affected employees, and the effort required to make the change. These five factors drive

https://doi.org/10.1515/9783110633702-011

the success of change projects and all can be applied to e-HRM implementation. For example, duration has historically been a critical risk with new HR technology projects but may be reduced with the use of Software as a Service (SaaS) systems that minimize customization. Integrity, or the skill level of the team, is often a risk with technology implementation projects and internal teams must often be supplemented with external experts from vendors or consulting companies. Commitment can be low for e-HRM projects among senior executives and employee groups more broadly. Austin (2015) described an e-HRM implementation project that was nearly derailed because the one dedicated change champion left the company. The effort component is related to ease of use. The easier the new system is to both implement and use, the higher the likelihood of project success. A thorough assessment will also uncover pockets of resistance in the organisation and help leaders address the resistance early in the project.

Organisational Change and e-HRM System Users

At the individual level, significant research has accumulated about user acceptance of new e-HRM systems and use of these systems. As noted by Bondarouk, Parry and Furtmueller (2017), there have been at least 168 different factors found to be empirically related to adoption of e-HRM since the 1970s. These factors can be organized into broad categories of technology, organisation, and people. Researchers have looked to several theories from the information systems literature to help explain and predict individual adoption outcomes. One such theory, the Technology Acceptance Model (TAM; Davis, 1989), stipulates that users are more likely to have favourable attitudes toward new systems and be more likely to use them when systems have two key characteristics: ease of use and perceived usefulness. Much research over the years has confirmed that these factors are an important role in individual employee decisions to adopt new HR technology. Having key stakeholders involved in the design and decision making about new systems promotes acceptance of the technology by enhancing ease of use and perceived usefulness, as well as giving user groups a stake in the new technology. More expanded theories such as the Unified Theory of Acceptance and Use of Technology (UTAUT) and other related derivations extend beyond system design factors to include the organisational environment (e.g., Venkatesh, Morris, Davis & Davis, 2003). The UTAUT includes facilitating conditions such as available resources and social influence. Resources include the technology infrastructure, appropriate documentation, and training.

Training is one common tool used to help employees adopt new HR technology. Training about the new system must be provided for effective and efficient use of the technology (e.g., Parry & Tyson, 2011), but not too far in advance of implementation such that employees could forget what they learned before the system is live. Consistent with the general literature on training transfer, employees must be given the opportunity to practice new skills related to e-HRM soon after training (Baldwin & Ford, 1988), ideally by applying them to the actual system. When employees use the HR technology irregularly (for example, only once a year to update their benefits during open enrollment) it may be more effective to provide performance supports rather than rely on training to produce positive attitudes and the correct user behaviors. Social support from managers and co-workers also play a role in adoption of these new technologies (Marler, Fisher & Ke, 2009), through factors such as perceived social support, more direct managerial pressure to use the technology, and workgroup norms about the technology. Managerial support and workplace norms also support transfer of trained skills to the workplace (Baldwin & Ford, 1988).

Organisational Change and HR Professionals

At the level of HR professionals or the HR department in general, organisational change issues focus on how the nature of the work changes for HR professionals. At the most basic level, HR professionals often need new skills to function effectively in a digitized HR environment (Bell, Lee & Yeung, 2006; Parry & Tyson, 2011) such as technology expertise and strategic HR knowledge, helping managers make better decisions. HR professionals also need to have a stronger relationship with the IT function, whether that is in-house or outsourced, and be able to communicate effectively with IT professionals. The need for more advanced technical skills has become even more pronounced as HR analytics have become more sophisticated and in demand by organisational managers as part of the e-HRM suite. In addition to participating in regular organisational training on new systems, Bell et al. (2006) suggested specific methods for helping HR professionals adapt to technological changes, such as experiential learning and error-based learning. Professional organisations such as the Society for Human Resource Management have also included technology and analytical skills in their HR professional competency models (SHRM, 2017). The SHRM competency model provides the foundation for testing and professional certification and is intended to guide university training as well as continued professional development, helping support organisational change for HR professionals.

HR professionals have been affected in more profound ways than most other employees by introduction of HR technology, as it may also change the way in which the HR department is structured. One of the early benefits of e-HRM was often positioned as the possibility to reduce the number of HR staff in organisations as day-to-day HR tasks are pushed to employees or managers through the use of employee self-service (ESS) and manager self-service (MSS) functions, or more easily centralized with the use of shared service centers. Evidence on the extent to which e-HRM has resulted in a reduced workforce and associated cost savings has been mixed (Bondarouk, et al., 2017) but it is very clear that the role of the HR professional has changed due to increased use of technology and this broader change must be addressed as part of organisational change efforts.

Continuing e-HRM Change

Much of the literature on change management in e-HRM has addressed the initial adoption of HR technology by an organisation. As this technology has become relatively standard over the years, it is important to also recognize unique issues that come about with system upgrades or adoption of subsequent HR technology systems. For example, Wiblen, Grant and Dery (2010) presented a case study in which a large organisation that had been using a proprietary HRIS for many years transitioned to using SAP for payroll and talent management. The resulting skill gap created a need to hire externally in order to obtain the necessary depth of SAP knowledge and skills. Naturally, this kind of change presents a threat to people who have been working with the legacy system and could easily result in resistance to change among affected employees. Another type of resistance to change related to past experience is cynicism (Reichers, Wanous & Austin, 1997). Employees who are cynical about implementation of a new system may have experienced technology system failures in the past (e-HRM or other IT) and may not trust the vendors or top managers who are promising an easy transition and wide-ranging benefits of the new system. Employee involvement and communication are the best ways to overcome cynicism, although truly cynical employees may not accept and adopt a new system until it is fully operational and demonstrating the promised benefits.

The challenges of organisational change related to e-HRM are clear and appear to be continuing with the progression of advanced technologies such as artificial intelligence rather than declining as e-HRM systems become more common. In their 2018 state of the e-HRM industry report, SierraCedar (2018) described change management as one of the most important factors related to effective implementation of e-HRM systems. They identified an overall culture of change management within an organisation as critical for creating positive HR technology outcomes. This means that companies use change management practices such as such as senior sponsorship, communication, documentation, project management, business process re-engineering and technology specific practices such as usability testing for every new technology implementation. In fact, sporadic use of change management practices was often worse than no change management at all. These practices are consistent with the TAM and UTAUT theories, promoting ease of use and providing necessary resources to employees.

Research Questions

Change management will doubtless continue to be a critical aspect of e-HRM implementation moving forward. Future research on this topic should continue addressing the intersections between the technology, organisational, and people factors identified by Bondarouk et al. (2017). As e-HRM technologies rely increasingly on artificial intelligence, individual employees' understanding of how the technology works is likely to decrease while simultaneously concerns for how it might be used for exploitative purposes will increase. It will be important to study how organisational change efforts can support employee trust in such technologies to facilitate full adoption and use. Research should also address change management fatigue (Austin, 2015) and resistance that are likely to arise from repeated adoption of upgraded and new e-HRM systems over time.

Further Readings

Austin, J. (2015). *Leading Effective Change: A Primer for the HR Professional.* Alexandria, VA: SHRM Foundation.

Bondarouk, T., Parry, E. & Furtmueller. E. (2017) Electronic HRM: Four decades of research on adoption and consequences, *The International Journal of Human Resource Management, 28:1,* 98–131.

Marler, J., Fisher, SL, & Ke, W. (2009). Employee self-service technology acceptance: A comparison of pre-implementation and post-implementation relationships. *Personnel Psychology, 62*(2), 327–358.

References

Baldwin, T. T., & Ford, J. K. (1988). Transfer of training: A review and directions for future research. *Personnel Psychology, 41*(1), 63–105.

Bell, B. S., Lee, S. W., & Yeung, S. K. (2006). The impact of e-HR on professional competence in HRM: Implications for the development of HR professionals. *Human Resource Management, 45*(3), 295–308.

Bondarouk, T., Schilling, D., & Ruël, H. J. M. (2016). eHRM adoption in emerging economies: The case of subsidiaries of multinational corporations in Indonesia. *Canadian Journal of Administrative Sciences, 33*(2), 124–137.

Davis, F. D. (1989). Perceived usefulness, perceived ease of use, and user acceptance of information technology. *MIS Quarterly,* 319–340.

Dorsey, D.W. (2002). Information Technology. In J. W. Hedge and E. D. Pulakos (Eds.) *Implementing Organizational Interventions* (pp. 110–132). Jossey-Bass. San Francisco.

Kotter, J.P. (1995). Leading change: Why transformation efforts fail. *Harvard Business Review.* 1–10.

Marler, JH and Fisher, SL. (2016). *Making HR Technology Decisions: A Strategic Perspective.* Business Expert Press. Singapore.

Nishii, L. H., Lepak, D. P., & Schneider, B. (2008). Employee attributions of the "why" of HR practices: Their effects on employee attitudes and behaviors, and customer satisfaction. *Personnel Psychology, 61*(3), 503–545.

Parry, E., & Tyson, S. (2011). Desired goals and actual outcomes of e-HRM. *Human Resource Management Journal, 21*(3), 335–354.

Reichers, A. E., Wanous, J. P., & Austin, J. T. (1997). Understanding and managing cynicism about organizational change. *Academy of Management Perspectives, 11*(1), 48–59.

Sierra-Cedar (2018). *Sierra-Cedar 2018–2019 HR Systems Survey White Paper, 21st Annual Edition.* Alpharetta, GA, retrieved from https://www.sierra-cedar.com/wp-content/uploads/sites/12/2019/02/Sierra-Cedar_2018-2019_HRSS_WhitePaper.pdf

Sirkin, H.L., Keenan, P., & Jackson, A. (2005). The hard side of change management. *Harvard Business Review, 83(10)*, 108–118.

Society for Human Resource Management. (2017). *The SHRM Body of Competencies and Knowledge.* Alexandria, VA.

Venkatesh, V., Morris, M. G., Davis, G. B., & Davis, F. D. (2003). User acceptance of information technology: Toward a unified view. *MIS Quarterly*, 425–478.

Wiblen, S., Grant, D. & Dery, K. (2010). Transitioning to a new HRIS: The reshaping of human resources and information technology talent. *Journal of Electronic Commerce Research, 11(4)*, 251–267.

Guido Hertel, Sarah M. Meeßen, and Miriam Höddinghaus

Trust in the Context of e-HRM

Human Resource Management (HRM) activities, such as recruitment, leadership, and personnel development often rely on social interactions. One crucial element of successful interactions is mutual trust. Indeed, trust has been shown to be correlated with effective HRM activities and performance in organizations in various ways (e.g., Breuer, Hüffmeier, & Hertel, 2016; Colquitt, Scott, & LePine, 2007). Digitalization of HRM might further increase the significance of trust due to reduced face-to-face interaction. Moreover, the introduction of electronic technologies in HRM (i.e., e-HRM) comes with considerable and partly disruptive changes in organizational processes, which can cause feelings of insecurity and strain both among employees and HRM representatives. In order to leverage the advantages of e-HRM applications, persons not only need to trust in their interaction partners, but also trust in these new processes and technologies. This entry reviews extant empirical research on trust in e-HRM contexts. In doing so, we consider both effects of electronic communication on trust development, and effects of trust on the usage of electronic technologies as central precondition for effective e-HRM.

Trust and Electronic Communication

In their seminal work, Mayer, Davis, and Schoorman (1995) defined trust as willingness to make oneself vulnerable to another party, irrespective of the ability to monitor or control that other party (Mayer et al., 1995, p. 712). Among the influential contributions of this approach is the explicit distinction between trust itself as experienced by the trusting party, and the perceived trustworthiness of a trusted party or object as determinant of trust. Moreover, Mayer et al. (1995) identified personal traits and situational risk perceptions as further determinants of experienced trust. Electronic technologies in HRM can affect all three types of trust determinants. For instance, electronically mediated communication can reduce the amount of transferred information, making judgments of trustworthiness more difficult. In a similar way, virtual work environments might be perceived as more risky due to reduced co-presence and control of other persons (e.g., Breuer et al., 2016). In addition to effects on interpersonal trust, e-HRM also requires trust in technology (e.g., McKnight, Carter, Thatcher, & Clay, 2011; Thielsch, Meeßen, & Hertel, 2018). If e-HRM applications are not perceived as reliable and trustworthy, they will not be used. For instance, a recent study in a simulated business setting shows that cognitive benefits of a decision support system for knowledge management only occurred if users trusted the information system (Hertel, Meeßen, Riehle, Thielsch, Nohe, & Becker, 2019).

https://doi.org/10.1515/9783110633702-012

In addition to such challenges, e-HRM can also provide benefits for trust in organizations. For instance, electronic communication technologies not only enable frequent interactions across spatial distance, but also high quality of these interactions, for instance, when using Virtual Reality applications (Montoya, Massey, & Lockwood, 2011). Moreover, automatic process documentation in electronic project management tools can secure more transparent and fair recognition of individual contributions (e.g., Breuer et al., 2016). Thus, in addition to considering potential challenging effects of e-HRM, it is also important to consider potential positive effects of HRM technologies for building trust.

Trust and e-Recruiting

Trust in the context of e-recruiting refers to individuals' willingness to rely on recruiting and selection systems that are technology-based. Important determinants of such willingness might be the perceived reliability and fairness of e-recruiting systems. Indeed, these systems might be seen as more powerful (high computing power) and fair (same algorithm for all applicants) as compared to traditional recruiting. However, so far, these potential advantages have not been acknowledged by applicants. Applicants judged e-recruiting as less fair than face-to-face procedures (e.g., Thielsch, Träumer, & Pytlik, 2012), and perceived information in online systems (e.g., electronic bulletin boards) as less credible than information from face-to-face interaction at a job fair (Cable and Yu, 2006). In a similar way, applicants judged selection via videoconferencing or telephone interviews as less fair than face-to-face interviews (Bauer, Truxillo, Paronto, Weekley, & Campion, 2004; Chapman, Uggerslev, & Webster, 2003), and evaluated interviewers in videoconferencing as less trustworthy than in face-to-face interviews (Sears, Zhang, Wiesner, Hackett, & Yuan, 2013). These reservations might change in the future when persons gain more experience with e-recruiting systems (Elsbach & Stigliani, 2019; Suen, Chen, & Lu, 2019). Indeed, "asynchronous" video interviews during which applicants' answers are recorded did not lead to lower attraction towards the organization than synchronous video interviews, even though applicants had more privacy concerns in asynchronous interviews (Langer, König, & Krause, 2017).

Given the need for fast and global recruitment strategies today, employers often have no choice but use online recruiting tools. Thus, it is important to design such applications in a trustworthy way. Indeed, even though applicants perceived company websites as less trustworthy than placement centres or business magazines (Mumford, 2012), company websites which conveyed the perception that an organization is trustworthy significantly increased applicants' acceptance of job offers from this company (Bermúdez-Edo, Hurtado-Torres, Aragón-Correa, 2010). However, employers should not investigate job candidates' private social network sites. Even though such investigations are quite popular, job seekers perceive such behaviour as severe privacy violation (Black, Stone, & Johnson, 2015), leading to distrust and negative effects on organizational attraction and acceptance of job offers (Stoughton, Thompson, & Meade, 2015).

Trust and e-Leadership

Developing social and trustful relationships is a key leadership task, and this is particularly true when leadership is predominantly mediated based on electronic communication technology (e-leadership; e.g., Kahai, Avolio, & Sosik, 2017). Therefore, building and maintaining trust has been noted as essential competence of e-leaders (e.g., Roman, Van Wart, Wang, Liu, Kim, & McCarthy, 2018). Empirical studies on the relation between leadership styles and trust in digital work settings suggest that participative leadership approaches are particularly suited for trust building, such as transformational leadership (e.g., Hoyt & Blascovich, 2003) or inspirational leadership (Joshi, Lazarova, & Liao, 2009). However, research still has to explore whether these leadership styles are also *more* effective in digital as compared to traditional work settings, and if so, why.

Studies focusing on more specific leadership behaviours in digital work settings have stressed that establishing clear communication norms is important to encourage honest and transparent communication (Malhotra, Majchrzak, & Rosen, 2007). Moreover, creating a secure non-critical atmosphere (McCallum & O`Connell, 2009), initial face-to-face meetings (Brake, 2006), and task delegation (Zhang, Tremaine, Egan, Milewski, O'Sullivan, & Fjermestad, 2009) have been found to foster trust in digital work settings. In addition, technology itself can support trust in leadership or reduce the need for trust, respectively. For example, 3D collaborative virtual environments can provide more visual cues (Montoya Massey, & Lockwood, 2011) and, thus, might support trust development in leader-follower interactions. Moreover, GPS tracking systems might reduce the need for trust in e-leadership settings, and even build trust if such control applications are perceived as legitimate by followers (Bruckes, Romeike, Hertel, & Schewe, 2018).

Trust and Virtual Collaboration

Trust has been discussed as a key driver especially in the context of virtual collaboration (e.g. Jarvenpaa & Leidner, 1999) because limited social cues increase the experienced need for trust as compensation of risks and uncertainties. Indeed, recent meta-analyses revealed that the relationship between trust and team effectiveness is stronger in virtual as compared to collocated teamwork (Breuer et al.,

2016; De Jong, Dirks, & Gillespie, 2016). In order to address this higher need for trust, particular emphasis might be placed on transparent and open communication in digital work settings, the choice of adequate and rich communication media, frequent and constructive feedback, and timely responses (e.g., Jarvenpaa, Cantu, & Lim, 2017). Moreover, the concept of "swift" trust has been introduced, relying more on social norms and standards (e.g., Meyerson, Weick, & Kramer, 1996) instead of time-consuming relationship building, particularly in the beginning of a team project (Jarvenpaa & Leidner, 1999). Finally, automatic documentation as part of electronic project management applications can reduce perceived risks of exploitation in teamwork contexts, and thus reduce the need of costly trust building interventions in virtual teams (Breuer et al., 2016).

Trust and e-Learning

Although trust is also important in personnel training and development, trust in the context of e-learning has been neglected in empirical research so far. Initial work can be found in the field of collaborative learning where the quality of an organizational knowledge management system correlated with higher levels of trust at work, which in turn were related to stronger knowledge sharing via the knowledge management system (Ho, Kuo, & Lin, 2012). Moreover, research comparing artificial (i.e., a computer algorithm and a humanoid robot) and human HR agents making personnel development decisions showed that ratings of perceived procedural justice (as aspect of trust) were quite similar (Ötting & Maier, 2018).

Future Research Directions

The reviewed literature shows that trust matters for effective e-HRM, and that trust can be facilitated by electronic technologies in the context of HRM. At the same time, research in this field is still in its infancy. Promising themes for further research include:
- trust as facilitating effect of e-HRM activities, particularly in so far neglected fields such as e-learning and virtual assessment
- trust reactions not only of applicants or employees but also of managers and HRM representatives, particularly because e-recruiting applications are often discussed as replacement of HRM professionals
- differences of trust and distrust reactions, and strategies to repair trust after trust breaches in e-HRM
- human-centred technology design that fosters trust and/or reduces the need for trust in e-HRM settings

Further Readings

Breuer, C., Hüffmeier, J., & Hertel, G. (2016). Does trust matter more in virtual teams? A meta-analysis of trust and team effectiveness considering virtuality and documentation as moderators. *Journal of Applied Psychology, 101*, 1151–1177.

Jarvenpaa, S., Cantu, C., & Lim, S. Y. (2017). Trust in virtual online environments. In Hertel, G., Stone, D., Johnson, R., & Passmore, J. (Eds.), *The Wiley Blackwell Handbook of the Psychology of the Internet at Work* (pp. 103–130). Chichester: Wiley-Blackwell.

McKnight, D. H., Carter, M., Thatcher, J.B., & Clay, P.F. (2011). Trust in a specific technology: An investigation of its components and measures. *ACM Transactions on Management Information Systems (TMIS), 2*(2), 1–15.

Thielsch, M. T., Meeßen, S. M., & Hertel, G. (2018). Trust and distrust in information systems at the workplace. *PeerJ, 6*:e5483.

References

Bauer, T. N., Truxillo, D. M., Paronto, M. E., Weekley, J. A., & Campion, M. A. (2004). Applicant reactions to different selection technology: Face-to-face, interactive voice response, and computer-assisted telephone screening interviews. *International Journal of Selection and Assessment, 12*(1-2), 135–148.

Bermúdez-Edo, M., Hurtado-Torres, N., & Aragón-Correa, J. A. (2010). The importance of trusting beliefs linked to the corporate website for diffusion of recruiting-related online innovations. *Information Technology and Management, 11*(4), 177–189.

Black, S. L., Stone, D. L., & Johnson, A. F. (2015). Use of social networking websites on applicants' privacy. *Employee Responsibilities and Rights Journal, 27*(2), 115–159.

Brake, T. (2006). Leading global virtual teams. *Industrial and Commercial Training, 38*(3), 116–121.

Bruckes, M., Romeike, P., Hertel, G., & Schewe, G. (2018). Trust and legitimate control: Longitudinal effects in supervisor-subordinate relationships. *Academy of Management Proceedings, 2018*(1), 14559.

Cable, D. M., & Yu, K. Y. T. (2006). Managing job seekers' organizational image beliefs: The role of media richness and media credibility. *Journal of Applied Psychology, 91*(4), 828–840.

Chapman, D. S., Uggerslev, K. L., & Webster, J. (2003). Applicant reactions to face-to-face and technology-mediated interviews: A field investigation. *Journal of Applied Psychology, 88*(5), 944–953.

Colquitt, J. A., Scott, B. A. & LePine, J. A. (2007). Trust, trustworthiness, and trust propensity: A meta-analytic test of their unique relationship with risk-taking and job performance. *Journal of Applied Psychology, 92*(4), 909–927.

De Jong, B. A., Dirks, K. T., & Gillespie, N. (2016). Trust and team performance: A meta-analysis of main effects, moderators, and covariates. *Journal of Applied Psychology, 101*(8), 1134–1150.

Elsbach, K. D., & Stigliani, I. (2019). New information technology and implicit bias. *Academy of Management Perspectives, 33*(2), 185–206.

Hertel, G., Meeßen, S. M., Riehle, D. M., Thielsch, M. T., Nohe, C., & Becker, J. (2019). Directed forgetting in organisations: The positive effects of decision support systems on mental resources and well-being. *Ergonomics, 62*(5), 597–611.

Ho, L. A., Kuo, T. H., & Lin, B. (2012). How social identification and trust influence organizational online knowledge sharing. *Internet Research, 22*(1), 4–28.

Hoyt, C. L., & Blascovich, J. (2003). Transformational and transactional leadership in virtual and physical environments. *Small Group Research*, *34*(6), 678–715.

Jarvenpaa, S. L., & Leidner, D. E. (1999). Communication and trust in global virtual teams. *Organization Science*, *10*(6), 791–815.

Joshi, A., Lazarova, M. B., & Liao, H. (2009). Getting everyone on board: The role of inspirational leadership in geographically dispersed teams. *Organization Science*, *20*(1), 240–252.

Kahai, S. S., Avolio, B. J., & Sosik, J. (2017). E-leadership. In Hertel, G., Stone, D., Johnson, R., & Passmore, J. (Eds.), *The Wiley Blackwell Handbook of the Psychology of the Internet at Work* (pp. 285–314). Chichester: Wiley-Blackwell.

Langer, M., König, C. J., & Krause, K. (2017). Examining digital interviews for personnel selection: Applicant reactions and interviewer ratings. *International Journal of Selection and Assessment*, *25*(4), 371–382.

Malhotra, A., Majchrzak, A., & Rosen, B. (2007). Leading virtual teams. Academy of *Management Perspectives*, *21*(1), 60–70.

Mayer, R. C., Davis, J. H., & Schoorman, F.D. (1995). An integrative model of organizational trust. *Academy of Management Review*, *20*(3), 709–734.

McCallum, S., & O'Connell, D. (2009). Social capital and leadership development: Building stronger leadership through enhanced relational skills. *Leadership and Organization Development Journal*, *30*(2), 152–166.

Meyerson, D., Weick, K. E., & Kramer, R. M. (1996). Swift trust and temporary groups. In R. M. Kramer & T. R. Tyler (Eds.), *Trust in Organizations: Frontiers of Theory and Research* (pp. 166–195). Thousand Oaks, CA: Sage.

Montoya, M. M., Massey, A. P., & Lockwood, N. S. (2011). 3D collaborative virtual environments: Exploring the link between collaborative behaviors and team performance. *Decision Sciences*, *42*(2), 451–476.

Mumford, T. V. (2012). Whom to believe: Recruiting information source credibility and organizational attractiveness. *Business and Management Research*, *1*(4), 63–80.

Ötting, S. K., & Maier, G. W. (2018). The importance of procedural justice in Human–Machine Interactions: Intelligent systems as new decision agents in organizations. *Computers in Human Behavior*, *89*, 27–39.

Roman, A. V., Van Wart, M., Wang, X., Liu, C., Kim, S., & McCarthy, A. (2018). Defining e-leadership as competence in ICT-mediated communications: An exploratory assessment. *Public Administration Review* https://doi.org/10.1111/puar.12980.

Sears, G. J., Zhang, H., Wiesner, W. H., Hackett, R. D., & Yuan, Y. (2013). A comparative assessment of videoconference and face-to-face employment interviews. *Management Decision*, *51*(8), 1733–1752.

Stoughton, J. W., Thompson, L. F., & Meade, A. W. (2015). Examining applicant reactions to the use of social networking websites in pre-employment screening. *Journal of Business and Psychology*, *30*(1), 73–88.

Suen, H. Y., Chen, M. Y. C., & Lu, S. H. (2019). Does the use of synchrony and artificial intelligence in video interviews affect interview ratings and applicant attitudes? *Computers in Human Behavior*, *98*, 93–101.

Thielsch, M. T., Träumer, L., & Pytlik, L. (2012). E-recruiting and fairness: the applicant's point of view. *Information Technology and Management*, *13*(2), 59–67.

Zhang, S., Tremaine, M., Egan, R., Milewski, A., O'Sullivan, P., & Fjermestad, J. (2009). Occurrence and effects of leader delegation in virtual software teams. *International Journal of e-Collaboration*, *5*(1), 47–68.

Barbara Imperatori

Implications of e-HRM for the Role of Employees

Research in the e-HRM domain has devoted efforts to study the e-HRM consequences both for the HR department (Marler & Fisher, 2013) and for the organization (Parry & Tyson, 2011). Nevertheless, it is unquestionable that e-HRM practices also have a great impact on employees by enabling them to be more aware and knowledgeable actors, as well as changing their relationships with the HR department.

The first part of this entry provides a summary of the main evidence-based implications of e-HRM for employees in organizations by considering three different foci: attitudes, knowledge, and perception of the HR department. Starting from this evidence, the second part focuses on their potential impact on *employee roles*.

Implications of e-HRM for Employees' Well-Being in Organizations

e-HRM and Employees' Attitudes

e-HRM practices provide the opportunity for employees to actively take part in their human resources management processes, thus developing positive attitudes towards work processes (Panayotopoulou et al., 2007). Research confirms that relational e-HRM practices make the content of the employment relationship transparent, therefore reducing possible biases and misunderstandings, and aligning the employees' and the organisation's expectations. Furthermore, the adoption of relational e-HRM systems is a way to signal the organizational support in shaping and reinforcing the employees' psychological contract, and enhancing their affective commitment and perception of procedural justice (Bissola & Imperatori, 2014). In addition, e-HRM practices enable employees to cope more effectively with their tasks by offering practical support and developmental opportunities. e-HRM enables local adaptation and greater personalization, thus negatively affecting employees' intention to quit.

Other results suggest a more complex relation among these variables. For instance, Maier et al. (2013) found that ease of use and perceived usefulness of the practices increase their acceptance and employees' job satisfaction. Voermans & van Veldhoven (2007) found that the employees who prefer strategic HR roles have a positive attitude towards e-HRM and the employees with a stronger preference for HR in an employee champion role tend to have negative attitudes towards e-HRM systems.

https://doi.org/10.1515/9783110633702-013

On the other hand, e-HRM devolves many operational activities to employees and this, not surprisingly also causes negative employee attitudes. The higher work load, the need to manage the technology changes, and the transformation of the ways of working could lead to technology stress, work and life unbalance, growing intention to quit and higher resistance to change (Olivas-Lujan et al., 2007; Maier et al., 2013). Preliminary research evidence suggests that a higher level of technology and change readiness could help to cope with the e-HRM techno stress (Hadziroh & Yusliza, 2015). Likewise, research indicates that e-HRM adoption could enhance employees' turnover intention. However, because the effect is mediated by job satisfaction, organizations can decrease turnover intentions by ensuring job satisfaction with different compensative measures, such as reward systems and work-life balance practices (Maier et al., 2013). Finally, the age matters: the older employees show resistance because they have not developed the proper basic qualifications and mind-sets (Sareen, 2015).

e-HRM and Employees' Knowledge

e-HRM systems help employees to carry out a range of self-development activities. Relational e-HRM practices, such as e-learning and web-based performance appraisal, support employees' competences (Ruël et al., 2004). Transformational e-HRM systems, such as knowledge sharing ones and networking platforms drive the alignment of employee mind-sets with the firm's strategy, thus supporting employees' awareness. Moreover, they enable the development of supporting communities of practice and knowledge management processes by helping employees to autonomously share and build new competences and skills, and crossing the organizational boundaries and constraints.

The growth of Employee Self Service (ESS) implementations had some relevant positive implications for employees' knowledge and skills. ESSs are web-based solutions providing employees with a browser interface to navigate relevant HR data and transactions, thus enabling real time access to their data without leaving their desktop. Therefore, employees are able to update their personal details, apply for leave, view their pay details and associated benefits, view internal job vacancies, book training and traveling solutions. The employees view the ESS as a tool for easier access to information for better decision-making (Marler & Dulebohn, 2005).

Finally, even if research on these topics is embryonic, a recent study, conducted in Pakistan, showed that e-HRM has a statistically significant positive effect on managers' perceptions of labor productivity (Iqbal et al., 2018). Research also suggests that e-HRM practices enhance the employees' creative performance, thus positively moderating the relationship between employees' creativity and organizational innovation (Lin, 2011).

e-HRM and Employees' Perception of the HR Department

e-HRM practices boost the visibility of career paths, training opportunities, and rewards, which in turn enable employees to self-manage their development and build a new relationship with the HR department (Ruel et al. 2004). e-HRM practices can shape a direct, individualized and regular relationship between employees and the HR department. They improve employee awareness, appreciation, and use of HR programs. Research reveals an increased service satisfaction and positive perceptions of general HRM effectiveness in employees (Bondarouk et al., 2009). Evidence confirms that operational e-HRM practices boost the perceived internal efficiency of the HR department, whereas relational and transformational e-HRM practices positively influence employees' perceptions of the HR departments' competence. Finally, a survey corroborates the hypothesis that relational e-HRM practices drive higher employees' trust towards the HRM department because they allow employees to clearly perceive the criteria underlining HRM policies (Bissola & Imperatori, 2014).

Finally, e-HRM could support HR devolution and facilitate a greater employees' empowerment as it fosters new direct communications between employees and the HR department. Despite agreement about the potential of e-HRM practices to enhance the workload of employees and managers, results about the greater empowerment of employees are still scarce (Parry & Tyson, 2011).

Table 13.1 summarizes the main evidence about the positive and negative outcomes of the e-HRM practices for employees and it also lists some of the drivers – both theoretically and empirically derived – that could support the positive ones and prevent the risks.

Table 13.1: e-HRM and employees.

EMPLOYEES' ATTITUDES	
Positive outcomes	**Negative outcomes**
– Affective commitment	– Technology stress
– Perceived procedural justice	– Work and life pressure
– Job satisfaction	– Growing intention to quit
– Decreasing intention to quit	– Resistance to change

Driver

employee level
- technology readiness
- preference about the strategic role of the HRM dept.
- age (competences and mindset)

e-HRM level
- ease of use
- usefulness

Table 13.1 (continued)

EMPLOYEES' ATTITUDES	
Positive outcomes	**Negative outcomes**

organization level
- HRM practices (reward and W&L balance)

EMPLOYEES' KNOWLEDGE	
Positive outcomes	**Negative outcomes**
– Competences	– Workload
– Self-management	– Responsibility
– Information and decision making	
– Productivity	
– Creative performance	

Drivers
employee level
- New competences
- Sense of entitlement

e-HRM level
- Relational and transformational e-HRM
- ESS tools

organization level
- Organizational culture
- POS and PSS

EMPLOYEES' PERCEPTION OF THE HR DEPT.	
Positive outcomes	**Negative outcomes**
– Trust	– Risk of a looser relationship
– Professional image (efficient and competent)	

Drivers
e-HRM level
- Operational and relational e-HRM
- *organization level*
- Organizational culture
- Internal communication
- New competences for the HR professionals

Implications of e-HRM for Employees' Roles in Organizations

e-HRM practices provide the opportunity for employees to take part in the organizational discussions, to be updated on the organizational developments, and to directly obtain information on the organization's people practices (Bondarouk & Ruël, 2009). They enable employees' self-development, thus empowering them to design and self-manage their career paths and learning activities (Marler & Dulebohn, 2005). Moreover, technology allows employees to have more autonomy also in consideration of the organization of their job; e-HRM solutions facilitate the work to be moved from inside to outside the organization, therefore permitting employees to decide where and when to perform their work activities. In addition, e-HRM provides collaborative functionalities to administer and coordinate different modes of collaboration among employees, for instance, employee self-service functionalities could be used to implement the intended empowerment of employees.

All these features suggest (and advocate) that e-HRM practices can provide a unique opportunity for employees, who could play a more proactive role within organizations, even if there is no agreement neither univocal evidence about these positive outcomes.

e-HRM and Job Crafting

By providing more information, enabling self-management practices, allowing for more freedom of choice, e-HRM practices seem to support the emergence of job crafting, which is the alteration of tasks or job characteristics based on the employees' own initiative (Bakker et al., 2012). Organizations can benefit from job crafting by complementing top-down job redesign approaches, achieving competitive advantage in attracting and retaining employees, and adjusting jobs for special groups of employees.

Conditions like job autonomy, job challenges, and their combination, were found to stimulate job crafting, while task interdependency hindered it. As technology enables organizations and supervision to be more controlling, these forces are likely to dampen perceived opportunities for job crafting. However, at the same time, e-HRM allows for less limiting practices in which flexible work hours, and flexible workplaces may accentuate opportunities to job craft. They foster more autonomy for employees and they can provide challenges through continuous communication and feedback across and within organizations. They can also help employees to better manage their interdependencies with other workers, thus encouraging them to craft their jobs.

e-HRM and Co-creation

Allowing for new forms and channels of collaboration, e-HRM technologies can improve the active role of employees within and across organizations, by engaging employees in co-creation processes and supporting their involvement into organizational innovation processes (Chesbrough 2006). Research proved that breakthrough ideas come from group activities, not from lone genius (Bissola et al., 2014). e-HRM systems can facilitate the flow of relevant knowledge among employees in order to create new products and services and develop capabilities that lead to new sources of value creation. The dialogical e-tools and the continuous exchanges made possible by the new technologies enable a higher employee participation in project works, and greater collaboration, thus giving voice to employees and facilitating collective sense-making processes. These, in turn, spawn novel ways of seeing the world and lead to the generation of new ideas.

In this vein, e-HRM systems could encourage the employees to a direct participation also to HRM activities. For the HRM professionals, participatory design methods – such as design thinking – embody the possibility to engage with employees and incorporate their suggestions in HRM solutions. These considerations suggest a new employee-HRM department relationship, where employees could personally participate to design and perform many HRM activities according to their needs.

Future Research

The new e-HRM practices seem to allow for a more proactive, aware and competent involvement of employees in the employee-organization relationship, by enabling a more valuable participation in all HR processes and higher employees' empowerment. On the other hand, detractors predict that e-HRM could be seen as a driver of higher organization remote control, thus reducing employees' freedom and enhancing organizational formalization and centralization. This could also increase the distance between HR department and employees, thus negatively affecting employees' wellbeing. This controversial scenario represents a tremendous chance for the HRM research domain. It provides stimuli to identify the drivers of a positive social change, and to develop and adopt e-HRM systems in a sustainable way, while also accounting for their implications for employees' roles. This means that there is a need to identify the constraints for a positive e-HRM adoption from the employees' point of view; support employees' mind-sets and competences to properly enact their new positive role; define the competences required for the future HR professionals in order to cope with these challenges.

In this scenario, HR professionals with competences in HRM, IT, and design methods will be uniquely positioned to make the HR function a sustainable and valuable contributor with and for employees and organizations. e-HRM represents a new realm for HRM, potentially opening up new career opportunities and transforming the impact HRM has on people, business, and society at large.

Further Readings

Chesbrough, H. (2006). *Open business models: How to thrive in the new innovation landscape.* Harvard Business Press.

Lee, H. W., Pak, J., Kim, S., & Li, L. Z. (2019). Effects of human resource management systems on employee proactivity and group innovation. *Journal of Management, 45*(2), 819–846.

Nishii, L. H., Lepak, D. P., & Schneider, B. (2008). Employee attributions of the "why" of HR practices: Their effects on employee attitudes and behaviors, and customer satisfaction. *Personnel Psychology, 61*(3), 503–545.

Petrou, P., Demerouti, E., & Schaufeli, W. B. (2018). Crafting the change: The role of employee job crafting behaviors for successful organizational change. *Journal of Management, 44*(5), 1766–1792.

References

Bakker, A. B., Tims, M., & Derks, D. (2012). Proactive personality and job performance: The role of job crafting and work engagement. *Human Relations, 65*(10), 1359–1378.

Bissola, R., & Imperatori, B. (2014). The unexpected side of relational e-HRM: Developing trust in the HR department. *Employee Relations, 36*(4), 376–397.

Bissola, R., Imperatori, B., & Trinca Colonel, R. (2014). Enhancing the creative performance of new product teams: an organizational configurational approach. *Journal of Product Innovation Management, 31*(2), 375–391.

Bondarouk, T. V., & Ruël, H. J. (2009). Electronic Human Resource Management: challenges in the digital era. *The International Journal of Human Resource Management, 20*(3), 505–514.

Chesbrough, H. (2006). *Open business models: How to thrive in the new innovation landscape.* Harvard Business Press.

Hadziroh, I. and Yusliza, M.Y. (2015), *"User characteristics as antecedents of techno stress towards EHRM: from experts' views"*, Procedia: Social and Behavioral Sciences, Vol. 172, pp. 134–141.

Iqbal, N., Ahmad, M., MC Allen, M., & Raziq, M. M. (2018). Does e-HRM improve labour productivity? A study of commercial bank workplaces in Pakistan. *Employee Relations, 40*(2), 281–297.

Lin, Y. S. (2011). Fostering creativity through education–a conceptual framework of creative pedagogy. *Creative education, 2*(03), 149.

Maier, C., Laumer, S., Eckhardt, A., & Weitzel, T. (2013). Analyzing the impact of HRIS implementations on HR personnel's job satisfaction and turnover intention. *The Journal of Strategic Information Systems, 22*(3), 193–207.

Marler, J. H., & Dulebohn, J. H. (2005). A model of employee self-service technology acceptance. In *Research in personnel and human resources management* (pp. 137–180). Emerald Group Publishing Limited.

Marler, J. H., Fisher, S. L., & Ke, W. (2009). Employee self-service technology acceptance: A comparison of pre-implementation and post-implementation relationships. *Personnel Psychology, 62*(2), 327–358.

Marler, J. H., & Fisher, S. L. (2013). An evidence-based review of e-HRM and strategic human resource management. *Human Resource Management Review, 23*(1), 18–36.

Meijerink, J. G., Bondarouk, T., & Lepak, D. P. (2016). Employees as active consumers of HRM: Linking employees' HRM competences with their perceptions of HRM service value. *Human Resource Management, 55*(2), 219–240.

Olivas-Lujan, M. R., Ramirez, J., & Zapata-Cantu, L. (2007). e-HRM in Mexico: adapting innovations for global competitiveness. *International Journal of Manpower, 28*(5), 418–434.

Panayotopoulou, L., Vakola, M., & Galanaki, E. (2007). E-HR adoption and the role of HRM: evidence from Greece. *Personnel Review, 36*(2), 277–294.

Parry, E., & Tyson, S. (2011). Desired goals and actual outcomes of e-HRM. *Human Resource Management Journal, 21*(3), 335–354.

Ruël, H., Bondarouk, T., & Looise, J. K. (2004). E-HRM: Innovation or irritation. An explorative empirical study in five large companies on web-based HRM. *Management revue*, 364–380.

Sareen, P. (2015). Study of employee satisfaction towards e-HRM system. *European Journal of Applied Business and Management, 1*(1).

Voermans, M., & van Veldhoven, M. J. P. M. (2007). Attitude towards E-HRM: an empirical study at Philips. *Personnel Review, 36*(6), 887–902.

Tanya Bondarouk
Employer Branding and Social Media

HR professionals have identified the power of information sharing for employer branding that could be obtained through the rapid growth of social media usage. Companies
have Facebook profiles to announce job openings, use LinkedIn to search for qualified
personnel and advertise new jobs on blogs, Twitter or YouTube. Creating an image of a
desirable and unique employer through social media has been a focus of attention in
the last decade, producing a new "hot" e-HRM topic: employer branding (Bondarouk
et al., 2013).

The attractiveness of employer branding, enhanced through the social media,
is rooted in the opportunities for HR professionals to get involved in activities beyond their traditional tasks. As with many new media technologies, employer
branding seems so promising once it is initiated through the social media. Thus,
recruiting is expected to become more interesting and efficient by tweeting a job
opening; head hunting could be better facilitated by the vast number of LinkedIn
profiles; employees could enhance their organizational image by blogging about
how it is to work in that company; and/or the number of good applicants could increase. In this entry I review the concept of employer branding and possibilities
that Social Media channels offer to enhance it.

Employer Branding Defined

The concept originated in the 1990s and started being widely used in the management world. It underwent various definitions during the years and development of
the academic material. Lievens and colleagues discuss employer branding as involving the development and communication of the culture of an organization as an employer, defining and delivering the employment experience (Lievens, Van Hove, &
Anseel, 2007). According to them, the basic principle is that all employees are consumers who must be recruited and retained. Departing from the discussion provided
by Backhaus and Tikoo (2004) and Brethon, Ewing, and Hah (2005), I suggest to define employer branding as *viewed as a long-term strategy of any given company,
aimed at both building a unique and desirable employer identity and managing the perceptions of prospective and current employees, in order to gain competitive advantage.*

Employer branding is believed to attract better candidates, as it helps them picture themselves as being a part of the corporation. By using employer branding, companies show how they differ from their competitors and why the best applicants
should choose to work for them. "A stronger employer brand fosters a positive image,
identity, reputation and encourages employees to identify with the organization"

https://doi.org/10.1515/9783110633702-014

(Brethon et al, 2005, p.151). In general, employer branding is viewed along three sub-dimensions:
- *Value proposition*: information on the organization's culture, management style, qualities of the current employees, current employees' image, etc. – an image of what the company can offer to its employee.
- *External marketing*: presenting the value proposition to recruiting companies or placement counselors to reach and attract the target population. Creating an unique image allows possible candidates to picture themselves working for the company, increasing the degree of commitment. Distinctiveness of the brand allows the firm to acquire distinctive human capital.
- *Internal marketing*: involves respecting the promises made to the employees before recruiting them and so it becomes a part of the organization's culture. It is meant to build a workforce that is difficult to imitate and committed to the organizational goals, but also to achieve an unique culture and increase employee retention.

In the literature there is an overlap between the concepts of organizational reputation, organizational attractiveness and employer branding. Table 14.1 displays broadly accepted definitions of the three concepts, that makes it visible that employer branding borrows certain characteristics from the concepts of organizational reputation, and organizational attractiveness. The noticeable difference is that in the proposed definitions organizational reputation is usually seen as a perception/judgement by stakeholders, customers, employees. Organizational attractiveness is defined as a degree of an appeal, and employer branding is seen as a process.

Table 14.1: Employer branding, organizational attractiveness, and organizational reputation defined.

Organizational reputation	a perception or judgement of stakeholders about the organization's ability to create value based on past actions. It provides a future prospect and it creates prominence for the organization.
Organizational attractiveness	a degree to which an individual would personally seek an organization as an employer, based on the favorable beliefs that an individual has of that organization, and the degree to which an individual would recommend the organization as an employer, based on the intention to act of that individual.
Employer branding	a process of creating the perception that an organization is a desirable place to work in order to attract, retain and motivate employees and therefore differentiate from competitors.

Employer Branding and Social Media

How to make the best use of social media; how to promote a company as the best employer; what if a job seeker receives negative information or feels the company does not offer enough information about the job openings? These are questions that marketing, HR professionals, public relations and advertising practitioners are trying to answer. The outcomes and benefits of the diffusion of information through social media could be of major interest for companies willing to establish a strong employer branding reputation. Put it stronger, if employer branding is not effectively implemented then organizations could lose qualified candidates.

Social media, defined by Kaplan and Haenlein (2010, p. 61) as *"a group of Internet-based applications that build on the ideological and technological foundations of Web 2.0, and that allow the creation and exchange of User Generated Content (UGC)"*, is a term that describes a wide variety of Information Technologies whose common denominator is the ability to connect users in ways that enable bridging distance, time, and other traditional barriers. As a part of social media, authors consider Social Networking Sites (SNS) to be the most utilized services within Web 2.0, whereby Facebook, Twitter, LinkedIn, and Instagram have attracted hundreds of millions of users which integrated these sites into their daily practices. Boyd & Ellison (2013, p. 211) defined social networking sites as *"[w]eb-based services that allow individuals to (1) construct a public or semi-public profile within a bounded system, (2) articulate a list of other users with whom they share a connection, and (3) view and traverse their list of connections and those made by others within the system. The nature and nomenclature of these connections may vary from site to site."*

Even though several "electronic facilities" have captured both general and business attention, it is clear that a high degree of environmental turbulence or high velocity exists, as both software (e.g., social networking sites such as LinkedIn, Xing, and Facebook; blogging sites such as Wordpress, Blogspot or Twitter; personal or organizational rich-media facilities like YouTube, Skype, and Spotify) and hardware platforms (e.g., tablets, smartphones, thinbooks and other emerging innovations) keep evolving at a very rapid pace. Whatever software or hardware context we may take, social media aims to complement or even replace traditional media and communication, and will be the locomotive via which the World Wide Web evolves during the next decade or so (Kaplan & Haenlein, 2010, p. 68).

It seems that organizations understand that social media may offer the possibility of promoting themselves at less cost, gaining competitive advantage and improving the quality of their service. How do different types of social media – social network sites, blogs, collaborative projects, content communities, virtual game worlds – contribute to employer branding?

For example, social media could enhance *Value Proposition* through their ability to provide organizational profiles, peer-to-peer communication, knowledge sharing, creating a trustworthy and loyal image; enhance *External Marketing* by creating a profile that represents the company, filtering information for specific target groups, reaching new and large audiences, searching for job candidates, timely and direct customer contact; and also enhance *Internal Marketing* through formal and informal communication with the employees, instant messaging and strengthening ties with and between employees (Bondarouk et al., 2013). Overall, HR professionals and business leaders get possibilities to take advantages of technical properties of social media to generate their own content (UGC) and communicate it to the external and internal customers.

The most important aspect of social media is that companies have to promote only what they already have. The advertised image of the company has to match the reality. Social media might be a fast way of communicating and spreading your values and intentions as an employer, but if the information is not true and turns out to be fake advertising, then the negative publicity will probably spread even faster.

Theoretically, employer branding, once employed via the social media channels, is well grounded on the assumption that human capital brings and retains value towards the firm, resulting in enhanced performance. This assumption is rooted in the classics of Resource Based View that characteristics of a firm's resources and their employment can contribute towards sustainable competitive advantage. External marketing establishes the firm as an employer of choice and therewith makes it possible to attract the best possible workers. Hereby it is assumed that the distinctiveness of the brand allows the firm to obtain distinctive human resources. Subsequently, the new hires develop a set of assumptions about employment related towards the brand. They will carry these assumptions into the future, hence supporting the values of the firm and increasing their commitment. The assumption is that internal marketing brings on a workforce that is hard for other firms to imitate, by routinely exposing the value proposition of the employer brand towards the workers. This should result in a workplace that is shaped around the corporate goals, enabling the firm to achieve a unique culture focused on doing business the firm's way (Backhaus & Tikoo, 2004).

Future research questions:
- What are the relationships between different types of brand, employer, organizational and individual career?
- What are the realized benefits of employer branding through the social media?

Further Readings

Davies,G., (2008). Employer branding and its influence on managers. *European Journal of Marketing,* 42 (5/6): 667–681.

Edwards, M.R. (2010). An integrative review of employer branding and OB theory. *Personnel Review,* 39 (1): 5–23.

Robertson, A., and Khatibi, A. (2013). The influence of employer branding on productivity-related outcomes of an organization. *IUP Journal of Brand Management, Vol. 10 (3),* pp. 1–17.

References

Bondarouk, T., Ruël, H., Axinia, E., & Arama, R. (2013). What is the future of employer branding through social media? Results of the Delphi study into the perceptions of HR professionals and academics. In: Bondarouk, T.V. and Olivas-Luijan, M.R. (2013) (Eds). *Social Media in Human Resource* Management. *Advanced Series in Management.* Vol. 12, (pp. 23–57). Emerald Group Publishing Limited: WA, UK.

Bondarouk, T., & Olivas-Luijan, MR. (2013). Social media and Human Resouce Management: it takes two to tango. In: Bondarouk, T.V. and Olivas-Luijan, M.R. (2013) (Eds). *Social Media in Human Resource* Management. *Advanced Series in Management.* Vol. 11 (pp. xi–xv), Emerald Group Publishing Limited: WA, UK.

boyd, D. and Ellison, N. B. 2013). Sociality through Social Network Sites. In Dutton, W. H. (Ed.), *The Oxford Handbook of Internet Studies.* Oxford: Oxford University Press, pp. 151–172.

Backhaus, K., & Tikoo S., (2004). Conceptualizing and researching employer branding. *Career Development International,* Vol. 9 (5): 501–517.

Brethon, P., Ewing, M. & Hah, L.L., (2005). Captivating company: dimensions of attractiveness in employer branding. *International Journal of Advertising,* 24: 151–173.

Kaplan, A.M., & Haenelein, M., (2010). Users of the world unite! The challenges and opportunities of social media. *Business Horizons,* 53: 59–68.

Lievens, F., Van Hoye, G. & Anseel, F. (2007). Organizational Identity and Employer Image: Towards a Unifying Framework. *British Journal of Management,* 2007, 18: 45–59.

Anna B. Holm
Virtual HRM and Virtual Organizing

The term virtual organization was coined by researchers at the beginning of 1990s to describe firms' increasing agility and digital connectivity (Davidow & Malone, 1992; Nagel & Dove, 1991). The spread of new network technologies during this period enabled both intra- and interorganizational collaboration across time and space, where distributed human and technological resources were electronically linked through the internet (Porter, 1993). Enterprise agility, or *virtuality*, could now be achieved by integrating three resources – technology, management and the workforce – into a coordinated, independent system (Nagel & Dove, 1991, p. 8). This led to the HR function, supported by information and communication technologies (ICTs), being sometimes referred to as virtual HRM (West & Berman, 2001). For example, Lepak and Snell (1998) define virtual HRM as "a network-based structure built on partnerships and typically mediated by information technologies to help the organization acquire, develop, and deploy intellectual capital".

From a phenomenological point of view, *virtual* as a characteristic is often attributed to phenomena simulated on a computer or computer network, or which occur or exist primarily online, within a virtual reality, or using virtual memory (Merriam-Webster English Dictionary Online, 2019). Thus, the term virtual suggests that, even though certain physical attributes are missing, the object still keeps its functionality through ICTs, e.g. from a computer's virtual memory to virtual pets, and from virtual departments to virtual organizations (Scholz, 1998). Virtual is also often a characteristic of collaborations enabled by technology, e.g. virtual teams and virtual communities of practice. However, this is not to say that the phenomenon in question does not exist physically, but rather that it is experienced by individuals through technology. Similarly, virtual HRM does not imply that HR work does not take place or does not exist in the real world, but rather that it is performed by individuals electronically, and that their collaboration is mediated by ICTs.

Thus, the concept of virtual HRM is just a broader phenomenological view of HRM, and simply suggests the use of "virtual technologies" (West & Berman, 2001) in HRM by means of "network-based structural arrangements" (Lepak & Snell, 1998). It is broad in scope, somewhat ambiguous, and lacks a clear definition that can guide researchers in studying e-HRM from an organizational perspective. Therefore, rather than viewing e-HRM as being equivalent to virtual HRM, scholars might find it more useful to regard it as a case of virtual organizing. Virtual organizing can be defined as the organization of activities facilitating time- and space-independent interaction and collaboration, and which requires the appropriate organization, technology and human agents. It is characterized by directionality and organizational levels, spans organizations' physical and legal boundaries, and may include organizational elements from

https://doi.org/10.1515/9783110633702-015

outside these boundaries, such as external partners, customers, and even society (Holm & Ulhøi, 2010). For instance, e-recruitment systems permit interaction between a hiring organization and job applicants, collaboration among hiring managers and recruiters, applicant screening and assessment – all performed asynchronously and from various locations. This turns recruitment into a time- and space-independent process facilitated by technological, organizational and individual elements at different levels of the organization, aimed at job-seekers from inside and outside (Holm, 2012).

Seen through the lens of virtual organizing, e-HRM comprises interdependent organizational, technological and socio-cognitive elements which are manifested, and can be studied, at different levels of the organization, i.e. from the individual employee to organizational levels, and may even include elements from the external environment (Holm, 2009). Examples of the various elements of virtual organizing of HRM are presented in Table 15.1. This view is supported by a number of other research contributions, e.g. Bondarouk, Parry and Furtmueller (2017) find that factors influencing the adoption of e-HRM can be divided into three areas: technology (T), organization (O), and people (P), which correspond to the three dimensions of virtual organizing presented in Table 15.1. They also find that the most important factors influencing both the adoption and consequences of e-HRM are "people

Table 15.1: Examples of elements of virtual organizing of HRM, i.e. e-HRM.

Dimension / Level	Organizational	Technological	Socio-cognitive
Employee	HR business partner, manager, assistant, line manager, routine	Client software, computers, network connectivity, automation	HR skills, technology acceptance, awareness
Groups / Teams	HR department, HR process, leadership, tasks	HR software, HR software modules, group networks	Group identity, inter-personal trust, team morale
Organization	HR policies, HR strategy, HR organization, top management	HR information system (HRIS), corporate website, ERP system, data security	Culture, ethics, cooperation
External partners and customers	External HR partners, IT vendors, job applicants, trade unions	Software as a service (SaaS), platforms, data repositories	Trust, formalization
Society	Labour markets, labour relations	Internet connectivity, web technologies	Computer literacy, cultural norms

Source: adapted from Holm and Ulhøi (2010)

factors", and are related to organizational cultures as well as employees and their acceptance of technology (Bondarouk et al., 2017). The authors call for e-HRM scholars to focus their research on these TOP groups of factors and to integrate them in studies in order to address the complexity of the e-HRM phenomenon. Strohmeier and Kabst (2009) find that e-HRM adoption is a multilevel process involving both individuals and firms at different organizational levels.

Viewing e-HRM as a case of virtual organizing allows investigating its manifestations and elements at different levels of analysis and in three interdependent dimensions, i.e. organizational, technological and socio-cognitive. Furthermore, the framework for studying virtual organizing presented in Table 15.1 provides a simple yet well-structured approach to studying e-HRM from an organizational perspective. It enables the researcher to outline the overall architecture of e-HRM in organizations and study its various components, as well as how they fit together, and also includes levels of analysis outside the focus organization, thus addressing the main challenges associated with research in virtual HRM (Lepak & Snell, 1998).

Employing a virtual organizing perspective to research in e-HRM can support research endeavours that seek to answer holistic research questions regarding the organizational elements of e-HRM. For example, future research might ask how the implementation of e-HRM on one organizational level effects e-HRM elements on another level, and how implementing e-HRM elements in one dimension requires specific solutions in another. In addition, e-HRM implementation might require organizational arrangements with suppliers, recipients or other stakeholders outside the formal boundaries of the organization, and these can be included in the analysis in various dimensions of virtual organizing. Moreover, since individuals are also an integral part of virtuality and virtual organizing, researchers can investigate which socio-cognitive elements, i.e. "people's factors", are pre-requisites for successful e-HRM adoption, and which new processes and practices might be necessary to ensure that they are in place.

Further Readings

Lepak, D. P., & Snell, S. A. (1998). Virtual HR: Strategic human resource management in the 21st century. *Human Resource Management Review, 8*(3), 215–234.

Bondarouk, T., Parry, E., & Furtmueller, E. (2017). Electronic HRM: four decades of research on adoption and consequences. *The International Journal of Human Resource Management, 28*(1), 98–131.

Holm, A. B. (2012). E-recruitment: The move towards a virtually organized recruitment process. In S. de Juana-Espinosa, J. A. Fernandez-Sanchez, E. Manresa-Marhuenda, & J. Valdes-Conca (Eds.), *Human resource management in the digital economy: creating synergy between competency models and information* (pp. 80–95). Hershey, PA: IGI Global.

Strohmeier, S. (2007). Research in e-HRM: Review and implications. *Human Resource Management Review, 17*(1), 19–37.

References

Bondarouk, T., Parry, E., & Furtmueller, E. (2017). Electronic HRM: four decades of research on adoption and consequences. *The International Journal of Human Resource Management, 28*(1), 98–131.

Davidow, W. H., & Malone, M. S. (1992). *The virtual corporation*. New York, NY: Harper Business.

Holm, A. B. (2009). *Virtual HRM: A case of e-recruitment*. Paper presented at the 3rd International Workshop on Human Resource Information Systems – HRIS 2009, Milan, Italy.

Holm, A. B. (2012). E-recruitment: The move towards a virtually organized recruitment process. In S. de Juana-Espinosa, J. A. Fernandez-Sanchez, E. Manresa-Marhuenda, & J. Valdes-Conca (Eds.), *Human Resource Management in the Digital Economy: Creating Synergy Between Competency Models and Information* (pp. 80–95). Hershey, PA: IGI Global.

Holm, A. B., & Ulhøi, J. P. (2010). A framework for conceptualising virtual organising. *International Journal of Business and Systems Research, 4*(3), 293–311.

Lepak, D. P., & Snell, S. A. (1998). Virtual HR: Strategic human resource management in the 21st century. *Human Resource Management Review, 8*(3), 215–234.

Merriam-Webster English Dictionary Online (2019). Merriam-Webster Inc.

Nagel, R., & Dove, R. (1991). *21st Century Manufacturing Enterprise Strategy*. Bethlehem, PA: Iaccoca Institute, Lehigh University.

Porter, A. L. (1993). Virtual companies reconsidered. *Technology Analysis & Strategic Management, 5*(4), 413–421.

Scholz, C. (1998). Towards the Virtual Corporation: A Complex Move along Three Axes. *Department of Management, University of Saarland, Germany*(62), 25.

Strohmeier, S., & Kabst, R. (2009). Organizational adoption of e-HRM in Europe: An empirical exploration of major adoption factors. *Journal of Managerial Psychology, 24*(6), 482–501.

West, J. P., & Berman, E. M. (2001). From traditional to virtual HR: Is the transition occurring in local government? *Review of Public Personnel Administration, 21*(1), 38–64.

Rita Bissola

Design Thinking and Implications for Organizational Design

The adoption of e-HRM into organizations has both supported and stimulated innovations, not only in terms of what technologies can be used to accomplish human resource tasks, but also as related to organizational design. Indeed, HRM systems act as coordination solutions in delivering people management practices to line managers and/or directly to employees (Ruël, Bondarouk, & Looise, 2004). This entry examines the theory and practice of design thinking and applies it to the context of organizational design and human resource management.

The Development of a Theory of Design Thinking for Management

Design was first created as a form of science opposite to natural sciences. In the design theorists' way of thinking, the science of design aims to create new artifacts, new forms, or new ideas, thus transforming reality, while natural sciences deal with the analysis of existence (Gregory, 1966; Simon, 1969). Schoen (1983) criticized Simon's (1969) positivist approach and proposed a more constructivist perspective based on the remark that designers usually face ambiguous, uncertain, messy situations, as opposed to well-structured problems as expected in the science of design. Schoen (1983) observes that designers tackle complex problems by getting involved in them, thus giving them the opportunity of intuition and mobilizing their artistic sensitivity, among others. He calls these processes "reflective practice".

The theoretical discourse around design – in this case specifically applied to management – was further developed by Richard Boland and Frank Collopy. Building on the observation of architect Frank Gehry's way of working, they note that managers are both designers and decision makers (Boland & Collopy, 2004). In their theory, they explicitly adopt the expression "design thinking" to describe the attitude of managers to solve ill-structured, open-ended problems, which is all but a rational process (Boland, 2004). From this perspective, design thinking is an abductive process of synthesis that permits solving highly ambiguous problems through collecting, organizing, reducing, and filtering data in order to obtain a plausible – though not necessarily best – solution (Kolko, 2010).

https://doi.org/10.1515/9783110633702-016

From Theory to Application of Design Thinking in Organizations

Concurrently with the development of a theory for management design thinking, interest in more practitioner-based studies has grown. The aim of these studies is understanding how designers work, what method and tools they use, to adopt them in managing organizations. Over time, a wide corpus of empirical research focused on identifying the instruments and systematic approaches which may enable employees and teams within companies to think and work like designers. Solutions like rapid prototyping, user observation, ethnographic methods, brainstorming, mind maps, and visualization of ideas were proved to be fundamental in order to concretely perform design thinking (Davis, 2010). Nevertheless, specific studies clearly mark the evolution of design thinking into managerial practice.

The stories of IDEO's successful way of working with product development innovations represent a pivotal reference in this domain (Johansson-Skoeldberg, Woodilla, Cetinkaya, 2013). Owing to the contributions drafted by its CEO Tim Brown, IDEO's design practice has become a generalized method to enhance innovation. He defines design thinking as *"a discipline that uses the designer's sensibility and methods to match people's needs with what is technologically feasible and what a viable business strategy can convert into customer value and market opportunity"* (Brown, 2008, p. 2). As a consequence of its human-centered focus, design thinking powers innovation because it allows for a thorough understanding of what people appreciate and need the most, and what they like or dislike about a particular product or service (Brown, 2008).

In this context, design thinking revolutionizes the product development process. From a predefined linear process of orderly steps where designers intervene in a downstream phase to provide a "beautiful wrapper" for the idea (Brown, 2008: 2), design thinking transforms innovation in a creative human-centered discovery process followed by iterative cycles of prototyping, testing, and refinement (Brown, 2008). From the design thinking perspective, innovation becomes a continuum comprising three sets of related activities (spaces) respectively called inspiration, ideation, and implementation. Inspiration consists in all the circumstances that can motivate the search for a solution. Ideation is the generation, development, test of ideas that could be a potential solution to the situation. Implementation concerns the transition of the selected idea into its application in the market production. The spaces are not linearly ordered, instead they compose an iterative process. Projects advance by means of going back and forth through these spaces (especially inspiration and implementation) as this process generates different ideas while searching for a viable solution. People are involved from the beginning, designers observe users and ask potential customers to discuss their needs, habits, and preferences during the whole design cycle. Users are members of diverse inter-functional teams and participate to the whole design process, thus directly contributing to shaping se-lected ideas and developing prototyping (Brown, 2008).

Besides design thinking as a way to foster innovation and provide more creativity, a second crucial discourse on design thinking depicts it as an effective approach to complex problem-solving and, therefore, considers it as a necessary competence for managers. The contribution of Roger Martin, who also worked with IDEO, mainly adds to this perspective (Johansson-Skoeldberg et al., 2013). By turning to examples of suc-cessful companies and developing the metaphor of the "knowledge funnel", Martin conceives design thinking as the interplay of analytical and intuitive thinking that al-lows the balancing of the exploration of new knowledge and the exploitation of the current one (Elsbach & Stigliani, 2018; Martin, 2009). In such a perspective, design thinking occurs as an ongoing process that equally employs abductive, deductive, and inductive logics. In order to face problems that present multiple possible solutions, de-sign thinking enhances the generation of new ideas (abduction), it requires predicting consequences (deduction), testing, and generalizing them (induction), thus defining a sort of cognitive and practical process for successful management (Martin, 2007).

Although there is an ample literature about the application of design thinking in the management realm, such corpus appears substantially heterogeneous with a clear distinction between the practice-based and the theoretically-based contribu-tions, which were developed independently. The main frameworks that synthetize the literature on design thinking agree on such a distinction and argue that the prac-titioner contributions prevail with respect to the theoretical developments of this domain, which is considered a limitation of the management design thinking dis-course (Elsbach & Stigliani, 2018; Johansson-Skoeldberg et al., 2013; Kimbell, 2011; Rylander, 2009). This opinion may be shared, yet, it should be noted that the litera-ture about design thinking in practice, its tools and phases, has the merit of enabling its concrete adoption in order to push innovation and find solutions to indeterminate organizational problems. For example, the HR department at FiveStars,[1] a customer loyalty and rewards platform founded in 2010, was first involved in a wide design thinking project to identify their own path for the improvement of their employee ex-perience. Having come to the decision that their HR strategy was to be warm, funny, and unapologetically authentic, and their aim to connect with people on a deeper level, they now regularly adopt design thinking tools – mainly brainstorming techni-ques at individual and team levels – to develop people management initiatives con-sistent with their HR strategy of increasing the employee experience value. Among these, they introduced the High Five Recognition Program that periodically en-courages employees to reflect and write five notes recognizing each other's value

---

1 https://www.ideou.com/blogs/inspiration/applying-design-thinking-to-hr-and-people-operations-at-fivestars retrieved in February 2020.

for something that made a difference. This is a way of recognizing valuable contributions and celebrating merit.

Design thinking proves to be particularly useful in designing e-HRM systems because it is human-centered, hence allowing for the involvement of employees from the beginning of the system design. This means that the employee experience and feedback as users of the technological tools are taken into consideration, in addition to their suggestions and needs. As a consequence, it is possible to obtain more efficient and engaging digital tools. For instance, DuPont redesigned its HR portal around the end users' experience which resulted in a dramatic reduction of time employees spend on routine HR tasks. Similarly, Australia and New Zealand Banking Group developed a user-friendly app which enables employees to carry out operational activities (e.g. managing their benefits and vacations) and collaborate with colleagues, thus also making these activities more exciting.[2]

Design Thinking Insights and Implications for Rethinking Organizational Design

Both streams of discourse about design thinking give rise to reflections that shed light on the organization studies seen as a science for design. Building on Simon's (1969) seminal work the *Science of the Artificial*, a first strand of research development relies on conceiving organization studies as a science for design where scientists are involved in envisioning and shaping organizational contexts in order to improve the human condition (Jelinek, Romme, & Boland, 2008). From this standpoint, organizations are much more than structure. Some scholars see them as protean social and enacted constructs where structure, understanding, and culture constantly co-evolve (Jelinek et al., 2008; Weick, 1979). Others conceive organizations as action streams or action nets, thus making the concept of organizational boundaries more nuanced (Czarniawska, 2004). This enables researchers to consider organizations as dynamic processes, hence overcoming the positivistic tradition that sees organizations as empirical objects essentially made of structure and control focusing almost exclusively on internal rationality, work flows, and efficiency.

The dynamic nature of organizations implies their ephemeral nature, which engages them in iterative loops of designing aimed at pursuing more desirable conditions related to multiple levels and types of functionality (e.g. including employees, clients, and society at large). As different people are constantly involved in organizations, random events, slippages, and serendipities within organizational entities,

---

2 https://www2.deloitte.com/us/en/insights/focus/human-capital-trends/2016/employee-experience-management-design-thinking.html retrieved in February 2020.

the desirable organizational conditions persistently evolve, leading companies to regular re-organization (Yoo, Boland, & Lyytinen, 2006).

The components of the iterative transformative process constituting the nature of organizations are the interplay of organizational entities, artifacts, and social circumstances. Such interactions generate new artifacts that define novel organizational conditions by modifying (or redesigning) the previous contexts. A further challenge to this dynamic is represented by the fact that artifacts are socially constructed through people interactions, which create meaning around these objects (Krippendorff, 2006).

All these arguments make it clear that organization in the design perspective is *necessarily messy, dynamic, iterative and responsive to circumstances* (Jelinek et al., 2008: 322), which prevents it from defining universal laws that do not halt the continuous redesign and redirection. This approach to organizational design makes it possible to explicit the micro-foundation of organizational forms, hence clarifying the path that leads to an organization entity. Moreover, the approach enhances the pursuit of multiple diverse aims in organization design other than just process efficiency, organizational functioning, and workload. For example, by involving employees in designing organizations, one can verify how a potential organizational solution can impact their motivation, thus converting such solution into a condition for identifying the preferable organizational alternative to implement in consideration of the employee's motivation. Design thinking entails the involvement of the users and/or beneficiaries of the project outcome. When employees take part in the design of the organizational structure, they contribute to shaping the resulting solution, which, therefore, will combine the company's as well as the employees' requirements, as opposed to the traditional approach to organizational design project. When design thinking is adopted, job design meets efficiency aims pursued by the company, but it also benefits from the suggestions offered by the employees' experience. Indeed, these will give their contribution and also state their aim, which is to avoid repetitive alienating tasks.

More recently, Elsbach and Stigliani (2018) claimed that there is a need for more theory on the organizational implications of adopting design thinking. In particular, they ventured on an in-depth literature review in order to investigate the relationship between design thinking and organizational culture. This study has the merit to overcome the traditional distinction between theoretical and practitioner-based research on design thinking. Indeed, the authors explore how the adoption of design thinking tools impacts organizational culture, and vice versa. In addition, they theorize on it by formalizing a theoretical framework to guide future research. In particular, they found that the adoption of need-finding tools, such as ethnographic interviews, support the development of the value of user focus. Similarly, evidence showed that the use of idea-generation tools, such as co-creation/co-design, positively impacts norms of collaboration, risk taking, and ambiguity. The authors also proved that the adoption of idea-testing tools, such as rapid prototyping, positively influences the development of cultures that enhance experimentation, learning from failure, and design-led strategic thinking. On the other side of the coin, they found confirmation that cultures promoting similar values better support the adoption of design thinking techniques.

Further Readings

Boland, Jr R.J., Collopy, F., Lyytinen, K., & Yoo, Y. (2008). Managing as designing: lessons for organization leaders from the design practice of Frank O. Gehry. *Design Issues*, 24(1): 10–25.

Buchanan, R. 1992. Wicked problems in design thinking. *Design Issues*, 8: 5–21.

Romme, A. G. L. 2003 Making a difference: Organization as design. *Organization Science* 14: 558–574.

Starbuck, W. H. (2006). *The production of knowledge: The challenge of social science research.* Oxford (UK): Oxford University Press.

References

Boland, R. J. (2004). Design in the Punctuation of Management Action. In Boland, R. & Collopy, F. (eds.) *Managing as Designing*. Stanford, CA, Stanford University Press: 106–112.

Boland, R. J., & Collopy, F. (2004). Design matters for management. In Boland, R. & Collopy, F. (eds.) *Managing as Designing*. Stanford, CA, Stanford University Press: 3–18.

Brown, T. (2008). Design thinking. *Harvard Business Review*, 86(6): 84–92.

Czarniawska, B. (2004). Management as the Designing of an Action Net. In Boland, R. & Collopy, F. (eds.) *Managing as Designing*. Stanford, CA, Stanford University Press: 102–105.

Davis, B. M. 2010. Creativity & innovation in business 2010 – Teaching the application of design thinking to business. *Procedia – Social and Behavioral Sciences*, 2 (4): 6532–6538.

Elsbach, K. D., & Stigliani, I. (2018). Design thinking and organizational culture: A review and framework for future research. Journal of Management, 44(6): 2274–2306.

Gregory, S. A. 1966. *The design method*. London, UK, Butterworth.

Jelinek, M., Romme, A. G. L., & Boland, R. J. (2008). Introduction to the special issue: Organization studies as a science for design: Creating collaborative artifacts and research. *Organization Science*, 29(3): 317–329.

Johansson-Sköldberg, U., Woodilla, J., & Çetinkaya, M. (2013). Design thinking: past, present and possible futures. *Creativity and innovation management*, 22(2): 121–146.

Kimbell, L. (2011). Rethinking design thinking: Part I. *Design and Culture*, 3(3): 285–306.

Kolko, J. 2010. Abductive thinking and sensemaking: The drivers of design synthesis. *Design Issues*, 26: 15–28.

Krippendorff, K. (2006). *The semantic turn: A new foundation for design*. Boca Raton, FL: CRC Press.

Martin, R. L. (2007). *The opposable mind: How successful leaders win through integrative thinking*. Cambridge, MA, Harvard Business School Press.

Martin, R. L. (2009). *The design of business: Why design thinking is the next competitive advantage*. Cambridge, MA, Harvard Business Press.

Ruël, H., Bondarouk, T., & Looise, J. K. (2004). E-HRM: Innovation or irritation. An explorative empirical study in five large companies on web-based HRM. *Management Revue*, 15(3): 364–380.

Rylander, A. (2009). Design thinking as knowledge work: Epistemological foundations and practical implications. *Design Management Journal*, 4(1): 7–19.

Schön, D. A. (1983). *The reflective practitioner: How professionals think in action*. Cambridge, MA, Basic Books.

Simon, H. A. (1969). *The sciences of the artificial*. 1st edn. Cambridge, MA, MIT Press.

Weick, K. E. (1979). *Enactment and organizing. The social psychology of organizing*. New York: Random House.

Yoo, Y., Boland, Jr R. J., & Lyytinen, K. (2006). From organization design to organization designing. *Organization Science*, 17(2): 215–229.

Part 4: **Theoretical Viewpoints**

Anna B. Holm
Institutional Theory Perspective

Institutional theory, in particular neo- or new institutional theory (NIT), is concerned with how broad social forces, ranging from explicit laws to implicit cultural understandings, influence, and are influenced by, the actions of organizations (Scott, 1994). One of the basic assumptions of NIT is that organizations are forced by various pressures, or institutions, to act in accordance with collectively held beliefs, rules and norms (DiMaggio & Powell, 1983). In the process, universal practices emerge as organizations benchmark against each other and copy practices that are believed to deliver certain outcomes (Farndale & Paauwe, 2007). As a result, organizations within certain domains are increasingly similar and tend to be organized around rituals of conformity to wider institutions (Meyer & Rowan, 1977), including their HRM strategies, policies and practices. For example, e-HRM adoption can be a consequence of 'copying' the behaviour of successful organizations or competitors.

The 'copying' process that makes organizations more homogeneous is referred to as *institutional isomorphism* (DiMaggio & Powell, 1983), and is characterized by three distinct mechanisms: 1) *coercive isomorphism*; 2) *mimetic isomorphism;* and 3) *normative isomorphism*. Coercive isomorphism results from both formal and informal pressures imposed on an organization by other organizations on whom they are dependent, and by expectations of the society in which the organization functions. Mimetic isomorphism results from organizations' tendency to model themselves on similar organizations that they perceive to be more legitimate or successful. Finally, normative isomorphism is associated with professionalization due to formal education and the growth and elaboration of professional networks, which together create 'a pool of almost interchangeable individuals who occupy similar positions across a range of organizations and possess a similarity of orientation and disposition' (DiMaggio & Powell, 1983).

Institutions

According to NIT, institutions are characterised by "more-or-less taken for granted repetitive social behaviour that is underpinned by normative systems and cognitive understandings that give meaning to social exchange and thus enable self-reproducing social order" (Greenwood, Oliver, Sahlin, & Suddaby, 2008, pp. 4–5). Institutions can be simple or highly contested, and may exist at a variety of levels, i.e. from a single individual to people in multiple countries (Van de Ven & Hargrave, 2004, p. 261). Examples of societal institutions include the market, the corporation, the professions, the state, the family, and religions (Thornton, Ocasio, & Lounsbury, 2012).

https://doi.org/10.1515/9783110633702-017

Institutions are composed of regulative, normative, and cultural-cognitive elements that, together with associated activities and resources, provide stability and meaning to social life (Scott, 2001, p. 48). In institutions, the regulative dimension is represented by rules, laws and sanctions, while the normative dimension is realised through normative systems such as routines, procedures, conventions, strategies, organizational forms, technologies, etc. (March & Olsen, 1984, p. 22). The cultural-cognitive dimension rests on the premise that the internal interpretive processes of individuals are shaped by external cultural frameworks and represented by belief systems and shared logics of action (Scott, 2001, p. 52). Thus, institutions provide the framework – regulative, normative, and cultural-cognitive – within which actors define and pursue their interests (Scott, 2001, p. 149).

Organizations are continuously influenced by their institutional context, which is made up of interacting agencies, such as professions and regulatory agencies (Hinings, Greenwood, Reay, & Suddaby, 2004, p. 307), and widespread social understandings that define what it means to be rational, also referred to as *rationalized myths* (Greenwood et al., 2008, p. 3). The latter are based on the rules, norms and beliefs surrounding economic activity that guide socially acceptable economic behaviour (Oliver, 1997), and which may constrain or empower social action (Scott, 2001, p. 55). Such rationalizations enable, and even require, participants to organize along prescribed lines (Meyer & Rowan, 1977).

Everyday activities that constitute a practice, including e-HRM practices, determine how actors interact, construct, and draw on physical and social features of the context (Jarzabkowski, Matthiesen, & Van de Ven, 2009, p. 288). Heikkilä (2013) study of e-HRM implementation in subsidiaries of American and European MNCs in China found that regulative, normative and cultural-cognitive institutional factors, such as labour law regulations, tax regulation, low HR professionalization, and the culture of 'guanxi' and 'money-oriented' mindset of Chinese employees, influenced e-HRM practices and undermined the strategic potential of e-HRM. Among other things, the local subsidiaries had to localize a number of e-HRM system modules, misused management performance systems, created additional work and costs for the HR function, and implemented tighter control of their subsidiaries. On the other hand, introducing HR technologies was easy, because Chinese employees are generally very open to new technologies and learning new technical skills.

Organizational Fields and Institutional Logics

NIT is based on two main premises, i.e. the demarcation of an *organizational field* as a unit and level of analysis, and the notion of *institutional logics*.

An organizational field consists of a community of organizations with a common meaning system, whose members interact more frequently with one another than with actors outside the field (Scott, 1994, pp. 207–208). According to DiMaggio and Powell (1983), an organizational field refers to "those organisations that, in aggregate, constitute a recognised area of institutional life: key suppliers, resource and product consumers, regulatory agencies, and other organisations that produce similar services or products". These can be organizational entities from a recognized area of institutional life, e.g. industries and business sectors that produce similar services or products (DiMaggio & Powell, 1983), and other organizations which influence their performance (Scott, 2001).

Organizational fields are characterized by distinctive field logics, also called institutional logics, which provide the organizing principles for field actors. These consist of formal and informal rules of action and interaction, that guide and constrain decision-makers (Thornton, 2004, p. 2), and which in turn underpins the appropriateness of organizational practices in given settings and at a particular time (Greenwood, Díaz, Li, & Lorente, 2010). Institutional logics are represented by socially constructed historical patterns of material practices, assumptions, values, beliefs, and rules, by which individuals organize time and space, and provide meaning to their social reality (Thornton & Ocasio, 1999). Belief systems and related practices guide and orient the behaviour of organizational field participants (Scott, 1994, p. 209; 2001, p. 139), and can differ fundamentally in the nature of their assumptions from field to field (Friedland & Alford, 1991). Organizational field actors at the interstices of divergent fields embody multiple institutional logics, and often build new organizational forms that bridge these logics (Thornton & Ocasio, 2008).

Holm (2014) employed the notion of institutional logics and the organizational field in her research on the adoption of e-recruitment practices in Denmark. In this study, the organizational field is defined as a community of organizations involved in providing recruitment-related services for external and internal parties, e.g. recruiting organizations, technology providers, head-hunters, search agencies, and professional associations. Although these organizations carry out different tasks, they influence the development of recruitment processes and practices at the organizational field level. The study found that many organizations adopted e-recruitment practices as a response to socio-cognitive and normative pressures from the wider society, e.g. labour markets, internet technologies, and changes in 'taken-for-granted' practices in their field. Moreover, the organizational field had evolved to include powerful new actors, such as internet-based job boards and HR technology providers.

Conducting Research in e-HRM from a NIT Perspective

The institutional approach is a good, albeit underutilised, theoretical approach to studying e-HRM in context, and, as noted by Strohmeier (2007), can cast a critical light on its consequences. NIT enables the researcher to explain how the institutional context influences the configuration of e-HRM and puts normative, regulative and socio-cognitive pressures on organizations to adopt various e-HRM practices as a means of gaining legitimacy (Marler & Fisher, 2013; Strohmeier, 2007). Marler and Fisher (2013) specifically mention the applicability of NIT for research on the implementation of e-HRM as a technological innovation to gain legitimacy and institutionalize the strategic HRM function. Furthermore, NIT can help gain a better understanding of how e-HRM enables the organization to reinforce strategic goals, conform to social norms, and comply with regulatory regimes.

Notwithstanding, e-HRM researchers can sometimes experience difficulties in designing and implementing their studies, since institutions are complex phenomena that interact across multiple levels of analysis and embody both content and process elements (Suddaby & Greenwood, 2009). Moreover, research from a NIT perspective needs to identify linkages between macro-institutional constructs, i.e. the ideational elements of institutions, and micro-institutional behaviours, i.e. the practical actions of individuals (Barley & Tolbert, 1997). In addition, given the many ways in which organizations are deeply embedded in institutional context (Scott, 2001, p. 82), an institutional approach also requires pluralistic research methods.

Scott's (2001) methodological framework for NIT research identified six levels of analysis: *world system*, *society*, *organizational field*, *organizational population*, *organization*, and *organizational subsystem*; and four types of carriers in which institutions are embedded: *symbolic systems*, *relationship systems*, *routines* and *artefacts* (pp. 77–83). Symbolic systems, or cultures, are inherent in the minds of individuals and operate within the organisation's environment. They may exist in the wider environment, e.g. at societal level, or be restricted to specific organizations. Relationship systems are often viewed as creating and enforcing codes, norms and rules, and as monitoring and sanctioning the activities of participants. Routines rely on 'patterned actions that reflect the tacit knowledge of actors: deeply ingrained habit and procedures based on inarticulated knowledge and beliefs' (p. 80). They underline much of the stability of organizational behaviour, accounting for reliable performance and organizational rigidities. Artefacts as institutional carriers, or material culture, are used in the performance of various tasks, and may be represented as complex technologies (e.g. hardware and software) which users interpret, appropriate and manipulate in various ways (Orlikowski, 1992, p. 408). One of the biggest challenges of the institutional approach, therefore, is to trace the interweaving of actions, processes, structures and material objects at multiple levels of analysis, i.e. individual, organisation, organisational field, etc., through the various categories of institutional carriers. Table 17.1 below presents a brief overview, including examples of NIT levels of analysis, actors, and institutional pillar carriers, of e-HRM research from a NIT perspective.

The NIT approach enables studying e-HRM in context, and combines a rational view of organizing with an ecological view of organizations. For example, researchers

Table 17.1: Institutional framework and carriers for research in e-HRM.

Level of analysis	Actors	Institutional pillar carriers		
		Regulative	Normative	Cultural-cognitive
World system	International Labour Organization; United Nations; international trade organizations, blocs and unions	International human rights conventions and laws; international labour conventions	International educational certification and accreditations; international professional charters	Human rights and freedoms; global mobility
Societal	National labour governmental agencies and bodies; professional associations; trade unions; educational institutions	Immigration policies; labour market regulations and laws; data protection regulations and laws	Educational policies; availability and dispersion of ICTs across social clusters and labour markets; HR education	Equal-opportunity employment; job mobility; equal pay; data privacy; fairness; discrimination
Organizational field	Organizations providing HR services; HR professional associations; HR technology providers	Personal data privacy protection regulations and laws	HR technologies; HR professional charters; data collection and exchange	Trust; cooperation; knowledge-sharing, competition
Organizational population	Public and private organizations; NGOs; HR professional associations and networks	Privacy protection acts; data protection regulations and laws	Organizational goals; collaborative networks	Organizational prestige and reputation; influence
Organization	Private and public organizations engaged in providing HR services	Labour protection, employment laws, acts and regulations; employment contracts	HR models and strategies; HR policies and processes; ERP systems; e-HRM systems; virtual teams	Organizational culture; talent philosophy; identity; mobility; employer brand
Organizational subsystem	HRM function and departments; worker unions and clubs	Organizational charters; employment contracts; collective bargaining	HR practices and procedures; payment schemes and benefits; e-HRM systems; HR documents	HR philosophy; employee identity; HR worker identity

can address the adoption of e-HRM as the outcome of mimetic mechanisms of bench-marking and the imitation of strategies of successful competitors. New e-HRM practices can also be analysed as a consequence of institutional change and insti-tutional pressures emanating from wider society, such as labour markets and in-ternet technologies. Researchers can also investigate how e-HRM is affected by changes in employment and data protection legislation, i.e. the regulative pillar of institutions and its carriers. Additional contributions to the legitimization of e-HRM practices in MNC subsidiaries in high- vs low-context locations (Child, 2000) can ad-vance the international dimension of e-HRM. Furthermore, future research in e-HRM can address such under-researched areas as the variations in e-HRM implementation and practice due to institutional pressures, the variation in e-HRM adoption due to the conflict between internal relational and external institutional contexts, and the institu-tionalization of e-HRM as a taken-for-granted mode of HR delivery.

Further Readings

DiMaggio, P. J., & Powell, W. W. (1983). The iron cage revisited: Institutional isomorphism and collective rationality in organizational fields. *American Sociological Review, 46*(2), 147–160.

Farndale, E., & Paauwe, J. (2007). Uncovering competitive and institutional drivers of HRM practices in multinational corporations. *Human Resource Management Journal, 17*(4), 355–375.

Kostova, T., & Roth, K. (2002). Adoption of an organizational practice by subsidiaries of multinational corporations: Institutional and relational effects. *Academy of Management Journal, 45*(1), 215–233.

Meyer, J. W., & Rowan, B. (1977). Institutionalized organizations: Formal structure as myth and ceremony. *American Journal of Sociology, 83*(2), 340–363.

Oliver, C. (1997). Sustainable competitive advantage: combining institutional and resource-based views. *Strategic Management Journal, 18*(9), 697–713.

Scott, W. R. (2008). *Institutions and Organizations: Ideas and Interests.* Thousand Oaks, CA: SAGE Publications.

Van de Ven, A. H., & Hargrave, T. J. (2004). Social, technical, and institutional change. In M. S. Poole & A. H. Van de Ven (Eds.), *Handbook of Organizational Change and Innovation.* New York, NY: Oxford University Press.

References

Barley, S. R., & Tolbert, P. S. (1997). Institutionalization and structuration: Studying the links between action and institution. *Organization Studies, 18*(1), 93–117.

Child, J. (2000). Theorizing about organizations cross-nationally. In J. L. Cheng & R. B. Peterson (Eds.), *Advances in International Comparative Management* (Vol. 13, pp. 27–76). Stamford, CT: JAI Press.

DiMaggio, P. J., & Powell, W. W. (1983). The iron cage revisited: Institutional isomorphism and collective rationality in organizational fields. *American Sociological Review, 46*(2), 147–160.

Farndale, E., & Paauwe, J. (2007). Uncovering competitive and institutional drivers of HRM practices in multinational corporations. *Human Resource Management Journal, 17*(4), 355–375.

Friedland, R., & Alford, R. (1991). Bringing society back in: Symbols, practices and institutional contradictions. In W. W. Powell & P. J. DiMaggio (Eds.), *The new institutionalism in organizational analysis*. Chicago and London: The Unversity of Chicago Press.

Greenwood, R., Díaz, A. M., Li, S. X., & Lorente, J. C. (2010). The multiplicity of institutional logics and the heterogeneity of organizational responses. *Organization Science, 21*(2), 521–539.

Greenwood, R., Oliver, C., Sahlin, K., & Suddaby, R. (2008). Introduction. In R. Greenwood, C. Oliver, K. Sahlin, & R. Suddaby (Eds.), *Organizational institutionalizm*. London, UK: SAGE Publications.

Heikkilä, J.-P. (2013). An institutional theory perspective on e-HRM's strategic potential in MNC subsidiaries. *The Journal of Strategic Information Systems, 22*(3), 238–251.

Hinings, C. R., Greenwood, R., Reay, T., & Suddaby, R. (2004). Dynamics of change in organizational fields. In M. S. Poole & A. H. Van de Ven (Eds.), *Handbook of organizational change and innovation*. New York, NY: Oxford University Press.

Holm, A. B. (2014). Institutional context and e-recruitment practices of Danish organizations. *Employee Relations, 36*(4), 432–455.

Jarzabkowski, P., Matthiesen, J., & Van de Ven, A. H. (2009). Doing which work? A practice approach to institutional pluralism. In T. B. Lawrence, R. Suddaby, & B. Leca (Eds.), *Institutional work: Actors and agency in institutional studies of organizations* (pp. 284–324). Cambridge, UK: Cambridge University Press.

March, J. G., & Olsen, J. P. (1984). The new institutionalism: Organizational factors in political life. *The American Political Science Review, 78*(3), 734–749.

Marler, J. H., & Fisher, S. L. (2013). An evidence-based review of e-HRM and strategic human resource management. *Human Resource Management Review, 23*(1), 18–36.

Meyer, J. W., & Rowan, B. (1977). Institutionalized organizations: Formal structure as myth and ceremony. *American Journal of Sociology, 83*(2), 340–363.

Oliver, C. (1997). Sustainable competitive advantage: Combining institutional and resource-based views. *Strategic Management Journal, 18*(9), 697–713.

Orlikowski, W. J. (1992). The duality of technology: Rethinking the concept of technology in organizations. *Organization Science*, (3), 398–427.

Scott, R. W. (1994). Conceptualizing organizational fields: Linking organizations and societal systems. In H.-U. Derlien, U. Gerhardt, & F. W. Scharpf (Eds.), *Systemrationalität und Partialinteresse. Festschrift für Renate Mayntz* (p. 544). Baden-Baden: Nomos.

Scott, R. W. (2001). *Institutions and Organizations* (2d ed.). Thousand Oaks, CA: SAGE Publications.

Strohmeier, S. (2007). Research in e-HRM: Review and implications. *Human Resource Management Review, 17*(1), 19–37.

Suddaby, R., & Greenwood, R. (2009). Methodological issues in researching institutional change. In D. Buchanan & A. Bryman (Eds.), *The SAGE handbook of organizational research methods* (pp. 176–195). London, UK: SAGE Publications.

Thornton, P. H. (2004). *Markets from culture: Institutional logics and organizational decisions in higher education publishing*. Stanford, CA: Stanford University Press.

Thornton, P. H., & Ocasio, W. (1999). Institutional logics and the historical contingency of power in organizations: Executive succession in the higher education publishing industry, 1958–1990. *American Journal of Sociology, 105*(3), 801–843.

Thornton, P. H., & Ocasio, W. (2008). Institutional logics. In R. Greenwood, C. Oliver, K. Sahlin, & R. Suddaby (Eds.), *The SAGE handbook of organizational institutionalism* (pp. 99–129). London, UK: SAGE Publications.

Thornton, P. H., Ocasio, W., & Lounsbury, M. (2012). *The Institutional Logics Perspective: A New Approach to Culture, Structure, and Process*. Oxford, UK: Oxford University Press.

Van de Ven, A. H., & Hargrave, T. J. (2004). Social, technical, and institutional change. In M. S. Poole & A. H. Van de Ven (Eds.), *Handbook of organizational change and innovation*. New York, NY: Oxford University Press.

Alessandra Lazazzara and Eleanna Galanaki

Resource-Based View Perspective in e-HRM Research

e-HRM is considered a mature practice in modern organizations and its adoption rate has significantly increased in recent decades. Although empirical evidence for the actual attainment of expected benefits from its application is scarce, e-HRM is believed to change the role of the HR function. Therefore, its adoption is likely to continue to rise over the coming years, given the advantages that such systems are expected to confer to organizations. More specifically, when adopting e-HRM, the main effects anticipated by companies include a more efficient and strategically oriented HRM function, to increase organizational innovativeness, and to boost competitive advantage.

To address the topic of e-HRM outcomes and goals, in this entry we look at the potential consequences of e-HRM, through the lens of the resource-based view (RBV) (Barney, 1991; Peteraf, 1993). This perspective has been very influential in many areas of HRM, particularly in the strategic HRM field, and it has been applied to identify which types of HRM systems and configurations lead to superior firm performance. Indeed, the RBV is usually applied to identify the kind of resources most likely to influence companies' competitive advantage. As one of the main weaknesses of current e-HRM research is its primarily non-theoretical character (Bondarouk et al., 2017), RBV may contribute to the theoretical foundation of e-HRM by explaining the relationships between adoption and consequences of e-HRM.

A Brief Overview of RBV

The literature on the RBV is now more than 30 years old (Barney, 1986; Wernerfelt, 1984) and is based on the idea that organizational success is the result of a mix of value-generating internal resources and market characteristics which impede competitive value erosion (Barney, 1991). In this view, firms are bundles of tangible and intangible resources and capabilities which can create a competitive advantage by differentiating themselves from competitors (Barney, 1991). Indeed, RBV assumes that the primary driver of the firm's durable competitive advantage and economic performance is a collection of physical, organizational, and human resources that have the attributes of VRIN, which stands for Valuable, Rare, Inimitable and Non-substitutable (Barney, 1991). According to the VRIN framework, resources are valuable when they are a significant source of profitability; rare when there is a scarcity of such resources and can only be acquired by one or very few companies; those resources should be hard to imitate; and should not be easily replaced by other

https://doi.org/10.1515/9783110633702-018

substitutes. Therefore, organizations may increase their competitive advantage by being more effective than competitors in developing and deploying such resources.

Moreover, the RBV relies on two critical assumptions deriving from the pioneering work of Edith Penrose (1959) who suggested that in order to provide competitive advantage, VRIN resources should be heterogeneous and immobile. The first assumption refers to heterogeneous distribution of valuable resources among firms which results in different strategies to compete. The value of such resources increases as they are bundled together to create idiosyncratic combinations which are able to solve firm-specific problems (Penrose, 1959; Spender & Grant, 1996). It follows that companies achieve competitive advantage by using their different bundles of resources and when such idiosyncratic combinations are so complex that others cannot easily duplicate or substitute for, these companies will outperform competitors (Barney, 1991; Peteraf, 1993). The second assumption is related to resources' immobility, which means that such resources do not move from one company to the other, therefore rivals cannot implement the same strategies.

Is e-HRM an Organizational Resource?

Several researchers have recommended the application of RBV in the e-HRM field. One of the first to suggest that RBV can contribute to the theoretical foundation of e-HRM research, in particular by explaining the relationship between the configuration and possible transformational consequences of e-HRM, is Strohmeier (2007). He affirmed that e-HRM and its specific sub-functions (e.g., e-recruiting, e-learning, e-communication) contribute to the company' success by providing the firm with human resources that fit to the VRIN characteristics. This means the e-HRM can be viewed as a lever to enhance the value of other organizational resources and capabilities, namely the human ones. Indeed, many authors have applied the RBV to the field of strategic HRM (Wright et al., 1994, 2001), suggesting that the core resources that contribute to the firm' success are the knowledge, skills and activities performed by the workforce. Moreover, in agreement with Penrose's (1959) view, human resources have been considered as the only resources capable of performing heterogeneously across different firms, being in this way the main sources of competitive advantage (Barney, 1986; Bowman & Ambrosini, 2000; Parry, 2011). Therefore, as in the case of the HRM function, whose role is fundamental in order to maximize the value created through the effective development and deployment of human resources (Marler, 2009), e-HRM can also be considered as a complementary resource that enhances the value of other organizational resources and capabilities.

In this view, e-learning, e-recruitment, e-selection, and other kinds of electronic human resources practices and policies are a way to attract, develop, and retain core human resources with VRIN characteristics. What makes a difference is not the technology itself, rather the complementarity between e-HRM practices and other internal resources that can generate idiosyncratic combinations which are harder for competitors to copy than stand-alone e-HRM policies and practices (Barney, 1991; Wright et al., 2001). The presence of e-HRM systems can increase the competitive advantage of the company by enhancing organizational resources. Indeed, what other competitors can do is to buy the same software packages or to use the same e-HRM service provider, but they will be never able to replicate the total effect given by the mix of complementary (i.e., e-HRM systems) and human resources which fulfil the four characteristics of being- valuable, rare, inimitable, and non-substitutable (Bharadwaj et al., 2007; Bhatt & Grover, 2005).

Moreover, according to the RBV, in order to truly create competitive advantage and value, e-HRM should be organisation-specific and innovatively exploited (Barney, 1991; Perez-Arostegui & Martinez-Lopez, 2014). In order to do so, on the one hand IT capabilities, namely the organization's ability to acquire and apply IT knowledge and to effectively manage the information generated, is an organization- specific asset that cannot be easily transferred. On the other hand, the HR function's and end-users's (e.g., line managers, employees) ability to implement e-HRM in order to create strategic value and achieve expected business results is a prerequisite to innovatively exploit technology (Perez-Arostegui & Martinez-Lopez, 2014). In a way, the accumulated experience and ability to implement e-HRM and technology at large in an organizationally- specific, tailored way, becomes itself a VRIN resource.

Several authors have also claimed that e-HRM facilitates the strategic transformation of the HR function, which can become an appreciated business partner by providing value to the organization (Ruël et al., 2007; Strohmeier, 2007). Moreover, it has been proposed that the potential of resource heterogeneity and immobility is greater when e-HRM is generated inside the firm through in-house resource investments (e.g., instead of buying and implementing a software package by a vendor), with a specific focus on developing interactions between HRM practices and e-HRM configurations, and considering firm-specific HR bundles.

Finally, according to the RBV, we can assume that e-HRM contributes to organizational success in two ways. First, it allows organizations to focus on and develop their VRIN resources by diminishing the resources that are spent on non-core, non-VRIN activities (e.g., by diminishing administrative and repetitive tasks) (Barney, 1991; Strohmeier, 2007). Second, e-HRM allows organizations to perform functions that were not possible to perform before. Functions such as HR metrics and HR goal setting and controling are becoming more and more easy with the use of technology. This means that now the majority of HRM departments can closely follow their costs, operation and outcomes, in ways that the identification of the sources of competitive advantage is more and more easy. This means that the ability to create value through e-HRM does not lie in the organizational possession of the technology but, rather, in how it is used to become strategic and contribute to expected outcomes (Lengnick-Hall & Lengnick-Hall, 2006).

Critical Examination of the RVB in the e-HRM Field

The debate about RBV in e-HRM research has involved many other authors (e.g., Bondarouk and Ruël, 2013; Maatman et al., 2010; Marler, 2009; Parry, 2011) who have discussed opportunities and threats from the adoption of the RBV in the e-HRM field. Parry (2011) is the first researcher who used the RBV framework as a basis for a large empirical study examining the role of e-HRM in increasing the value of the HR function. Although her research has made an important contribution to the field of e-HRM research by rooting it within a sound theoretical framework, it showed that the use of e-HRM improves the HR function capability to contribute to the competitive advantage of the firm and increases its role in delivering the business strategy, but it does not allow to reduce costs by completing transactional activities more efficiently. Other studies have recently questioned that e-HRM enables the HRM function to develop into a strategic business partner and proposed that the causal order that defines e-HRM as a determinant of organizational outcomes should be reversed, given that e-HRM may be more plausibly viewed as the result of a strategic decision-making process by the HR function (see Marler & Parry, 2016).

Some of the most predominant critiques on the RBV in HRM research are related to the static and equilibrium-based nature of the model, which disregards the challenges of the external dynamic environment (see Bondarouk & Ruël, 2013). To address this weakness, Bondarouk and Ruël (2013) advanced the RBV adoption in e-HRM research by combining it with the *dynamic capabilities approach*. They proposed that e-HRM would enable HRM dynamic capabilities, namely the capacity of the HRM function to identify the need or opportunity for change, formulate a response and implement a course of action (Helfat et al., 2007). However, their single case study revealed that e-HRM did not enable the strategic capabilities of the HRM function, nor its operational capability.

In conclusion, the debate on RBV in the e-HRM field and the expected consequences in terms of HRM strategic value has yet to reach a definitive conclusion. On the one hand, RBV constitutes a promising theoretical framework. However, the multilevel nature of e-HRM and its outcomes (i.e., individual, HR function, organizational) make the integration with other theoretical frameworks like dynamic capabilities, institutional logics or configurational approaches imperative. On the other hand, very few empirical studies have investigated e-HRM consequences under a RBV perspective, so more RBV-driven studies are still needed in order to fully evaluate the potential of the RBV approach in the e-HRM field.

Further Readings

Barney, J. (1991), "Firms resources and sustained competitive advantage", *Journal of Management*, Vol. 17 No. 1, pp. 99–120.

Liang, T., You, J. and Liu, C. (2010) 'A Resource-Based perspective in information technology and firm performance: A meta-analysis', *Industrial Management & Data*, Vol. 110 (8): pp. 1138–1158.

Parry, E. (2011), "An examination of e-HRM as a means to increase the value of the HR function", *International Journal of Human Resource Management*, Vol. 22 No. 5, pp. 1146–1162.

References

Barney, J. (1986), "Organizational culture: Can it be a source of sustained competitive advantage?", *Academy of Management Review*, Vol. 11 No. 3, pp. 656–665.

Barney, J. (1991), "Firms resources and sustained competitive advantage", *Journal of Management*, Vol. 17 No. 1, pp. 99–120.

Bharadwaj, S., Bharadwaj, A. and Bendoly, E. (2007), "The performance effects of complementarities between information systems, marketing, manufacturing, and supply chain processes", *Information Systems Research*, Vol. 18 No. 4, pp. 437–453.

Bhatt, G.D. and Grover, V. (2005), "Types of information technology capabilities and their role in competitive advantage: an empirical study", *Journal of Management Information Systems*, Vol. 22 No. 2, pp. 253–277.

Bondarouk, T., Parry, E. and Furtmueller, E. (2017), "Electronic HRM: four decades of research on adoption and consequences", *The International Journal of Human Resource Management*, Routledge, Vol. 5192 No. November, pp. 1–34.

Bondarouk, T. and Ruël, H. (2013), "The strategic value of e-HRM: Results from an exploratory study in a governmental organization", *The International Journal OfHuman Resource Management*, Vol. 24 No. 2, pp. 391–414.

Bowman, C. and Ambrosini, V. (2000), "Value Creation Versus Value Capture: Towards a Coherent Definition of Value in Strategy", *British Journal of Management*, Vol. 11, pp. 1–15.

Helfat, C.E., Finkelstein, S., Mitchell, W., Peteraf, M.A., Singh, H., Teece, D.J. and Winter, S.G. (2007), *Dynamic Capabilities: Understanding Strategic Change in Organizations*, Blackwell Publishing, Oxford.

Lengnick-Hall, C.A. and Lengnick-Hall, M.L. (2006), "HR, ERP, and Knowledge for Competitive advantage", *Human Resource Management*, Vol. 45 No. 2, pp. 179–194.

Maatman, M., Bondarouk, T. and Looise, J.C. (2010), "Conceptualizing the Capabilities and Value Creation of HRM Shared Service Models", *Human Resource Management Review*, Vol. 20, pp. 327–339.

Marler, J. (2009), "Making human resources strategic by going to the net: reality or myth?", *International Journal of Human Reosurce Management*, Vol. 20 No. 3, pp. 515–527.

Marler, J.H. and Parry, E. (2016), "Human resource management, strategic involvement and e-HRM technology", *The International Journal of Human Resource Management*, Vol. 5192 No. December, pp. 1–21.

Parry, E. (2011), "An examination of e-HRM as a means to increase the value of the HR function", *International Journal of Human Resource Management*, Vol. 22 No. 5, pp. 1146–1162.

Penrose, E.T. (1959), *The Theory of the Growth of the Firm*, Oxford University Press, Oxford.

Perez-Arostegui, M. and Martinez-Lopez, F. (2014), "IT Competence-Enabled Business Performance and Competitive", in Martinez-Lopez, F.J. (Ed.), *Handbook of Strategic E-Business Management [Progress in IS]*, Springer, Berlin, Heidelberg, pp. 109–138.

Peteraf, M.A. (1993), "The cornerstones of competitive advantage: A resource-based view", *Strategic Management Journal*, Vol. 12, pp. 95–117.

Ruël, H.J.M., Bondarouk, T.V. and Van der Velde, M. (2007), "The Contribution of E-Hrm to Hrm Effectiveness", *Human Relations*, Vol. 29 No. 3, pp. 280–291.

Spender, J.C. and Grant, R.M. (1996), "Knowledge and the firm: Overview", *Strategic Management Journal*, Vol. 17, pp. 5–9.

Strohmeier, S. (2007), "Research in e-HRM: review and implications'", *Human Resource Management Review*, Vol. 17, pp. 19–37.

Wernerfelt, B. (1984), "A resource-based view of the firm", *Strategic Management Journal*, Chichester, Vol. 5 No. 2, pp. 171–180.

Wright, P.M., Dunford, B.B. and Snell, S.A. (2001), "Human Resources and the Resource-Based View of the Firm", *Journal of Management*, Vol. 27, pp. 701–721.

Wright, P.M., McMahan, G.C. and McWilliams, A. (1994), "Human resources and sustained competitive advantage: A resource-based perspective", *International Journal of Human Reosurce Management*, Vol. 5, pp. 301–326.

Part 5: **Social Issues of e-HRM**

Jamie A. Gruman and Alan M. Saks
e-Socialization

Organizational socialization, which is often referred to as on-boarding in industry, refers to the "introductory events and activities by which individuals come to know and make sense out of their newfound work experiences" (Katz, 1980, p. 88). It is "a learning and adjustment process that enables an individual to assume an organizational role that fits both organizational and individual needs" (Chao, 2012, p. 582), and in which new hires must learn new attitudes, behaviours, and ways of thinking (Klein & Weaver, 2000). *E-socialization,* or *e-onboarding*, is the process of leveraging information and communication technologies (ICTs) to enable this process and help newcomers adjust by learning the attitudes, behaviours, and skills required to perform their new jobs, fulfil their new roles, and operate successfully in organizations (Gruman & Saks, 2018).

Traditional socialization and e-socialization practices lead to three sets of successive outcomes: newcomer capital (human and social capital), newcomer adjustment (e.g., role clarity), and socialization outcomes (e.g., job satisfaction) (Gruman & Saks, 2018). However, because ICTs can alter communication processes, patterns of social interaction, and the flow of information (Stone & Lukaszewski, 2009), the effect of e-socialization practices on these outcomes might differ from traditional socialization practices. Such differences are likely to be contingent on the degree of virtuality of the ICT's – the greater the virtuality the greater the differences (Gruman & Saks, 2018).

There is very little research on this issue. Whether, and the ways in which, e-socialization helps or hinders the ability of newcomers to learn about and integrate into new roles is largely an open question. Along these lines, below we offer some research-based ideas that warrant empirical attention.

e-Orientation

The socialization process usually begins with an orientation program that occurs immediately after being hired during which newcomers are introduced to their new job, colleagues, and the organization (Klein & Weaver, 2000). Such programs help newcomers learn and adjust to their new roles (e.g., Saks, 1994). However, preliminary research suggests that e-socialization processes that include e-orientation programs compromise newcomer learning, adjustment, and socialization outcomes (Wesson & Gogus, 2005). Newcomers obtain subtle and tacit information about their new job, role, and organization by observing co-workers and supervisors (Ostroff & Kozlowski, 1992). E-socialization processes that involve high levels of

https://doi.org/10.1515/9783110633702-019

virtuality may interfere with newcomers' ability to observe colleagues, develop tacit knowledge, learn, and adjust to new roles. The greater the virtuality, the greater the interference.

e-Training

Training is sometimes part of the socialization process that helps newcomers adjust to their new roles (Feldman, 1989). Although e-training that occurs as part of the e-socialization process might be adequate for allowing newcomers to learn task-related knowledge, it can compromise the development of newcomers' social capital. Brown and Van Buren (2007) suggest that e-training might make it less likely that trainees will develop common norms of conduct and a shared vision, and although e-training may make it easier to associate with more people, fostering and sustaining relationships with those people is more difficult. This is likely to compromise all three outcomes associated with e-socialization. As with e-orientation, the deleterious effects of e-training that occur as part of the e-socialization process are likely to be moderated by the degree of virtuality.

e-Socialization Agents

Socialization agents are organizational insiders who aid in the adjustment of new-comers through actions such as providing feedback, information, and resources (Klein & Heuser, 2008). Contemporary models of socialization highlight the value of socialization agents and social capital for successful socialization (Jokisaari & Nurmi, 2013). Indeed, it has been suggested that the primary activity that hastens the socialization process is the frequency with which newcomers interact with insiders (Reichers, 1987). However, as noted by Driskell, Radtke and Salas (2003), "interaction that is mediated by technology may lead to less intimacy and difficulty in establishing relationships" (p. 303). Compared to traditional socialization agents, e-socialization agents may be less influential because opportunities for social interaction are decreased, communication difficulties are liable to increase, and communication is likely to be more task-focused than socially-focused. These conditions might compromise newcomers' social capital and socialization outcomes such as affective commitment, which Johnson, Bettenhausen, and Gibbons (2009) observed among team members who engaged in a high level of computer-mediated communication. That said, e-socialization may benefit newcomers by promoting the development of weak ties and structural holes which allow newcomers to leverage a wider network (Fang, Duffy, & Shaw, 2011). In the end, e-socialization agents will have a more difficult time establishing relationships with newcomers and the degree of virtuality will moderate this effect.

e-Socialization Tactics

Socialization tactics are "the ways in which the experiences of individuals in transition from one role to another are structured for them by others in the organization" (Van Maanen & Schein, 1979, p. 230). Socialization tactics can be institutionalized, which reflect a highly structured socialization process that reduces uncertainty and replicates the organizational status quo, or individualized, which is a less structured, and potentially more anxiety-producing process that encourages newcomers to question the status quo and find their own approaches to their roles. Institutionalized tactics are positively associated with all three sets of outcomes noted earlier (Lapointe, Vandenberghe, & Boudrais, 2014; Saks, Uggerslev, & Fassina, 2007). However, there is reason to believe that e-socialization tactics are likely to be more individualized, largely because a central characteristic of new work systems is self-management (Gephart, 2002). For example, in the Wesson and Gogus (2005) study cited earlier, the computer-based orientation that produced inferior outcomes was a more individualized, self-guided process, unlike the traditional, more institutionalized orientation program in which newcomers engaged in collective structured activities. Because they are more likely to be individualized, e-socialization tactics are likely to produce less human and social capital, weaker adjustment, and interfere with the development of socialization outcomes. Designing e-socialization programs to include more institutionalized tactics may counteract these effects.

e-Proactive Behaviours

A final area in which ICT's may influence the socialization process involves proactive behaviours, which concern "anticipatory action that employees take to impact themselves and/or their environments" (Grant & Ashford, 2008, p. 8). Proactive behaviours such as information seeking and relationship building have been shown to be positively associated with newcomer adjustment and socialization outcomes (Ashford & Black, 1996; Morrison, 1993). However, in e-socialization, it may be less likely that newcomers will engage in e-proactive behaviours. Gruman, Saks and Zweig (2006) found that institutionalized socialization tactics are positively associated with proactive behaviour. However, as noted above, e-socialization tactics are more likely to be individualized than institutionalized. In the end, e-socialization is likely to reduce the number of e-proactive behaviours in which newcomers engage, as well as how frequently they engage in them. The degree of virtuality will moderate these relationships.

Socialization Resources Theory

If e-socialization is to be effective, an appropriate strategy is to design socialization programs based on socialization resources theory (SRT). According to SRT, effective socialization involves providing newcomers with resources prior to entry (e.g., getting in touch with the newcomer before they enter the organization), immediately after entry (e.g., assign a buddy or mentor to each newcomer), following orientation (supervisor provides newcomers with support), and after the formal socialization/on-boarding period (e.g., follow-up and stay in touch with newcomers) (Saks & Gruman, 2012).

Although SRT focuses on traditional socialization practices, it can easily be adapted for the purposes of e-socialization. Thus, many of the 17 socialization resources identified by Saks and Gruman (2012) can be provided to newcomers through e-socialization prior to entry, immediately after entry, following orientation, and after the formal socialization/on-boarding period. Research is needed on how e-socialization programs can be made more effective by providing socialization resources to newcomers throughout the socialization/on-boarding process.

Future Research

E-socialization presents many new opportunities and challenges for the way organizations help new employees learn and become adjusted and socialized to their roles. However, there is very little research on how ICTs influence newcomer adjustment, and how the outcomes associated with e-socialization differ from those achieved through traditional socialization. This is a new area of research that is of particular importance given the frequency with which employees change jobs and the increased rate at which newcomers are socialized in the contemporary workforce.

It is important to note that the relationships among e-socialization practices and outcomes may change over time. We have suggested that the degree of virtuality will moderate the relationship among e-socialization practices and outcomes. However, advances in ICT's may alter the nature of virtuality itself and modify these relationships. As noted by Landers (2019), the relationships we observe between human behaviour and technology are likely to vary as the technologies change. Research is necessary to understand the effect of e-socialization practices on newcomer capital, adjustment and socialization outcomes, and early findings need to be supplemented with conceptual replications to understand how these effects may change over time as technology progresses. To be most effective, e-socialization programs should provide newcomers with numerous socialization resources throughout the socialization process.

Further Readings

Gruman, J. A., & Saks, A, M. (2018). E-socialization: The problems and promise of socializing newcomers in the digital age. In J. H.Dulebohn, & D. L. Stone (Eds.), *The brave new world of eHRM 2.0* (pp. 111–139). Charlotte, NC: Information Age Publishing.

Saks, A. M., & Gruman, J. A. (2012). Getting newcomers on-board: A review of socialization practices and introduction to socialization resources theory. In C. Wanberg (Ed.), *The Oxford handbook of organizational socialization* (pp. 27–55). New York: Oxford University Press.

Wesson, M. J. & Gogus, C. I. (2005). Shaking hands with a computer: An examination of two methods of organizational newcomer orientation. *Journal of Applied Psychology, 90*, 1018–1026.

References

Ashford, S. J., & Black, J. S. (1996). Proactivity during organizational entry: The role of desire for control. *Journal of Applied Psychology, 81*(2), 199–214.

Brown, K. G., & Van Buren, M. E. (2007). Applying a social capital perspective to the evaluation of distance training. In S. M. Fiore & E. Salas (Eds.), *Toward a Science of Distributed Learning* (pp. 41–63). Washington, DC. American Psychological Association.

Chao, G. T. (2012). Organizational socialization: Background, basics, and a blueprint for adjustment at work. In S. W. J. Kozlowski (Ed.), *The Oxford Handbook of Organizational Psychology* (pp. 579–614). New York: Oxford University Press.

Driskell, J. E., Radtke, P. H., & Salas, E. (2003). Virtual teams: Effects of technological mediation on team performance. *Group Dynamics: Theory, Research, and Practice, 7*, 297–323.

Fang, R., Duffy, M. K., & Shaw, J. D. (2011). The organizational socialization process: Review and development of a social capital model. *Journal of Management, 37*, 127–152.

Feldman, D.C. (1989). Socialization, resocialization, and training: Reframing the research agenda. In I.L. Goldstein (Ed.), *Training and development in organizations* (pp. 376–416). San Francisco: Jossey-Bass.

Gephart, R. P. (2002). Introduction to the brave new workplace: organizational behavior in the electronic age. *Journal of Organizational Behavior, 23*, 327–344.

Grant, A. M., & Ashford, S. J. (2008). The dynamics of proactivity at work. *Research in Organizational Behavior, 28*, 3–34.

Gruman, J. A., & Saks, A, M. (2018). E-socialization: The problems and promise of socializing newcomers in the digital age. In J. H. Dulebohn, & D. L. Stone (Eds.), *The brave new world of eHRM 2.0* (pp. 111–139). Charlotte, NC: Information Age Publishing.

Gruman, J. A., Saks, A. M., & Zweig, D. I. (2006). Organizational socialization tactics and newcomer proactive behaviors: An integrative study. *Journal of Vocational Behavior, 69*, 90–104.

Johnson, S. K., Bettenhausen, K., & Gibbons, E. (2009). Realities of working in virtual teams: Affective and attitudinal outcomes of using computer-mediated communication. *Small Group Research, 40*, 623–649.

Jokisaari, M., & Nurmi, J-E. (2013). Getting the right connections? The consequences and antecedents of social networks in newcomer socialization. In C. R. Wanberg (Ed.), *The Oxford handbook of organizational socialization* (pp. 78–96). New York: Oxford University Press.

Katz, R. (1980). Time and work: Toward an integrative perspective. In B. Staw and L. L. Cummings (Eds.), *Research in organizational behavior* (vol. 2, pp. 81–127). Greenwich CT: JAI Press.

Klein, H. J., & Heuser, A. E. (2008). The learning of socialization content: A framework for researching orientating practices. *Research in Personnel and Human Resources Management, 27*, 279–336. Emerald Group.

Klein, H. J., & Weaver, N. A. (2000). The effectiveness of an organizational-level orientation training program in the socialization of new hires. *Personnel Psychology, 53*, 47–66.

Landers, R. N. (2019). The existential threat to I-O Psychology highlighted by rapid technological change. In R. N. Landers (Ed.), *Cambridge Handbook of Technology and Employee Behavior* (pp. 3–21). New York, NY: Cambridge University Press.

Lapointe, E., Vandenberghe C., & Boudrais, J-S. (2014). Organizational socialization tactics and newcomer adjustment: The mediating role of role clarity and affect-based trust relationships. *Journal of Occupational and Organizational Psychology, 87*, 599–624.

Morrison, E. W. (1993). Newcomer information seeking: Exploring types, modes, sources, and outcomes. *Academy of Management Journal, 36*, 557–589.

Reichers, A. E. (1987). An interactionist perspective on newcomer socialization rates. *Academy of Management Review, 12*, 278–287.

Saks, A. M. (1994). A psychological process investigation for the effects of recruitment source and organization information on job survival. *Journal of Organizational Behavior, 15*, 225–244.

Saks, A. M., & Gruman, J. A. (2012). Getting newcomers on-board: A review of socialization practices and introduction to socialization resources theory. In C. Wanberg (Ed.), *The Oxford handbook of organizational socialization* (pp. 27–55). New York: Oxford University Press.

Saks, A. M., Uggerslev, K. L., & Fassina, N. E. (2007). Socialization tactics and newcomer adjustment: A meta-analytic review and test of a model. *Journal of Vocational Behavior, 70*, 413–446.

Stone, D. L., & Lukaszewski, K. M. (2009). An expanded model of the factors affecting the acceptance and effectiveness of electronic human resource management systems. *Human Resource Management Review, 19*, 134–143.

Ostroff, C., & Kozlowski, S. W. J. (1992). Organizational socialization as a learning process: The role of information acquisition. *Personnel Psychology, 45*(4), 849–874.

Van Maanen, J., & Schein, E. H. (1979). Toward a theory of organizational socialization, In B.M Staw (Ed.), *Research in Organizational Behaviour*, (Vol. 1, pp. 209–264). Greenwich, CT: JAI Press.

Wesson, M. J. & Gogus, C. I. (2005). Shaking hands with a computer: An examination of two methods of organizational newcomer orientation. *Journal of Applied Psychology, 90*, 1018–1026.

Surinder Kahai
e-Leadership

Advances in and widespread adoption of information and communication technologies (ICTs) are rapidly changing how we interact with, perceive, influence, and be influenced by others. Since these processes are critical ingredients of leadership, exercising and experiencing leadership is changing too. Moreover, with ICTs changing access to information, the kind that is collected and processed, and where and how it is used and presented, the ways for leaders to derive their influence are changing too (Avolio & Kahai, 2003). Beyond the potential to change the processes and basis of influence, ICTs may be redefining the target of leadership. Increasing deployment of ICTs and the accompanying automation are changing the nature of work, the workers we employ, the expected competencies, and the decisions we make. In fact, rapid advances in artificial intelligence (AI) are fueling the question of what work will remain for us to lead and what decisions will remain for the leader to make in the future (Manyika, 2017). This entry discusses what the new context enabled by ICTs means for leadership, starting with a discussion of different views on this issue.

Do ICTs Make a Difference for Leadership?

For some, the answer is 'no'. They argue that leaders still have to be competent, caring, and benevolent (Sutton, 2010) or they still need to relate to and personally engage others (Champy, 2010). For others, the digital revolution requires the development of new competencies that have to be blended with skills important in traditional settings (Van Wart, Roman, Wang, & Liu, 2019). Some argue that leadership and its development are changing because ICTs are altering the basis of leadership by changing how information is acquired, stored, interpreted, and disseminated (Avolio & Kahai, 2003; Kahai, 2012). Avolio, Sosik, Kahai, and Baker (2014) take this argument further and make the case that ICTs are changing the source of leadership, how leadership is transmitted and received, and the context that embeds leadership. On the other hand, some scholars claim that ICTs mute leadership by attenuating emotions (Purvanova & Bono, 2009) or by making it unnecessary (Kahai, Sosik, & Avolio, 2004). Another viewpoint argues that digitization might improve leadership effectiveness or help its emergence by providing transparency into behaviors and performance of team members (Reeves, Malone, & Driscoll, 2008).

The seemingly contradictory viewpoints can be reconciled using Yammarino, Dansereau, and Kennedy's (2001) integrative leadership model, which describes five focus areas in leadership research: fundamental human processes, leadership

https://doi.org/10.1515/9783110633702-020

core processes, leadership outcomes or tactics of putting together core processes, outcomes of core processes, and substitutes for leadership. Scholars claiming that leadership remains unchanged are focusing on a leader's core processes and their outcomes. Scholars who argue that leadership and its development are changing focus on how ICTs change fundamental human processes underlying leadership and are, in turn, shaped by them. Scholars who claim that ICTs mute leadership or make it unnecessary are generally focusing on neutralizers and substitutes. Scholars who point to ICTs improving leadership effectiveness or helping its emergence are focusing on ICTs as enhancers.

What is e-Leadership?

Using their original definition of e-leadership (Avolio, Kahai, & Dodge, 2001) in which they employ the vocabulary of that time and refer to ICTs as Advanced Information Technology (AIT), Avolio et al. (2014, p. 107) define e-leadership as "a social influence process embedded in both proximal and distal contexts mediated by AIT that can produce a change in attitudes, feelings, thinking, behavior, and performance". They provide this definition to capture the rich and complex dynamic between ICTs and leadership – how ICTs affect leadership and how leadership affects ICTs. They don't see ICTs as fixed objects that affect leadership; instead, they are shaped by the culture, the system of performance measurement and rewards, and the knowledge, skills, and attitudes of users within the context in which they are used – all of which are influenced by leadership. Thus, while ICTs affect leadership, they are affected in turn by leadership. This definition implies that in ICT dominated contexts, leadership does not remain the same as in traditional contexts. It recognises the rich dynamic between ICTs and leadership. It accommodates leader qualities for behaviors that would be relevant in the new contexts as well as the mechanisms by which those qualities or behaviors might influence individuals, groups, or organisations.

While the above definition affords generalizability, its lack of precision has prompted more precise versions. Van Wart et al. (2019, p. 83) define e-leadership as, "the effective use and blending of electronic and traditional methods of communication" and include in it "an awareness of current ICTs, selective adoption of new ICTs for oneself and the organisation, and technical competence in using those ICTs selected". Li, Liu, Belitski, Ghobadian, and Regan (2016) identify qualities that describe a leader who is successful at achieving alignment between and information technology (IT) function and business. These include agile leadership, hybrid skill development, architectural view, digital entrepreneurship, value creator, and value protector. Richter and Wagner (2014) focus on the process of social influence in an organisational context dominated by social media and refer to it as leadership 2.0. Purvanova and Kenda (2018) argue that virtual work introduces paradoxes or tensions – technology dependence tensions, geographic dispersion tensions, and human capital tensions – and paradoxical virtual leadership or leadership that synergistically exploits these paradoxes is essential. Pulley, Sessa, and Malloy (2002), too, see e-leadership as balancing the paradoxes introduced by ICTs.

e-leadership captures two parts of a dynamic: how ICTs shape leadership and how leadership shapes ICTs. Since ideas about how leadership may shape ICTs follow from a separate entry, I focus on the former aspect of e-leadership.

How ICTs Shape Leadership

Findings suggest that ICTs make a difference for leadership. In same-place meetings supported by Group Support Systems (GSS), while GSS-enabled anonymity may help transformational leadership be more impactful for effects that rely on group salience, it can replace transformational leadership for outcomes such as idea flexibility (Sosik, Kahai, & Avolio, 1998). GSS-enabled anonymity may also reduce the impact of transactional leadership by reducing the potency of contingent rewarding (Sosik et al., 1997). However, its presence can cause directive leadership to be seen as informational rather than as controlling (Kahai et al., 1997). Other GSS features may make a difference for leadership too. For instance, statistical feedback provided by a GSS may conflict with the leader and neutralize the leader's impact (Hiltz, Johnson, & Turoff, 1991).

In virtual team settings, the losses in group processes due to virtuality have been blamed for some of the effects related to leadership. For instance, the inability of some personality variables (extraversion and emotional stability) that predict transformational leadership in face-to-face teams to do the same in virtual teams has been attributed to the lack of nonverbal cues (Balthazard, Waldman, & Warren, 2009). Yet, some argue that the losses in group processes due to virtuality create a situation that is ripe for core leadership processes and tactics to be shared or have an even larger impact by compensating for the losses. In support, Geister, Konradt, and Hertel (2006) found that when virtual team members provided feedback about the team's process to the team, motivation, satisfaction, and performance of members improved. Purvanova and Bono (2009) found that transformational leadership had a stronger impact on performance in virtual teams than in face-to-face teams. Hill and Bartol (2016) found that the effect of empowering team leadership became stronger with increasing dispersion in geographically distributed teams. Evidence also suggests that virtuality may increase the impact of leadership that highlights the identity and vision of the collective (e.g., inspirational leadership) by reducing attention to interpersonal differences and increasing team members' sensitivity to cues emphasizing the team and its social identity (Joshi, Lazarova, & Liao, 2009).

Findings suggest that leadership in the age of social media is likely to emergent and informal, with others recognising someone to be a leader (Johnson, Safadi, &

Faraj, 2015). In online communities enabled by social media, governance tends to be bottom-up and, even when there are formal hierarchies, those in formal leadership positions are not necessarily seen as leaders (Johnson et al., 2015). Visible actions and the quality and quantity of text communication end up predicting leadership emergence (Eseryel & Eseryel, 2013; Huffaker, 2010). According to Luther and Bruckman (2008), the nature of work in certain online communities, such as one focused on computer-animated movies, may introduce unique challenges that can neutralize a leader's efforts. Using tweets related to the Occupy movement, Bennett, Segerberg, and Walker (2014) suggest that small transactions or networking micro-operations of individual participants (i.e., tweets, retweets, posting links, adding multiple hashtags, etc.) help weave together different smaller networks into a larger network and create coherence and rationality in actions. By doing so, these micro-operations end up substituting for collective action that is normally inspired by a leader in traditional social movements.

Evidence on how cloud computing may be shaping leadership is limited. Emerging evidence, however, suggests that the gig platforms enabled by cloud computing have the potential to disintermediate the middle management layer from the chain of command, as we see in the case of Uber which does not need supervisors to manage its drivers (Rosenblat & Stark, 2016).

Opportunities for future research on how ICTs shape leadership abound. Smartphones have created the potential for research on how back-channel communication, i.e., communication which occurs simultaneously with the main communication but is secondary to it, affects leadership in same-place meetings. A variety of back-channel communication is possible: between the leader and outsiders, between the leader and those the leader is meeting, between those the leader is meeting and outsiders, or that among those meeting the leader. By redrawing both the physical boundaries of same-place meetings and of what is socially acceptable in them (Dennis, Rennecker, & Hansen, 2010), such communication can change the direction of the leader, the emergence of a new leader, the relationships among followers, the capability of the whole group, and the formation of coalitions or cliques. In virtual teams, the topic of how leaders can contribute to the development and well-being of members of their teams is ripe for future research. Though a distinct set of skills or competencies is needed to operate virtually (Krumm, Kanthak, Hartmann, & Hertel, 2016), organisations often provide little help for its development and, consequently, it is left to team leaders to help their team develop. Since social networks enabled by social media consist of a large number of highly interconnected and constantly changing nodes which make them unpredictable, these networks can be considered as complex systems (Kahai, 2012). In such systems, leadership can also emerge from the interaction among nodes in addition to that from individuals or formal positions associated with those nodes (Uhl-Bien, Marion, & McKelvey, 2007). With research on this possibility having just begun (e.g. Bennett et al., 2014), there is tremendous potential for future research to study this. Significant changes in the nature of work and disruption to ranks of leaders are just around the corner due to AI backed cloud computing. Future research should investigate what aspects of leadership will be retained by humans and what will be replaced by ICTs.

Further Readings

The following sources are likely to provide good coverage of e-leadership and associated sub-fields as well as a sense of more recent conversations on the topic: (a) descriptions and conceptualisations of the e-leadership phenomena by Avolio and colleagues (Avolio et al., 2001; Avolio et al., 2014; Kahai, 2012), (b) a review of the e-leadership literature by Kahai et al. (2017) (for a briefer review and the addition of implications of AI backed cloud computing for leadership, see Kahai (2018)), (c) a framework for thinking about effective virtual team leadership developed by Bell and Kozlowski (2002), and (d) a recent conceptual article on paradoxical virtual leadership by Purvanova and Kenda (2018).

References

Avolio, B. J., & Kahai, S. S. (2003). Adding the" E" to e-leadership: How it may impact your leadership. *Organizational Dynamics, 31*(4), 325–338.

Avolio, B. J., Kahai, S., & Dodge, G. E. (2001). E-leadership: Implications for theory, research, and practice. *The Leadership Quarterly, 11*(4), 615–668.

Avolio, B. J., Sosik, J. J., Kahai, S. S., & Baker, B. (2014). E-leadership: Re-examining transformations in leadership source and transmission. *The Leadership Quarterly, 25*(1), 105–131.

Balthazard, P. A., Waldman, D. A., & Warren, J. E. (2009). Predictors of the emergence of transformational leadership in virtual decision teams. *The Leadership Quarterly, 20*(5), 651–663.

Bell, B. S., & Kozlowski, S. W. (2002). A typology of virtual teams: Implications for effective leadership. *Group & Organization Management, 27*(1), 14–49.

Bennett, W. L., Segerberg, A., & Walker, S. (2014). Organization in the crowd: peer production in large-scale networked protests. *Information, Communication & Society, 17*(2), 232–260.

Champy, J. (2010, May 4). Does leadership change in a web 2.0 world? *HBR Blog Network*. Retrieved from http://blogs.hbr.org/imagining-the-future-of-leadership/2010/05/does-leadership-change-in-a-we.html

Dennis, A. R., Rennecker, J. A., & Hansen, S. (2010). Invisible whispering: Restructuring collaborative decision making with instant messaging. *Decision Sciences, 41*(4), 845–886.

Eseryel, U. Y., & Eseryel, D. (2013). Action-embedded transformational leadership in self-managing global information systems development teams. *The Journal of Strategic Information Systems, 22*(2), 103–120.

Geister, S., Konradt, U. & Hertel, G. (2006). Effects of process feedback on motivation, satisfaction and performance in virtual teams. *Small Group Research, 37*(5), 459–489.

Hill, N. S., & Bartol, K. M. (2016). Empowering leadership and effective collaboration in geographically dispersed teams. *Personnel Psychology, 69*(1), 159–198.

Hiltz, S. R., Johnson, K., & Turoff, M. (1991). Group decision support: The effects of designated human leaders and statistical feedback in computerized conferences. *Journal of Management Information Systems, 8*(2), 81–108.

Huffaker, D. (2010). Dimensions of leadership and social influence in online communities. *Human Communication Research, 36*(4), 593–617.

Johnson, S. L., Safadi, H., & Faraj, S. (2015). The emergence of online community leadership. *Information Systems Research, 26*(1), 165–187.

Joshi, A., Lazarova, M. B., & Liao, H. (2009). Getting everyone on board: The role of inspirational leadership in geographically dispersed teams. *Organization Science, 20*(1), 240–252.

Kahai, S. (2018). E-leadership: An essential part of doctoral leadership education. In Hyatt, L. & Allen, S. (Eds.), *Advancing Doctoral Leadership Education Through Technology* (pp. 11–35). Edward Elgar.

Kahai, S. S. (2012). Leading in a digital age: What's different, issues raised, and what we know. In M. C. Bligh, & R. E. Riggio (Eds.), *Exploring distance in leader-follower relationships: When near is far and far is near* (pp. 63–108). New York, NY: Taylor & Francis/Routledge Publishing.

Kahai, S., Avolio, B., & Sosik, J. (2017). E-leadership. In Hertel, G. Stone, D., Johnson, R. & Passmore, J. (Eds.), *The Wiley Blackwell handbook of the psychology of the internet at work* (pp. 285–314). Chichester: John Wiley & Sons, Ltd.

Kahai, S. S., Sosik, J. J., & Avolio, B. J. (2004). Effects of participative and directive leadership in electronic groups. *Group & Organization Management, 29*(1), 67–105.

Kahai, S. S., Sosik, J. J., & Avolio, B. J. (1997). Effects of leadership style and problem structure on work group process and outcomes in an electronic meeting system environment. *Personnel Psychology, 50*(1), 121–146.

Krumm, S., Kanthak, J., Hartmann, K., & Hertel, G. (2016). What does it take to be a virtual team player? The knowledge, skills, abilities, and other characteristics required in virtual teams. *Human Performance, 29*(2), 123–142.

Li, W., Liu, K., Belitski, M., Ghobadian, A., & O'Regan, N. (2016). e-Leadership through strategic alignment: An empirical study of small-and medium-sized enterprises in the digital age. *Journal of Information Technology, 31*(2), 185–206.

Luther, K., & Bruckman, A. (2008). Leadership in online creative collaboration. In *Proceedings of the 2008 ACM conference on Computer Supported Cooperative Work* (pp. 343–352). New York, NY: ACM.

Manyika, J. (2017, May). *Technology, jobs, and the future of work*. Retrieved from http://www.mckinsey.com/global-themes/employment-and-growth/technology-jobs-and-the-future-of-work

Pulley, M. L., Sessa, V., & Malloy, M. (2002). E-Leadership: A Two-Pronged Idea. *T+ D, 56*(3), 35–46.

Purvanova, R. K., & Bono, J. E. (2009). Transformational leadership in context: Face-to-face and virtual teams. *The Leadership Quarterly, 20*(3), 343–357.

Purvanova, R. K., & Kenda, R. (2018). Paradoxical virtual leadership: Reconsidering virtuality through a paradox lens. *Group & Organization Management, 43*(5), 752–786.

Reeves, B., Malone, T. W., & O'Driscoll, T. (2008). Leadership's online labs. *Harvard Business Review, 86*(5), 58–66.

Richter, A., & Wagner, D. (2014). Leadership 2.0: Engaging and supporting leaders in the transition towards a networked organization. In *Proceedings of the 2014 47th Hawaii International Conference on System Sciences* (pp. 574–583). Washington, DC: IEEE Computer Society.

Rosenblat, A., & Stark, L. (2016). Algorithmic labor and information asymmetries: A case study of Uber's drivers. *International Journal Of Communication, 10*, 27. Retrieved from http://ijoc.org/index.php/ijoc/article/view/4892

Sosik, J. J., Avolio, B. J., & Kahai, S. S. (1997). Effects of leadership style and anonymity on group potency and effectiveness in a group decision support system environment. *Journal of Applied Psychology, 82*(1), 89–103.

Sosik, J. J., Kahai, S. S., & Avolio, B. J. (1998). Transformational leadership and dimensions of creativity: Motivating idea generation in computer-mediated groups. *Creativity Research Journal, 11*(2), 111–121.

Sutton, R. (2010, June 9). What every new generation of bosses has to learn. *HBR Blog Network.* Retrieved from http://blogs.hbr.org/cs/2010/06/good_bosses_have_a_passion_for.html

Uhl-Bien, M., Marion, R., & McKelvey, B. (2007). Complexity leadership theory: Shifting leadership from the industrial age to the knowledge era. *The Leadership Quarterly, 18*(4), 298–318.

Van Wart, M., Roman, A., Wang, X., & Liu, C. (2019). Operationalizing the definition of e-leadership: Identifying the elements of e-leadership. *International Review of Administrative Sciences, 85*(1), 80–97.

Yammarino, F. J., Dansereau, F., & Kennedy, C. J. (2001). Viewing leadership through an elephant's eye: A multiple-level multidimensional approach to leadership. *Organizational Dynamics, 29*(3), 149–163.

Stefan Strohmeier
Sustainable Electronic HRM

Sustainability – defined as ". . . meet the needs of the present without compromising the ability of future generations to meet their own needs" (World Commission on Environment and Development, 1987) – constitutes a prominent concept discussed in a broad range of different domains, among them also the business domain. In the business domain, sustainability is prevalently seen as a highly promising approach that is able to overcome the notorious ecological and social externalities of the current economic activities.

Research on Sustainable Electronic HRM

Relating to business subdomains, sustainability is also discussed in Human Resource Management (e.g. Ehnert et al., 2014) and Digital Information Technologies (DIT) (e.g. Hilty & Aebischer, 2015). In the interim, in both domains there is a growing body of research and related knowledge (see the reviews of de Stefano et al., 2018 and Asadi & Dahlan, 2017). It is respectively discussed what sustainability means for the domain and how HRM and DIT can contribute to more sustainability. In both areas, sustainability has become a prominent concept and it is obvious that both, HRM and DIT, can make considerable contributions to sustainability. However, since the two sustainability research streams are completely separated, the intersection, i.e. *sustainable electronic HRM*, is not considered so far. Insights on how DIT and HRM do and should interact in affecting sustainability are thus missing. The concept of sustainable electronic HRM therefore seems to be relevant, however is not researched and thus not well understood at present (Strohmeier, 2014).

Conceptualisation of Sustainable Electronic HRM

Aiming at a conceptualisation of sustainable electronic HRM there is a broad agreement to understand sustainability as an overarching corporate objective to which HRM as DIT should contribute. Following this understanding, HRM and DIT can be understood as two interacting means, which (should) contribute to sustainability as an end and which consequently are understood as sustainable if doing so (Strohmeier, 2014; see Figure 21.1).

Constituting the core objective of sustainable electronic HRM, *sustainability* is commonly understood as a multi-dimensional concept that simultaneously refers to

https://doi.org/10.1515/9783110633702-021

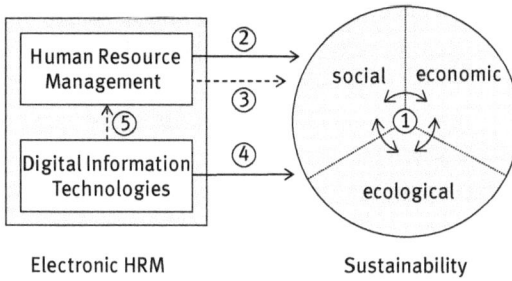

```
Human Resource          ②
Management      --------→      social | economic
         ↑⑤              ③          ↖ ①↘
                                    ↗ ① ↖
Digital Information     ④          ↘   ↙
Technologies      ----→         ecological
```

Electronic HRM   Sustainability

⟶ *primary effects* ---→ *secondary effects* ⟷ *interaction effects*

Figure 21.1: Sustainable Electronic HRM.

economic, ecological, and social objectives (e.g. Ehnert et al., 2014; Hilty & Aebischer, 2015). The resulting trisection of objectives is frequently designated as "triple bottom line" (e.g. Elkington, 1994). *Economic sustainability* refers to the enduring reproduction of financial resources, i.e. organisational practices must persistently ensure that the capital invested yields returns on investment sufficient for both skimming and reinvestment. *Ecological sustainability* refers to the enduring reproduction of natural resources, i.e. organisational activities must persistently comply with the rate of natural reproduction when consuming and the rate of natural absorption when polluting natural resources. *Social sustainability* refers to the enduring reproduction of human resources, i.e., organizational activities must persistently enable human wealth, health, education, etc. Following this tripartite model of sustainability, organisations are understood as sustainable, and thus, successful if they realise these three dimensions simultaneously (e.g. Dyllick & Hockerts, 2002). Consequently, HRM and DIT are also understood as sustainable if they are systematically adjusted towards simultaneous support of these three dimensions. In both domains, there are, however, also research contributions that selectively aim at the social dimension ("socially responsible HRM" respectively "socially responsible DIT"; e.g. Sharma et al., 2011 and Salb et al., 2011) or the ecological dimension ("green HRM" respectively "green DIT"; e.g. Jackson et al., 2011 and Murugesan, 2008). It is crucial to understand that the three dimensions of sustainability show *interaction effects* (effect 1; e.g. Dyllick & Hockerts, 2002). A first variety of an interaction refers to mutual reinforcement, i.e. contributing to one dimension also contributes to one or both of other sustainability dimension(s). Reinforcement effects are unproblematic since the objectives of sustainability can be met simultaneously. A second and very frequent variety of interaction effects, however, refers to mutual trade-offs between the dimensions, i.e., contributing to one dimension of sustainability detracts from one or both of other dimension(s) (e.g. Norman & McDonald, 2004). Trade-off effects are evidently problematic since objectives cannot be simultaneously met then.

As a first component of sustainable electronic HRM, *HRM* affects sustainability (see Figure 21.1). *Primary effects* emerge as direct effects of HRM itself, initially without or before an application of DIT (effect 2). Using the example of recruiting, there are direct effects of recruiting on all three sustainability dimensions. Economic sustainability is influenced by the costs of recruiting such as fees for job ads. Ecological sustainability is influenced by the consumptions of materials and energy such as physical transport of candidates to job interviews. Social sustainability is influenced by (non-)employment decisions which on their part determine the social status of applicants. Thus, a first challenge of sustainable electronic HRM is to uncover how HRM itself can be made more sustainable and directly contribute to the triple bottom line, what might be termed "sustainability *of* HRM". *Secondary effects* emerge indirectly as consequences of the workforce provided by HRM, while such effects initially occur without or before the application of DIT (effect 3). Again using the example of recruiting: the recruiting and employing a certain type of employees – consciously or unconsciously – influences sustainability since the work output of these employees will show direct effects on the economic, ecological and social dimension. To put it simply, recruiting candidates that fit the versatile sustainability requirements of their jobs and an organisation will contribute to sustainability while non-fitting candidates will detract from sustainability. Generalising this statement, a second challenge of sustainable electronic HRM is to uncover how HRM based on its versatile practices can contribute to organisational sustainability, what might be termed as "sustainability *by* HRM".

As a second component of sustainable electronic HRM, the employed DIT also affects the sustainability (see Figure 21.1). *Primary effects* are again direct effects of digital information technologies applied in HRM on the triple bottom line (effect 4 / Hilty & Aebischer, 2015). This comprises effects due to the physical existence of DIT, i.e., economic, ecological and social effects of the physical production, application and disposal of versatile hardware and network components. Again using recruiting as an example: there are economic effects due to the costs of purchasing, implementing and maintaining e-recruiting technologies. Moreover, there are direct ecological effects of technologies, which refer to material and energy consumption in producing hardware, energy consumption in utilising hardware and an ongoing production of waste by the cyclical replacement of hardware components (e.g. Hilty & Aebischer, 2015). Finally, there are direct social consequences of digital technologies, which refer to working conditions in the physical production, application and disposal of recruiting technology, for instance, socially unsustainable working conditions in the production of mobile devices. Thus, a third challenge of sustainable electronic HRM is to uncover how DIT in HRM can be made more sustainable and directly contribute to the triple bottom line what might be termed as "sustainability *of* DIT" (Hilty & Aebischer, 2015). *Secondary effects* refer to changes of HRM due to the application of DIT, and thus to induced changes of the primary and secondary sustainability effects of HRM (effect 5). Using the example of digital recruiting technologies, these, of course, change recruiting and thus the primary and secondary effects of recruiting on the triple bottom line. Regarding the economic sustainability, recruiting technologies, for instance, might offer automation effects that cut overall recruiting costs and improve recruiting efficiency. Regarding the ecological sustainability, recruiting technologies might show effects such as reduced paper use or reduced travel to job interviews. Regarding social sustainability, recruiting technologies might, for instance, discriminate applicants without access to digital technologies ("digital divide") and prevent them from getting a job. However, *rebound effects* uncover that secondary improvements of sustainability by DIT may also induce actions due to digital technologies, which reduce or even overcompensate improvements (e.g. Gossart, 2015). The latter subcase of overcompensation is also referred to as *backfire effect*. For instance, recruiting technologies initially improved recruiting efficiency enormously and contributed to the economic sustainability of HRM. However, the possibility of effortless electronic applications induced a massive increase of hardly suitable applications in many organisations what reduced or even overcompensated the economic efficiency gains of technology – therewith being an economic rebound effect. A fourth challenge of sustainable electronic HRM there with is to uncover how DIT can be used in HRM in order to improve the primary and secondary effects of HRM on the triple bottom line, what might be termed as "sustainability *by* DIT" (Hilty & Aebischer, 2015).

Definition of Sustainable Electronic HRM

Summarising the above, electronic HRM shows primary effects on sustainability ("sustainability *of* electronic HRM") and secondary effects on sustainability ("sustainability *by* electronic HRM"). Depending on the concrete realisation of electronic HRM, primary and secondary effects might contribute to, but also detract from sustainability. Moreover, rebound effects might weaken or even overcompensate positive contributions of electronic HRM to sustainability. Finally, interaction effects frequently imply trade-offs between the three sustainability dimensions and necessitate compromises and balancing between the objectives. This allows deriving a *definition* of sustainable electronic HRM: *Sustainable electronic HRM refers to the purposeful primary ("sustainability of electronic HRM") and secondary ("sustainability by electronic HRM") contributions to and balancing of economic, ecological and social objectives of the corporation.*

Future Directions in Sustainable Electronic HRM

Due to compelling ethical and rational reasons, it is virtually impossible to ignore sustainability and not to aim at a sustainable design of electronic HRM. Sustainable electronic HRM thus constitutes an imperative. Based on the above, however, realising sustainable electronic HRM presents a substantial challenge. Sustainability requires an ongoing handling of tenacious conflicts and an ongoing search for workable compromises in electronic HRM (and beyond). The notorious incompatibility of economic, ecological and social objectives thus constitutes both the core potential *and* the core problem of the sustainability concept in electronic HRM (Strohmeier, 2014).

Future work needs to adopt and elaborate the concept of sustainability while three interrelated core research tasks refer to the *conceptual, empirical and practical elaboration* of sustainable electronic HRM (Strohmeier, 2014). Regarding a future conceptual elaboration, the complex effects categories need a deeper clarification. For instance, the secondary effects of HRM (how the workforce provided by HRM [not] contributes to organisational sustainability) are not well understood at present. In the same way, further effects need a deeper consideration. Regarding an empirical elaboration, the lack of empirical insights entails a broad range of different research opportunities and necessities. For instance, the number and kind of already performed sustainability activities and their impacts are of interest, including the research of ambivalence of effects and rebound effects. Regarding a practical elaboration, there is a clear need to develop procedures, methods and tools that support practice in realising sustainable electronic HRM. With regard to the difficulties in realising the triple bottom line, this should also include an identification of expectable trade-offs and – where possible – suggestions on workable compromises. Given the tension between the imperative to realise sustainability (also) in electronic HRM and the highly nascent state of knowledge on the realisation of sustainable electronic HRM, the future execution of these research tasks constitutes an urgent obligation.

Further Readings

Ehnert, I., Harry, W., & Zink, K. J. (2014). Sustainability and HRM. An introduction to the field. In I. Ehnert, W. Harry, & K.J. Zink, K.J. (Eds.), *Sustainability and Human Resources. Developing Sustainable Business Organizations* (pp. 3–32). Berlin Heidelberg: Springer.

Hilty, L. M., & Aebischer, B. (2015). ICT for sustainability: An emerging research field. In L.M. Hilty, & B. Aebischer (Eds.), *ICT Innovations for Sustainability* (pp. 1–34). Berlin Heidelberg: Springer.

Strohmeier, S. (2014). Sustainable Electronic Human Resources Management: Why Information Technology Matters in Sustainable Human Resources Management. In J. Zentes & C. Scholz (Eds.), *Beyond Sustainability* (pp. 219–243). Baden-Baden: Nomos Verlagsgesellschaft.

References

Asadi, S., & Dahlan, H. M. (2017). Organizational research in the field of Green IT: A systematic literature review from 2007 to 2016. *Telematics and Informatics, 34*(7), 1191–1249.

De Stefano, F., Bagdadli, S., & Camuffo, A. (2018). The HR role in corporate social responsibility and sustainability: A boundary-shifting literature review. *Human Resource Management, 57*(2), 549–566.

Dyllick, T., & Hockerts, K. (2002), Beyond the business case for corporate sustainability, *Business Strategy and the Environment, 11*(2), 130–141.

Ehnert, I., Harry, W., & Zink, K. J. (2014). Sustainability and HRM. An introduction to the field. In I. Ehnert, W. Harry, & K.J. Zink, K.J. (Eds.), *Sustainability and Human Resources. Developing Sustainable Business Organizations* (pp. 3–32). Berlin Heidelberg: Springer.

Elkington, J. (1994). Towards the suitable corporation: Win-win-win business strategies for sustainable development, *California Management Review, 36*(2), 90–100.

Gossart, C. (2015). Rebound effects and ICT: A review of the literature. In L.M. Hilty, & B. Aebischer (Eds.). *ICT Innovations for Sustainability* (pp. 435–448) Berlin Heidelberg: Springer.

Hilty, L. M., & Aebischer, B. (2015). ICT for sustainability: An emerging research field. In L.M. Hilty, & B. Aebischer (Eds.), *ICT Innovations for Sustainability* (pp. 1–34). Berlin Heidelberg: Springer

Jackson, S.E., Renwick, D.W., Jabbour, C.J., & Müller-Camen, M. (2011). State-of-the-art and future directions for Green Human Resource Management: Introduction to the special issue, *German Journal of Research in Human Resources, 25*(2), 99–116.

Murugesan, S. (2008). Harnessing green IT: Principles and practices. *IT Professional, 10*(1), 24–33.

Norman, W., & MacDonald, C. (2004). Getting to the bottom of "triple bottom line", *Business Ethics Quarterly, 14*(2), 243–262.

Salb, D., Friedman, H. H., & Friedman, L. W. (2011). The role of information technology in fulfilling the promise of corporate social responsibility, *Computer and Information Science, 4*(4), 2–9.

Sharma, S., Sharma, J., & Devi, A. (2011). Corporate social responsibility: The key role of Human Resources Management. In R. Simons (Ed.), *Human Resource Management: Issues, Challenges and Opportunities* (pp. 9–18). Oakville: Apple Academic Press.

Strohmeier, S. (2014). Sustainable Electronic Human Resources Management: Why Information Technology Matters in Sustainable Human Resources Management. In J. Zentes & C. Scholz (Eds.), *Beyond Sustainability* (pp. 219–243). Baden-Baden: Nomos Verlagsgesellschaft.

World Commission on Environment and Development (1987). *Our common future.* Oxford: Oxford University Press.

Sharna Wiblen
Talent Management and Digitalised Talent Management

Talent management permeates the corporate lexicon as organisations endeavour to deploy people for strategy execution and competitive advantage. The first serious discussions of "talent management" emerged during the late 1990s with the publication of the "War for Talent" (Chambers, Foulton, Handfield-Jones, Hankin, & Michaels Ill, 1998). The "War for Talent" deployed references to the scarcity of qualified, valuable and relevant people-based resources, to promote powerful battle like imagery. Organisations were encouraged to fight and compete (against the competition) for this significant resource. Strategic approaches to workforce management were the key mechanism to ensure effective management of the "best people" and "talent".

Despite vast technological innovations and changes in commercial realities such as the increase in knowledge-based work, and decrease in manufacturing, talent management practices prevail in importance. The quality of an organisation's internal workforce is paramount to organisational success with competitors unable to replicate the human element of any business, which constantly supports "people are an organisation's greatest asset" rhetoric. Thus, effective management of employees, and the most valuable employees – aka talent – is vital for all organisations regardless of size, industry, and geographic location. Notwithstanding the inherent relationship between people, strategy execution and arguments that talent management contributes positively to organisational and financial performance (Cappelli, 2008; Collings, 2014), industry-based survey's frequently finds that this strategic activity presents both opportunities and challenges (see PwC Annual Global CEO Surveys).

Definitions and Perspectives of Talent Management

There are various definitions and different frameworks which can be utilised to guide our approach to talent management. Earlier definitions suggested that talent management was a specific set of practices, functions or activities (Lewis & Heckman, 2006). Practices included talent acquisition, recruitment and selection, talent identification, talent development, succession planning, and talent retention. Talent, therefore, was synonymous with human capital. From this perspective, talent management aligns with strategic human resource management and on this basis may merely involve the re-branding of traditional human resource management.

https://doi.org/10.1515/9783110633702-022

A widely accepted definition operating in parallel is offered by Collings and Mellahi (2009, p. 304) which frames talent management as the mobilisation of specific individuals into key positions: "strategic talent management as activities and processes that involve the systematic identification of key positions which differentially contribute to an organisations sustainable competitive advantage, the development of a talent pool of high potential and high performing incumbents to fill these roles, and the development of a differentiated human resource architecture to facilitate filling these positions with the best available incumbent and to ensure their continued commitment to the organisation."

Another, more practical way, to understand and appreciate what talent management "is", is to consider the activities required of actors to realise the promoted (beneficial) outcomes. Wiblen (2019, p. 154) suggests that talent management is "[a] judgment-orientated activity, where humans make judgments about [the value] of other humans. These judgments, while mediated by various contextual factors and variables (such as technology), should be informed by and aligned to, current and future strategic ambitions and goals."

This definition recognises that actors within organisations use talent management – whether talent identification, talent development, and talent retention – as a mechanism to decide which individuals are privy to talent management practices. That is, actors, make judgments about the value of individuals within their workforces. Individuals judged as of greater value than their counterparts are afforded additional resources and development opportunities. Perceptions of value are influenced by various micro (individual-level), meso (functional and team) and macro (organisational, industry, country) discourses.

Notwithstanding definitional debates, conceptualisations of talent and talent management are contextually specific with each organisation required to decide who and what is talent and how to manage talent subjects via certain practices within the context of their strategic ambitions and goals.

Prevailing Talent Management Debates

Exclusive versus Inclusive

A notable and dominate tension focuses on whether the practice of talent management applies to some (exclusive) or all (inclusive) employees. Exclusive advocates argue that workforce differentiation is the core foundational activity of talent management and that the unequal allocation of resources key. Resources, such as development opportunities and stretch assignments, are only afforded to individuals who are of higher value and contribute directly to the pursuit and realisation of current or future strategic ambitions and goals.

The alternative, inclusive perspective operates in parallel. The "everybody is talent" approach (Wiblen, 2016) asserts that all individuals are talent. The talent inherent in each of these individuals underpins the primary reasoning for why they have been selected as employees of the organisation. Everyone will illustrate a certain level of "potential" which the organisation will seek to develop and exploit. These are 'inclusive' or 'whole of workforce' approaches to talent. Consequently, such advocates will guide organisations to implement talent management policies and processes that are inclusive and apply to the entire workforce. This conceptualisation is frequently resisted by talent management advocates (Lepak & Snell, 1999; Lewis & Heckman, 2006; McDonnell, Lamare, Gunnigle, & Lavelle, 2010) who believe that while the mantra that every individual employee possesses talent and should be developed to increase their contribution to organisational performance is both appealing and admirable, it is hardly strategic.

Consistent or Flexible Approach

Organisations are required to identify the individuals afforded access to development and retention practices. Debates rage, however, whether the systematic (aka consistent) approaches proposed by Collings and Mellahi (2009) is most effective. Talent management systems are valuable because and the value-based criteria on which to judge employees is defined and individuals are privy to a consistent process (Iles, Chuai, & Preece, 2010; Stainton, 2005), thus creating greater transparency in the "what" and the "how" of workforce differentiation. Consistent processes, however, may limit perceptions of "talent" resulting in the identification of "talent clones" (McDonnell, 2011) or the ability to recognise idiosyncrasy and diversity (Highhouse, 2008; Mäkelä, Björkman, & Ehrnrooth, 2010).

A more nuanced understanding and the enactment of practices which possess dexterity and fluidity may enable organisations to react to changes in market conditions and external factors. Flexibility, rather than consistency, may be essential in the current VUCA (volatile, uncertain, complex and ambiguous) environment.

Digitalised Talent Management

Digitalised talent management – the use of IT in talent management – afford organisations with access to various pre-designed and pre-configured "systems" to manage their workforces and their "talent". Many technology vendors, such as SAP, Oracle, and Workday, provide Human Resource and Line managers with software-as-a-service capabilities which encourage integration and represent the mechanisms through which organisations enact the systematic and consistent processes detailed in certain talent management definitions. Technology affords a mechanism to define "talent" as organisations are required to outline the skills, capabilities and attributes individuals are evaluated against in traditional annual performance review processes. Technology vendors provide organisations with the capabilities and workflow processes required to evaluate an individual "performance" and "potential". That is, technology dictates the "how" of talent management and permits the systematic and consistent evaluation where all individuals are allocated numerical scores (usually out of 5). Some senior stakeholders assert that "talent" can be identified by using technology, whereby the embedded algorithms (largely vendor designed and commonly referred to as the "black-box") rank all individuals. Workforce rankings are used to generate "talent lists", with the workforce ranked from the highest performer or with the highest potential to the lowest performer and those with lower potential. Senior executives (whether HR or line managers) decide whether a specific proportion of the workforce (as a percentage %) or a specific number individuals are deemed "talent", allocated to the internal talent pool. Processes appear to happen automatically with little need for HR intervention. Vendors also claim that technology facilitates faster and more accurate decision-making and gives organisations access to "best-practices". E-talent management is also framed as the primary mechanism for procedural justice because individuals are subjected to the same process. There are also assertions that e-talent management and the associated consistent practices allow HR practitioners to develop greater objectivity and balance in their decisions. The rhetoric that technology enables objectivity in talent management, while appealing and compelling as a risk mitigation strategy, is fraught with danger in practice. While technology captures and stores data, metrics and analytics about "talent", humans input the data into the system at the beginning of the talent management process. Therefore, data represents and quantifies the human evaluators' perceptions of an individuals performance, potential and relative value.

An alternative viewpoint asserts that numerical performance and potential scores captured and ranked via materially-embedded processes outline above are the start of the workforce differentiation process. Numerical evaluations inform subsequent cognition-based activities in which certain stakeholders talk about the value of specific individuals within the context of the organisations operational and strategic needs. Stakeholders are encouraged to share various information about an individual with stakeholders encouraged to arrive at collegiate (albeit sometimes contested) agreement. Individuals deemed to possess the defining characteristics of "talent" are allocated resources and invested in disproportionately. Access to talent development occurs regardless of decisions about the value of the technologically-enabled or human-conversational process.

Despite the increased rhetoric about evidence and data-driven decision making, the use of information technology in the identification and management of talent varies. A possible explanation for the marginalisation of talent management "systems" is that actors differ in perceptions about whether you should "measure" or "observe" talent. Some actors believe that you can, and should, quantitively and numerically represent judgments about an individual's value. Advocates of an observable approach assert that talented individuals perform in a certain way, with talent a performative construct. There is no requirement to employ technologically-enabled processes because actors "know talent when they see it". Thus, humans, rather than technology, are responsible for making judgments about the value of individuals and whether they illustrate the defining characteristics of "talent".

Future Research Directions

Ongoing debates about "who" should be tasked with talent management – humans or technology – will amplify and become more complex as organisations make decisions about which talent management (and HRM) processes benefit from automation and those which require human intervention and agency. As we transition to more digitalised ways of working and as more technological innovations emerge, HR, senior stakeholders and researchers alike will have many questions including; what factors enable or constrain the appropriation of digitalised talent management? Will organisations continue to "buy" talent management technology and adopt the talent definitions and processes embedded within technology or will organisations design proprietary systems to ensure talent management practices aligned to current and future strategic ambitions? What's the role of HR functions and executives in talent management in the future? Will HR be excluded or play a prominent role?

Further Readings

McDonnell, A., Collings, D., Mellahi, K., & Schuler, R (2017). Talent management: a systematic review and future prospects. *European Journal of International Management* 11 (1)86–128 (Literature review)

Gallardo-Gallardo, E., & Thunnissen, M. (2016). Standing on the shoulders of giants? A critical review of empirical talent management research. *Employee Relations, 38*(1), 31–56. (Literature review of empirical studies)

Gallardo-Gallardo, E., Dries, N., & González-Cruz, T. F. (2013). What is the meaning of 'talent' in the world of work? *Human Resource Management Review, 23*(4), 290–300. (Talent definitions and conceptualisations)

Tansley, C. (2011). What do we mean by the term "talent" in talent management? *Industrial and Commercial Training, 43*(5), 266–274. (Talent definitions and conceptualisations)

References

Cappelli, P. (2008). Talent Management for the Twenty-First Century. *Harvard Business Review*, *86*, 74–81.

Chambers, E. G., Foulton, M., Handfield-Jones, H., Hankin, S. M., & Michaels III, E. G. (1998). The War For Talent *McKinsey Quarterly* (3), 44–57.

Collings, D. G. (2014). The Contribution of Talent Management to Organization Success. In K. Kraiger, J. Passmore, N. R. Dos Santos, & S. Malvezzi (Eds.), *The Wiley-Blackwell Handbook of the Psychology of Training, Development, and Performance Improvement* (pp. 247–260). Online John Wiley & Sons, Ltd.

Collings, D. G., & Mellahi, K. (2009). Strategic talent management: A review and research agenda. *Human Resource Management Review*, *19*(4), 304–313.

Highhouse, S. (2008). Stubborn Reliance on Intuition and Subjectivity in Employee Selection. *Industrial and Organizational Psychology*, *1*(3), 333–342.

Iles, P., Chuai, X., & Preece, D. (2010). Talent Management and HRM in Multinational companies in Beijing: Definitions, differences and drivers. *Journal of World Business*, *45*(2), 179–189.

Lepak, D. P., & Snell, S. A. (1999). The Human Resource Architecture: Toward a Theory of Human Capital Allocation and Development *Academy of Management Review*, *24*(1), 31–48. doi:10.5465/amr.1999.1580439

Lewis, R. E., & Heckman, R. J. (2006). Talent management: A critical review. *Human Resource Management Review*, *16*(2), 139–154.

Mäkelä, K., Björkman, I., & Ehrnrooth, M. (2010). How do MNCs establish their talent pools? Influences on individuals' likelihood of being labeled as talent. *Journal of World Business*, *45*(2), 134–142.

McDonnell, A. (2011). Still Fighting the War for Talent? Bridging the Science Versus Practice Gap. *Journal of Business and Psychology*, *26*(2), 169–173.

McDonnell, A., Lamare, R., Gunnigle, P., & Lavelle, J. (2010). Developing Tomorrow's Leaders-Evidence of Global Talent management in Multinational Companies *Journal of World Business*, *45*(2), 150–160.

Stainton, A. (2005). Talent management: Latest buzzword or refocusing existing processes?. *Competency and Emotional Intelligence*, *12*(1), 39–43.

Wiblen, S. (2016). Framing the usefulness of eHRM in talent management: A case study of talent identification in a professional services firm. *Canadian Journal of Administrative Sciences*, *33*(2), 95–107. doi:10.1002/cjas.1378

Wiblen, S. (2019). e-Talent in Talent Management. In M. Thite (Ed.), *e-HRM: Digital Approaches, Directions and Applications* (pp. 153–171). Milton Park Routledge.

Debora Jeske and Thomas S. Calvard
Risk Management in the Age of e-HRM

Risk management involves many different aspects and practices within organisations. HR is often involved in many of these, particularly as HR departments become increasingly digital. As more and more processes go online, e-HRM is also increasingly tasked with managing risks that arise due to the adoption of digital processes and services by employers, employees and applicants, in addition to traditional risks (Becker & Smidt, 2016). Risk management describes the practice of identifying risks in e-HRM practices, the analysis of existing and prospective risks, and the development of risk reduction or mitigation approaches. The following sections outline some major e-HRM-related risk examples and impacts in more detail.

Data Risks

One of the first risks concerns the management of *data risks* (Calvard & Jeske, 2018). Most HR functions such as recruitment and payroll also have access to personal information about (past and present) employees, applicants, temporary workers and other contract workers. Ensuring that data is kept securely is one of the main responsibilities for HR staff, but also one of the main challenges, as interconnected databases and online access to Enterprise Resource Systems also open up new avenues by which data can be compromised. Cyberattacks are an organisational concern – beyond just the IT function (Creelman, 2019). Extra diligence is required to secure this extensive data. Multifactor authentication becomes increasingly important, as does the technical expertise of HR, as this function increasingly employs more and more tools (e.g., chatbots and apps), the use of which requires due consideration of their security and usability. Data breaches of HR data can damage the employer's reputation and affect their ability to retain and hire new talent. This means data accident handling and breach strategies are therefore also part of the new e-HRM agenda (Calvard & Jeske, 2018).

The degree to which rewards are awarded for risky business decision-making is also a concern in this domain. This applies to how data is mined and used for business decisions, and where the data originated from (as well as the extent to which it may be triangulated and used for other purposes than initially indicated, see Calvard & Jeske, 2018). Similarly, the use of HR data for risk-based monitoring of employees on site and in access control management tools (e.g., the use of personal information such as finger prints on access control panels) can also fall under the purview of risk management as such information may be shared across multiple systems and even sites. This means data risks (e.g., leak or breach) increase exponentially.

https://doi.org/10.1515/9783110633702-023

Legal and Financial Risks

Not far behind data risks are *legal risks*. These increase as e-HRM professionals change and trial new processes and practices. These include the use of algorithms in selection which may result in biased outcomes (Oppenheim, 2018). There is a need to ensure compliance (e.g., adherence to rules and audits) and to insure against risks that are changing fast with the emergence of algorithms to support existing HR processes (e.g., the filtering of suitable applicants in selection and talent management). These activities also increase the exposure of the company to legal risks that may in turn increase the risks to the business as well (Creelman, 2019). Legal risks connect to *financial risks*. Poor ethical practices may expose the company to legal consequences, which may include significant financial fines, according to GDPR guidelines (2018). The amount of the fine may vary depending on the nature of the infringement, the intentional or negligent nature associated with non-compliance, data type, and many other legal and policy criteria (GDPR EU, 2019).

In the UK, following the 2008 financial crisis, this led to the mandatory appointment of Chief Risk Officers among financial institutions (Creelman, 2019). In recent years, the emergence of new roles and job titles such as Chief Data Officers (CDOs), Chief Information Officers (CIO) and Chief Information Security Officers (CISOs) demonstrate how digital services are impacting appointments and therefore risk management staffing. A UK Institute of Employment Studies (2019) report discusses risk management in relation to HR, and the discussion around AI may be particularly noteworthy for HR professionals. Finally, risk management in the age of greater uncertainty is discussed by Madhani (2017), who also identifies various HR options to tackle uncertainty due to risk.

Adverse Impact Risks

The above risks may also increase the *risk of adverse impact* due to the type of traditional and non-traditional selection practices that employer adopt. Adverse impact is generated when certain groups are selected more often than other groups (e.g., selection appears to result in hires from a majority group rather than a minority group). This may be the result of deliberate discrimination (also called disparate treatment). Information is not objective or free of social and cultural biases (Chowdhury & Mulani, 2018), which means that algorithms constructed on the basis of such information will not be free of bias. Algorithms used in selection may also be trained on materials that subsequently bias outcomes (e.g., information about predominantly male white workers; Bousquet, 2018), resulting in adverse impact. In other words, many employers may also need to embrace risk management in terms of how they train, use and evaluate algorithms for fairness as part of robust HR practices.

A related issue is cyber-vetting and social media screening which can generate a variety of legal and ethical issues (Jeske & Shultz, 2016, 2019; Holland & Jeske, 2017, 2018). Depending on the job in question and the use of social media for personal rather than professional purposes, applicants may self-select out of the process (Jeske & Shultz, 2019). This may also reduce diversity and inadvertently discourage individuals from applying to certain positions (Jeske, Lippke, & Shultz, 2019). Using digital footprints in selection can mean applicants are disadvantaged when they do not use the right social media, do not have a social media profile, or do not update their profile regularly. As a result, it becomes increasingly important for HR to jointly, with other departments, devise new means to train managers on behavioural biases when using online information that may also impact the business' risk exposure, in both the HR domain as well as the financial domain (Adam, Fernando, & Golubeva, 2015). The emergence of HR analytics also plays into this domain as analytical results will need to be tested in terms of their impact on analytical workforce models (Baesens, de Winne & Sels, 2017). Trusting algorithms without question increases the risks of HR engaging in practices that foster discriminatory or other negative outcomes.

Reputational Risks

This brings us to the management of *reputational risk* (Becker & Smidt, 2016), management of which often falls to HR. Poor applicant management, poor employee treatment, and data leaks may be quickly revealed in the public domain via the emergence of employer review sites such as Glassdoor (Jeske & Holland, 2019). Employees also engage in employer vetting via such sites, which means poor management increases the workload for HR trying to manage the online profile and image of the employer. Many HR professionals now regularly monitor employer review sites and respond to both positive and negative reviews in order to reduce the potential fallout. The emergence of virtual career fairs also requires HR professionals to adopt new processes and systems for managing employer reputational risks (Stenberg Vik, Nørbech, & Jeske, 2018).

Health and Safety Risks

Risk management also extends to work environments where employees face abuse or threats, creating *new health and safety issues*. In most instances, hostile work environments are discussed as physical spaces (Bader, Schuster, and Dickmann, 2019). However, some online work involves virtual environments that may increase distress and create mental health issues. One example are individuals who work as content moderators and review graphic and disturbing online content on a company's online sites. These roles may be relatively poorly paid but carry the risk of significant distress over time (BBC, 2018). This means that as some jobs require more online interaction, the health and safety parameters also shift. Existing research on call centres and hostile work environments (e.g., Bader et al., 2019) may be informative for health and safety risk management in virtual environments. Relatedly, preventing and adequately responding to cyberbullying instances at work is another domain that falls under e-HRM risk management responsibilities (Webb, 2017). Not taking account of these issues is likely to increase the aforementioned and interrelated legal and reputational risks.

Risk Implications for HR Professionals

Risk management today is an increasingly inter-departmental priority that requires cross-functional collaboration to succeed. This might involve HR representatives sitting on risk committees (Creelman, 2019), providing training to HR professionals involved in risk audits, and having regular exchanges with risk professionals in insurance and other organisational units (Creelman, 2019). HR may be able to inform risk management initiatives by bringing in new e-HRM issues to the table for discussion. This means that tackling risk management may also require more technical expertise, practice and training among HR professionals (Cohen, 2015).

Further Readings

Despite the work on risk management to date, the relationship to e-HRM trends has not been explored in detail. Research questions remain, such as what the pros and cons are of using algorithms in HR. Another question relates to how HR can develop new risk management protocols and tools for emerging roles (e.g., such as content moderator jobs). Despite these research gaps, a number of resources exist that may be informative for readers. This includes the work on risk management in HR by Becker and Smidt (2016), and the work on data risk management in HR by Calvard and Jeske (2018). Moreover, Cagliano, Grimaldi and Rafele (2015) produced a theoretical framework to develop project risk management techniques which may be a useful resource for e-HRM professionals taking on risk management responsibilities related to the identification, the monitoring, response to, and analysis of, risk. Project approaches may be particularly helpful as many e-HRM initiatives are initially tried as pilot projects. Other resources also discuss risk mitigation in relation to outsourcing (Cappelli, 2011) and ethical practice (Cohen, 2015; Falkenberg, 2019).

References

Adam, T. R., Fernando, C. S., & Golubeva, E. (2015). Managerial overconfidence and corporate risk management. *Journal of Banking & Finance*, *60*, 195–208. doi: 10.1016/j.jbankfin.2015.07.013

Bader, B., Schuster, T., & Dickmann, M. (2019). Managing people in hostile environments: lessons learned and new grounds in HR research. *The International Journal of Human Resource Management*, *30*(20), 2809–2830. doi: 10.1080/09585192.2018.1548499

BBC (2018, April 26). Meet the people who watch terrible things online. BBC. Available at: https://www.bbc.com/news/av/technology-43901236/meet-people-who-review-facebook-s-reported-content (accessed 30 June 2019).

Becker, K. and Smidt, M. (2016). A risk perspective on human resource management: A review and directions for future research. *Human Resource Management Review*, *26*(2), 149–165. doi: 10.1016/j.hrmr.2015.12.001

Baesens, B., De Winne, S., & Sels, L. (2017). Is your company ready for HR analytics?. *MIT Sloan Management Review*, *58*(2), 20–22. http://ilp.mit.edu/media/news_articles/smr/2017/58210.pdf

Bousquet, C. (2018, August 31). Algorithmic Fairness: Tackling Bias in City Algorithms. Available at: https://datasmart.ash.harvard.edu/news/article/algorithmic-fairness-tackling-bias-city-algorithms (accessed 15 July 2019).

Cagliano, A. C., Grimaldi, S., & Rafele, C. (2015). Choosing project risk management techniques. A theoretical framework. *Journal of Risk Research*, *18*(2), 232–248. doi: 10.1080/13669877.2014.896398

Calvard, T.S. & Jeske, D. (2018). Developing human resource data risk management in the age of big data. *International Journal of Information Management*, *43*(2018), 159–164. doi: 10.1016/j.ijinfomgt.2018.07.011

Cappelli, P (2011). HR sourcing decisions and risk management. *Organizational Dynamics*, *40*, 310–316. doi: 10.1016/j.orgdyn.2011.07.008

Chowdhury, R. & Mulani, N. (2018, October 24). Auditing Algorithms for Bias. Harvard Business Review. Available at: https://hbr.org/2018/10/auditing-algorithms-for-bias (accessed 15 July 2019).

Cohen, D. J. (2015). HR past, present and future: A call for consistent practices and a focus on competencies. *Human Resource Management Review*, *25*(2), 205–215. doi: 10.1016/j.hrmr.2015.01.006

Creelman, D. (2019). Why HR pros should start talking about risk. *HR Future*, *2019*(Jan 2019), 12–13.

Falkenberg, L. (2019, April n.d.). Working with AI – Guidelines for ethical conducting a digitized working world. Available at: https://www.dotmagazine.online/issues/ai-intelligence-in-the-digital-age/working-with-ai-guidelines-for-ethical-conduct-in-a-digitalized-working-world (accessed 30 June 2019).

GDPR (2018). General Data Protection Regulation Available at: https://gdpr-info.eu/ (accessed 15 July 2019).

GDPR EU (2019). Web learning resources for the EU General Data Protection Regulation. Fines and Penalties. Available at: https://www.gdpreu.org/compliance/fines-and-penalties/ (accessed 15 July 2019).

Holland, P., & Jeske, D. (2017). The changing role of social media at work: Implications for Recruitment and Selection, in T. Bondarouk, H. Ruel, & E. Parry (Eds). *Electronic HRM in the Smart Era*. Emerald Publishing.

Holland, P., & Jeske, D. (2018) The Cyber-vet or not to Cyber-vet: An Ethics Question for HRM. In A. Malik (Ed). *trategic Human Resource Management and Employment Relations: An International Perspective*. Singapore, Springer.

Institute for Employment Studies (2019). *Which way now for HR and organisational changes? IES Perspectives on HR 2018*. January Report. Brighton, UK: Institute for Employment Studies.

Jeske, D., & Shultz, K. (2016). Using social media content for screening in recruitment and selection: pros and cons. *Work, Employment & Society, 30*(3), 535–546. doi: 10.1177/0950017015613746

Jeske, D., & Shultz, K.S. (2019). Social media screening and content effects: Implications for applicant reactions. *International Journal of Manpower;* 40(1), 73–86.

Jeske, D., Lippke, S., & Shultz, K.S. (2019). Predicting self-disclosure in recruitment in the context of social media screening. *Employee Rights and Responsibilities. 31*(2), 99–112.

Jeske, D. & Holland, P. (2019). Employer and Employee Vetting: Reputation management challenges. In P. Holland (Ed), *Contemporary HRM issues in the 21st century* (Ch. 10, pg. 149–158). Bingley, UK: Emerald Publishing.

Madhani, P. M. (2017). Enhancing return on HR investments: Risk management with real options approach. *Compensation & Benefits Review, 49*(1), 38–55. doi: 10.1177/0886368718757310

Oppenheim, M. (2018, October 11). Amazon scraps ‚sexist AI' recruitment tool. Available at: https://www.independent.co.uk/life-style/gadgets-and-tech/amazon-ai-sexist-recruitment-tool-algorithm-a8579161.html (accessed 30 June 2019).

Stenberg Vik, Å., Nørbech, B.C., & Jeske, D. (2018). Virtual career fairs: Perspectives from Norwegian recruiters and exhibitors. Future Internet. ePub. Available at: https://www.mdpi.com/1999-5903/10/2/19/htm (accessed 30 June 2019).

Webb, D. (2017, November 15). What employers can do to stop cyber bullying at work. Available at: https://www.personneltoday.com/hr/what-employers-can-do-to-stop-cyber-bullying-at-work/ (accessed 30 June 2019).

Michael E. Wasserman and Sandra L. Fisher

Sailing in Stormy Weather: Digitalization, Ethics and e-HRM

Human resource (HR) professionals are navigating through another new wave of technological change, an era where artificial intelligence, facial recognition, autonomous vehicles, data mining, and an ever-increasing array of digital tools are radically redefining the relationships among organizations and their workforce (Nica, 2018). The latest wave of digitalization impacts all aspects of HR systems, including job design, strategic staffing, recruiting, selection, onboarding, training, employee development, and more (Bondaruk & Ruel, 2009; Parry & Strohmeier, 2014). These new digital technologies can certainly improve efficiency (reviewing job candidate resumes) and worker safety (using robotics to reduce exposure to dangerous substances or repetitive physically stressful movements). These technologies can make lives better (Tambe, Cappelli, & Yakubovich, 2019; Wasserman & Mahmoodi, 2017). However, this new digital era also comes with a radically changing ethical context. Much damage can be done by new technology to workers, their families, and their communities (Lewis, 2019). Thus, HR researchers and practitioners need to work towards a clearer understanding of how technology can be used to benefit multiple stakeholders in the employment relationship (Marler & Fisher, 2018), balancing fair treatment of employees with benefits for workplaces and communities. These are difficult issues with no easy answers. This entry examines two key ethical challenges stemming from the application of e-HRM in organizations; justice with how data are used, and responsibilities organizations have with more extensive contracting practices beyond organizational boundaries.

Ethical Decisions and Frameworks in e-HRM

Human resource managers are in a position to, at a minimum, address some of these issues by focusing on the workplace. In organizations of all sizes and in all industries, HR managers are facing new types of decisions about which digital technologies to deploy and how to deploy them. We are at a critical juncture as we confront the realities of the digital technologies we are using, and the business models we are embracing: *Who is responsible for making ethical decisions? The organization? Outsourced partners that make products or provide services under contract? Or the makers of the technology we buy and deploy within our own organizations?* Once we gain clarity on these questions, then the relevant question becomes, *are there decision models that will help us make sure that the decisions we make help both*

https://doi.org/10.1515/9783110633702-024

organizations and employees? There is clearly an urgent need for revisiting the ethical guidelines that we use to make decisions about the role humans play in our organizations, how they are treated, how they treat each other, and what we expect in terms of attitudes and behaviors (Royakkers, Timmer, Kool, & van Est, 2018).

In order to better understand the ethics of this latest technological age, an exploratory conversation among HR professionals is needed. The starting point for this conversation lies in understanding past research and adapting/using what we know to point us toward what we need to do next. To help us, we can borrow three traditional frameworks and use those to identify "what could possibly go wrong" with the current wave of technology. This foundation then helps build a concise toolkit of best practices and leads to concrete recommendations for how to think about ethics and e-HRM.

Three traditional frameworks that can help make sense of these ethical challenges are:

1. *Kantian ethics* is based on the principle that people should not be treated solely as a means to an end (Kant, 1964; Greenwood, 2002). Rawls (1972) built on this notion, making the case that we must recognize the universal right of individuals to live and work in a just society, where the rights of individuals to exist as ends in themselves requires the need for social contracts and institutions to enforce these contracts. Greenwood (2002) connects the concept of Rawlsian justice to the justification for HRM in organizations, that is, to propel companies to provide training, meaningful jobs, career pathways, mentoring, etc. For example, Kantian ethics are important when we think about using data collected from employees or contractors, particularly those with less power.

2. *Utilitarian ethics* is based on making decisions that gain the greatest good for the greatest number of people (Greenwood, 2002). This also can be used to justify the existence of HRM – to act as a balance to the notion that a corporation exists to maximize shareholder value (Greenwood, 2002). The premise is that others beyond shareholders are affected by decisions made by managers, and that the impact of these others should be considered as part of any decision. For example, utilitarian ethics are important when considering whether companies should hire full-time employees or rely on temporary workers or contingent contractors.

3. *Stakeholder theory* builds on Kantian and Utilitarian ethics but takes a slightly different approach by looking at groups other than shareholders as stakeholders. Corporations should be managed for the benefit of these many stakeholder groups, which include employees along with suppliers and community residents in locations where the firm operates (Freeman, 1984; Greenwood & Freeman, 2011). For example, stakeholder theory is important when companies make decisions to move from human-driven to autonomous delivery vehicles.

Guiding Principles for Ethical Use of HR Technology

We can use these three frameworks to create guidelines that researchers and managers should be considering as they consider technologies that shift the relationship between organizations and workers, such as artificial intelligence, facial recognition, machine learning, and the like. It is important to examine the extent to which such technologies might benefit management or stakeholders at the expense of workers, leading to the HRM system being viewed as exploiting workers for the financial gain of the firm (Guest, 2002; Nishii, Lepak & Schneider, 2008). Two guiding principles are evident:

1. *Considering Justice*: Justice relates to deciding what is fair. The concept of organizational justice is well-known to HR researchers and practitioners. (Miller, 1996). Justice relates neatly to ethical decision making (see, for example, Rawls, 1972). Two types of justice are particularly important: Informational justice (Greenberg, 1993) and procedural justice (Alexander & Ruderman, 1987). *Informational justice* relates to perceptions that information was used fairly when making decisions and that relevant information was shared with relevant parties. In applications such as using data scraped from social media sites to guide hiring or promotion decisions, this form of justice could be important. *Procedural justice* relates to perceptions that the process used to make decisions is fair. Applying a concept of fairness requires considering impacts on oneself in relation to other stakeholders, in that the outcomes for employees and community members are equally as valuable as the outcomes for owners (those who control the capital used to fund the business). Miller (1996) calls this *comparative judgment* about fairness. Thus, HR researchers and managers need to consider decisions about the development and deployment of digital tools, projects, and services in ways that consider the inherent fairness of the adoption to all relevant stakeholders. Such consideration involves four steps:
   - identifying relevant stakeholders
   - estimating benefits and costs for each stakeholder group
   - evaluating those benefits and costs comparatively
   - committing to a process that is transparent and communicated clearly to justify decisions
2. *Considering Contracts*: Outsourcing does not mean offloading an organization's ethical responsibilities. Increasingly, organizations are 'contracting out' work rather than doing it themselves. There are two main mechanisms for this contracting out: outsourcing to other companies and outsourcing out to freelance individuals. There are two important issues here: one is that when firms contract out work to outside companies, this does not mean the companies are offloading their ethical responsibilities. Customers and regulators should hold firms accountable for the content and assembly of their products, regardless of whether the subcomponents or raw materials were created by the company that

sells the product or not. It includes environmental impact, wages, working conditions, and product quality. Secondly, the treatment of contract workers should be considered similarly, or in comparison to, employees. These decisions are especially important in the case of wage rates, benefits, working conditions, and opportunities for development and advancement. As noted elsewhere in this volume, the use of technology allows organizations to easily contract with freelancers and gig workers for one-time projects. The ethical implications of this contracting mode need to be considered as part of HR strategy.

How do researchers and practitioners use the Kantian, Utilitarian, and Stakeholder frameworks and the consideration of both justice and contracts going forward? The dilemma we face as a field is balancing people and profit given rapid technological shifts. Do we want technology to save money or make people's lives better? Can we do both, improving the HR function and employee well-being simultaneously (Guest, 2002; Guest, 2017)? If we have to choose one goal over the other, how do we balance this choice? What questions should we be asking ourselves? What metrics do we look at to help us decide? What trade-offs are acceptable, and what ethical guidelines should be clear limits to the decisions that we make?

Ethical Statements about e-HRM

Three possible areas for future consideration of ethics in decision making about e-HRM are evident:

1. How should explorations about e-HRM technologies include the alignment of ethical and legal standards? What responsibility do researchers have to identify ethical and legal issues related to the HR technologies about which they present and publish? While these issues are under such strenuous debate, we might argue that all papers dealing with e-HRM technologies should be expected to have a section dealing with the ethical issues of that technology. A complicating factor is that across international borders, different cultures and countries have different ethical and legal standards that must be taken into account.

2. Researchers may be able to help shape industry or professional ethical standards on the use and implementation of e-HRM technologies. Industry or professional association ethical standards are imperfect mechanisms, but they are a starting point and important statement on values that are intended to guide practitioners' decision making. For example, the Society for Human Resource Management offers a code of ethics for HR professionals that addresses the use of information (SHRM, 2014), but as of this writing it does not discuss the ethics of technology more broadly. Researchers in the field of e-HRM can help identify the stakeholder tradeoffs inherent in use of these technologies.

3. Tilt towards 'technoethics' or 'digital ethics'. Technoethics is not a new term – it dates back to at least the 1970s (see for example. Bunge, 1977). It highlights the ethical implications of technology. Bunge (1977) noted that people who develop technology have a special responsibility not just to their employer, but to all of humanity, to thoughtfully consider the direct and indirect impacts the work they do has on the rest of the world. This is a very important point. Medical doctors take the Hippocratic Oath to do no harm. Those of us who study the creation and deployment of technology into the workplace ought to have the same perspective. This becomes especially important as advanced HR technology becomes less evident to those affected by it, as noted with the concerns for "explainability" of AI (Tambe, et al., 2019). We need to deploy a tilt towards technoethics in both what we do and what we study in the world of HR, including job descriptions, selection criteria, performance management, and rewards. Technoethics needs to be embedded in every technology company's culture and into how we train the next generation of academic HR researchers.

We suggest three potential future research areas to enhance our understanding of digitalization and ethics in e-HRM.
1. Understanding the impact of data privacy and security on employee well-being, employee attraction and retention, and development of human capital.
2. Understanding the role of transparency in the selection process for both employees and gig workers when artificial intelligence either supports or makes the decisions.
3. Understanding the implications of national and organizational culture on ethical orientations toward data privacy and security in HR, the use of machine learning and algorithms for hiring and promotion, and collaborative work between robots and humans.

The weather may be stormy, but researchers and practitioners have maps and tools that have helped us navigate in the past, several of which were identified above. We will need to use these tools to address ethical decisions about employee tracking, data collection from employees and customers, AI-based hiring algorithms, full-time vs. contracting decisions, and privacy in the workplace (Douglas, 2018). The challenge is clear, but with focused attention, a good map, and reliable tools, safe passage is possible.

Further Readings

Bogen, M. & Rieke, A. (December 2018). Help wanted: An examination of hiring algorithms, equity, and bias. Upturn, Washington, DC. Available at www.upturn.org/hiring-algorithms

Kellogg, K. C., Valentine, M. A., & Christin, A. (2020). Algorithms at work: The new contested terrain of control. *Academy of Management Annals*, *14*(1), 366–410.

Tambe, P., Cappelli, P., & Yakubovich, V. (2019). Artificial intelligence in human resources management: challenges and a path forward. *California Management Review*, *61*(4), 15–42.

References

Alexander, S., & Ruderman, M. (1987). The role of procedural and distributive justice in organizational behavior. *Social Justice Research*, *1*(2), 177–198.

Bondarouk, T.V. and Ruël, H.J.M. (2009), Electronic human resource management: challenges in the digital era, *International Journal of Human Resource Management*, *20*(3), 505–514.

Bunge, M. (1977). Towards a technoethics. *The Monist*, *60(1)*, 96–107.

Douglas, E. (2018, April 11). How should HR balance AI and ethics? *Human Resources Director*, Accessed at: https://www.hcamag.com/ca/news/general/how-should-hr-balance-ai-and-ethics/129768

Freeman, R.E. (1984). *Strategic Management: A Stakeholder Approach*. Pitman: Boston.

Greenberg, J. (1993). The social side of fairness: Interpersonal and informational classes of organizational justice. In R. Cropanzano (Ed.), *Justice in the Workplace: Approaching Fairness in Human Resource Management*: 79–103. Hillsdale, NJ: Lawrence Erlbaum.

Greenwood, M.R. (2002). Ethics and HRM: A review and conceptual analysis. *Journal of Business Ethics*, *36*(3), 261–278.

Greenwood, M., & Freeman, R.E. (2011). Ethics and HRM: The contribution of stakeholder theory. *Business & Professional Ethics Journal*, 269–292.

Guest, D. (2002). Human resource management, corporate performance and employee wellbeing: Building the worker into HRM. *The Journal of Industrial Relations*, *44(3)*, 335–358.

Guest, D.E. (2017). Human resource management and employee well-being: Towards a new analytic framework. *Human Resource Management Journal*, *27*(1), 22–38.

Kant, I. (1964). *Groundwork of the Metaphysic of Morals*. Harper: New York.

Lewis, N. (2019). What is HR's ethical responsibility in the digital transformation age? SHRM.com. Accessed at: https://www.shrm.org/resourcesandtools/hr-topics/technology/pages/hr-ethical-responsibility-digital-transformation.aspx

Marler, J. & Fisher, S.L. (November 2018). Have we gone too far? Reconsidering the role of employee stakeholders in eHRM. Paper presented at the 7th International Conference on eHRM, Milan, Italy.

Miller, P. (1996). Strategy and the ethical management of human resources. *Human Resource Management Journal*, *6*(1), 5–18.

Nica, E. (2018). Will robots take the jobs of human workers? Disruptive technologies that may bring about jobless growth and enduring mass unemployment. *Psychosociological Issues in Human Resource Management*, *6*(2), 56–61.

Nishii, L.H., Lepak, D.P., & Schneider, B. (2008). Employee attributions of the "why" of HR practices: Their effects on employee attitudes and behaviors, and customer satisfaction. *Personnel Psychology*, *61(3)*, 503–545.

Parry, E., & Strohmeier, S. (2014). HRM in the digital age–digital changes and challenges of the HR profession. *Employee Relations 36*(4):.

Rawls, J. (1972). *A Theory of Justice*. Oxford, Clarendon.

Royakkers, L., Timmer, J., Kool, L., & van Est, R. (2018). Societal and ethical issues of digitization. *Ethics and Information Technology*, *20*(2), 127–142.

Society for Human Resource Management (2014). Code of Ethics. Available at https://www.shrm.org/about-shrm/pages/code-of-ethics.aspx.

Tambe, P., Cappelli, P., & Yakubovich, V. (2019). Artificial intelligence in human resources management: challenges and a path forward. *California Management Review, 61*(4), 15–42.

Wasserman, M.E., and Mahmoodi, F. (2017, 1st Quarter). Disruptive technologies: Should you give them the green light? *CSCMP's Supply Chain Quarterly*, 24–29.

Debora Jeske
Introducing e-Internships

Internships continue to be an important part of the journey into employment. They are "temporary (non-permanent) work placements that reflect a period of transition from higher education to the world of work" (Bayerlein & Jeske, 2018a, p. 29). This entry introduces computer-mediated internships: e-internships (also known as virtual internships). These internships emerged about ten years ago (see van Dorp, 2008). This development was fostered by the emergence of new software and virtual collaboration tools. As in the case of traditional internships, e-internships serve to provide a learning experience to the e-intern, often as a means to qualify the person for new roles, a new career and employment. However, some characteristics set e-internships apart from traditional internships. First, e-internships are not necessarily location bound nor are they by default a transition from education into employment (they may also represent a transitional period between different careers). Second, e-interns may be trained entirely online by a supervisor or peers. Third, almost all work is completed using online platform, shared software and tools. And fourth, many e-interns are not enrolled in educational institutions (although the majority of e-interns are students). e-internship formats are therefore particularly suitable to roles and tasks that are heavily computer-mediated in real life as well. To date, there is no evidence that suggests e-internships are any less effective than traditional internships in teaching new cognitive and technical skills, although affective learning outcomes may be harder to obtain (Bayerlein & Jeske, 2018a).

The current entry will briefly introduce the two forms of e-internships that exist, but will focus specifically on the second form (applied e-internships with employers). Following this introduction, the entry will outline the unique value proposition and challenges that arise for managers who wish to run the organisationally-applied e-internships.

e-Internships Forms

Two different types of e-internships are known today (Bayerlein & Jeske, 2018a). The first form includes *simulated internships* that are indeed virtual: Interns may complete tasks in a simulated work environment which presents them with the same challenges that they may face in the workplace (Bayerlein, 2015; Ruggiero & Boehm, 2016, 2017). This e-internship is a popular option for many educational institutions that run them as these e-internships allow students to build and learn skills in a virtual work environment while the lecturers can also assess their performance in these settings (e.g., accounting, engineering). Many of these e-internships

https://doi.org/10.1515/9783110633702-025

do not reflect the length of more traditional internships. However, in those cases, students are also able to get academic credit for completing specific internships.

The second and more applied form of *e-internships* (and the focus of this entry) are those internships that are essentially an extension of teleworking practices: e-interns work with an actual employer, using online tools, platforms, and teams (Jeske & Axtell, 2016a, 2016b). The intern (not necessarily a student, however) is engaging with an organisation as part of an internship that may last several weeks to a year (two thirds of such internships last 6 to 12 weeks, see Jeske & Axtell, 2018b). Most e-interns will be working part-time (rather than full-time). But like traditional interns, many may be offered employment after completing their e-internship, especially if they are situated in the same country as the e-internship provider. Given their flexibility, these e-internships are an increasingly interesting for organisations regardless of location and size (e.g., a number of service providers specialize in marketing e-internships online on behalf of larger companies and public organisations, particularly in the USA, Australia and India).

e-Internship Prominence and Characteristics

To date, these e-internships have been observed across the globe in most countries and across most continents (Jeske & Axtell, 2013, 2016a, 2017). Overall, they tend to be more popular in geographically large countries such as the USA and India (Jeske & Axtell, 2016a). Such e-internships may be located across various time zones and countries (which may not be the case with the simulated e-internships that are run by universities). e-interns may work in a number of different roles. These include predominantly marketing activities (including branding and design), programming (of websites, programmes, databases), and often complete work related to analytical tasks (frequently in start-ups; Jeske & Axtell, 2018a). However, e-interns may also work in roles related to online journalism, customer care (including eHealth solutions or online counselling) and other people-oriented roles (Jeske & Axtell, 2013). The nature of employers is very varied, as e-interns may work for any number of organisations, starting from government bodies, charities, museums, multinational businesses, to academic institutions and start-ups.

Organisational Implementation

The implementation of e-internship programmes requires careful planning for HR and the managers supervising e-interns. A few examples demonstrate what is required. First, the national regulation of payment of interns and legal protection of interns while at work vary significantly across countries, sectors, and organisations

(Jeske & Axtell, 2013, 2018a). As e-interns might work across national boundaries, organisations have to pay attention to several different legislative frameworks (particularly when the organisations are small and not multi-nationals). Clarifying the legal requirements will therefore be important for HR professionals. In addition to the legal ramifications a second point is worth noting: Managing interns with different cultural backgrounds may require new training for managers who have hitherto only managed local interns. Cultural values may vary (Stone et al., 2007) and therefore affect how practices and policies are interpreted by both managers and e-interns. Giving due consideration to cross-cultural situations and how they may be managed effectively will be important steps for managers to consider (Nardon & Steers, 2014). Good communication, expectation and process management will be essential to ensure the right candidates are recruited and both e-interns and employer benefit from the internship experience.

Third, managers of e-interns will need to have the appropriate ICT tools and skills in order to train their e-interns and to manage their performance effectively (not all e-interns will have access to or experience with relevant tools). Fourth, it is important to ensure that managers have the interpersonal and supervisory skills to instruct, motivate and manage their e-interns. As part of this process, managers of e-interns need to consider what kind of relational investment they are willing to make and the resulting psychological contract they are building (transitional, relational or balanced; Rousseau, 1995). Research suggests that all forms of contracts can be found among e-internships. e-internship characteristics associated with balanced or relational contracts tend to feature training, more structured internships, at least some degree of collaboration with others (inter-dependent team work) (Jeske & Axtell, 2018a). A variety of e-internship providers use online peer coaching (see also Parker et al., 2014). Peer coaching or mentoring is possible when organisations have several interns working for them simultaneously. Such activities can be facilitated via social media platforms and the appointment of experienced e-interns to help manage the onboarding process, support the knowledge exchange and engage in online community building.

Organisational Benefits

e-Internships feature unique value for organisations of all sizes. A few are briefly introduced. First, such e-internships enable even small organisations to access talent from which staff can learn and who they may also be able to mentor in turn (Jeske & Axtell, 2016b). This can be enriching for small organisations who lack the resources to hire new talent and whose staff seeks the exchange with others. This is particularly enriching for start-ups that are keen to increase the (temporary) intellectual capital while building the business (Jeske & Axtell, 2016a). This brings us to the second point: e-internships afford a degree of flexibility that allows even small organisations such as charities, small business or start-ups to accommodate interns, In addition, the option to work across different time zones and days of the week means that many e-interns are not by default bound to regular working hours. This allows many organisations as well as interns to work in parallel or sequentially on tasks. Third, such internships allow organisations to increase diversity by recruiting interns from all walks of life (Jeske & Axtell, 2016a; Kraft et al., 2019). e-internships are not just of interest to students (Jeske & Axtell, 2014), but also working professionals and individuals who are unable to take traditional internships for a variety of reasons (Jeske & Axtell, 2016a). This includes those with family responsibilities, those with limited financial means, and those who are geographically limited (e.g., due to remote location or disabilities that impact individuals' ability to travel or commute).

Further Readings

A number of research gaps and questions remain. First, due to the lack of work in this domain, it is not entirely clear how simulated internships and applied e-internships can be best integrated in employer and educational internship programmes, despite their increasing popularity across many countries. Secondly, it would be helpful if employers and academics would exchange their experiences and approaches as interns are likely to become more diverse over time, particularly considering that many people pursue multiple careers paths. A number of resources are available for e-internships with employers as well as simulated e-internships (such as Bayerlein, 2015; Jeske & Bayerlein, 2018b).

References

Bayerlein, L. & Jeske, D. (2018a). Student learning opportunities in traditional and computer-mediated internships. *Education + Training*, 60(1), 27–38. doi: 10.1108/ET-10-2016-0157

Bayerlein, L. & Jeske, D. (2018b). The potential of computer-mediated internships for higher education. *International Journal of Educational Management*, 32(4), 526–537. doi: 10.1108/IJEM-11-2016-0254

Jeske, D., & Axtell, C.M. (2013). E-internship prevalence, characteristics, and research opportunities. In P. Kommers, P. Isaias, & L. Rodrigues (Eds). *Proceedings of the IADIS International Conference on e-Society*, Lisbon, Portugal 12–16 March, 201–208.

Jeske, D., & Axtell, C.M. (2014). e-Internships: prevalence, characteristics and role of student perspectives. *Internet Research*, 24(4), 457–473. doi: 10.1108/IntR-11-2012-0226

Jeske, D., & Axtell, C.M. (2016a). Global in small steps: e-internships in SMEs. *Organizational Dynamics*, 45(1), 55–63. doi: 10.1016/j.orgdyn.2015.12.007

Jeske, D., & Axtell, C.M. (2016b). How to run successful e-internships: a case for organizational learning. *Development and Learning in Organizations: An International Journal*, 30(2), 18–21. doi: 10.1108/DLO-09-2015-0073.

Jeske, D., & Axtell, C.M. (2017). Effort and rewards effects: Appreciation and self-rated performance in e-internships. *Social Sciences*, 6(4), 154. doi:10.3390/socsci6040154.

Jeske, D., & Axtell, C.M. (2018a). The nature of relationships in e-internships: A matter of psychological contract, communication and relational investment. *The Journal of Work and Organizational Psychology*, 34(2), 113–121. ePub. doi: https://doi.org/10.5093/jwop2018a14

Jeske, D., & Axtell, C.M. (2018b). Virtuality in e-internships: A descriptive account. In A. Lazazzara, R. C. D. Nacamulli, C. Rossignoli, & S. Za, *Organizing in the digital economy. At the interface between social media, human behaviour and inclusion*. Springer: Lecture Notes in Information Systems and Organisation (LNISO).

Kraft, C., Jeske, D., & Bayerlein, L. (2019). Seeking diversity? Consider virtual internships. *Strategic HR Review* (in press).

Nardon, L. & Steers, R. M. (2014). Managing cross-cultural encounters: putting things in context. *Organizational Dynamics*, 43, 138–145.

Stone, D. L., Stone-Romero, E. F. & Lukaszewski, K. M. (2007). The impact of cultural values on the acceptance and effectiveness of human resource management policies and practices. *Human Resource Management Review*, 17, 152–165.

Bayerlein, L. (2015). Curriculum innovation in undergraduate accounting degree programmes through 'virtual internships'. *Education+Training*, 57, 673–684.

Parker, P., Kram, K. E. & Hall, D. T. (2014). Peer coaching: an untapped resource for development. *Organizational Dynamics*, 43, 122–129.

Rousseau, D. M. (1995*), Psychological contracts in organizations: Understanding written and unwritten agreements*. Thousand Oaks, CA: Sage.

Van Dorp, K.-J. (2008). A premier European platform for clearing e-internships. *British Journal of Educational Technology*, 39, 175–179. doi: 10.1111/j.1467-8535.2007.00731.x

Part 6: **Functional Areas of e-HRM**

Andrea R. Neely and John L. Cotton
e-Mentoring

As workplace communication is increasingly facilitated by technology (Purcell & Rainie, 2014), computer-mediated communication becomes a necessity. In this entry, we explore one computer-mediated relationship: e-mentoring. E-mentoring is the process through which informal, career relevant knowledge, social capital, and psychosocial support are transmitted from a mentor to a protégé (Bozeman & Feeney, 2007) through computer-mediated communication (Hamilton & Scandura, 2003). Based on current theorizing and research, we briefly: (a) give a short introduction and history of e-mentoring, (b) explicate the importance of e-mentoring, (c) outline important advantages and disadvantages of e-mentoring, and (d) discuss the specific opportunities and challenges it presents.

Designed for the same reasons as traditional, face-to-face mentoring, the purpose of e-mentoring programs is to provide the socialization and enculturation of younger employees (Boyle & Boice, 1998) and generate mentoring relationships that may not have been available otherwise (Ragins & Cotton, 1991). Similar to the earliest mentoring programs, e-mentoring provides a tool for career growth and advancement for individuals (e.g., minorities, women) who would have never received it (Bierema & Merriam, 2002; Single & Single, 2005).

Importance of e-Mentoring

Like mentoring, e-mentoring benefits both the protégé and mentor. First, e-mentoring benefits protégés by increasing their social and professional networks (Headlam-Wells, Gosland, & Craig, 2005), giving them access to new resources (e.g., job opportunities), and expanding their knowledge, skills, and abilities (Higgins & Thomas, 2001; de Janasz, Ensher, & Huen, 2008). It facilitates the growth and development of interpersonal communication skills (Adams & Crews, 2004), written communication skills (Fodeman, 2002), teamwork skills (Fodeman, 2002) and reflective skills (Headlam-Wells, Gosland, & Craig, 2006; Shrestha, May, Edirisingha, Burke, & Linsey, 2009). Self-esteem and self-efficacy can also be enhanced with e-mentoring (Adam & Crews, 2004; DiRenzo, Weer, & Linnehan, 2013).

Second, e-mentoring benefits the mentor. Previous research asserts that mentors gain similar outcomes (e.g., self-esteem, self-efficacy) from their participation in e-mentoring relationships (Adams & Crews, 2004). They can also improve their own network, gain new knowledge, and job-related assistance through e-mentoring (Ensher, Grant-Vallone, & Marelich, 2002). Mentoring experience can enhance

https://doi.org/10.1515/9783110633702-026

constructive feedback skills (Forret, 1996), coaching skills (Gilles & Wilson, 2004), update technical skills (Gilles & Wilson, 2004), and improve work practices (Lopez-Real & Kwan, 2005).

Advantages and Disadvantages

E-mentoring provides the following advantages over traditional mentoring: communication autonomy, increased pool of mentors, and cost effectiveness. First, unlike traditional mentoring, mentors and protégés have the benefit of communication autonomy since they determine when, where, and how (e.g., communication mechanism) they communicate. As long as both parties have access to the internet, they can communicate anywhere and at any time (Bierema & Hill, 2005; Headlam-Wells et al., 2005; Kirk & Orlinger, 2003). This communication autonomy also allows them to decide between synchronous or asynchronous communication mechanisms so they are not required to respond immediately, and can review the exchanges at any time (Headlam-Wells et al., 2005). For many mentors and protégés, this flexibility in communication is both the primary advantage and incentive to choosing e-mentoring over more traditional mentoring.

Second, unlike face-to-face mentoring, e-mentoring increases the pool of potential mentors and protégés (Bierma & Hill, 2005) both inside and outside the organization. Within organizations, junior employees are often intimidated by older or higher-ranking employees and this may reduce the likelihood that mentoring relationships will occur (Kasprisin, Single, Single, & Muller, 2003). Without the hierarchical framework inside the organization, both protégés and mentors may be more likely engage in e-mentoring. Other online platforms and organizations (e.g., ementor for military personnel, Risk Management Association's e-mentor for banking professionals) connect potential mentors and protégés from different organizations.

By increasing the potential mentor pool, e-mentoring also mitigates power distance to facilitate egalitarian relationships, which is beneficial for women and minorities. Building relationships between people from different cultures, genders, and ethnicities is easier in e-mentoring as it can conceal individual characteristics (Bierema & Merriam, 2002). Since the interaction is faceless (assuming there is no video conferencing; Ensher & Murphy, 2007), e-mentoring has the potential to reduce stereotypes and stigmas (e.g., age, gender, race). In e-mentoring, the visual cues that reinforce certain biases, stereotypes, and proclivities are not an issue. Therefore, it may alleviate inherent disadvantages for underrepresented groups such as women and minorities.

Third, because the only technological requirement for e-mentoring is internet access, e-mentoring is typically a less expensive alternative to face-to-face mentoring programs (Headlam-Wells et al., 2005; Johnson & Brown, 2017). Unlike e-mentoring, traditional mentoring requires more consideration of time (e.g. when and how long), and space/location (e.g., where given the nature of the conversation).While training staff and budgets may be dwindling, e-mentoring may serve as a cost-effective way to improve the effectiveness of distance training and education (Jossi, 1997).

E-mentoring provides the following disadvantages compared to traditional mentoring: interaction frequency and reciprocal self-disclosure as impediments to building quality relationships. First, it may be more difficult to build and maintain trusting relationships in e-mentoring. E-mentoring participants may have fewer opportunities for reinforcement cues to encourage individuals to maintain these relationships (Single & Single, 2005). Because these online relationships begin or end with such ease, a lack of commitment may result (Bierma & Hill, 2002). For any mentoring, interaction frequency is critical to initiating and maintaining relationship (DiRenzo, Linnehan, Shao, & Rosenberg, 2010). The higher the interaction frequency, the more likely protégés perceive vocational and psychosocial support and mentors experience satisfaction with protégés (Murphy, 2011).

Second, reciprocal self-disclosure may be more difficult in e-mentoring relationships (Shpigelman, Weiss, & Reiter, 2009); this is important as it promotes openness and closeness in relationships. Some researchers suggest that e-mentoring may be less personable than traditional mentoring relationships (Hinds & Kiesler, 1995). There may be some topics which individuals are cautious to discuss online (Adams & Crews, 2004) which may hamper communication. However, one study suggests that reciprocal self-disclosure was increased in technology-mediated communication due to visual anonymity (Joinson, 2001).

Opportunities and Challenges

We lack rigorous empirical research on e-mentoring and its effectiveness (Ensher & Murphy, 2007; Murphy 2011). We discuss two primary opportunities and challenges for e-mentorship research: difficulty of studying relationships as their development is time contingent and the difficulty of technology. First, relationships are difficult to study, as they require empirical studies that are longitudinal in nature. Similar to traditional mentoring, e-mentoring research needs longitudinal research to establish temporal precedence for causal inferences between e-mentoring and important outcomes (e.g., productivity, performance, job satisfaction) (Scandura & Pellegrini, 2007). Additionally, longitudinal studies are necessary to elucidate the dynamic, interactional process of e-mentoring (Allen, Eby, O'Brien, & Lentz, 2008).

Second, unlike traditional communication, e-mentoring has the potential to invade the privacy of both parties. For example, email, online forums, messenger messages are captured in public record (Kirk & Olinger, 2003). Hacking also presents a threat to confidentiality online. When individuals experience privacy concerns, subsequent justice issues may create a situation where they are less likely to accept or more likely to leave a job (Stone-Romero, Stone, & Hyatt, 2003). If privacy concerns can impact the likelihood of accepting or quitting a job, it may similarly impact the likelihood of participants' initiation of e-mentoring relationships.

Further Readings

Bagley, E. A., & Shaffer, D. W. (2015). Stop talking and type: Comparing virtual and face-to-face mentoring in an epistemic game. *Journal of Computer Assisted Learning, 31*(6), 606–622.

de Janasz, S. C., & Godshalk, V. M. (2013). The role of e-mentoring in protégés' learning and satisfaction. *Group and Organization Management, 38*(6), 743–774.

DiRenzo, M. S., Linnehan, F., Shao, P., & Rosenberg, W. L. (2010). A moderated mediation model of e-mentoring. *Journal of Vocational Behavior, 76*(2), 292–305.

Ensher, E. A., & Murphy, S. E. (2007). E-mentoring: Next-generation research strategies and suggestions. In B. R. Ragins & K. E. Kram (Eds.), *The handbook of mentoring at work: Theory, research, and practice* (pp. 299–322). Thousand Oaks, CA: Sage.

Neely, A.R., Cotton, J.L., & Neely, A.D. (2017). E-mentoring: A model and review of the literature. *AIS Transactions on Human-Computer Interaction, 9*(3), 220–242.

References

Adams, G., & Crews, T. B. (2004). Telementoring: A viable tool. *Journal of Applied Research for Business Instruction, 2*(3), 1–4.

Allen, T. D., Eby, L. T., O'Brien, K. E., & Lentz, E. (2008). The state of mentoring research: A qualitative review of current research methods and future research implications. *Journal of Vocational Behavior, 73*(3), 343–357.

Bierema, L. L., & Hill, J. R. (2005). Virtual mentoring and HRD. *Advances in Developing Human Resources, 7*(4), 556–568.

Bierema, L. L., & Merriam, S. B. (2002). E-mentoring: Using computer mediated communication to enhance the mentoring process. *Innovative Higher Education, 26*(3), 211–227.

Boyle, P., & Boice, B. (1998). Best practices for enculturation: Collegiality, mentoring, and structure. *New Directions for Higher Education, 1998*(101), 87–94.

Bozeman, B., & Feeney, M. K. (2007). Toward a useful mof Mentoring: A conceptual analysis and critique. *Administration & Society, 39*(6), 719–739.

De Janasz, S. C., Ensher, E. A., & Heun, C. (2008). Virtual relationships and real benefits: using e-mentoring to connect business students with practicing managers. *Mentoring & Tutoring: Partnership in Learning, 16*(4), 394–411.

DiRenzo, M. S., Linnehan, F., Shao, P., & Rosenberg, W. L. (2010). A moderated mediation model of e-mentoring. *Journal of Vocational Behavior, 76*(2), 292–305.

DiRenzo, M. S., Weer, C. H., & Linnehan, F. (2013). Protégé career aspirations: The influence of formal e-mentor networks and family-based role models. *Journal of Vocational Behavior, 83*(1), 41–50.

Ensher, E. A., Grant-Vallone, E. J., & Marelich, W. D. (2002). Effects of perceived attitudinal and demographic similarity on protégés' support and satisfaction gained from their mentoring relationships. *Journal of Applied Social Psychology, 32*(7), 1407–1430.

Ensher, E. A., & Murphy, S. E. (2007). Next generation research strategies and suggestions. In B. R. Ragins & K. E. Kram (Eds.), *The handbook of mentoring at work: Theory, research, and practice*. SAGE.

Fodeman, D. (2002). Telementoring. *Technology and Learning*, *23*(4), 28–30.

Forret, M. L. (1996). Issues facing organizations when implementing formal mentoring programmes. *Leadership & Organization Development Journal; Bradford*, *17*(3), 27–30.

Gilles, C., & Wilson, J. (2004). Receiving as well as giving: mentors' perceptions of their professional development in one teacher induction program. *Mentoring & Tutoring: Partnership in Learning*, *12*(1), 87–106.

Hamilton, B. A., & Scandura, T. A. (2003). E-mentoring: Implications for organizational learning and development in a wired world. *Organizational Dynamics*, *31*(4), 388–402.

Headlam-Wells, J., Gosland, J., & Craig, J. (2005). "There's magic in the web": E-mentoring for women's career development. *Career Development International*, *10*(6/7), 444–459.

Headlam-Wells, J., Gosland, J., & Craig, J. (2006). Beyond the organisation: The design and management of E-mentoring systems. *International Journal of Information Management*, *26*(5), 372–385.

Higgins, M. C., & Thomas, D. A. (2001). Constellations and careers: Toward understanding the effects of multiple developmental relationships. *Journal of Organizational Behavior*, *22*(3), 223–247.

Hinds, P., & Kiesler, S. (1995). Communication across boundaries: Work, structure, and use of communication technologies in a large organization. *Organization Science*, *6*(4), 373–393.

Johnson, R., & Brown, K. G. (2017). E-learning. In G. Hertel, D. L. Stone, R. Johnson, & J. Passmore (Eds.), *Handbook of the psychology of the Internet at work*. London: Wiley/Blackwell.

Joinson, A. (2001). Self-disclosure in computer-mediated communication: The role of self-awareness and visual anonymity. *European Journal of Social Psychology*, *31*, 177–192.

Jossi, F. (1997). Mentoring in changing times. *Training; Minneapolis*, *34*(8), 50–54.

Kasprisin, C. A., Single, P. B., Single, R. M., & Muller, C. B. (2003). Building a better bridge: Testing e-training to improve e-mentoring programmes in higher education. *Mentoring & Tutoring: Partnership in Learning*, *11*(1), 67–78.

Kirk, J. J., & Olinger, J. (2003). *From traditional to virtual mentoring*. Retrieved from Education Resources Information Center website: https://eric.ed.gov/?id=ED475467

Lopez-Real, F., & Kwan, T. (2005). Mentors' perceptions of their own professional development during mentoring. *Journal of Education for Teaching*, *31*(1), 15–24.

Murphy, W. M. (2011). From e-mentoring to blended mentoring: Increasing students' developmental initiation and mentors' satisfaction. *Academy of Management Learning & Education*, *10*(4), 606–622.

Purcell, K., & Rainie, L. (2014). *Technology's impact on workers*. Washington, D.C.: Pew Research Center.

Ragins, B. R., & Cotton, J. L. (1991). Easier said than done: Gender differences in perceived barriers to gaining a mentor. *Academy of Management Journal*, *34*(4), 939–951.

Scandura, T. A., & Pellegrini, E. K. (2007). Workplace mentoring: Theoretical approaches and methodological issues. In T. D. Allen & L. T. Eby (Eds.), *The blackwell handbook of mentoring: A multiple perspectives approach*. John Wiley & Sons.

Shpigelman, C.-N., Weiss, P. L., & Reiter, S. (2009). E-mentoring for all. *Computers in Human Behavior*, *25*(4), 919–928.

Shrestha, C. H., May, S., Edirisingha, P., Burke, L., & Linsey, T. (2009). From face-to-face to e-mentoring: Does the "e" add any value for mentors? *International Journal of Teaching and Learning in Higher Education*, *20*(2), 116–124.

Single, P. B., & Single, R. M. (2005). E-mentoring for social equity: Review of research to inform program development. *Mentoring & Tutoring: Partnership in Learning*, *13*(2), 301–320.

Stone-Romero, E. F., Stone, D. L., & Hyatt, D. (2003). Personnel selection procedures and invasion of privacy. *Journal of Social Issues*, *59*(2), 343–368.

Anthony S. Boyce and Christine E. Boyce

Talent Identification in the Digital Age: Moving from Selection to e-Selection

The modern employment landscape is radically changing. As of this writing, almost one-third of the world's 7.7 billion people were born since 2001 – i.e., "Generation Z" (Miller & Lu, 2018), global life expectancy is increasing at the fastest rate since the 1960s (World Health Organization [WHO], n.d.), and global talent shortages[1] have reached a 12-year high (ManpowerGroup, 2018b). The skills individuals have now are not the same ones they will need in the future; sixty-five percent of the jobs Generation Z will perform do not even exist yet (ManpowerGroup, 2018a). In this complex environment, new strategies for selecting talent are a prerequisite for organizational success.

Regardless of the processes involved (e.g., resumé screen, cognitive abilities test, interview), the goal of talent selection remains the same: fairly and efficiently identify individuals most likely to perform the job successfully. This requires an understanding of what success on the job looks like and an understanding of the characteristics (e.g., knowledge, skills, abilities, personality traits) that enable someone to perform well. Armed with this understanding, the problem of selection becomes one of efficiently measuring whether someone possesses the characteristics required for successful job performance. For the purposes of this entry, we consider all selection methods (e.g., resumé screens, interviews, or any other approach that chooses one job seeker, whether active or passive, over another) to be relevant.

Brief History of Employment Selection

Formal selection of employees via a standardized process has a history dating back to Imperial China (Elman, 2009), and a modern history dating back to Robert Yerkes and his work on the Army Alpha and Army Beta tests used to select recruits into the United States Army during World War I. While the former example illustrates that humankind has long sought ways to identify "the best person for the job," the latter served to cement assessments as an efficient method of doing so. The earliest approaches to testing

---

1 Given publishing timelines, this chapter was written prior to the COVID-19 pandemic. At the time of our writing, broad-based talent shortages were being experienced by organizations around the globe. In the short period of time since this entry was approved for publication, the nature of the labor market and global unemployment rates have changed dramatically. Despite these factors, we believe the fundamental ideas and direction expressed in this entry remain relevant and accurate, perhaps even more so in a world where social distancing and technology-mediated interaction are becoming the new normal.

https://doi.org/10.1515/9783110633702-027

groups of people and identifying those most likely to perform well were not without controversy or challenge (Army Alpha, n.d.); however, the administrative benefits of using assessments to process and classify large numbers of people were quickly noticed and set the stage for high-volume, high-stakes testing in the future.

Assessments and the field of selection have since evolved in both incremental and revolutionary ways. Scoring of selection procedures (including assessments, resumés, and other evaluation methods) became more standardized and rigorous; improvements were made in the understanding of how test questions functioned, and researchers explored the relationship between test scores and job performance. This progress was punctuated by major changes that became the earliest e-selection methods, like adapting paper-based processes for use in (proctored and eventually unproctored) internet-based settings and then developing equivalent versions for use on mobile devices. As methods for evaluating the effectiveness and utility of different selection approaches continued to advance, selection processes became cheaper, faster, more accurate, more user-friendly, and as a result, ubiquitous.

In a landmark paper published in 1998, Frank Schmidt and John Hunter summarized 85 years of research in talent selection and the validity of 19 selection procedures used to predict job and training performance. Their analysis included everything from graphology (handwriting samples) to methods of cognitive ability and solidified the dominance of some of the most common selection methods in use today, namely cognitive ability, work sample, and personality tests. At that time, while the internet was finding its way and the stage was being set for large-scale online assessment use, talent selection was still a mostly analog process, with individuals responding to job postings in newspapers or via word of mouth.

e-Selection 1.0 to 2.0

In the 20+ years since Schmidt and Hunter's paper, talent selection has undergone another revolutionary transformation. Though the categories of selection methods they identified remain, the internet and associated technologies (e.g., processing power, handheld computers, mobile broadband) have caused a sea change to occur as companies have moved from analog selection (paper-based, face-to-face, and manual) to e-selection (digital, remote, and automated). This macro-level trend toward digitization leads us to formally define e-selection as any selection method, whether used alone or in concert with others, that is delivered in a digital format or contains digitized elements (e.g., a mobile assessment combined with an in-person interview, a video-based interview scored by artificial intelligence). By this definition, while internet testing alone can be considered a form of e-selection, it is, already, a relatively antiquated and simple one.

The digitization of selection has centered around four desired objectives:

- *Efficiency*: reducing the amount of human time and effort involved in the selection process by automating repeatable, transactional tasks
- *Accuracy*: increasing the precision with which selection methods identify people most likely to be successful on the job by harnessing greater amounts of relevant data with more sophisticated prediction algorithms
- *Experience*: enhancing user-friendliness and overall candidate experience by incorporating technologies that make applying to a job quicker, more interesting, and more engaging
- *Compliance*: ensuring adherence to maturing and increasingly prescriptive data privacy, information technology security, and user accessibility standards (e.g., Global Data Protection Regulation [GDPR], and Web Content Accessibility Guidelines [WCAG])

Consider a common process we might call "e-selection 1.0." A job becomes available and is posted online via a job board, where an individual can search for it and apply. His resume is reviewed by a recruiter, who calls the candidate for a brief pre-screen interview. Having met the minimal qualifications, the candidate advances to the next stage, an online personality assessment that takes 45 minutes to complete, and an online cognitive abilities assessment that takes 30 minutes to complete. After his scores are reviewed and determined to fit within the predefined qualification standards, he is invited for an in-person behavioral interview and a chance to meet the hiring manager, tour his potential place of work and ask questions about the role. Successfully passing this stage, a conditional job offer is made.

Now consider a more fully digitized version of the same process, or "e-selection 2.0." A job becomes available and its description is shared with an internal recruiter who scans her own human resources database to identify any individuals in the organization who possess the skills and experience needed to be successful. Then, she uses an automated web scraping tool to extract data from thousands of potential candidates' public social media profiles, identifying individuals who possess the characteristics of interest and may be presently employed elsewhere. She also places a posting for the job on social media and an online job board that distributes the posting across many other job boards, collects resumes from applicants, and uses artificial intelligence to prioritize the individuals most likely to succeed. She selects 50 potential candidates to pursue.

Next, she proactively reaches out to these 50 individuals using chatbot software (i.e., an artificial intelligence-based software program that engages in simple, automated conversations with end users) that emails them a video about the job, and for external candidates, a link to the company's website. Via the chatbot, candidates open the email, review its content, and schedule a phone call with the recruiter to learn more. She tracks which individuals open the email, which view the video and/or website, and which schedule a time to connect with her via phone.

Of the 50 individuals, 20 open the email, 15 schedule a phone call, and 10 express interest after the phone call. Those 10 are asked to provide their e-signatures on a waiver that acknowledges their data is being collected to make a selection decision and describing who will see the data and where it will be housed. All 10 agree and are then invited to complete a digital interview, where questions are displayed on a computer screen and they respond via their webcam while their answers are recorded. A computer program using artificial intelligence scores the interview responses based on language, tone of voice, and facial expression, and determines that 5 of the 10 individuals should advance. Each completes a 15-minute, mobile-friendly assessment including a brief simulation of the job and measures of personality and cognitive ability. The assessment is a computerized adaptive test that uses highly sophisticated algorithms to determine each individual's level of cognitive ability and personality traits. It contains gamified elements, making it a fun and engaging experience for the candidates. Combining the results of these assessments indicates three of the five are a better fit for the role than the others. Those three are interviewed by phone or in person by the hiring manager, mostly as a formality, and a selection decision is made.

Benefits and Challenges of e-Selection 2.0

While not much research exists yet on the benefits of e-selection 2.0, there are a few key differences that have the potential to yield more positive outcomes:
- Despite the number of steps involved in the process, recruiter time per considered candidate is reduced, considering that e-selection has the potential to access data from thousands of potential candidates at the earliest stages; later in the process, recruiters can spend more time with candidates who have already been vetted in some way and are more likely to be successful.
- Candidates are able to access information about the organization and the job at whatever time is convenient for them – viewing a video, clicking on a website, and/or engaging with a chatbot any time of day or night.
- The introduction of gamified elements and immersive narratives to the job simulation can create a fun and engaging assessment experience (Weidner & Short, 2019).
- Predictive validity may be enhanced by combining multiple methods and sources of data and using artificial intelligence-based scoring techniques to more accurately measure candidate characteristics (Adler, Boyce, & Caputo, 2017).

That said, moving to a completely digitized approach can also present some challenges, including:

- less of a "personal touch" for some of the candidates early in the recruiting fun-nel (e.g., those who submit their resumes via a job board)
- a need to train recruiters and hiring managers on new tools, processes, and ap-proaches – including helping them serve as level one "technical support" for in-dividuals who may have trouble navigating the digital elements of the process
- the introduction of digital processes may require candidates to possess a level of digital fluency beyond what is required for the job
- time and cost associated with maintaining the various elements of the process (e.g., training and retraining artificial intelligence-based scoring algorithms)

Future Research Questions

As with many areas of human resource management being transformed by technol-ogy, additional research is needed to determine whether, how, and to what extent the potential benefits of using an e-selection process arise and are driven by the dif-fering features and components of these processes. For example, at this time, re-search on candidate reactions to some methods (e.g., digital versus live interviews; mobile versus computer-based assessments) suggests that candidates are somewhat less in favor of the e-selection method (e.g., Arthur & Traylor, 2019; Langer, König, & Papathanasiou, 2019), but whether these less favorable reactions outweigh the poten-tial benefits in efficiency or reaching a broader talent pool is unknown. Other critical questions include:

- Do e-selection methods result in bias against protected or vulnerable sub-groups (e.g., racial or ethnic minorities, persons with disabilities, individuals of lower socioeconomic status)?
- What are the legal and privacy implications of adding artificial intelligence (e.g., evaluating an individual's social media profile, automatically scoring a digital interview) to the talent identification process?
- Are these methods readily transferrable and equivalent globally across cultures and languages?

Further Readings

Technology is transforming the way we work, and those organizations who select the best talent will maintain a competitive advantage. E-selection methods are gaining in power and growing in popularity to meet these needs. For additional information on how these changes will impact selection in the future, we encourage the interested reader to explore the past and future work of some leading thinkers on this topic (in alphabetical order by last name): Seymour Adler, Tomás Chamorro-Premuzic, Robert

Guion, Richard Landers, Paul Sackett, and Nancy Tippins. Of particular use are works by Scott, Bartram, and Reynolds (2017) and Farr and Tippins (2017). We also encourage a review of the standards governing the use of assessment and selection methods, which are available in the following publications: *Uniform Guidelines on Employee Selection Procedures* (http://www.uniformguidelines.com/), *Principles for the Validation and Use of Personnel Selection Procedures* (https://www.apa.org/ed/ accreditation/about/policies/personnel-selection-procedures.pdf), *The Standards for Educational and Psychological Testing* (https://www.apa.org/science/programs/ testing/standards), and *The International Test Commission Guidelines* (https://www. intestcom.org/page/5#).

References

Adler, S., Boyce, A. S., & Caputo P. M. (2017). The promise and challenges of internet delivery of employment testing. In J. Scott, D. Bartram, & D. Reynolds (Eds.), *Next Generation Technology-Enhanced Assessment: Global Perspectives on Occupational and Workplace Testing*. New York: Cambridge University Press.

Arthur, W., & Traylor, Z. (2019). Mobile assessment in personnel testing. In R. N. Landers (Ed.), *The Cambridge Handbook of Technology and Employee Behavior* (pp. 179–207). Cambridge, UK: Cambridge University Press.

Army Alpha and Army Beta. (n.d.) Retrieved June 25, 2019, from https://psychology.iresearchnet. com/industrial-organizational-psychology/i-o-psychology-history/army-alpha-and-army-beta/).

Elman, B. A. (2009). Civil service examinations. In *Berckshire Encyclopedia of China*. (Vol. 1, pp. 405–410). Great Barrington, Massachusetts: Berkshire Publishing Group.

Farr, J. L., Tippins, N. T. (Eds.). (2017). Handbook of Employee Selection, 2nd Edition. New York, NY: Routledge.

Langer, M., König, C. J., & Papathanasiou, M. (2019). Highly automated job interviews: Acceptance under the influence of stakes. *International Journal of Selection and Assessment*, *27*(3), 217–234.

ManpowerGroup (2018). *Skills Revolution 2.0*. ManpowerGroup.

ManpowerGroup (2018). *Solving the Talent Shortage: Build, Buy, Borrow and Bridge*. ManpowerGroup.

Miller, L. J., & Lu, W. (2018, August 20). Gen Z Is Set to Outnumber Millennials Within a Year. *Bloomberg*, p. 1. Retrieved from https://www.bloomberg.com/news/articles/2018-08-20/gen-z-to-outnumber-millennials-within-a-year-demographic-trends

Schmidt, F. L., & Hunter, J. E. (1998). The validity and utility of selection methods in personnel psychology: Practical and theoretical implications of 85 years of research findings. *Psychological Bulletin*, *124*(2), 262–274.

Scott, J. C., Bartram, D., & Reynolds, D. H. (Eds.). (2017). *Next Generation Technology-Enhanced Assessment Global Perspectives on Occupational and Workplace Testing*. Cambridge, UK: Cambridge University Press.

Weidner, N., & Short, E. (2019). Playing with a purpose: The role of games and gamification in modern assessment practices. In R. N. Landers (Ed.), *The Cambridge Handbook of Technology and Employee Behavior* (pp. 151–178). Cambridge, UK: Cambridge University Press.

World Health Organization. (n.d.). *Global Health Observatory Data*. Retrieved August 2, 2019 from https://www.who.int/gho/mortality_burden_disease/life_tables/situation_trends_text/en/

Stefan V. Dumlao, Anjelica M. Mendoza, and Stephanie C. Payne

Performance Monitoring in the 21st Century

It becomes increasingly difficult for supervisors to directly observe their subordinates' performance as organisations grow in size, become more geographically dispersed, or require work that does not lend itself to direct observation (e.g., service calls, knowledge work). In order to overcome this barrier, organisations regularly monitor employees' performance electronically. Electronic performance monitoring (EPM) is the utilisation of electronic instruments or devices to collect, store, analyse, and report the performance of an individual or a group (Nebeker & Tatum, 1993). EPM is a method of monitoring employees, and encompasses a broad range of organisational activities. The complexity of EPM can vary. For example, in order to track employees' arrival and departure from the workplace one might use something as simple as a time clock, or something as complex as a series of wireless hubs that detect when an employees' badge is in close proximity.

EPM has clear benefits for organisations; it facilitates the documentation of performance, and the delivery of performance feedback. That being said, prior to implementation, it is important to consider employees' attitudes and reactions towards being monitored. This entry provides a brief overview of EPM research, emerging trends in EPM, practical considerations surrounding the utilisation of EPM technologies, best practices for implementing EPM, and closes with future directions for EPM research.

A Look Back at EPM Research

Research on the antecedents and outcomes of EPM began in the mid-1980's, when societal consciousness of monitoring began to form and it started to become feasible for organisations to deploy EPM technologies (Alge & Hansen, 2014). In 1987, the U.S. Congress Office of Technology Assessment published a report on the impact of organisational computer and telephonic surveillance on employees, which likely contributed to an increase in scholarly interest into the 1990s. Early research focused on the mere presence of EPM, rather than the differential impact that the type, features, or characteristics of the monitoring had on outcomes (Ravid, Tomczak, White, & Behrend, 2020). Since then, EPM has grown to include the monitoring of electronic communications (e.g., text messages, e-mails), internet behaviour (e.g., internet surfing on the job, social media usage on and off the job), location, and more recently, physiological activity and health.

https://doi.org/10.1515/9783110633702-028

Investigations have focused on both the antecedents and outcomes of EPM, though more heavily on the latter category. Chen and Ross (2005) proposed a research framework for the study of antecedents of EPM, focusing on managerial trust in employees and organisational culture. Stanton (2000) proposed a research framework for investigating outcomes and employee reactions to EPM. Documented negative outcomes of EPM include increased individual job stress (Aiello & Kolb, 1995), turnover intentions (Heavey, Holwerda, & Hausknecht, 2013), perceived invasion of privacy, and decreased perceptions of procedural justice (McNall & Roch, 2007), job satisfaction, and organisational commitment (Wells, Moorman, & Werner, 2007). It should be noted that research rarely keeps pace with technological innovations, so these findings may need to be revisited or clarified as new technology emerges.

Emerging Trends in EPM

As computers have grown more interconnected, there has been an exponential rise in the number of different sources organisations can use to monitor and collect employee performance data. The result is that organisations have rich, but potentially fragmented stories about their operations. Consequently, one emerging trend in EPM is the utilisation of workforce analytics tools and techniques to synthesise these data. The integration and synthesis of data can be facilitated by artificial intelligence, which can aid in the automatized coding of non-numeric data, such as behaviours recorded by video monitoring.

Another emerging area of EPM is monitoring via sensors worn by employees as an accessory or as part of their work equipment. Over the past decade, the variety and complexity of wearable accessories has grown substantially, and wearable EPM programmes are gaining popularity (Cascio & Montealegre, 2016). Wearable sensors are capable of gathering physiological data about the wearer, capturing data about the immediate environment, and communicating with nearby connected devices. These data, in turn, can be used to document information such as the number of face-to-face interactions between employees (e.g., Olguín et al., 2009), location (e.g., Choi, Hwang, & Lee, 2017), and safe behaviours (e.g., Gatti & Migliaccio, 2012). Organisations also use wearables to encourage healthy behaviours, either by providing employees with wearable devices to wear outside of work, or by incentivising a "bring-your-own-wearable" programme. Researchers interested in utilising wearables to monitor participants may find Chaffin et al. (2017) and Matusik et al. (2019) helpful when designing studies. Compared to earlier EPM methods, wearable sensors capture a greater volume and variety of data across a number of different contexts; as a result, some wearable EPM programmes may pose unique legal and ethical challenges.

Considerations for Utilising EPM in Practice

Electronic tools to support the observation and assessment of performance have been customised to serve the needs of many industries. Generally, EPM has been found to increase performance when appropriately implemented (Bhave, 2014). Within manufacturing, EPM allows the organisation to assess the efficiency of its procedures and identify where performance can be improved. EPM can also be used to measure the transfer of training by tracking post-training performance. Wearable technologies also show promise for monitoring safe behaviours in high-risk occupations like construction. Behrend et al. (2019) summarise a host of job and individual characteristics that may create circumstances which lead to positive (and negative) EPM outcomes. It is likely that the adoption and impact of EPM will grow in tandem with the increasing capabilities of monitoring technologies.

In addition to considering the benefits of EPM, organisations should also consider the legal rights and protections afforded to their employees. The relevant laws and regulations may vary by state, nation, or region. In Australia, workplace surveillance regulations vary by state, and in the United States a handful of states have imposed method-specific (e.g., e-mail) and area-specific (e.g., changing rooms) restrictions on workplace monitoring. Under U.S. federal law, employers generally have the right to monitor their employees for a legitimate business purpose without notifying them, as long as employees do not have a reasonable expectation of privacy (Sprague, 2007). Other regions and nations impose more restrictive limitations. For example, the General Data Protection Regulation (GDPR) protects individuals in the European Union and the European Economic Area from unauthorised collection of personal data. Under the GDPR, organisations are legally obligated to obtain consent from data subjects (e.g., employees, customers) and must comply with other regulatory requirements. Kidwell and Sprague (2009) offer a foundation in legal concerns surrounding EPM globally, with the caveat that relevant laws may have changed since its publication (e.g., GDPR became enforceable in 2018), and more recently Sprague (2018) reviewed laws in the United States relevant to workplace monitoring.

Beyond the legal permissibility of EPM, organisations should also consider the ethical responsibility they have to their employees. Alder (1998) notes it is not EPM itself that is ethical or unethical, but rather how it is used. Laptop computers and smartphones have facilitated flexible work arrangements, but have also obscured the boundary between work and nonwork. Wearable monitors may further blur this boundary. Employees' ethical views can significantly influence how they react to being monitored, resulting in different levels of trust in the organisation and how fair they judge the monitoring to be (Alder, Schminke, Noel, & Kuenzi, 2008). West and Bowman (2016) provide a brief summary of ethical considerations both in opposition to and in favour of the implementation of EPM. Ethical considerations are also inextricably linked to business decisions. The unethical use of an EPM programme can lead to a host of negative outcomes for employees, exposing the organisation to unnecessary reputational risk, if not legal or economic risk, all of which can have a negative impact on the business overall. Both legally and ethically speaking, organisations should be fair and reasonable when applying EPM, and avoid violating their employees' rights.

Best Practices for Implementing EPM

The outcomes of an EPM programme are linked to how it is implemented. Based on a review of empirical evidence and theory, Tomczack et al. (2018) proposed five best practice recommendations for the implementation of EPM technologies in organisations. Organisations that wish to appropriately utilise EPM should (1) be transparent with employees about EPM use, (2) be aware of employee reactions to being monitored, (3) use EPM for learning and development rather than deterrence (i.e., ensure that EPM data is not used punitively), (4) restrict EPM to only work-related behaviours, and (5) consider organisational makeup when implementing an EPM system (i.e., communication and utilisation of EPM is dependent on the characteristics of the job and the structure of the organisation). In addition to these, an organisation might also be well-advised to carefully consider what to monitor in order to achieve the desired outcome (e.g., increased performance). As with direct monitoring, there are different implications for whether a target behaviour or output is monitored, and whether the monitoring emphasises the *quantity* or the *quality* of performance. Following these recommendations may mitigate negative outcomes associated with monitoring.

Future Directions

The extant EPM literature has focused primarily on the outcomes of EPM or specific antecedents, such as job characteristics (Alge & Hansen, 2014; Behrend et al., 2019). Very little research has focused on the impetus of managers' decision to implement EPM, or the impact that managers' attitudes have on the design of an EPM programme. Do managers who have less trust in their employees tend to communicate the purpose of a programme more poorly? What is the relative importance of the antecedents of EPM implementation (e.g., organisational context vs. monitoring characteristics) with different outcomes? When EPM is used both punitively and developmentally (e.g., police body cameras), what drives employees' reactions? Despite three decades of research, there is still much to be learned about EPM, due in no small part to the continued innovation of monitoring technologies. Additional background readings are listed below, and those interested in further discussion of future research directions are referred to Ravid et al. (2020).

Further Readings

Alge, B. J., & Hansen, S. D. (2014). Workplace monitoring and surveillance research since 1984: A review and agenda. In M. D. Coovert & L. F. Thompson (Eds.), *The psychology of workplace technology* (pp. 209–237). New York, NY: Routledge.

Kidwell, R. E., & Sprague, R. (2009). Electronic surveillance in the global workplace: Laws, ethics, research and practice. *New Technology, Work and Employment, 24*, 194–208. doi: 10.1111/j.1468-005X.2009.00228.x

Stanton, J. M. (2000). Reactions to employee performance monitoring: Framework, review, and research directions. *Human Performance, 13*, 85–113. doi: 10.1207/S15327043HUP1301_4

References

Aiello, J. R., & Kolb, K. J. (1995). Electronic performance monitoring: A risk factor for workplace stress. In S. L. Sauter, & L. R. Murphy, (Eds.) *Organizational risk factors for job stress* (pp. 163–179). Washington, DC, US: American Psychological Association.

Alder, G. S. (1998). Ethical issues in electronic performance monitoring: A consideration of deontological and teleological perspectives. *Journal of Business Ethics, 17*, 729–743. doi: 10.1023/A:1005776615072

Alder, G. S., Schminke, M., Noel, T. W., & Kuenzi, M. (2008). Employee reactions to internet monitoring: The moderating role of ethical orientation. *Journal of Business Ethics, 80*, 481–498. doi: 10.1007/s10551-007-9432-2

Alge, B. J., & Hansen, S. D. (2014). Workplace monitoring and surveillance research since 1984: A review and agenda. In M. D. Coovert & L. F. Thompson (Eds.), *The psychology of workplace technology* (pp. 209–237). New York, NY: Routledge.

Behrend, T. S., White, J., & Ravid, D. (2019). Moderating effects of person and job characteristics on digital monitoring outcomes. *Current Opinion in Psychology*. Advance online publication. doi: 10.1016/j.copsyc.2019.07.042

Bhave, D. P. (2014). The invisible eye? Electronic performance monitoring and employee job performance. *Personnel Psychology, 67*, 605–635. doi:10.1111/peps.12046

Cascio, W. F., & Montealegre, R. (2016). How technology is changing work and organizations. *Annual Review of Organizational Psychology and Organizational Behavior, 3*, 349–375. doi: 10.1146/annurev-orgpsych-041015-062352

Chaffin, D., Heidl, R., Hollenbeck, J. R., Howe, M., Yu, A., Voorhees, C., & Calantone, R. (2017). The promise and perils of wearable sensors in organizational research. *Organizational Research Methods, 20*, 3–31. doi: 10.1177/1094428115617004

Chen, J. V., & Ross, W. H. (2005). The managerial decision to implement electronic surveillance at work: A research framework. *International Journal of Organizational Analysis, 13*, 244–268. doi: 10.1108/eb029006

Choi, B., Hwang, S., & Lee, S. (2017). What drives construction workers' acceptance of wearable technologies in the workplace?: Indoor localization and wearable health devices for occupational safety and health. *Automation in Construction, 84*, 31–41. doi: 10.1016/j.autcon.2017.08.005

Gatti, U. C., Migliaccio, G. C., Bogus, S. M., & Schneider, S. (2014). An exploratory study of the relationship between construction workforce physical strain and task level productivity. *Construction Management and Economics, 32*, 548–564. doi: 10.1080/01446193.2013.831463

Heavey, A. L., Holwerda, J. A., & Hausknecht, J. P. (2013). Causes and consequences of collective turnover: A meta-analytic review. *Journal of Applied Psychology, 98*, 412–453. doi: 10.1037/a0032380

Kidwell, R. E., & Sprague, R. (2009). Electronic surveillance in the global workplace: Laws, ethics, research and practice. *New Technology, Work and Employment, 24*, 194–208. doi: 10.1111/j.1468-005X.2009.00228.x

Matusik, J. G., Heidl, R., Hollenbeck, J. R., Yu, A., Lee, H. W., & Howe, M. (2019). Wearable bluetooth sensors for capturing relational variables and temporal variability in relationships: A construct validation study. *Journal of Applied Psychology, 104*, 357–387. doi: 10.1037/apl0000334

McNall, L. A., & Roch, S. G. (2007). Effects of electronic monitoring types on perceptions of procedural justice, interpersonal justice, and privacy. *Journal of Applied Social Psychology, 37*, 658–682. doi: 10.1111/j.1559-1816.2007.00179.x

Nebeker, D. M., & Tatum, B. C. (1993). The effects of computer monitoring, standards, and rewards on work performance, job satisfaction, and stress. *Journal of Applied Social Psychology, 23*(7), 508–536. doi: 10.1111/j.1559-1816.1993.tb01101.x

Olguín, D. O., Waber, B. N., Taemie, K., Mohan, A., Ara, K., & Pentland, A. (2009). Sensible organizations: Technology and methodology for automatically measuring organizational behavior. *IEEE Transactions on Systems, Man & Cybernetics: Part B, 39*(1), 43–55. doi: 10.1109/TSMCB.2008.2006638

Ravid, D., Tomczak, D. L., White, J., & Behrend, T. S. (2020). EPM 20/20: A review, framework, and research agenda for electronic performance monitoring. *Journal of Management, 46*, 100–126. doi: 10.1177/0149206319869435

Sprague, R. (2007). From Taylorism to the Omnipticon: Expanding employee surveillance beyond the workplace. *John Marshall Journal of Computer & Information Law, 25*, 1–36.

Sprague, R. (2018). Survey of (mostly outdated and often ineffective) laws affecting work-related monitoring. *Chicago-Kent Law Review, 93*, 221–256.

Stanton, J. M. (2000). Reactions to employee performance monitoring: Framework, review, and research directions. *Human Performance, 13*, 85–113. doi: 10.1207/S15327043HUP1301_4

Tomczak, D. L., Lanzo, L. A., & Aguinis, H. (2018). Evidence-based recommendations for employee performance monitoring. *Business Horizons, 61*, 251–259. doi: 10.1016/j.bushor.2017.11.006

U.S. Congress, Office of Technology Assessment. (1987). *The electronic supervisor: New technology, new tensions* (OTACIT-333). Washington, DC: U.S. Government Printing Office.

Wells, D. L., Moorman, R. H., & Werner, J. M. (2007). The impact of the perceived purpose of electronic performance monitoring on an array of attitudinal variables. *Human Resource Development Quarterly, 18*, 121–138. doi: 10.1002/hrdq.1194

West, J. P., & Bowman, J. S. (2016). Electronic surveillance at work: An ethical analysis. *Administration & Society, 48*, 628–651. doi: 10.1177/0095399714556502

Michael E. Wasserman and Sandra L. Fisher

e-Learning

E-learning is a broad term covering the use of digital tools and resources to deliver training and development to learners. We apply the term e-learning to include more specific applications and terms such as web-based instruction (WBI) and technology-based training. E-learning has substantially shifted the practice of training in organisations. Training is now accessible anytime, anywhere and learner expectations for flexibility and training quality have increased. In this entry we trace key developments and outline future directions in e-learning research and practice. We first discuss approaches to training design and development. We then examine individual differences related to learning processes and outcomes. We discuss evidence of training effectiveness related to different training approaches, looking at both short-term learning and training transfer. Finally, we review emerging training technologies, including mobile learning, augmented reality (AR), and virtual reality (VR).

Design and Development

Training designers face many choices about which knowledge and skills to include in training programs and how best to achieve learning goals. The move toward informal technology-mediated knowledge sharing has created a shift toward learner-centered and socially-constructed training design (Kraiger, 2008; Noe, Clarke, & Klein, 2014). E-learning technology facilitates design choices that may enhance learning under certain conditions, by changing four dimensions of the training process: where, who, when, and how training is developed and delivered (see Table 29.1).

One primary choice in e-learning training design is the extent to which learning should be self-directed, or the amount of control provided to the learner. Learner control is defined as "a constellation of both learner and instruction-centric constructs describing a general situation in which learners are given increased discretion over behaviors regarding formal learning events" (Brown, Howardson, & Fisher, 2016, p.268). In e-learning environments, learners can be given control over a range of features, including instructional pace, topic sequence, content, amount of feedback provided, and type of media (Karim & Behrend, 2014; Kraiger & Jerden, 2007; Granger & Levine, 2010; Howardson, Orvis, Fisher & Wasserman, 2016). Research has found that the degree of control learners have over the training environment is generally positively related to learning. However, some learners make suboptimal choices and learn less (Fisher, Howardson, Wasserman, & Orvis, 2017).

https://doi.org/10.1515/9783110633702-029

Table 29.1: Changes in Training Environments due to e-Learning.

Where	Physical location is no longer an access barrier. Users can learn on-the-job, while travelling, from home, or at an alternative workspace such as a coworking space.
Who	Employees at any location may access e-learning. Since phones and tablets have built-in accessibility features (large text, text-to-voice, etc.), inclusion of users that might be limited in terms of classroom learning because of sight, hearing, or mobility differences is facilitated.
When	Training becomes available around the clock and across time zones. Learners can access training when it fits their schedule, rather than when classrooms or trainers are available. Microlearning allows learning in short time spans.
How	E-learning technology, both on the server side (the learning platform) and the user side (smartphones and tablets), opens up additional training methodologies and design elements such as learner control, error-based training and adaptive training. Learners can co-create learning content.

Error-based training and adaptive training are examples of training design elements made easier in e-learning. Simulation techniques allow designers to create error situations that have a positive motivational impact on trainees. Advances in algorithm design and artificial intelligence allow program designs that adapt to user actions and learning trajectories rather than making adjustments at fixed intervals, which increases learning (Brown et al., 2016). The flexibility of e-learning, particularly when using mobile devices, is allowing the design of micro-learning, or learning just a snippet of information or a tiny component of a skill (Pandey, 2016). This type of training often occurs on the job site, so learners can directly access information and skills relevant to the task at hand rather than having to recall knowledge learned in a classroom setting in the past. This further blurs the line between informational and instructional resources (Brown, Charlier, & Pierotti, 2012). Thus, in addition to choices about delivery methods and technologies, e-learning has brought more design choices about which knowledge and skills should be included in formal training and which should be provided through informal on-the-job tools and resources.

Individual Differences

Another important aspect of e-learning is its ability to accommodate individual differences among many learners simultaneously. In fact, the continued shift toward learner-centered training design places a heavier emphasis on individual learner characteristics such as ability, motivation, learning styles, or personality. As instructor control over what happens in the training environment decreases, the impact of individual differences on learning processes and outcomes increases. Many interactions between characteristics have been identified, as well as relationships between design features and learner characteristics (Bell, Tannenbaum, Ford, Noe & Kraiger, 2017; Gully & Chen, 2010). Regarding ability, for example, trainees with greater cognitive ability and prior knowledge generally learn better with more learner control (Brown et al. 2016). Motivation to learn and mastery goal orientation are both associated with positive learning outcomes in e-learning (Brown, 2005, Orvis et al., 2009). There is evidence that if trainees are low in these motivational characteristics, interventions can increase them within the training context enhance learning (Brown et al., 2016).

Researchers have generally concluded that there is little evidence that learning styles (e.g., verbal learners vs. visual learners) significantly impact learning (Pashler, McDaniel, Rohrer & Bjork, 2008). However, Orvis, Russo, Wasserman, & Fisher (2011) found some evidence supporting the effectiveness of matching available e-learning tools to individual learning preferences as reflected by personality traits. Personality can have a direct influence on individual success with e-learning, as demonstrated by findings that conscientious individuals are more successful in programs with high learner control (Bell et al., 2017). Research in this area has also examined preference for learner control as an important individual difference.

Training Effectiveness

Studies on the relative effectiveness of e-learning compared to face-to-face training techniques have generally shown that e-learning can be at least as effective as face-to-face (Sitzmann, Kraiger, Stewart & Wisher, 2006). These results come with the caveat that poorly designed training can exist in any format. Thus, it is critical to examine the features included in any training program rather than focusing on the distinction between face-to-face, blended, or fully online learning (Bell et al., 2017). E-learning has made it easier to gather training evaluation data, whether that is re-action data at the end of training, short term learning, or longer-term learning. Technologies such as virtual reality may make it easier to assess new skills gained from training in a variety of high-fidelity scenarios.

Transfer of training continues to be a concern in the e-learning environment. When using e-learning for compliance-based training with low levels of learner motivation and engagement, associated knowledge transfer might be expected to be quite low. Transfer can be supported through the digital availability of training information and job aids, such as the microlearning tools described above. E-learning technologies offer both advantages and risks of measuring transfer outcomes over time. It becomes easier to reach trainees months after the training program has ended, collecting more within-person data over time to model individual transfer curves (Huang, Ford & Ryan, 2016). Mobile technologies may be used to capture knowledge based outcomes through questionnaires or gather video evidence of skill based outcomes (Wasserman & Fisher, 2017) although there is greater risk with some of these techniques that users are relying on external information sources to complete the assessments, reducing the validity of the assessments. Technology-supported measurement techniques may also be used with face-to-face training programs, creating a new type of blended learning and assessment experience.

Key Technologies

Advances in technology offer new opportunities for designing and managing e-learning, but also threaten to outpace the science of training. Here we address some of the key technologies currently featured in e-learning. Certainly this list is not exhaustive and there are other important technologies being applied in e-learning, but this list features technologies that can be implemented in a variety of learning contexts. Learning management systems (LMS) and mobile technologies are regularly implemented. Augmented reality (AR), virtual reality (VR), artificial intelligence (AI), and machine learning (ML) all are in or about to enter the training mainstream as costs decline while reliability and usability improve.

Learning management systems (LMS): These are web-based portals that organize and track learning progress for each learner. They range from simple open-source tools to complex subscription-based cloud-hosted software-as-a-service (SaaS) solutions. All are designed to automate and simplify the training process for learners and managers. All are only as good as the content that populates them, and depend on an organizational culture that supports training. More advanced features of LMS including AI and ML can generate learning suggestions for users (Borghini et al., 2017), and advanced analytics can generate predictive guidance for managers to evaluate performance potential of individual employees. Features in development include using AI and ML to identify unconscious bias during training assessment (Borghini et al., 2017).

Mobile technologies: Mobile training has become common. But, it is an open question as to whether users who are accessing mobile training are learning effectively. Distractions are more frequent outside a classroom, and a mobile device regularly bombards users with notifications of incoming texts, voicemails, news updates, and social media mentions (Wasserman & Fisher, 2017). The phone or tablet may be effective for specific microlearning, but mobile technologies are unlikely the best tool for a distraction-free environment that supports complex or deep learning. Thus, for training designers, the external environment now matters more. Learners could be engaged in mobile training while in the gym, walking down the street, or when using public transportation. All of these environments have risks and distractions not present in classrooms. The variance in training environments needs to be considered by learners and training managers, both from a learning effectiveness perspective and perhaps even from a learner safety perspective.

Augmented Reality (AR) and Virtual Reality (VR): Augmented reality is where numbers, words, or graphics are made visible on top of a real-time image of the world. This is typically accomplished through the lens of a smartphone or tablet camera, adding a new dimension to mobile learning, or less commonly through the lenses of 'smart glasses' such as those introduced by Google and Snapchat. These applications allow users to augment the live image with important data, offering an opportunity to learn something new. For example, someone learning how to fix a machine could view that machine through the mobile phone camera and the AR system could label the different parts of the machine, listing the repair steps. This type of resource may be better categorized as informational rather than instructional (Brown et al., 2012) if it is used as a job aid rather than a learning tool.

VR is a step beyond AR in complexity. In an immersive VR training environment, the learner wears goggles or sits in a room with no external lighting or stimulus. The learner is then visually and auditorily surrounded by a digitally constructed environment created using 360-degree cameras or built using computer generated imaging. The learner feels as if they are interacting in this created world, rather in the world they physically occupy. Devices may provide haptic feedback (physical vibrations delivered through connected devices) to learners about the accuracy of their movements or decisions. Organizations have successfully used VR-based training tools to teach complex skills with significant decision making components (Bailenson, 2018). VR training can provide high fidelity learning and practice environments for skills that are performed infrequently or under dangerous conditions, such as surgical skills or managing a retail store on the busiest shopping day of the year.

Future Research Questions

Bell et al. (2017) called for training research that focuses on the features and conditions of training. One important condition is the duration of e-learning programs. Training design research should examine how techniques such as micro-learning can lead to effective skill development and transfer. It is currently unclear if micro-learning approaches can help learners develop complex skills that require long periods of instruction and practice. Researchers should examine the extent to which micro-learning instruction can lead to compilation of larger bodies of knowledge or complex skills, and how micro-learning might support retention of material over time.

Second, research should examine the impact of VR technologies on the use of learner control features. With true immersive VR that requires use of specific hardware, training may lose the "anytime, anywhere" features that have been attractive in e-learning. Further, learners with a high desire for control may have negative re-actions to tightly structured VR environments (Howardson et al., 2018). Training designers must balance cost concerns with learner control as they create programs with multiple choice points and learner options.

Finally, we encourage interdisciplinary research on how techniques borrowed from artificial intelligence can help improve key components of the training process. E-learning sits at the intersection of computer engineering, computer science, data analytics, and human resource management – we need to get both researchers and practitioners together if we want to maximize the future benefits of e-learning.

Further Readings

Brown, K.G., Howardson, G., & Fisher, S.L. (2016). Learner control and e-learning: Taking stock and moving forward. *Annual Review of Organizational Psychology and Organizational Behavior* 3(1),267–291.

Noe, R.A., Clarke, A.D.M., & Klein, H.J. (2014). Learning in the twenty-first-century workplace. *The Annual Review of Organizational Psychology and Organizational Behavior, 1,* 245–75.

References

Bailenson, J. (2018). *Experience on Demand: What Virtual Reality Is, How It Works, and What It Can Do.* W. W. Norton & Company.

Bell, B.S., Tannenbaum, S.I., Ford, J.K., Noe, R.A., & Kraiger, K. (2017). 100 years of training and development research: What we know and where we should go. *Journal of Applied Psychology, 102(3),* 305–323.

Borghini, G., Aricò, P., Di Flumeri, G., Sciaraffa, N., Colosimo, A., Herrero, M.T., . . . Babiloni, F. (2017). A New Perspective for the Training Assessment: Machine Learning-Based Neurometric for Augmented User's Evaluation. *Frontiers in Neuroscience, 11,* 325. doi:10.3389/fnins.2017.00325

Brown, K.G. (2005). An examination of the structure and nomological network of trainee reactions: a closer look at" smile sheets". *Journal of Applied Psychology, 90(5),* 991–1001.

Brown, K., Charlier, S., & Pierotti, A. (2012). E-Learning at Work: Contributions of Past Research and Suggestions for the Future. *International Review of Industrial and Organizational Psychology, 27,* 89–114.

Brown, K.G., Howardson, G., & Fisher, S.L. (2016). Learner control and e-learning: Taking stock and moving forward. *Annual Review of Organizational Psychology and Organizational Behavior 3(1),* 267–291.

Fisher, S.L, Howardson, G., Wasserman, M.E, & Orvis, K. (2017). How Do Learners Interact with e-learning? Examining Patterns of Learner Control Behaviors. *AIS Transactions on Human-Computer Interaction, 9(2),* 75–98.

Granger, B. P., & Levine, E. L. (2010). The perplexing role of learner control in e-learning: Will learning and transfer benefit or suffer? *International Journal of Training and Development, 14(3),* 180–197.

Gully, S., & Chen, G. (2010). Individual differences, attribute-treatment interactions, and training outcomes. In S. W. J. Kozlowski & E. Salas (Eds.), SIOP Organizational Frontiers Series. *Learning, Training, and Development in Organizations* (pp. 3–64). New York, NY: Routledge/ Taylor & Francis Group.

Howardson, G., Orvis, K.A., Fisher, S.L. & Wasserman, M.E. (2017). The Psychology of Learner Control in Training: A Multilevel, Interactionist Framework. In KG Brown (Ed.) *The Handbook of Workplace Training and Employee Development*. Cambridge University Press.

Huang, J. L., Ford, J. K., & Ryan, A. M. (2016). Ignored no more: Within-person variability enables better understanding of training transfer. *Personnel Psychology, 70*(3), 557–596.

Karim, M.N. & Behrend, T.S. (2014). Reexamining the nature of learner control: Dimensionality and effects on learning and training reactions. *Journal of Business Psychology, 29(1)*, 87–99.

Kraiger, K. (2008). Transforming our models of learning and development: Web-based instruction as enabler of third-generation instruction. *Industrial and Organizational Psychology, 1(4)*, 454–467.

Kraiger, K., & Jerden, E. (2007). A meta-analytic investigation of learner control: Old findings and new directions. In S. M. Fiore & E. Salas (Eds.), *Toward a science of distributed learning* (pp. 65–90). Washington, DC: American Psychological Association.

Noe, R.A., Clarke, A.D.M., & Klein, H.J. (2014). Learning in the twenty-first-century workplace. *The Annual Review of Organizational Psychology and Organizational Behavior, 1*, 245–75.

Orvis, K., Brusso, R., Wasserman, M.E., & Fisher, S.L. (2011). E-nabled for e-learning? The moderating role of personality in determining the optimal degree of learner control in an e-learning environment. *Human Performance, 24(1)*, 60–78.

Orvis, K. A., Fisher, S. L., & Wasserman, M. E. (2009). Power to the people: Using learner control to improve trainee reactions and learning in web-based instructional environments. *Journal of Applied Psychology, 94*(4), 960.

Pandey, A. (2016 March 28). 10 benefits of micro-learning based training. *e-Learning Industry*. Available at https://elearningindustry.com/10-benefits-microlearning-based-training

Pashler, H., McDaniel, M., Rohrer, D., & Bjork, R. (2008). Learning styles: Concepts and Evidence. *Psychological Science in the Public Interest, 9(3)*, 106–119.

Sitzmann, T., Kraiger, K., Stewart, D., & Wisher, R. (2006). The comparative effectiveness of web-based and classroom instruction: A meta-analysis. *Personnel Psychology, 59*(3), 623–664.

Wasserman, M.E. & Fisher, S.L. (2017). One (Lesson) for the Road? What We Know (and Don't Know) about Mobile Learning. In KG Brown (Ed.) *The Handbook of Workplace Training and Employee Development*. Cambridge University Press.

Anna B. Holm
e-Recruiting

E-recruiting, also referred to as web-based (Parry & Wilson, 2009) or online recruit-ment (Cappelli, 2001), refers to recruitment practices and activities carried out by an organisation, through electronic means (Lee, 2005), for the primary purpose of identifying, attracting (Barber, 1998, p. 5) and influencing the job choices of compe-tent applicants (Ployhart, 2006) in order to fill vacancies effectively and efficiently (Lee, 2005). E-recruitment assumes a number of different forms, including advertis-ing on websites (Heery & Noon, 2001, p. 112; Parry & Tyson, 2008; Thompson, Braddy, & Wuensch, 2008), advertising on internet job boards and internet directo-ries (Borstorff, Marker, & Bennett, 2007), e-recruitment systems for the collection of applications, data management and coordination, also called hiring management systems (Cappelli, 2001), and search engines and online résumé databases for iden-tifying and attracting potential applicants (Lee, 2005). E-recruitment is increasingly used as a means of marketing the organization, and is even integrated into overall marketing and employer-branding campaigns (Cappelli, 2001). In other words, the term is rather broad and refers to different sets of recruitment practices, activities and tools, and is considered an umbrella term covering practically all recruitment-related activities which use, or are supported by, the Internet and related informa-tion and communication technologies (ICTs) (Holm, 2012). From an e-HRM perspec-tive, e-recruitment represents a case of relational e-HRM that supports the basic business process of hiring employees (Ruël, Bondarouk, & Looise, 2004).

Benefits of e-Recruitment

Research on e-recruitment has shown that the shift from paper-based to ICT-enabled recruitment has a number of rational underpinnings. First, e-recruiting permits employers to communicate to a wider group of potential applicants with-out drastically increasing costs (Breaugh & Starke, 2000). Second, e-recruiting is known to reduce administrative burdens in the hiring process, freeing resources for assessment and selection (Singh & Finn, 2003). Third, it is significantly more cost-efficient than a paper-based recruitment process (Maurer & Liu, 2007). Fourth, the technology enables managers to combine recruitment with more stra-tegic tasks, such as employer branding (Cappelli, 2001). Apart from rational con-siderations, employers switch to e-recruitment due to the social and technological pressures of their societies, where most applicants expect recruitment to take place online (Holm, 2014).

https://doi.org/10.1515/9783110633702-030

Research on e-recruiting has so far been dominated by topics including applicants' perception of corporate career websites, e-recruitment system design, e-recruitment source effectiveness, and organisation of e-recruitment. However, researchers have become increasingly interested in the evolving practice of mobile recruitment (m-recruitment) and recruitment through social network sites (SNS), or social media. The most significant of these for the implementation of e-recruitment are corporate career websites, the use of SNS, e-recruitment system design, and data protection.

Corporate Career Websites

Corporate websites are considered to be one of the most important sources of recruitment (CIPD & HAYS, 2017; SHRM, 2016), where employers, beside posting vacancies, also host a job application process through integration with the e-recruitment system. Corporate websites also facilitate rich communication activities related to employer branding (Backhaus & Tikoo, 2004), the most important element of the recruitment process (Lievens, 2007). Moreover, if a corporate website succeeds in providing both accessible and effective information, it can facilitate an appropriate *self-selection* behaviour (Cober, Brown, Keeping, & Levy, 2004), resulting in a better person–organization (PO) or person-job (PJ) fit of new hires (Kristof-Brown, 2000; Pfieffelmann, Wagner, & Libkuman, 2010).

Research has found that successful recruitment requires websites to provide adequate information richness, interactivity, vividness, and aesthetic appeal (Maurer & Liu, 2007). The amount of information that organisations provide about themselves and open positions has been found to correlate positively with the attraction of prospective applicants (Williamson, King, Lepak, & Sarma, 2010). Furthermore, user experience regarding the ease of use and navigability of the website, as well as its aesthetic features (e.g. colour scheme, pictures and animations), have a positive impact on the engagement of applicants (Allen, Mahto, & Otondo, 2007). If well-designed, these features may also signal the innovativeness of the organization and thus play a role in attracting applicants, perhaps even matching them with the organization (Cober, Brown, Levy, Cober, & Keeping, 2003). Moreover, positive perceptions of prospective employers are strong predictors of ultimate job choice and the intention to accept a job (Chapman, Uggerslev, Carroll, Piasentin, & Jones, 2005). Thus, employers need to constantly promote their career websites (Allen et al., 2007), which must be viewed as an integrated part of recruitment practices, in order to ensure their attraction to and engagement of future jobseekers (Chapman et al., 2005).

Advertising vacancies on paid job boards, such as Monster and CareerBuilder, as well as free job boards, can be both a way to point jobseekers to the career website and a good recruitment source. In the case of searching for applicants with specific educational training or for specific industries, specialized job boards can be a more effective option, however (Holm & Haahr, 2019, pp. 177–178). For example, Allretailjobs, which provides job listings for the retail industry in the USA, boasts a résumé database of over 1.5 million retail résumés. However, as with corporate websites, job boards are primarily effective at reaching active jobseekers (Phillips & Gully, 2015, p. 179).

Social Network Sites

Social Network Sites (SNS), also referred to as social media, are web-based services where people can create a profile and create and share connections to view each other's profiles and updates (Melanthiou, Pavlou, & Constantinou, 2015). The most popular SNS for employee recruitment in the western hemisphere are LinkedIn, Facebook, Twitter, Instagram and Snapchat, which increasingly serve as an arena for interactions between individuals and employers (Roth, Bobko, Van Iddekinge, & Thatcher, 2013). SNS are widely used as a recruitment source, since they provide easy access to a large pool of both active and passive jobseekers. Furthermore, recruiters systematically trawl SNS for information, to analyse their data, match SNS users with vacancies, and select and contact potential candidates (Brown & Vaughn, 2011; Van Iddekinge, Lanivich, Roth, & Junco, 2016). SNS are also actively employed as a communication channel for corporate employer-branding efforts. In addition, organizations also encourage existing employees to act as employer-brand ambassadors and job referrers on SNS. When employees help fill vacant positions, they are often rewarded. Notwithstanding, it can be a challenge for employers to motivate employees to like and share company postings (Cervellon & Lirio, 2017).

SNS provide quick access to a large amount of unfiltered information on candidates, which is increasingly being used for online screening, or *cybervetting* (Berkelaar & Buzzanell, 2014). By gaining access to non-work-related information, employers can potentially gain insights into an applicant's identity (Berkelaar & Buzzanell, 2014), personality (Schroeder & Cavanaugh, 2018), and activities, including drug or alcohol use. Although organizations assume that cybervetting can reveal an individual's "true" identity (Jeske & Shultz, 2016), the information on SNS is often inaccurate, outdated and untrustworthy, and does not necessarily reflect an individual's professional behaviour (Slovensky & Ross, 2012). Moreover, screening candidates on SNS invades people's privacy and can reveal sensitive information, such as sexual orientation, race, political views, and religious beliefs, and with it the potential for discrimination. The fact is, however, that recruiters continue to intensify their use of cybervetting (Schroeder & Cavanaugh, 2018), while individuals increasingly want to distinguish between professional and private online domains (Jeske & Shultz, 2016).

SNS technology is constantly evolving and is increasingly integrated with third-party software providers and e-recruitment systems, offering diverse services to candidates, organizations and recruitment agencies. Consequently, SNS have become new digital platforms where employers engage with users for recruiting, searching and screening potential employees (Brown & Vaughn, 2011).

e-Recruitment / Applicant Tracking Systems

E-recruitment systems, also often referred to as Applicant Tracking Systems (ATS), have become a standard tool for managing the entire hiring process, from advertising vacancies to making a hiring decision. Most e-recruitment systems offer integration with external recruitment sources, such as job boards and social network sites (SNS), and even pre-screen applicants. The systems are typically offered online as Software-as-a-Service (SaaS), or as part of a wider Enterprise Resource Planning (ERP) system. In some cases, e-recruitment systems are enhanced with technology to evaluate applicants on pre-defined criteria, such as education, job experience, loyalty to employers, and personality, based on their résumés and their profiles on SNS and other sites used for data mining. (For additional information see the entry "Applicant Tracking System".)

Data Protection in e-Recruitment

In a digitized recruitment process, organizations process personal data when they collect, store or delete it. In the European Union, employers must comply with the General Data Protection Regulation (GDPR), which came into force on May 25, 2018 (European Commission, 2016). This states that 'personal data' means any information relating to an identified or identifiable natural person, i.e. 'data subject'. However, the GDPR also covers processing activities outside the European Union when the personal data of data subjects derive from the EU. The GDPR also has specific rules for the transfer of personal data outside the EU, which has direct implications for moving data to or from an EU-based system, including when the data just passes through a server in an EU member state.

Article 5 of the GDPR states that seven principles must be observed whenever personal data is processed: 1) lawfulness, fairness and transparency, 2) purpose limitation, 3) data minimization, 4) accuracy, 5) storage limitation, 6) integrity and confidentiality, and 7) accountability (European Commission, 2016). According to these principles, recruitment processes will continuously need to consider why, how much, and how long personal data is needed. They will also have to consider whether unsolicited applications can be received, shared, and stored in regular email inboxes; what applicants must be informed about when submitting applications; whether their systems are capable of deleting personal data; what to do once applicants demand that their personal data is deleted; and how to assure that every employee knows when and how to ensure the proper deletion of personal data. Organizations must be able to demonstrate compliance with the overriding principles of GDPR. If recruitment platforms, screening software, etc. process personal data in a way that contravenes the GDPR, then the organization concerned might be subject to substantial fines.

Future Research Questions

Research in e-recruitment has been scarce in recent years, mainly due to the fact that e-recruitment has become an umbrella term for a wide range of technology-supported recruitment practices. Nonetheless, future research contributions can still address questions related to e-recruitment process efficiency and effectiveness for hiring organisations. For example, more studies are needed to assess the quantity vs. quality of information for hiring decisions. The current tendency is to acquire as much information as possible about applicants to establish a person-environment fit with the use of data analytics, data mining and even artificial intelligence. However, this approach often leads to collecting sensitive data in violation of national laws and regulations. Moreover, additional information collected without candidates' consent might have little value for assessment outcomes, and even damage organisational reputation.

Another line of research can investigate how applicants' perceptions of e-recruitment and employers are evolving depending on the technological complexity of recruitment tools. The balancing act for recruiters is to make an impression of a modern, technologically advanced organisation, yet to provide a personalised experience to each potential candidate. In this context, e-recruitment processes and tools need to approximate a human approach and permit a high degree of customization for each category of applicants. Thus, scholars can investigate the use, the degree and effects of human-centred technologies on recruitment outcomes.

Further Reading

Cappelli, P. (2001). Making the most of on-line recruiting. *Harvard Business Review, 79*(3), 139–146.
Holm, A. B. (2012). E-recruitment: Towards an ubiquitous recruitment process and candidate relationship management. *Zeitschrift fuer Personalforschung, 26*(3), 241–259.
Williamson, I. O., King, J. E., Lepak, D., & Sarma, A. (2010). Firm reputation, recruitment web sites, and attracting applicants. *Human Resource Management, 49*(4), 669–687.

References

Allen, D. G., Mahto, R. V., & Otondo, R. F. (2007). Web-based recruitment: Effects of information, organizational brand, and attitudes toward a web site on applicant attraction. *Journal of Applied Psychology, 92*(6), 1696–1708.

Backhaus, K., & Tikoo, S. (2004). Conceptualizing and researching employer branding. *Career Development International, 9*(5), 501–517.

Barber, A. E. (1998). *Recruiting Employees*. Thousand Oaks, CA: SAGE Publications.

Berkelaar, B. L., & Buzzanell, P. M. (2014). Cybervetting, person–environment fit, and personnel selection: Employers' surveillance and sensemaking of job applicants' online information. *Journal of Applied Communication Research, 42*(4), 456–476.

Borstorff, P. C., Marker, M. B., & Bennett, D. S. (2007). Online recruitment: Attitudes and behaviours of job seekers. *Journal of Strategic E-commerce, 5*(1&2), 1–23.

Breaugh, J. A., & Starke, M. (2000). Research on employee recruitment: So many studies, so many remaining questions. *Journal of Management, 26*(3), 405–434.

Brown, V. R., & Vaughn, E. D. (2011). The writing on the (Facebook) wall: The use of social networking sites in hiring decisions. *Journal of Business and Psychology, 26*(2), 219–225.

Cappelli, P. (2001). Making the most of on-line recruiting. *Harvard Business Review, 79*(3), 139–146.

Cervellon, M., & Lirio, P. (2017). When employees don't 'like' their employers on social media. *MIT Sloan Management Review, 58*(2), 63–70.

Chapman, D. S., Uggerslev, K. L., Carroll, S. A., Piasentin, K. A., & Jones, D. A. (2005). Applicant attraction to organizations and job choice: A meta-analytic review of the correlates of recruiting outcomes. *Journal of Applied Psychology, 90*(5), 928–944.

CIPD, & HAYS. (2017). *Resourcing and Talent Planning: Survey Report 2017*. Retrieved from London, UK: https://www.cipd.co.uk/Images/resourcing-talent-planning_2017_tcm18-23747.pdf

Cober, R. T., Brown, D. J., Keeping, L. M., & Levy, P. E. (2004). Recrutment on the net: How do organizational web sites characteristics influence applicant attraction? *Journal of Management, 30*(5), 23.

Cober, R. T., Brown, D. J., Levy, P. E., Cober, A. B., & Keeping, L. M. (2003). Organizational web sites: Website content and style as determinants of organizational attraction. *International Journal of Selection and Assessment, 11*(2/3), 158–169.

Heery, E., & Noon, M. (2001). E-recruitment. In *Dictionary of Human Resource Management* (pp. 112). Oxford, UK: Oxford University Press.

Holm, A. B. (2012). E-recruitment: The move towards a virtually organized recruitment process. In S. de Juana-Espinosa, J. A. Fernandez-Sanchez, E. Manresa-Marhuenda, & J. Valdes-Conca (Eds.), *Human Resource Management in the Digital Economy: Creating Synergy Between Competency Models and Information* (pp. 80–95). Hershey, PA: IGI Global.

Holm, A. B. (2014). Institutional context and e-recruitment practices of Danish organizations. *Employee Relations, 36*(4), 432–455.

Holm, A. B., & Haahr, L. (2019). E-recruitment and Selection. In M. Thite (Ed.), *e-HRM: Digital Approaches, Directions & Applications* (pp. 172–195). London and New York: Routledge.

Jeske, D., & Shultz, K. S. (2016). Using social media content for screening in recruitment and selection: Pros and cons. *Work, Employment and Society, 30*(3), 535–546.

Kristof-Brown, A. L. (2000). Perceived applicant fit: Distinguishing between recruiters' perceptions of person-job and person-organization fit. *Personnel Psychology, 53*, 643–671.

Lee, I. (2005). The evolution of e-recruiting: A content analysis of fortune 100 career web sites. *Journal of Electronic Commerce in Organizations, 3*(3), 57–68.

Lievens, F. (2007). Employer branding in the Belgian Army: The importance of instrumental and symbolic beliefs for potential applicants, actual applicants, and military employees. *Human Resource Management, 46*(1), 51–69.

Maurer, S. D., & Liu, Y. (2007). Developing effective e-recruiting websites: Insights for managers from marketers. *Business Horizons, 50*(4), 305–314.

Melanthiou, Y., Pavlou, F., & Constantinou, E. (2015). The use of social network sites as an e-recruitment tool. *Journal of Transnational Management, 20*(1), 31–49.

Parry, E., & Tyson, S. (2008). An analysis of the use and success of online recruitment methods in the UK. *Human Resource Management Journal, 18*(3), 257–274.

Parry, E., & Wilson, H. (2009). Factors influencing the adoption of online recruitment. *Personnel Review, 38*(6), 655–673.

Pfieffelmann, B., Wagner, S. H., & Libkuman, T. (2010). Recruiting on corporate web sites: Perceptions of fit and attraction. *International Journal of Selection and Assessment, 18*(1), 40–47.

Phillips, J. M., & Gully, S. M. (2015). *Strategic Staffing, Global Edition*. Harlow, UK: Pearson Education Limited.

Ployhart, R. E. (2006). Staffing in the 21st century: New challenges and strategic opportunities. *Journal of Management, 32*, 868–897.

Regulation (EU) 2016/679 of The European Parliament and The Council on the protection of natural persons with regard to the processing of personal data and on the free movement of such data, and repealing Directive 95/46/EC (General Data Protection Regulation), 59 C.F.R. (2016).

Roth, P., L., Bobko, P., Van Iddekinge, C., H., & Thatcher, J., B. (2013). Social media in employee-selection-related decisions: A research agenda for uncharted territory. *Journal of Management, 42*(1), 269–298.

Ruël, H., Bondarouk, T., & Looise, J. K. (2004). E-HRM: innovation or irritation. An explorative empirical study in five large companies on web-based HRM. *Management Review, 15*(3), 364–380.

Schroeder, A. N., & Cavanaugh, J. M. (2018). Fake it 'til you make it: Examining faking ability on social media pages. *Computers in Human Behavior, 84*, 29–35.

SHRM. (2016). *Talent Acquisition: Recruitment. Key Findings*. Retrieved from https://www.shrm.org/hr-today/trends-and-forecasting/research-and-surveys/Documents/Talent-Acquisition-Recruitment.pdf

Singh, P., & Finn, D. (2003). The effects of information technology on recruitment. *Journal of Labor Research, 24*(3), 395–408.

Slovensky, R., & Ross, W. H. (2012). Should human resource managers use social media to screen job applicants? Managerial and legal issues in the USA. *info, 14*(1), 55–69.

Thompson, L. F., Braddy, P. W., & Wuensch, K. L. (2008). E-recruitment and the benefits of organizational web appeal. *Computers in Human Behavior, 24*(5), 2384–2398.

Van Iddekinge, C. H., Lanivich, S. E., Roth, P. L., & Junco, E. (2016). Social media for selection? Validity and adverse impact potential of a facebook-based assessment. *Journal of Management, 42*(7), 1811–1835.

Williamson, I. O., King, J. E., Lepak, D., & Sarma, A. (2010). Firm reputation, recruitment web sites, and attracting applicants. *Human Resource Management, 49*(4), 669–687.

Stephanie C. Payne and Anjelica M. Mendoza
e-Performance Management

Electronic performance management (e-PM) is the application of information technology to the evaluation of employee performance. At the core of e-PM is the continuous measurement and development of the performance of individuals and teams to facilitate alignment with the organisation's strategic goals for performance management (PM; Aguinis, 2013). PM systems include setting performance expectations, observing performance, integrating performance-related information, evaluating employees relative to expectations over time, providing informal and formal feedback, and coaching employees for improvement (Schleicher et al., 2018). The adoption of these systems has flourished and e-PM is one of the most prevalent types of talent management applications in electronic human resource management (eHRM). Indeed, in a survey of a diverse sample of 1,636 organisations, 81% reported that they have adopted or plan to adopt e-PM systems (Sierra-Cedar, 2018). This high rate of adoption is further substantiated by the 57% of organisations that reported plans to increase their spending on e-PM systems within the next twelve months (Sierra-Cedar, 2018). The e-PM market has grown exponentially in both providers and capabilities to meet the rising demand. This entry provides a brief review of the available e-PM research, e-PM's promised capabilities and limitations, unanswered research questions, and best practices for organisations seeking to implement an e-PM system.

e-PM's Promise and Capabilities

The development of and transition to e-PM has taken place during a time where there have been a growing number of calls to abolish traditional (paper & pencil) performance appraisal (PA) ratings (Adler et al., 2016). A PA is typically characterized as an annual or biannual evaluation in which the supervisor delivers feedback about employee performance by generating ratings on a standardised form. The supervisor and employee review the numerical ratings and the employee signs the form to acknowledge the supervisor's assessment of their performance. The form is then placed in the employee's personnel file.

Payne, Mendoza, and Horner (2018) propose that e-PM technology enhancements influence the PM process in the following five ways. e-PM (a) automates, (b) documents, (c) integrates, (d) structures, and (e) makes the evaluation process more accessible. Briefly, within an e-PM system, communication, data analyses, and reporting tasks can be automated reducing the amount of time and effort devoted to these tasks (Krauss & Snyder, 2009; Pulakos, 2004). e-PM systems also serve as repositories of data concerning various PM-related processes and outcomes; thus, to a certain extent

https://doi.org/10.1515/9783110633702-031

e-PM systems document, store, and archive an extensive amount of performance-related data (Farr et al., 2013). Since e-PM systems are often integrated into a broader e-HRM system and some interface with other systems (e.g., performance monitoring), data from these systems can potentially populate directly into the e-PM system. e-PM systems impose structure on the process which should be customised to how managers within the organisation have decided the various related procedures should be implemented. The structure also likely facilitates standardisation of the process within the organisation. Finally, e-PM systems make it easy to access performance-related data and to conduct PM-related tasks. In fact, they are likely to present the data in aesthetically pleasing charts and graphs.

Krauss and Snyder (2009) identified a number of elements that can be automated and ways that technology can potentially enhance the PM process by making it less labour-intensive for the supervisor. Many of these enhancements are operational or procedural. For example, the e-PM system can be programmed to send supervisors reminders to generate ratings and conduct feedback sessions and alert others when these tasks are not completed in a timely fashion. Payne et al. (2018) propose that e-PM technology enhancements (e.g., automation) lead to immediate outcomes concerning goals, ratings, and feedback (e.g., linking of goals to ratings), followed by more distal outcomes which include user perceptions and reactions (e.g., ease of use, frustration with the system) and system-level outcomes (e.g., resource savings).

Theoretically, all PM processes can be supported by the use of e-PM and may prove to resolve some of the known challenges associated with traditional PA and PM (see Adler et al., 2016; Pulakos & O'Leary, 2011). When part of a broader e-HRM system, e-PM data can be linked to and enhance other HR processes including recruitment, selection, development, and compensation. e-PM can retrieve and populate relevant data (e.g., position description, duties, task statements, goals, definitions) from other e-HRM modules to customise screens for individual employees and to give the rater easy access to applicable information. For example, rather than rating employees on a generic set of performance dimensions, each employee could be evaluated on the task statements listed in his/her position description. This information could be populated with real-time changes directly from the position description. An embedded e-PM system can also link data across HR processes, allowing for the calculation of an endless number of HR analytics. For instance, performance ratings could be aggregated by recruitment sources or pre-employment test scores allowing for an analysis of the quality of hires or validation of selection tools.

Some e-PM programs incorporate more social aspects where employees are encouraged or prompted to give each other feedback and recognition. The solicited feedback is often brief and facilitates more frequent contributions from sources at different organisational levels. Feedback may be organised around company values (e.g., documenting incidents when an employee behaves in accordance with a company value) or incorporated into more formalised annual or semi-annual reviews.

Organisations can also post feedback publicly (via a company intranet) for others to comment on or "like." When posted for others, it may include pictures and other visually appealing graphics. Some of these social elements incorporate gamification in which employees earn badges or other reinforcements for contributing.

e-PM Research

In the research literature, e-PM has been given many names including Electronic Performance Support Systems (Raybould, 1990), Business Performance Management (Neely, 1999), technology-based performance management systems (Pulakos, 2009), Electronic Performance Measurement Systems (Keong Choong, 2014), and Electronic Performance Appraisal (Levy, Tseng, Rosen, & Lueke, 2017). Unfortunately, the science behind e-PM is lagging considerably behind the practice. Relatively few empirical studies that have examined the effectiveness of e-PM or something similar. We provide a very brief summary of e-PM-related research to date.

Early examinations of e-PM implementation appear as case studies. For example, the Air Force Research Laboratory's move to web-based forms resulted in a reduced workload for supervisors and streamlined management's ability to make administrative decisions through the examination of performance distributions (Grote, 2000). In 2002, Neary outlined the process TRW, Inc. took when implementing a new e-PM system. Based on observations gathered for two years following the system's implementation, Neary concluded that the system was viewed positively by stakeholders and allowed the organisation to better leverage their HR data.

To date, we know of only two empirical examinations of e-PM. The first compared traditional paper & pencil PAs to emailed PA (Kurtzberg, Naquin, & Balkin, 2005). Across three studies, Kurtzberg and colleagues found that using e-mail resulted in more negative appraisals which were mediated by reduced feelings of social obligation. The second examination was conducted when the PM system at a large university was moved from a paper & pencil format to an online PA system (Payne, Horner, Bosswell, Schroder, & Stine-Cheyne, 2009). Through a survey of employee reactions, the authors found that employees viewed the online review system more favourably in terms of rater accountability and employee participation compared to the previous paper & pencil system. However, they also found that employees perceived the feedback from the online system to be of lower quality.

Limitations of e-PM

Whereas e-PM offers promising solutions to some PM challenges, e-PM is not without limitations. It is important to acknowledge that just like any other software system, its value is a function of its usability, design, and ability to facilitate (and not inhibit) the critical human resource management PM process. Anecdotally, we have heard of various challenges with these systems that often reflect imposing too much structure (e.g., requiring a second-level supervisor to sign-off when there isn't one currently in place) or forcing a one-size fits all solution on an organisation that needs to have more flexibility (e.g., due to having multiple employment relationships like sub contractors). Sometimes, there are are easy programming solutions (e.g., allowing for more than one attachment), but not all issues are easily addressed (not interfacing well with another software system). We have also learned that retaining files indefinitely on the cloud poses new challenges of purging files that are legally mandated to be destroyed on a regular basis in some countries.

Both e-PM capabilities and adoption are growing rapidly and have outpaced empirical research by a decade. It is evident that there is a large gap between the first e-PM systems and the capabilities of the e-PM systems currently available. Only the very first transition from paper & pencil systems to web-hosted forms have been empirically examined (Kurtzberg et al., 2005; Payne et al. 2009). To our knowledge, there is no empirical research that examines the advantages of advanced e-PM capabilities, like the delivery of more frequent performance feedback. Further research is needed in order to empirically test the benefits and challenges of e-PM.

Future Research Questions

Given the promise and limitations of these systems, organisations interested in implementing e-PM should carefully consider the intended utilisation and purposes of PM. Rather than the piecemeal adoption of specific e-PM tools, best practice would be to consider PM as a complete system. Given the limited empirical comparisons between e-PM and traditional PM systems, organisations are likely to benefit from empirical studies testing the promised improvements e-PM offers. Payne et al. (2018) offer multiple propositions and research questions comparing e-PM ratings to traditional PA ratings. For example, they propose that e-PM ratings can be screened for rater errors, which should result in higher levels of employee satisfaction with the ratings. They also propose that e-PM presents the opportunity to provide more feedback and more timely feedback than traditional (yearly) PAs. Rigorous empirical studies are needed to determine if these propositions come to fruition. Finally, management should also communicate the proposed benefits of e-PM systems in order to ensure support from supervisors and follow-up with all stakeholders to address any unforeseen challenges that occur during implementation.

Further Readings

Krauss, A. D., & Snyder, L. A. (2009). Technology and performance management. In J.W. Smither
& M. London (Eds.), *Performance management: Putting research into practice* (pp. 445–491).
San Francisco, CA: Jossey-Bass.

Payne, S. C., Mendoza, A. M., & Horner, M. T. (2018). Electronic performance management: Does
altering the process improve the outcome? In D. L. Stone & J. H. Dulebohn (Eds.), *The brave
new world of e-HRM 2.0* (pp. 189–215). Charlotte, NC: Information Age.

Schleicher, D. J., Baumann, H. M., Sullivan, D. W., Levy, P. E., Hargrove, D. C., & Barros-Rivera,
B. A. (2018). Putting the system into performance management systems: A review and agenda
for performance management research. *Journal of Management, 44*, 2209–2245. doi:10.1177/
0149206318755303

References

Adler, S., Campion, M., Colquitt, A., Grubb, A., Murphy, K., Ollander-Krane, R., & Pulakos,
E. D. (2016). Getting rid of performance ratings: Genius or folly? A debate. *Industrial and
Organizational Psychology: Perspectives on Science and Practice, 9*, 219–252. doi:10.1017/iop.
2015.106

Aguinis, H. 2013. *Performance management* (3rd ed.). Upper Saddle River, NJ: Pearson Prentice
Hall.

ClearCompany (2019, March 21). *Performance Management System.* http://www.clearcompany.
com/performance-management

Farr, J. L., Fairchild, & Cassidy, S. E. (2013). Technology and performance appraisal.
In M. D. Coovert & L. F. Thompson (Eds.) *The psychology of workplace technology* (pp. 76–98).
London, UK: Taylor and Francis.

Keong Choong, K. (2014). The fundamentals of performance measurement systems: A systematic
approach to theory and a research agenda. *International Journal of Productivity and
Performance Management, 63*, 879–922. doi:10.1108/ijppm-01-2013-0015

Krauss, A. D., & Snyder, L. A. (2009). Technology and performance management. In J.W. Smither
& M. London (Eds.), *Performance management: Putting research into practice* (pp. 445–491).
San Francisco, CA: Jossey-Bass.

Kurtzberg, T. R., Naquin, C. E., & Belkin, L. Y. (2005). Electronic performance appraisals: The effects
of e-mail communication on peer ratings in actual and simulated environments.
Organizational Behavior and Human Decision Processes, 98, 216–226. doi: 10.1016/
j.obhdp.2005.07.001

Levy, P. E., Tseng, S. T., Rosen, C. C., & Lueke, S. B. (2017). Performance Management: A Marriage
between Practice and Science–Just Say "I do". In *Research in personnel and human resources
management* (pp.155–213). Bingley, UK: Emerald Publishing Limited.

McNall, L. A., & Roch, S. G. (2009). A social exchange model of employee reactions to electronic
performance monitoring. *Human Performance, 22*, 204–224. doi:10.1080/
08959280902970385

Neary, D. B. (2002). Creating a company-wide, on-line, performance management system: A case
study at TRW Inc. *Human Resource Management, 41*, 491–498. doi:10.1002/hrm.10056

Neely, A. (1999). The performance measurement revolution: Why now and what next? *International
Journal of Operations & Production Management, 19*, 205–228. doi:10.1108/
01443579910247437

Payne, S. C., Horner, M. T., Boswell, W. R., Schroeder, A. N., & Stine-Cheyne, K. J. (2009). Comparison of online and traditional performance appraisal systems. *Journal of Managerial Psychology, 24*, 526544. doi: 10.1108/02683940910974116

Payne, S. C., Mendoza, A. M., & Horner, M. T. (2018). Electronic performance management: Does altering the process improve the outcome? In D. L. Stone & J. H. Dulebohn (Eds.), *The brave new world of e-HRM 2.0* (pp. 189–215). Charlotte, NC: Information Age.

Pulakos, E. D. (2004). *Performance management: A roadmap for developing, implementing and evaluating performance management systems*. Alexandria, VA: SHRM Foundation

Pulakos, E. D. (2009). *Performance management: A new approach for driving business results*. Chichester, UK: Wiley-Blackwell.

Pulakos, E. D., & O'Leary, R. S. (2011). Why is performance management broken? *Industrial and Organizational Psychology: Perspectives on Science and Practice, 4*, 146–164. doi:10.1111/j. 1754-9434.2011.01315.x

Raybould, B. (1990). Solving human performance problems with computers a case study: Building an electronic performance support system. *Performance Improvement, 29*, 4–14. doi:10.1002/pfi.4160291004

Schleicher, D. J., Baumann, H. M., Sullivan, D. W., Levy, P. E., Hargrove, D. C., & Barros-Rivera, B. A. (2018). Putting the system into performance management systems: A review and agenda for performance management research. *Journal of Management, 44*, 2209–2245. doi:10.1177/0149206318755303

Sierra-Cedar (2018). *2018–2019 HR systems survey white paper*, 21st Annual Edition. Alpharetta, GA: Sierra-Cedar.

Stanton, J. M. (2000). Reactions to employee performance monitoring: Framework, review, and research directions. *Human Performance, 13*, 85–113. doi:10.1207/s15327043hup1301_4

Sladjana Nørskov and John P. Ulhøi
The Use of Robots in Job Interviews

In the wake of robotics and the extensive use of IT for critical HR tasks such as personnel selection, the adoption of robots seems to be the next logical step for future e-HRM practices. Based on state-of-the-art literature in the field of human-robot interaction (HRI), two types of robots are discussed:

(i) embodied physical agents and (ii) embodied virtual agents. Particular attention is directed towards the advantages and disadvantages of using physical versus virtual presence of artificial agents in job interviews by integrating HRM research with HRI research. The article also focuses on the potential of robots to remedy the problem of discrimination in relation to the job interview.

Embodied Virtual and Physical Agents

Robotics has recently attracted attention for its applicability, feasibility and effects in personnel selection (e.g. Kumazaki et al., 2017, Nørskov et al., 2019, Smith et al., 2014). In this context, robotics is applied as embodied virtual agents and embodied physical agents. Embodiment in the domain of artificial agents refers to "the dynamical coupling among brain (control), body, and environment"[1] (Pfeifer et al., 2007, p. 1088), and applies to situations where an algorithm in itself is insufficient but "requires a physical instantiation, a body" (Pfeifer and Scheier, 1999, p. 649). The focus of this article is thus on the phenomenon of robotic agents in job interviews – both AI-based (fully or semi-autonomous robots) and non-AI-based (e.g. teleoperated robots).

Embodied virtual agents are digitally generated visual characters that simulate the actions and behaviors of humans and other creatures (Fridin and Belokopytov, 2014, Li, 2015). Such agents appear in different applications such as e-commerce, computer games, training simulators, film, virtual tutors, etc. in order to humanize online experiences and make them more interpersonal (Fridin and Belokopytov, 2014). On the other hand, *embodied physical agents* have a physical body and are physically collocated agents in a user's environment, such as social robots. While these two types of embodied artificial agents are at each end of the continuum that ranges from physical to virtual embodiment, an artificial agent, however, can also be a hybrid of the two types (Li, 2015).

---

1 Anthropomorphic ascriptive terms such as "body" and "brain" should, however, be used with caution as they may lead to making "fictionalist analogues" that superimpose human categories on artificial agents, for better or worse. (Seibt, 2017, p. 14).

https://doi.org/10.1515/9783110633702-032

To better understand how robots may be employed in job interviews, and what advantages and disadvantages this option may entail, it is important to distinguish between an artificial agent's:(i) physical embodiment, (ii) physical presence, and (iii) social presence (Li, 2015, Thellman et al., 2016). Physical embodiment entails having a physical "body" that can be physically present in a user's environment. Such agents are also referred to as copresent robots. However, a physically embodied agent can also be telepresent, and is referred to as a telepresent robot. A telepresent robot interacts with people through a computer, a television or a projector screen (Li, 2015), and should not be confused with virtual agents, since those are digitally generated and only exist in the digital space (Holz et al., 2009). Regarding the first two factors – i.e., physical embodiment and physical presence – a review of research on physically present robots, telepresent robots and virtual agents found that physically present robots generated more favourable responses, they were perceived to perform better, and to be more persuasive and engaging. No perceptual differences were found between telepresent robots and virtual agents (Li, 2015). This suggests that an artificial agent's physical presence rather than its physical embodiment is central to eliciting favourable psychological responses. Humans are also more likely to empathize with a physically present agent compared with a virtual alternative (Seo et al., 2015). The third factor, the level of social presence of artificial agents, has been found to determine how answers are responded to and what type of information is revealed. Interactions involving higher social presence, e.g. face-to-face interviews, involve more social desirability bias compared with computer-distributed questionnaires (Richman et al., 1999). When compared with embodied virtual agents, embodied physical agents are able to elicit a greater sense of social presence (Lee et al., 2006) and more favourable emotional responses and attitudes related to user enjoyment, trust toward the agent, attraction to the agent, etc. (Li, 2015). However, greater social presence of the artificial agent may in turn increase the risk of users' socially desirable responses (Schuetzler et al., 2018).

Using Robots to Overcome Imperfections in Existing Selection Practices

In the job interview, a key area of concern is related to the fairness of selection methods (Robertson and Smith, 2001). Due to being "a fundamentally interpersonal process" (Rivera, 2012, p. 1000), the job interview as a method is particularly exposed to subjective impressions and affective processes that are known to bias the selection process (e.g. García et al., 2008). While research has proposed a variety of ways to increase the perceived fairness of the selection process, e.g. by giving feedback, providing selection information, etc., implicit biases in the job interview, however, remain an unresolved issue (for a recent review see McCarthy et al., 2017).

In trying to resolve this problem, embodied physical agents (social robots) are now being tested for their applicability in job interviews to ensure objectivity and to increase applicants' fairness perceptions (Nørskov et al., 2019). Robotics holds promises of addressing parts of the job interview setup associated with implicit biases, such as visual cues in face-to-face communication, that potentially give rise to unintended discrimination of applicants (Rivera, 2012). To reduce discriminative biases associated with the employee interview, the use of robots as a fair proxy communication device during the job interview has been proposed (Seibt and Vestergaard, 2018). *Fair proxy communication* is defined as "a specific communicational setting in which a teleoperated robot is used to remove perceptual cues of implicit biases in order to increase the perceived fairness of decision-related communications" (Seibt and Vestergaard, 2018, p. 1).

In addition, as job interviews are generally perceived as a stressful situation for applicants, job interview training has also become an area of application for robotics. Interview training is one of the factors that have shown to have a positive effect on job applicants' interview performance and therefore on the outcome of the job interview, i.e. whether they are offered a job or not (Maurer et al., 2008). Job interview training involving either embodied virtual agents (e.g. virtual characters) or embodied physical agents (e.g. android robots) has been found to be able to facilitate job interview skills, improve job interview performance, improve the participants' self-confidence, reduce their stress levels and improve their nonverbal communication skills (e.g. Kumazaki et al., 2019).

Applicant Reactions, Organizational Reputation and Robot Design

In the context of job interviews, where artificial agents become a type of representative for the hiring organization, the ability of embodied virtual agents to easily adapt their visual appearance to applicants' preferences may have a positive impact on applicants' organizational attraction (Turban and Dougherty, 1992). On the other hand, a stronger perceived physical and social presence of embodied physical agents may be better able to engage job interviewees and generate more positive reactions and attitudes. This may not only have a positive effect on the perception and reputation of the recruiting organization, but also on the quality of the interviews as a basis for the hiring decision.

The design of an artificial agent for personnel selection is relevant not only because it may act as a representative for the organization, but also because it influences the interaction between external stakeholders, such as job applicants, and the artificial agent. For instance, the degree of an artificial agent's anthropomorphism has been found to influence how humans perceive social presence of the agent (Nowak and Biocca, 2003). Humans also tend to interact with computers and robots similar to the way they interact with other humans, thus transferring social rules of politeness, conformity, reciprocity, recognition, but also gender stereotypes, same-ethnicity favoritism and even racial prejudice to their interaction with artificial agents (Eyssel and Hegel, 2012, Gong, 2008, Nørskov and Nørskov, 2019). Finally, verbal and non-verbal behaviors of an artificial agent also tend to influence the quality and the outcome of the interaction between a job applicant and the agent, including applicant reactions to the interview process such as fairness perceptions.

In general, the use of robotics in personnel selection has the potential to overcome some of the current limitations related to unintentional discrimination of applicants (Nørskov et al., 2019). More empirical research, however, is needed to determine (i) how different design characteristics of both embodied virtual and physical agents are able to facilitate job interviews in a way that improves applicant reactions while being able to identify the best candidate for the hiring organization, and (ii) whether and how the use of these agents to mediate or facilitate job interviews affects applicants' perceptions of the hiring organization.

Further Readings

Lee, K. M., Jung, Y., Kim, J., & Kim, S.R. (2006). Are physically embodied social agents better than disembodied social agents?: The effects of physical embodiment, tactile interaction, and people's loneliness in human-robot interaction. *International Journal of Human-Computer Studies*, *64*(10), 962–973.

Li, J. (2015). The benefit of being physically present: A survey of experimental works comparing copresent robots, telepresent robots and virtual agents. *International Journal of Human-Computer Studies*, *77*, 23–37.

Nørskov, S., Damholdt, M. F., Ulhøi, J. P., Jensen, M. B., Mathiasen, M. K., Ess, C. M., & Seibt, J. (2019). *Fairness perceptions in job interviews: using a teleoperated robot as a fair proxy*. Paper presented at the European Group for Organizational Studies (EGOS) Colloquium, Edinburgh, United Kingdom.

References

Eyssel, F., & Hegel, F. (2012). (S)he's got the look: Gender stereotyping of robots. *Journal of Applied Social Psychology*, *42*(9),2213–2230.

Fridin, M., & Belokopytov, M. (2014). Embodied robot versus virtual agent: Involvement of preschool children in motor task performance. *International Journal of Human-Computer Interaction*, *30*, 459–469.

García, M. F., Posthuma, R. A., & Colella, A. (2008). Fit perceptions in the employment interview: The role of similarity, liking, and expectations. *Journal of Occupational and Organizational Psychology*, *81*, 173–189.

Gong, L. (2008). The boundary of racial prejudice: Comparing preferences for computer-synthesized White, Black, and robot characters. *Computers in Human Behavior, 24*(5), 2074–2093.

Han, S., Jiang, Y., Humphreys, G. W., Zhou, T., & Cai, P. (2005). Distinct neural substrates for the perception of real and virtual visual worlds. *NeuroImage, 24*(3), 928–935.

Holz, T., Dragone, M., & O'Hare, G. M. P. (2009). Where robots and virtual agents meet: a survey of social interaction research across Milgram's reality-virtuality continuum. *International Journal of Social Robotics, 1*(1), 83–93.

Huffcutt, A. I. (2011). An empirical review of the employment interview construct literature. *International Journal of Selection and Assessment, 19*, 62–81.

Kumazaki, H., Warren, Z., Corbett, B. A., Yoshikawa, Y., Matsumoto, Y., Higashida, H., . . . Kikuchi, M. (2017). Android robot-mediated mock job interview sessions for young adults with autism spectrum disorder: a Pilot study. Frontiers in psychiatry, 8, 169.

Kumazaki, H., Muramatsu, T., Yoshikawa, Y., Corbett, B. A., Matsumoto, Y., Higashida, H., . . . Kikuchi, M. (2019). Job interview training targeting nonverbal communication using an android robot for individuals with autism spectrum disorder. *Autism*(E-publication ahead of print). Retrieved from https://journals.sagepub.com/doi/abs/10.1177/1362361319827134.

Lee, K. M., Jung, Y., Kim, J., & Kim, S. R. (2006). Are physically embodied social agents better than disembodied social agents?: The effects of physical embodiment, tactile interaction, and people's loneliness in human-robot interaction. *International Journal of Human-Computer Studies, 64*(10), 962–973.

Li, J. (2015). The benefit of being physically present: a survey of experimental works comparing copresent robots, telepresent robots and virtual agents. *International Journal of Human-Computer Studies, 77*, 23–37.

Maurer, T. J., Solamon, J. M., & Lippstreu, M. (2008). How does coaching interviewees affect the validity of a structured interview? *Journal of Organizational Behavior, 29*(3), 355–371.

McCarthy, J. M., Bauer, T. N., Truxillo, D. M., Anderson, N. R., Costa, A. C., & Ahmed, S. M. (2017). Applicant perspectives during selection: a review addressing "So what?," "What's new?," and "Where to next?". *Journal of Management, 43*(6), 1693–1725.

Nowak, K. L., & Biocca, F. (2003). The effect of the agency and anthropomorphism on users' sense of telepresence, copresence, and social presence in virtual environments. *Presence: Teleoperators & Virtual Environments, 12*(5), 481–494.

Nørskov, M., & Nørskov, S. (2020). Social robots and recognition. *Philosophy & Technology*, 33(1), 5–8.

Nørskov, S., Damholdt, M. F., Ulhøi, J. P., Jensen, M. B., Mathiasen, M. K., Ess, C. M., & Seibt, J. (2019). *Fairness perceptions in job interviews: using a teleoperated robot as a fair proxy*. Paper presented at the European Group for Organizational Studies (EGOS) Colloquium, Edinburgh, United Kingdom.

Pfeifer, R., Lungarella, M., & Iida, F. (2007). Self-organization, embodiment, and biologically inspired robotics. *Science, 318*(5853), 1088–1093.

Pfeifer, R., & Scheier, C. (1999). *Understanding Intelligence*. Cambridge, MA: MIT Press.

Richman, W. L., Kiesler, S., Weisband, S., & Drasgow, F. (1999). A meta-analytic study of social desirability distortion in computer-administered questionnaires, traditional questionnaires, and interviews. *Journal of Applied Psychology, 84*(5), 754–775.

Rivera, L. A. (2012). Hiring as cultural matching: The case of elite professional service firms. *American Sociological Review, 77*(6), 999–1022.

Robertson, I. T. & Smith, M. (2001). Personnel selection. *Journal of Occupational and Organizational Psychology, 74*, 441–472.

Schuetzler, R. M., Giboney, J. S., Grimes, G. M., & Nunamaker Jr, J. F. (2018). The influence of conversational agent embodiment and conversational relevance on socially desirable responding. *Decision Support Systems, 114*, 94–102.

Seo, S. H., Geiskkovitch, D., Nakane, M., King, C., & Young, J. E. (2015). *Poor thing! Would you feel sorry for a simulated robot?: A comparison of empathy toward a physical and a simulated robot.* Proceedings of the Tenth Annual ACM/IEEE International Conference on Human-Robot Interaction. Portland, Oregon, USA.

Smith, M. J., Ginger, E. J., Wright, K., Wright, M. A., Taylor, J. L., Humm, L. B., . . . Fleming, M. F. (2014). Virtual reality job interview training in adults with autism spectrum disorder. Journal of Autism and Developmental Disorders, 44(10), 2450–2463.

Thellman, S., Silvervarg, A., & Ziemke, T. (2016). *Physical vs. virtual agent embodiment and effects on social interaction.* Paper presented at the Intelligent Virtual Agents: 16th International Conference, IVA 2016, Los Angeles, CA, USA.

Turban, D. B., & Dougherty, T. W. (1992). Influences of campus recruiting on applicant attraction to firms. *Academy of Management Journal, 35*(4), 739–765.

Sebit, J. (2017). Towards an ontology of simulated social interaction: varieties of the "as if" for robots and humans. In R. Hakli & J. Seibt (Eds.), *Sociality and normativity for robots: philosophical inquiries into human-robot interactions* (pp. 11–39). Cham: Springer.

Seibt, J., & Vestergaard, C. (2018). Fair proxy communication: using social robots to modify the mechanisms of implicit social cognition. *Research Ideas and Outcomes, 4*, e31827.

Anna B. Holm
Applicant Tracking Systems

An Applicant Tracking System (ATS) is a single piece of software that supports the hiring process using a common database containing job and applicant information (Eckhardt, Laumer, Maier, & Weitzel, 2014). It is often offered as a stand-alone, web-based, software-as-a-service (SaaS) subscription application, or a wider-system integrated IT solution, such as a module in HRIS (HR.com, 2019). An ATS is also often referred to as an e-recruitment system (Holm, 2012), a hiring management system (HMS) (Bussler & Davis, 2002; Cappelli, 2001), a candidate management system, and a talent management or acquisition system (Reynolds & Dickter, 2017; Schweyer, 2010). The variety of labels reflects the contemporary application of the software for people resourcing, which in most cases goes beyond the administrative nature of early ATSs.

Most of the original ATS vendors have expanded their original offerings, and the term ATS is not sufficient to describe the range of their solutions (Schweyer, 2010). Contemporary systems can store job descriptions, generate job requisition analyses, automatically store all applications and résumés submitted via the internet, scan résumés, create applicant profiles, generate automatic responses to applicants, schedule and track interviews and other assessments, produce staffing statistics and cost analyses, generate mailing lists and labels, and perform many other data processing operations (Phillips & Gully, 2015, p. 393). Some vendors create talent acquisition suites that include a core ATS backbone together with the ability to carry out recruitment marketing, sourcing and onboarding, all under the same vendor roof. Many ATSs have thus become full-service recruiting platforms that enable employers to oversee the entire hiring process (Brienza, 2018) with added candidate relationship-management functions (Zielinski, 2015). Unsurprisingly, such systems are often considered an integral part of organisations' talent acquisition programmes (HR.com, 2019).

Applicant Screening

ATSs are capable of conducting basic applicant screening and background checks, which helps reduce the time spent on weeding out unsuitable applicants (Heneman III, Judge, & Kammeyer-Mueller, 2015, p. 218). Moreover, they are able to mine résumés to generate detailed profiles of candidates that include education, social background, skills, behavioural attributes, work history, and salary requirements. Typical tools for mining include keyword parsing and text search. Parsing tools automatically deconstruct the résumé and arrange relevant data into fields (e.g. education, contact information), and keyword search detects words and phrases that are

https://doi.org/10.1515/9783110633702-033

relevant for the vacancies. Recruiters can then contact high-scoring applicants and engage in more targeted communications with them. Similar applicant data can be potentially tracked from social media postings and other online activity (Reynolds & Dickter, 2017). However, one of the major drawbacks of using ATS tracking software is its limitations in matching candidates to the right job postings and missing qualified applicants (HR.com, 2019). Furthermore, the résumé format might be insufficient to reveal crucial competencies of a job-seeker. Notwithstanding, although ATS screening tools cannot replace human screeners entirely, they can be invaluable in narrowing down the number of applicants a recruiter must handle and improve the efficiency of large-scale recruiting processes. Other essential candidate characteristics can then be determined with the help of more advanced screening, assessment, and interviewing techniques (Reynolds & Dickter, 2017).

An ATS can help pre-screen applicants by carrying out online pre-screening tests or qualification questionnaires. Recruiters can use ATSs to carry out a range of assessments of job-related knowledge and relevant skills. For example, automated testing systems can include embedded audio, video, and animated graphics as part of the question stimuli and permit a wide range of response formats, such as hotspots, drag and drop, and other interactive controls (Reynolds & Dickter, 2017). ATSs can also provide managers with interview and selection guidelines and facilitate the interview process. Recruiters can store interview protocols, summary notes, and applicant ratings in the system. Some systems even offer biometric tools such as voice analysis and facial recognition to confirm interviewee identity and aid in scoring (Reynolds & Dickter, 2017). Moreover, some systems offer intuitive interfaces that can be integrated with third-party recruiting technologies, such as video interviewing, skills assessments, personality and cognitive assessments, and gaming, thus creating extended recruitment and selection ecosystems (Zielinski, 2015).

Data Analytics

ATS vendors increasingly offer cloud-based environments with enhanced user and applicant experience, and routinely integrate the most popular job boards and social networks into their ATS job advertisement, job application and applicant screening capabilities (Zielinski, 2015). For example, applicants' online presence on Web 2.0 sites can be mined for data which reflects their personality (Faliagka, Tsakalidis, & Tzimas, 2012). Using programs such as Linguistic Inquiry and Word Count (LIWC) to extract linguistic data from texts such as blogs and posts gives recruiters an indication of the author's personality traits (Oberlander & Nowson, 2006).

Apart from keeping records, an ATS can also automatically track some of the important hiring metrics, such as time-to-fill / time-to-hire (the number of days from job vacancy to hiring), yield ratio (the percentage of applicants from a particular recruitment source), acceptance rate (the percentage of applicants who accept offered jobs), and cost of recruitment (the sum of advertising costs, agency fees, referral bonuses and other costs divided by the number of hires) (Snell, Morris, & Bohlander, 2016, pp. 186–188). In addition, ATSs can process the data and generate reports on the key performance indicators (KPIs) of the entire recruiting process. Recruiters' work can thus be monitored and, if necessary, improved (Eckhardt et al., 2014). Research has also found that by using an ATS that supports the design and evaluation of KPIs, the cycle time of the recruiting process can be shortened significantly through business process controlling and process analysis (Laumer, Maier, & Eckhardt, 2015). Data from an ATS can thus help recruiters improve hiring efficiency by speeding up the hiring process (Phillips & Gully, 2015, pp. 393–394) and fine-tuning the entire recruitment process (McCrory & Mueller, 2000).

Communication with Applicants

ATSs ease communication with candidates, especially after they apply or are rejected. For example, they provide recruiters with a pop-up e-mail form to use for rejected applicants so as not to keep them waiting unnecessarily. Many ATSs also enable the integration and management of job marketing on social network sites (SNS) so that recruiters can push jobs out to social networks, carry out content marketing, and measure how social interactions drive engagement with a candidate community (Zielinski, 2015). ATSs also offer a number of benefits to job applicants. For example, job-seekers can easily apply for jobs from their desktop or mobile device, either directly or via social media, and receive real-time updates. Some ATS providers even enable job-seekers to apply with social media profiles (Weber, 2013). Once selected for a job, applicants can, via an ATS, receive and accept or reject a job offer, retrieve information about the job, the employing organisation, the new workplace, and, in some cases, communicate with future colleagues through a dedicated tool (Laumer et al., 2015). Nonetheless, according to some industry reports, many ATSs still fail at offering candidates a personalized experience (see e.g. HR.com, 2019).

Efficiency Concerns

In practice, the reasons for using an ATS are predominately driven by the need to improve the efficiency of the talent acquisition process, with the main sought-after benefits being reduced time to hire, improved candidate screening, easier management of applications and résumés, and better talent acquisition metrics (HR.com, 2019). Despite the apparent cost-savings, however, large organisations still spend an estimated 7% of their external recruitment budgets on ATSs. An ATS alone can cost from about €5,000 to millions of euros (Weber, 2012). Additional costs are incurred from having to train end users to properly use the systems, which is considered crucial for ATS deployment. HR personnel must possess the knowledge and skills to utilise the various functionalities in the different steps of the recruiting process. Therefore, recruiters need to learn such things as content development for career web pages, how to post job ads on online job boards, communication with applicants and hiring managers, search of applicant pool databases, etc. In addition, recruiters might need to acquire specific skills in order to use social media and data-mining in recruiting, e.g. how to perform online marketing and search-engine optimisation (Eckhardt et al., 2014). Thus, a crucial requirement for recruiters using ATSs is to be open to new technological developments in e-recruitment and keep their knowledge and skills up-to-date (Eckhardt, Brickwedde, Laumer, & Weitzel, 2011).

The additional costs of using an ATS derive from its potential vulnerability under a possible cyber-attack, as well as the safe storage and management of personally identifiable information (PII) on candidates. ATS users must therefore ensure that the systems are compliant with data privacy regulations, that they are kept up-to-date, and that software bugs are fixed as soon as they are discovered (Dorsey, Martin, Howard, & Coovert, 2017). Cybersecurity work requires a unique set of skills, and training recruiters in cybersecurity is thus also a prerequisite of employing ATSs.

Future Research Questions

Although widely implemented across hiring organisations (HR.com, 2019) research on the effect of hiring systems on the efficiency and, more importantly, the effectiveness of an ATS-enabled recruiting process is still scarce. Future research might evaluate the impact on ATSs of social media integration in the application process, and whether this creates synergies, generates more qualified candidates, or benefits employers in other ways, e.g. leading to improved employer attractiveness and higher intention to apply among qualified job-seekers. Another line of research could evaluate the value of using big data from ATSs for various stages of talent acquisition and corresponding recruitment, selection and onboarding tasks. More research effort could also be put into studying the use of mobile devices for job applications, applicant screening, candidate testing and communication via ATSs. Finally, future research contributions could investigate the transformation of the recruitment profession due to rapidly advancing complex technologies, such as Artificial Intelligence (AI), and their impact on recruiters' job profiles and competencies.

Further Readings

Eckhardt, A., Laumer, S., Maier, C., & Weitzel, T. (2014). The transformation of people, processes, and IT in e-recruiting: Insights from an eight-year case study of a German media corporation. *Employee Relations, 36*(4), 415–431.

Laumer, S., Maier, C., & Eckhardt, A. (2015). The impact of business process management and applicant tracking systems on recruiting process performance: An empirical study. *Journal of Business Economics, 85*(4), 421–453.

Reynolds, D. H., & Dickter, D. N. (2017). Technology and Employee Selection. In J. Farr & N. Tippins (Eds.), *Handbook of Employee Selection* (pp. 855–873). New York, NY: Routledge.

References

Brienza, L. (2018). 5 reasons why an applicant tracking system makes sense. *Canadian HR Reporter, 31*(1), 13.

Bussler, L., & Davis, E. (2002). Information systems: The quiet revolution in human resource management. *Journal of Computer Information Systems, 42*(2), 17–20.

Cappelli, P. (2001). Making the most of on-line recruiting. *Harvard Business Review, 79*(3), 139–146.

Dorsey, D. W., Martin, J., Howard, D. J., & Coovert, M. D. (2017). Cybersecurity issues in selection. In J. Farr & N. Tippins (Eds.), *Handbook of Employee Selection* (pp. 913–930). New York, NY: Routledge.

Eckhardt, A., Brickwedde, W., Laumer, S., & Weitzel, T. (2011). The need for a recruiter 2.0 for hiring it talent – the case of a German software manufacturer. In J. Luftman (Ed.), *Managing IT Human Resources: Considerations for Organizations and Personnel* (pp. 325–339). Hershey, PA: IGI Global.

Eckhardt, A., Laumer, S., Maier, C., & Weitzel, T. (2014). The transformation of people, processes, and IT in e-recruiting: Insights from an eight-year case study of a German media corporation. *Employee Relations, 36*(4), 415–431.

Faliagka, E., Tsakalidis, A., & Tzimas, G. (2012). An integrated e-recruitment system for automated personality mining and applicant ranking. *Internet Research, 22*(5), 551–568.

Heneman III, H. G., Judge, T. A., & Kammeyer-Mueller, J. (2015). *Staffing Organisations* (8th ed.). Mishawaka, IN: Pangloss Industries in collaboration with McGraw Hill.

Holm, A. B. (2012). E-recruitment: The move towards a virtually organized recruitment process. In S. de Juana-Espinosa, J. A. Fernandez-Sanchez, E. Manresa-Marhuenda, & J. Valdes-Conca (Eds.), *Human Resource Management in the Digital Economy: Creating Synergy Between Competency Models and Information* (pp. 80–95). Hershey, PA: IGI Global.

HR.com. (2019). *The State of Applicant Tracking System – 2019*. Retrieved from http://www.hr.com

Laumer, S., Maier, C., & Eckhardt, A. (2015). The impact of business process management and applicant tracking systems on recruiting process performance: An empirical study. *Journal of Business Economics, 85*(4), 421–453.

McCrory, M., & Mueller, D. (2000). Nebraska "whole picture" recruitment: From paperwork to "people work" featuring the personic applicant tracking system. *Public Personnel Management, 29*(4), 505–510.

Oberlander, J., & Nowson, S. (2006). *Whose thumb is it anyway? Classifying author personality from weblog text*. Paper presented at the Proceedings of the COLING/ACL 2006 Main Conference Poster Sessions.

Phillips, J. M., & Gully, S. M. (2015). *Strategic Staffing, Global Edition*. Harlow, UK: Pearson Education Limited.

Reynolds, D. H., & Dickter, D. N. (2017). Technology and Employee Selection. In J. Farr & N. Tippins (Eds.), *Handbook of Employee Selection* (pp. 855–873). New York, NY: Routledge.

Schweyer, A. (2010). *Talent management systems: Best practices in technology solutions for recruitment, retention and workforce planning*. Etobicoke, Canada: John Wiley & Sons.

Snell, S., Morris, S., & Bohlander, G. (2016). *Managing Human Resources*. Boston, MA: Cengage Learning.

Weber, L. (2012, January 24). Your Résumé vs. Oblivion. *The Wall Street Journal*.

Weber, L. (2013, March 25). McDonald's Caters to Job-Seekers on the Go. *The Wall Street Journal*. Retrieved from https://blogs.wsj.com/atwork/2013/03/25/mcdonalds-caters-to-job-seekers-on-the-go/

Zielinski, D. (2015, October 1). 7 Reasons to Love Your ATS. *HR Magazine*.

Christopher J. Hartwell and Regan Eggli
Social Media Screening in Employee Selection

Screening applicant social media (SM) information during the hiring process is a growing trend in organizations. To most effectively understand and utilize SM, organizations and researchers should understand different types of SM, what information is likely to be found, what job-related criteria can possibly be measured using SM, and the potential challenges.

Defining Social Media Screening

Social media (SM) refers to internet-based platforms that allow users to develop and share content with each other (Landers & Schmidt, 2016). *SM screening (SMS)*, also known as SM assessment, is the review of SM information for use in employment decisions (Roth, Bobko, Van Iddekinge, & Thatcher, 2016). The most commonly used SM platforms for conducting SMS are LinkedIn and Facebook (Hartwell & Campion, 2020; SHRM, 2016). SMS is a major component of *cybervetting*, which is when online information is used to make employment decisions (Berkelaar & Harrison, 2017). The practice of using SMS has likely been around since the advent of SM, but was first measured by CareerBuilder in 2006 and the Society for Human Research Management (SHRM) in 2008. SHRM conducted four total SMS surveys (SHRM, 2008, 2011, 2013, 2016), while CareerBuilder has conducted ten (2006, 2008, 2009, 2012, 2013, 2014, 2015, 2016, 2017, 2018). Compiling these survey results, Figure 34.1 shows the percentage of hiring managers using SMS has risen substantially, from 12% (2006) to 70% (2017, 2018) for CareerBuilder and from 13% (2008) to 39% (2015) for SHRM.

Research on Social Media Screening

SMS research has trailed behind professional practice. In fact, one recent review of technology in human resources failed to even mention SMS (Stone, Deadrick, Lukazewski, & Johnson, 2015), though other recent reviews gave SMS adequate attention (McFarland & Ployhart, 2015; Roth et al., 2016). The first empirical look into SMS was a 2009 study using undergraduate student raters to examine the Facebook profiles of other students (Kluemper & Rosen, 2009). This and two subsequent studies (Kluemper, Rosen, & Mossholder, 2012) demonstrated validity in rating personality

https://doi.org/10.1515/9783110633702-034

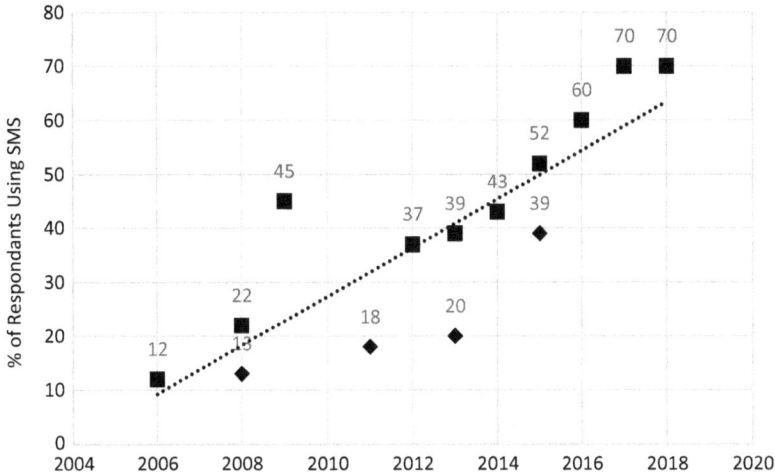

Figure 34.1: Percentage of CareerBuilder (square) and SHRM (diamond) respondents using SMS.

traits using SMS, and the latter also demonstrated that SM-based hireability ratings correlated with job performance ratings. In 2019, Roulin and Levashina found that LinkedIn-based SMS had good interrater reliability, temporal stability, and validity (correlating with self-report ratings and later career success).

Not all research has demonstrated such positive results. Using recruiters to rate student Facebook profiles on general suitability and 10 work-related criteria, Van Iddekinge, Lanivich, Roth, & Junco (2016) found that very few ratings correlated with supervisor-rated job performance or turnover. Result from another study suggest that using SMS may increase ambiguity in decision making (Pike, Bateman, & Butler, 2017). Finally, research has shown that Facebook-based SMS may impact applicant reactions by increasing perceptions of privacy invasiveness, lowering perceptions of fairness, and lowering organizational attractiveness (Madera, 2012; Stoughton, Thompson, & Meade, 2015).

Impact of Social Media Screening

The widespread use of SMS can substantially impact selection decisions. For example, 57% of recent CareerBuilder survey respondents have rejected a candidate based on SMS (CareerBuilder, 2018). Thus, continued research on SMS is essential to understand whether the practice is valuable in employee selection. As it currently stands, researchers have cautioned against using SMS in practice, citing a lack of a consistent research demonstrating SMS validity and utility (e.g., Kluemper et al., 2012; Ployhart, 2012; Roth et al., 2016). But Figure 34.1 shows that these calls have gone unheeded. Researchers and practitioners alike would benefit from a larger body of research examining which criteria are measurable using SMS, how SMS can be structured to increase reliability and validity, how applicants react to the process, and the legal and ethical implications.

In contrast to most traditional selection procedures, where information is actively solicited from applicants (e.g., applications, assessments, interviews), SMS represents a *passive selection procedure* that does not require direct applicant input. Instead, organizational representatives review applicant SM information previously posted online. There are pros and cons to this approach. The positives include the likelihood that SMS uncovers unique information because the SM context activates a broader identity than that activated in high-stakes selection procedures (Hartwell & Campion, 2020). Inasmuch as the unique information from SMS can be reliably interpreted and validly related to skills, abilities, or personal characteristics that predict effective job performance, it adds value to the selection process. However, whether SMS provides reliable and valid information is debatable, and there are various issues associate with SMS.

Challenges with Social Media Screening

One issue or challenge with SMS is that organizations do not utilize SMS in a consistent, structured way. Structuring a selection process increases reliability and, in turn, increases the likelihood to achieving valid, useful results. Such a process has shown promise in various selection procedures, most notably with job interviews (Levashina, Hartwell, Morgeson, & Campion, 2014). The interviewing context is somewhat similar to that of SMS because a rater is tasked with making judgments about applicants using qualitative information. Not surprisingly, many SMS articles cite the interview structure literature as a good starting point for structuring SMS (Kluemper, 2013; Roth et al., 2016; Van Iddekinge et al., 2016). The structured interview framework developed by Campion, Palmer, and Campion (1997), which identifies 15 structural components, could be adapted to the SMS context.

Second, SMS may be too broad of a concept, as SM platforms vary in purpose and the information shared by users. Thus, results of prior research using Facebook to represent SMS may not generalize when using LinkedIn (or vice versa). Some recent research distinguishes between *professional-based SMS* – SMS using a SM platform designed for professional use (e.g., LinkedIn) – and *personal-based SMS* – SMS using a SM platform designed for personal use (e.g., Facebook) (Nikolaou, 2014; Roulin & Bangerter, 2013). Professional-based SMS is likely to uncover deeper information about work-related experience and professional identity, while personal-based SMS is likely to uncover broader information about personality, an individual's identity outside of the workplace, and interpersonal style, among other factors (Hartwell & Campion, 2020).

A third, but related, conceptual issue is understanding the purpose of SMS. Hartwell (2018) identified two major approaches to SMS based on the purpose of the screen. The first approach is a *screen-in approach*, in which the purpose of the SMS is to assess whether the applicant has the requisite job qualifications to move on in the selection process. Because this approach is focused on work-related information, professional-based SMS is likely to be most effective. Conversely, a screen-out approach is a SMS in which the purpose is to uncover red flags or *faux pas* (e.g., drug use, racist views) that would disqualify the applicant from further consideration (Roulin, 2014). This type of information is most likely to be discovered using personal-based SMS. Which SMS approach(es) used, if any, should be based on the organizational and job characteristics.

Finally, the acceptability of SMS needs to be carefully considered. One type of acceptability is from a legal standpoint. Depending on national and local laws, SMS may be a considered a violation of privacy or lead to discrimination or adverse impact (Davison, Maraist, & Bing, 2011; Thomas, Rothschild, & Donegan, 2015). Another form of acceptability refers to applicant reactions. If applicants react negatively to SMS, the organization could lose highly qualified candidates that self-select out of the applicant pool. However, applicant reactions are likely to differ between professional-based and personal-based SMS or the SMS approach used (Aguado, Rico, Rubio, & Fernández, 2016).

Future Research on Social Media Screening

There are many avenues for future SMS research. First, more research is needed regarding validity and reliability of SMS, especially since the available research is inconclusive. Second, research that examines how SM information influences perceptions and decision making of recruiters and hiring managers is needed. As Figure 34.1 demonstrates, SMS is being used in the hiring process, so understanding the impact of this practice on perceptions and decision making, even outside of validity and reliability, is imperative. Third, future research should examine whether structuring SMS can increase reliability and validity in a similar manner to how structure has increased these psychometric properties in interviewing. Given that SMS is generally done informally and often covertly, there is likely much psychometric benefit to be had from standardizing the process. But whether these benefits are strong enough to encourage SMS as a formal part of a selection process remains to be seen.

Fourth, acceptability of SMS needs to be better understood, but from a legal perspective and from an applicant perspective. Privacy invasiveness concerns arising from the use of SMS by an unintended audience (recruiters and hiring mangers) are one major concern. Fifth, many researchers assume that applicant faking in social media contexts is less of a concern than in traditional selection procedures, but empirical research on the topic is lacking. Finally, in all of these future research directions, care should be taken to differentiate between SM platforms with different features and purposes, such as between professional and personal SM types. Another differentiation may be between long-term SM platforms – in which the information you share is saved indefinitely – and short-term SM platforms – in which the information shared is only available for a short period of time (usually 24 hours). Some social media platforms (e.g., Facebook, Instagram) allow you to share both long-term and short-term information. Dependent on the SM type/platform, the information available, validity/reliability, and acceptability of SMS, are likely to be different. Understanding these differences would help practitioners more effectively utilize SMS during the hiring process.

Future Research Questions

1. How valid and reliable is SMS during the hiring process?
2. How does SMS influence perceptions and decision making during the hiring process?
3. Does structuring the SMS process increase psychometric properties and overall utility?
4. How is SMS during the hiring process perceived by applicants?
5. How does applicant impression management and faking manifest itself in SMS?
6. What differences in research questions 1–5 are found when moderated by SM type (e.g., professional vs. personal SM)?

Further Readings

Roth et al. (2016): This article provides a research agenda for studying SMS, including almost 20 testable propositions and research questions.

Landers and Schmidt (2016): This book includes 16 chapters that give a broad look at SMS for both researchers and practitioners, including current application, practical guidelines, and challenges and limitations.

Hartwell and Campion (2020): This article surveyed HR professionals regarding their perceptions and use of SMS, including how specific content influences their perceptions of candidates.

SHRM (2016): This report in a PowerPoint slide format details the results of SHRM's most recent survey on how SMS is currently being used in organizations, including how the recent results compare to prior SHRM surveys on the topic.

CareerBuilder (2018): This press release details the results of CareerBuilder's most recent survey gives the most up-to-date information regarding how and why hiring managers and HR professionals are using SMS.

References

Aguado, D., Rico, R., Rubio, V. J., & Fernández, L. (2016). Applicant reactions to social network web use in personnel selection. *Journal of Work and Organizational Psychology*, *32*, 183–190. DOI: 10.1016/j.rpto.2016.09.001

Berkelaar, B. L., & Harrison, M. A. (2017). Cybervetting. *The International Encyclopedia of Organizational Communication*, 1–7. DOI: 10.1002/9781118955567.wbieoc054

Buster, M. A., Roth, P. L., & Bobko, P. (2005). A process for content validation of education and experienced-based minimum qualifications: An approach resulting in federal court approval. *Personnel Psychology*, *58*, 771–799. DOI: 10.1111/j.1744-6570.2005.00618.x

Campion, M. A., Palmer, D. K., & Campion, J. E. (1997). A review of structure in the selection interview. *Personnel Psychology*, *50*, 655–702. DOI: 10.1111/j.1744-6570.1997.tb01488.x

CareerBuilder (2006, October 26). One-in-four hiring managers have used Internet search engines to screen job candidates; one-in-ten have used social networking sites, CareerBuilder.com survey finds. Retrieved from http://www.careerbuilder.com/

CareerBuilder (2008, September 10). One-in-five employers use social networking sites to research job candidates, CareerBuilder.com survey finds. Retrieved from http://www.careerbuilder.com/

CareerBuilder (2009, June 10). More employers screening candidates via social networking sites. Retrieved from http://www.careerbuilder.com/CareerBuilder (2013, July 2). More employers finding reasons not to hire candidates on social media, finds CareerBuilder survey. Retrieved from http://www.careerbuilder.com/

CareerBuilder (2012, April 18). Thirty-seven percent of companies use social networks to research potential job candidates, according to new CareerBuilder Survey. Retrieved from http://www.careerbuilder.com/

CareerBuilder (2013, July 2). More employers finding reasons not to hire candidates on social media, finds CareerBuilder survey. Retrieved from http://www.careerbuilder.com/

CareerBuilder (2014, June 26). Number of employers passing on applicants due to social media continues to rise, according to new CareerBuilder survey. Retrieved from http://www.careerbuilder.com/

CareerBuilder (2015, May 14). 35 percent of employers less likely to interview applicants they can't find online, according to annual CareerBuilder social media recruitment survey. Retrieved from http://www.careerbuilder.com/

CareerBuilder (2016, April 28). Number of employers using social media to screen candidates has increased 500 percent over the last decade. Retrieved from http://www.careerbuilder.com/

CareerBuilder (2017, June 15). Number of employers using social media to screen candidates at all-time high, finds latest CareerBuilder study. Retrieved from http://www.careerbuilder.com/

CareerBuilder (2018, August 9). More than half of employers have found content on social media that caused them not to hire a candidate, according to recent CareerBuilder survey. Retrieved from http://www.careerbuilder.com/

Davison, H. K., Maraist, C., Bing, M. N. (2011). Friend or foe? The promise and pitfalls of using social networking sites for HR decisions. *Journal of Business Psychology*, *26*, 153–159. DOI: 10.1007/s10869-011-9215-8

Hartwell, C. J. (2018). Social media and e-HRM. In M. Thite (Ed.), *e-HRM: Leveraging digital technology to transform HRM*. New York, NY: Routledge Publishing.

Hartwell, C. J., & Campion, M. A. (2020). Getting social in selection: How social networking website content is perceived and used in hiring. *International Journal of Selection and Assessment*, *28*, 1–16. doi: 10.1111/ijsa.12273

Kluemper, D. H. (2013). Social network screening: Pitfalls, possibilities, and parallels in employment selection. In T. Bondarouk & M. R. Olivas-Luajn (Eds.), *Advanced series in management: Social media in human resources management*. Bingley, UK: Emerald.

Kluemper, D. H., & Rosen, P. A. (2009). Future employment selection methods: Evaluating social networking web sites. *Journal of Managerial Psychology, 24*, 567–580. DOI: 10.1108/02683940910974134

Kluemper, D. H., Rosen, P.A., & Mossholder, K. W. (2012). Social networking websites, personality ratings, and the organizational context: More than meets the eye? *Journal of Applied Social Psychology, 42*, 1143–1172. DOI: 10.1111/j.1559-1816.2011.00881.x

Landers, R. N. & Schmidt, G. B. (Eds.) (2016). *Social media in employee selection and recruitment: Theory, practice, and current challenges*. Geneva, Switzerland: Springer International. DOI: 10.1007/978-3-319-29989-1

Levashina, J., Hartwell, C. J., Morgeson, F. P., & Campion, M. A. (2014). The structured employment interview: Narrative and quantitative review of the recent literature. *Personnel Psychology, 67*, 241–293. DOI: 10.1111/peps.12052

Madera, J. M. (2012). Using social networking websites as a selection tool: The role of selection process fairness and job pursuit intentions. *International Journal of Hospitality Management, 31*, 1276–1282. DOI: 10.1016/j.ijhm.2012.03.008

McFarland, L. A., & Ployhart, R. E. (2015). Social media: A contextual framework to guide research and practice. *Journal of Applied Psychology, 100*, 1653–1677. DOI: 10.1037/a0039244

Nikolaou, I. (2014). Social networking web sites in job search and employee recruitment. *International Journal of Selection and Assessment, 22*, 179–189. DOI: 10.1111/ijsa.12067

Pike, J. C., Bateman, P. J., & Butler, B. S. (2017). Information from social networking sites: Context collapse and ambiguity in the hiring process. *Information Systems Journal, 28*, 729–758. DOI: 10.1111/isj.12158

Ployhart, R. E. (2006). Staffing in the 21st century: New challenges and strategic opportunities. *Journal of Management, 32*, 868–897. DOI: 10.1177/0149206306293625

Ployhart, R. E. (2012). Social media in the workplace: Issues and strategic questions. *SHRM Foundation Executive Briefing*, 1–5. Retrieved from http://www.shrm.org/

Roth, P. L., Bobko, P., Van Iddekinge, C. H., & Thatcher, J. B. (2016). Social media in employee-selection-related decisions: A research agenda for uncharted territory. *Journal of Management, 42*, 269–298. DOI: 10.1177/0149206313503018

Roulin, N. (2014). The influence of employers' use of social networking websites in selection, online self-promotion, and personality in on likelihood of *faux pas* postings. *International Journal of Selection and Assessment, 22*, 80–87. DOI: 10.1111/ijsa.12058

Roulin, N. & Bangerter, A. (2013). Social networking websites in personnel selection: A signaling perspective on recruiters' and applicants' perceptions. *Journal of Personnel Psychology, 12*, 143–151. DOI: 10.1027/1866-5888/a000094

Roulin, N., & Levashina, J. (2019). LinkedIn as a new selection method: Psychometric properties and assessment approach. *Personnel Psychology, 72*, 187–211. DOI: 10.1111/peps.12296

Society for Human Resource Management [SHRM] (2008). Online technologies and their impact on recruitment strategies: Using social networking websites to attract talent. Retrieved from http://www.shrm.org/

Society for Human Resource Management [SHRM] (2011). SHRM research spotlight: Social media in the workplace. Retrieved from http://www.shrm.org/

Society for Human Resource Management [SHRM] (2013). SHRM survey findings: Social networking websites and recruiting/selection [PowerPoint slides]. Retrieved from http://www.shrm.org/

Society for Human Resource Management [SHRM] (2016). SHRM survey findings: Using Social Media for Talent Acquisition – Recruitment and Screening [PowerPoint slides]. Retrieved from http://www.shrm.org/

Stone, D. L., Deadrick, D. L., Lukaszewski, K. M., & Johnson, R. (2015). The influence of technology on the future of human resource management. *Human Resource Management Review, 25,* 216–231. DOI: 10.1016/j.hrmr.2015.01.002

Stoughton, J. W., Thompson, L. F., & Meade, A. W. (2015). Examining applicant reactions to the use of social networking websites in pre-employment screening. *Journal of Business Psychology, 30,* 73–88. DOI: 10.1007/s10869-013-9333-6

Taylor, P. J., Pajo, K., Cheung, G. W., & Stringfield, P. (2004). Dimensionality and validity of a structured telephone reference check procedure. *Personnel Psychology, 57,* 745–772. DOI: 10.1111/j.1744-6570.2004.00006.x

Thomas, S. L., Rothschild, P. C., & Donegan, C. (2015). Social networking, management responsibilities, and employee rights: The evolving role of social networking in employment decisions. *Employee Responsibilities and Rights Journal, 27,* 307–323. DOI: 10.1007/s10672-014-9250-5

Van Iddekinge, C. H., Lanivich, S. E., Roth, P. L., & Junco, E. (2016). Social media for selection? Validity and adverse impact potential of a Facebook-based assessment. *Journal of Management, 42,* 1811–1835. DOI: 10.1177/0149206313515524

Part 7: **Serving Different Audiences**

Emma Parry
Generations

A "generation" is commonly defined as 'an identifiable group that shares birth years, age, location and significant life events at critical developmental stages' (Kupperschmidt, 2000, p. 66). The literature suggests that each generation shares a different set of values and attitudes, as a result of their shared events and experiences while growing up, specifically in their formative years (late teens). The notion of a generation has received a lot of attention in the early part of the 21st century from both academics and practitioners; particularly in relation to how differences in their values and attitudes might affect their expectations and preferences as an employee and consumer.

The literature generally refers to four generations: Veterans (born 1925–1942); Baby Boomers (born 1943–1960); Generation X (born 1961–1981); and Generation Y or Millennials (born 1982–1999) (Howe & Strauss, 2007). More recent is the addition of a fifth generation – Generation Z (Reeves & Oh, 2008; Gibson, 2015), born from 2000 onwards, who's members are mostly still in education.

It is important to consider generational differences for a number of reasons. As explained by Ng & Parry (2016), a comparison of generational differences in terms of work values, attitudes, and career expectations is helpful in informing current HRM policies and practices in order to benefit future generations of workers and to manage intergenerational conflict. The idea of generations is relevant for this text as one of the main trends that is suggested to shape the attitudes of a generation is technological advancement.

This entry will consider the theoretical background of generations as well as reviewing the nature and quality of current empirical research in this area. This entry will also consider the role of technology in shaping the attitudes and values of the younger generations.

Theoretical Background

The notion of "generations" is commonly ascribed to the sociologist Karl Mannheim and his seminal paper "The Problem of Generations" (1952). Mannheim conceptualised a generation as a group of individuals with the same year of birth that share a common social location in history. This location means that these individuals are subjected to a limited range of potential experience, which predisposes them to a particular mode of thought and behaviour. Mannheim emphasized that year of birth alone was not sufficient for someone to belong to a generation; they must also be in a position to share common experience with other members, so that they have

https://doi.org/10.1515/9783110633702-035

a "distinct consciousness of that historical position . . . [and are] shaped by the events and experiences of that time" (Gilleard, 2004. P.108). This idea has been taken up by scholars focusing on the notion of collective memories (Schuman & Scott, 1989) and extended to include cultural characteristics of a period such as music or fashion (Edmunds & Turner, 2002; Holdbrook & Schindler, 1989, 1994; McMullin et al., 2007). Most importantly for this chapter, one of the main drivers of attitude change across generations, is said to be technological advancement with those who were born into particular types of technology ("digital natives") having different attitudes to those who were not.

Empirical Evidence on Generational Differences

The idea of generational differences has received significant attention from academics and a very large number of papers have been published since 2000. It is therefore impossible to review all of the available evidence in this brief entry. A number of reviews of this literature have been produced that cover this topic in more detail (see for example: Lyons & Kuron, 2014; Ng & Parry, 2016; Parry & Urwin, 2011; Twenge, 2010).

The characteristics that have been found to differ between generations are summarized in the Table 35.1. Much of the research has been focused on Generation Y due to their dominance in the workforce.

Much less is known about Generation Z compared to other generations due to their fairly young age. They are suggested to value security, traditional beliefs and the family unit as well as being more responsible (Williams & Page, 2011) confident, optimistic, and imaginative (Matthews, 2008).

Several authors have expressed their concerns about the quality of the evidence on which the idea of generations is based (see for example Costanza & Finklestein, 2015; Parry & Urwin, 2011). This is for a number of reasons. First, most research about generational differences uses cross-sectional research designs which are problematic in their failure to distinguish between cohort (generational), age (maturation) and period (the time in which the research was conducted) effects (Parry & Urwin, 2011; Rhodes, 1983). A few scholars have used longitudinal research in order to overcome these problems (Smola & Sutton, 2002; Twenge, Campbell, Hoffman, & Lance, 2008; Parry & Urwin, 2017), but the majority of research still relies on cross sectional studies. Second, research generally does not consider attributes of 'social space' other than birth year, such as geographical location or gender (Parry, 2014). Third, a number of scholars have suggested that the generations described above are not valid outside of the western world. For example, qualitative work from Parry, et al (2014)'s research across several countries suggested that generational characteristics differ according to national context.

Table 35.1: Summary of generational differences.

Characteristic	Summary of difference	Example citations
Loyalty	Lower in X than BB	Smola & Sutton (2002)
Work centrality	Lower in X than BB	Smola & Sutton (2002)
Patience	Declines with younger generations	Leung (2004); Parker-Pope (2010)
Dependence on technology	Declines with younger generations	Leung (2004); Parker-Pope (2010)
Self esteem	Increases with younger generations	Gentile, Twenge & Campbell (2010); Twenge & Campbell (2001)
Narcissism	Increases with younger generations	Twenge & Campbell (2009)
Individualism	Increases with younger generations	Foster, Campbell & Twenge (2003)
Valuing prestige/status	Increases in older generations	Hansen & Levy (2012)
Valuing autonomy	Increases in older generations	Hansen & Levy (2012)
Valuing extrinsic work factors	Increases in younger generations	Hansen & Levy (2012); Twenge et al. (2010)
Valuing leisure time	Increases in younger generations	Twenge et al. (2010); Becton et al. (2014)

Source: adapted from Ng & Parry (2016)

The Role of Technological Advancement in Driving Generational Difference

Technological advancement has commonly been suggested as a trend that drives change in attitudes and values and thus leads to differences between generations. For example, McMullin et al. (2007) identified computing as a marker of culture through which generations can be formed. Research has suggested that the digital age has led to an increasing impatience and a greater dependency on technology in millennials (Leung, 2004; Parker-Pope, 2010), with several authors describing millennials as "digital natives", as they are the first generation to grow up with technology (see for example Gursoy, Chi & Karadag 2013). Despite this, there is little research that examines the impact of technological advancement on attitudes directly. Research in this area is much needed.

More important in relation to e-HRM perhaps is the evidence pertaining to generational differences in use and comfort with technology. For example, a study by Van Volkom, Staplet & Amaturo (2014) found that those in older generations described more difficulties in using mobile phones and websites compared to younger generations, while younger generations reported more reliance on technology (evidenced by higher anxiety when they left their mobile phone at home) and a greater impact of technology on their communication behavior. This suggests that younger generations might have a greater acceptance of – and expectation for – the use of technology in human resource management. However, no research could be found that tests the suggestion that different generations might approach e-HRM differently, although some studies have found positive effects of e-HRM in samples of millennial employees (see for example Bissola 2014). Generally it is clear that there is a lack of empirical research on this topic: this needs to be addressed.

The practitioner press has emphasized the importance of digital approaches to HRM in satisfying younger generations. For example, Gayescki (2015) described research by Accenture that predicted that HR information and processes would need to be more integrated and accessible. Gayescki suggested that the HR function needed to be more like a digital marketing department in order to satisfy Generation Z's requirement for mass customization. Gayescki also commented that Generation Z were used to using statistics about themselves (e.g. from wearable devices) so could be encouraged to self-manage within organisations. These comments suggest a slightly different role for digital HRM in the future in order to use and provide data about employees, in order to individualize jobs and rewards and to empower employees to manage themselves.

Conclusions

The idea of generations has been adopted by both HR practitioners and academics, despite the flaws in the evidence behind it. What is clear is that attitudes are changing over time and that technological advancement is one driver of this. It is also likely that as employees' experiences of technology generally change across time, so will their expectations regarding the use of e-HRM. Empirical evidence regarding this idea however is sparse, with no real evidence that compares the use or attitudes of different generations towards e-HRM. This is a gap that needs to be addressed in the future.

Future Reading

Parry E. (2014). *Generational diversity at work: new research perspectives*. UK: Routledge.

References

Becton, J. B., Walker, H. J., & Jones-Farmer, A. (2014). Generational differences in workplace behavior. *Journal of Applied Social Psychology*, *44*(3), 175–189.

Bissola, R, (2014). The unexpected side of relational e-HRM: developing trust in the HR department. *Employee Relations*, *36*(4), 376–397.

Costanza, D.P., & Finklestein, L.M. (2015). Generationally based differences in the workplace: is there a *there* there? *Industrial and Organizational Psychology*, *8*(3), 308–323.

Edmunds, J. & Turner, B. (2002). *Generational consciousness, narrative and politics*. MD: Rowman & Littlefield.

Foster, J.D., Campbell, W.K., & Twenge, J.M. (2003). Individual differences in narcissism: Inflated self-views across the lifespan and around the world. *Journal of Research in Personality*, *37*(6), 469–486.

Gayescki, D. (2015). Will Generation Z even care about HR technology? *Workforce Solutions Review*, *6*(3), 9–11

Gentile, B., Twenge, J.M., & Campbell, W.K. (2010). Birth cohort differences in self-esteem, 1988–2008: A cross-temporal meta-analysis. *Review of General Psychology*, *14*(3), 261–268.

Gibson, C. (2015, December 3). Gen Z, iGen, Founders: What should we call the post-millennials? *Washington Post*. . Retrieved from https://www.washingtonpost.com/lifestyle/style/gen-z-igen-founders-what-should-we-call-the-post-millennials/2015/12/03/38a102b2-99d2-11e5-94f0-9eeaff906ef3_story.html?postshare=8391449617846120&tid=ss_tw

Gilleard, C. (2004). Cohorts and generations in the study of social change. *Social Theory and Health*, *2*, 106–119.

Gursoy, D., Chi, G. & Karadag, E. (2013). Generational differences in work values and attitudes among frontline and service contract employees. *International Journal of Hospitality Management*, *32*, 40–48.

Hansen, J.I.C., & Leuty, M.E. (2012). Work values across generations. *Journal of Career Assessment*, *20*(1), 34–52.

Holdbrook, M.B. & Schindler, R.M. (1989). Some exploratory findings on the development of musical tastes. *Journal of Consumer Research*, *16*, 119–124.

Holdbrook, M.B. & Schindler, R.M. (1994). Age, sex and attitude toward the past as predictors of consumers' aesthetic tastes for cultural products. *Journal of Marketing Research*, *31*, 412–422.

Howe, N. & Strauss, W. (2007). The next 20 years: how customer and workforce attitudes will evolve. *Harvard Business Review*, July-August, 41–52.

Kupperschmidt, B. (2000). Multigenerational employees: strategies for effective management. *Health Care Manager*, *19*, 65–76.

Leung, L. (2004). Net-generation attributes and seductive properties of the internet as predictors of online activities and internet addiction. *Cyber Psychology and Behavior*, *7*(3), 333–348.

Lyons, S. & Kuron, L. (2014). Generational differences in the workplace: a review of the workplace and directions for future research. *Journal of Organizational Behavior*, *35*(1), 139–157.

Mannheim, K. (1952). The problem of generations. In Kecskemeti P. (Ed.). *Essays on the Sociology of Knowledge* (276–322). London: Routledge & Kegan Paul.

Matthews, V. (2008). Generation Z, *Personnel Today*, *13*(4), 48–52.

McMullin, J., Comeau, T. & Jovic, E. (2007). Generational affinities and discourses of difference: a case study of highly skilled information technology workers. *British Journal of Sociology*, *58*, 86–103.

Ng, E.S.W. & Parry, E. (2016). Multigenerational research in human resource management. In: Buckley, R., Halbesleben J. & Wheeler A. (Eds). *Review in Personnel and Human Resource Management*, UK: Emerald. Pp. 1–41.

Parker-Pope, T. (2010). An ugly toll of technology: Impatience and forgetfulness. *New York Times*, June 6.

Parry, E. (2014). *Generational Diversity at Work: New Research Perspectives*. Abingdon, UK: Routledge.

Parry, E., Unite, J., Chudzikowski, K., Briscoe, J.P., & Shen, Y. (2014). Generational differences in the factors influencing career success across countries. In E. Parry (Eds,), *Generational Diversity at Work: New Research Perspectives* (pp. 204–231). Abingdon, UK: Routledge.

Parry, E. & Urwin, P. (2017). The evidence base for generational differences: where do we go from here? *Work, aging and retirement*, *3*(2), 140–148.

Parry, E., & Urwin, P. (2011). Generational differences in work values: a review of theory and evidence. *International Journal of Management Reviews*, *13*(1), 79–96.

Reeves, T. C., & Oh, E. (2008). Generational differences. In J. M. Spector, M. D. Merrill, J. van Merrienboer, & M. P. Driscoll (Eds.), *Handbook of research on educational communications and technology* (3rd ed.) (pp. 295–303). Mahwah, NJ: Lawrence Erlbaum.

Rhodes, S. (1983). Age-related differences in work-attitudes and behaviour: A review and conceptual analysis. *Psychological Bulletin*, *93*(2), 328–367.

Schuman, H. & Scott, J. (1989). Generations and collective memories. *American Sociological Review*, *54*, 359–381.

Smola, K.W., & Sutton, C.D. (2002). Generational differences: Revisiting generational work values for the new millennium. *Journal of Organizational Behavior*, *23*(SPI), 363–382.

Twenge, J.M. (2010). A review of the empirical evidence on generational differences in work attitudes. *Journal of Business and Psychology*, *25*(2), 201–210.

Twenge, J.M., & Campbell, W.K. (2001). Age and birth cohort differences in self-esteem: A cross-temporal meta-analysis. *Personality and Social Psychology Review*, *5*(4), 321–344.

Twenge, J.M., & Campbell, W K. (2009). *The narcissism epidemic: Living in the age of entitlement*. New York, NY: Simon and Schuster.

Twenge, J.M., Campbell, S.M., Hoffman, B.J., & Lance, C.E. (2010). Generational differences in work values: Leisure and extrinsic values increasing, social and intrinsic values decreasing. *Journal of Management*, *36*(5), 1117–1142.

Twenge, J.M., Campbell, S.M., Hoffman, B.J., & Lance, C.E. (2008). Generational differences in work values: leisure and extrinsic values increasing, social and intrinsic values decreasing. *Journal of Management*, *36*(5), 1117–1142.

Van Volkom, M., Staplet, J.C. & Amaturo, V. (2014). Revisiting the digital divide: generational differences in technology use in everyday life. *North American Journal of Psychology*, *16*(3), 557–574.

Williams, K.C., & Page, R.A. (2011). Marketing to Generations. *Journal of Behavioural Studies in Business*, *3*, 1–17.

Jeroen Meijerink

Gig Work and Online Labour Platforms' Use of e-HRM

Platform-enabled gig work (here after: gig work) is a particular type of contingent labour which is enabled by the use of digital technologies developed and maintained by platform firms such as Uber, Deliveroo or Amazon Mechanical Turk (Cassady, Fisher, & Olsen, 2018; Kuhn & Maleki, 2017; Meijerink & Keegan, 2019). Although the term gig work is used here, other concepts have been coined to describe platform-enabled contingent work, such as: crowdsourcing (Ellmer & Reichel, 2018; Nakatsu, Grossman, & Iacovou, 2014), elancing (Aguinis & Lawal, 2013), (in)dependent contracting (Kuhn & Maleki, 2017), "work on demand via app" (Aloisi, 2016) and interim/ freelance project work (Keegan, Ringhofer, & Huemann, 2018).

Defining Platform-Enabled Gig Work

Although contingent labour is in itself not new, the combination of the following features make gig work distinctive from other types of temporary work (Stanford, 2017). First, gig work involves paid work executed by freelancers. As such, rather than being employed, gig workers are independent contractors who – in principle – are free to decide when, where and for who they want to work. Although frequently violated by online labour platforms (see also section on "HRM without employment"), gig workers also (should) have discretion over the rates they charge (Aloisi, 2016; Kuhn & Maleki, 2017). As such, gig work is performed outside the confines of an organisation and/or employment relationship. Second, gig work involves the performance of fixed-term activities. These activities can be both short lived (such as delivering meals, performing a taxi ride or coding a piece of software) as well as more long term in nature (such as performing household activities on a repeated basis or taking part in a long-term consultancy project) (Nakatsu et al., 2014). Moreover, these activities can take place solely online – like eLancing (Aguinis & Lawal, 2013; Kässi & Lehdonvirta, 2018) – or be performed in the real world such as "work on demand via app" (Aloisi, 2016). Lastly, gig work involves a triangular relationship between a gig worker, a requester and an online platform firm (Breidbach, Brodie, & Hollebeek, 2014; Jacobides, Cennamo, & Gawer, 2018; Meijerink & Keegan, 2019). Through this relationship, requesters (which can be organisations as well as individual consumers) seek to outsource a fixed-term activity to a freelancer. The outsourcing of these activities is facilitated by online labour platforms such as Uber, Deliveroo or Upwork, which essentially act as intermediaries between gig workers and requesters. The key purpose of online labour platforms is thus to match the supply of and demand for

https://doi.org/10.1515/9783110633702-036

labour by connecting gig workers and requesters who are remote from one another, yet, wish to transact. To do so, online labour platforms rely on digital technologies to algorithmically dispatch orders (Duggan, Sherman, Carbery, & McDonnell, 2020; Lee, Kusbit, Metsky, & Dabbish, 2015), transact automated payments (Kuhn & Maleki, 2017) and create trust by means of online rating schemes (Pavlou & Gefen, 2004).

Online labour platforms are different from other types of lab labour or market intermediaries such as social network sites (e.g. LinkedIn). Whereas online labour platforms remain involved when gig workers and requesters transact, social network sites withdraw from the triangular relationship once a match is made. The same goes for headhunting agencies that do not remain when worker-requester transactions are taking place, for instance, as they do not facilitate payments or performance appraisal (Bonet, Cappelli, & Hamori, 2013). Moreover, online labour platforms are different from temp agencies as the latter employ those working for them, while the former work with independent contractors (Meijerink & Keegan, 2019). Taken together, platform-enabled gig work is therefore defined here as "[f]ixed-term activities which requesters (i.e. organizations or individual consumers) outsource on-demand to a self-employed gig worker with the help of an intermediary platform firm which installs an online platform that matches and manages gig workers and requestors, yet without actually employing gig workers and instituting an employment relationship with them" (Meijerink & Keegan, 2019,: 217)

e-HRM for Coordinating Platform Ecosystems

Online labour platforms establish semi-regulated marketplaces where supply and demand for labour is matched and managed. Put differently, and in line with the triangular relationship discussed before, online labour platforms maintain a platform ecosystem of semi-autonomous, yet interdependent workers, requesters and online platform firm (Jacobides et al., 2018; Wareham, Fox, & Cano Giner, 2014). These actors are interdependent as they either supply labour (i.e. gig workers), demand labour (i.e. requesters) or match labour supply and demand (i.e. online platform firm) – while remaining semi-autonomous entities. All platform ecosystem actors are critical, such that the ecosystem malfunctions when one group of actors stops transacting with the other actors. For instance, gig workers are dissatisfied and may leave the platform ecosystem if too little requesters are available (i.e. too little income to be earned), while requesters are dissatisfied if too little gig workers are available (i.e. activities cannot be outsourced).

To coordinate platform ecosystems, online labour platforms rely on a range of electronic human resource management (e-HRM) activities, including: online performance management systems (Cassady et al., 2018; Pavlou & Gefen, 2004), automated task allocation and division of labour (Duggan et al., 2020; Ellmer, 2015;

Kuhn & Maleki, 2017), dynamic pricing / compensation schemes (Lee et al., 2015; Rosenblat, 2018) and information sharing (Cassady et al., 2018). Gig workers are subject to these e-HRM activities to ensure they comply with the interest of the platform firms as well as those of requesters.

In platform ecosystems, requesters are also subject to e-HRM activities to ensure they comply with the platform firm's rules and meet the interests of gig workers (Meijerink & Keegan, 2019). Research shows that requesters' actions are controlled by means of e-HRM activities such as online performance management systems for expelling non-compliant requesters from the platform (Kuhn & Maleki, 2017), e-selection where platform firms make use of social network sites such as Tripadvisor to recruit requesters, holding pay in escrow (Kuhn & Maleki, 2017; Pavlou & Gefen, 2004), or algorithmically restricting the number/type of gig workers that requesters can hire (Meijerink, Keegan, & Bondarouk, 2019).

Conceptualising the HRM System for Gig Workers

The studies of Ellmer and Reichel (2018), Cassady et al. (2018) and Meijerink et al. (2019) provide a good overview of the (e)HRM activities used by online labour platforms for managing gig workers and/or requesters. Although online labour platforms install HRM activities in bundles, extant classifications of HRM systems do not readily apply to the gig work context. For instance, clustering HRM activities into ability-, motivation-, and opportunity-enhancing HRM (Jiang, Lepak, Hu, & Baer, 2012) does not translate well as online labour platforms often invest very little into the abilities of gig workers. Moreover, since gig workers are freelancers, they are limitedly provided with opportunity-enhancing HRM such as participation in decision making. Given the freelance status of gig workers, it is more important for online platforms to attract workers to their platforms, ensure they accept many orders, and meet requester's needs (Ellmer, 2015; Meijerink et al., 2019; Rosenblat, 2018). Following Meijerink et al. (2019), I propose to cluster the HRM activities of gig workers into the following three dimensions (see also Figure 36.1):

1) *Presenteeism-enhancing HRM activities* which ensure gig workers decide to obtain work via a given platform. These activities may include employer branding, surge prices and referral schemes;
2) *Immersion-enhancing HRM activities* that motivate gig workers to continue serving requesters via a given platforms. Examples of such activities are: automated task allocation and division of labour, personalised compensation, and incentive schemes;
3) *Performance-enhancing HRM activities* which motivate gig workers to meet requesters' wishes. These activities can include online performance management systems and information sharing.

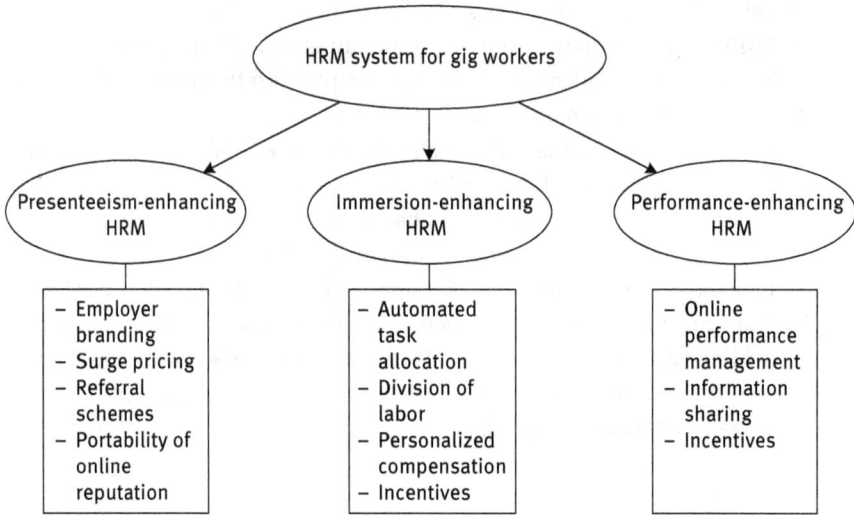

Figure 36.1: HRM system for gig workers.

HRM without Employment as Institutional Complexity

Online labour platforms create a situation of "HRM without employment", that is, the use of HRM activities by online labour platforms for controlling gig workers (and requesters), without establishing an employment relationship and holding that the platform firm is a neutral intermitter between supply and demand (Meijerink & Keegan, 2019). This situation has sparked many court cases around the world that centre on the false self-employment of gig workers and need to reclassify gig workers as employees (Aloisi, 2016; Daskalova, 2018; Kessler, 2015). Academics conceptualised the control over gig workers by means of (e)HRM of online platforms without establishing employment relationships as institutional complexity (Frenken, Vaskelainen, Fünfschilling, & Piscicelli, 2018; Meijerink et al., 2019). Institutional complexity occurs when organisations face incompatible prescriptions from different institutional logics (Greenwood, Raynard, Kodeih, Micelotta, & Lounsbury, 2011). In the case of gig work, these incompatible institutional logics include the 'corporation logic' (i.e. treating gig workers as if they are employed by a corporation that controls employee behaviour by means of HRM) and the 'market logic' (i.e. gig workers are independent who compete on a free, unregulated market by setting prices themselves). Research shows that online labour platforms address the institutional complexity associated with "HRM without employment" by delegating/outsourcing e-HRM responsibilities to requesters (and gig workers) through the online platform (Meijerink et al., 2019).

As such, in platform-enabled gig workers, e-HRM activities serve to uphold a platform ecosystem which in turns also facilitates the implementation of e-HRM activities.

Future Research Questions

Following available insights on e-HRM and gig work, I propose the following questions for future research:

- Which worker, platform and requester characteristics explain why requesters engage in performance appraisal (e.g. leaving online reviews) on online labour platforms?
- In what way do online labour platforms address institutional complexity associated with "HRM without employment" and how does this differ across institutional contexts / countries as well as across different institutional logics?
- Through which mechanisms do presenteeism-, immersion- and performance-enhancing HRM activities relate to gig worker behaviour?
- How do platform ecosystems evolve over time and which role do HRM activities play in such processes?
- What are the implications of algorithmic (HR) management for workers, requesters and (HR) professionals?

Further Readings

Cassady, E. A., Fisher, S. L., & Olsen, S. (2018). Using e-HRM to manage workers in the platform economy. In J. H. Dulebohn & D. Stone (Eds.), *The Brave New World of e-HRM 2.0* (pp. 217). Charlottee: Information Age Publishing.

Kuhn, K. M., & Maleki, A. (2017). Micro-entrepreneurs, Dependent Contractors, and Instaserfs: Understanding Online Labor Platform Workforces. *The Academy of Management Perspectives, 31*(3), 183–200.

Meijerink, J. G., & Keegan, A. (2019). Conceptualizing human resource management in the gig economy: Toward a platform ecosystem perspective. *Journal of Managerial Psychology, 34*(4), 214–232.

Stanford, J. (2017). The resurgence of gig work: Historical and theoretical perspectives. *The Economic and Labour Relations Review, 28*(3), 382–401.

References

Aguinis, H., & Lawal, S. O. (2013). eLancing: A review and research agenda for bridging the science–practice gap. *Human Resource Management Review, 23*(1), 6–17.

Aloisi, A. (2016). Commoditized workers: Case study research on labor law issues arising from a set of on-demand/gig economy platforms. *Comparative Labor Law & Policy Journal, 37*(3), 653–690.

Bonet, R., Cappelli, P., & Hamori, M. (2013). Labor market intermediaries and the new paradigm for human resources. *Academy of Management annals, 7*(1), 341–392.

Breidbach, C., Brodie, R., & Hollebeek, L. (2014). Beyond virtuality: from engagement platforms to engagement ecosystems. *Managing Service Quality, 24*(6), 592–611.

Cassady, E. A., Fisher, S. L., & Olsen, S. (2018). Using e-HRM to manage workers in the platform economy. In J. H. Dulebohn & D. Stone (Eds.), *The Brave New World of e-HRM 2.0* (pp. 217). Charlottee: Information Age Publishing.

Daskalova, V. (2018). Regulating the New Self-Employed in the Uber Economy: What Role for EU Competition Law. *German Law Journal, 19*, 461.

Duggan, J., Sherman, U., Carbery, R., & McDonnell, A. (2020). Algorithmic Management & App-Work in the Gig Economy: A Research Agenda for Employment Relations & HRM. *Human Resource Management Journal, 30*(1), 114–132.

Ellmer, M. (2015). The digital division of labor: socially constructed design patterns of Amazon Mechanical Turk and the governing of human computation labor. *Momentum Quarterly, 4*(3), 174–186.

Ellmer, M., & Reichel, A. (2018). Crowdwork from an HRM perspective—integrating organizational performance and employee welfare. *University of Salzburg: Working Paper, 1.*

Frenken, K., Vaskelainen, T., Fünfschilling, L., & Piscicelli, L. (2018). An Institutional Logics Perspective on the Gig Economy. doi:10.31235/osf.io/uqn9v

Greenwood, R., Raynard, M., Kodeih, F., Micelotta, E. R., & Lounsbury, M. (2011). Institutional complexity and organizational responses. *Academy of Management Annals, 5*(1), 317–371.

Jacobides, M. G., Cennamo, C., & Gawer, A. (2018). Towards a theory of ecosystems. *Strategic Management Journal.*

Jiang, K., Lepak, D. P., Hu, J., & Baer, J. C. (2012). How does human resource management influence organizational outcomes? A meta-analytic investigation of mediating mechanisms. *Academy of Management Journal, 55*(6), 1264–1294.

Kässi, O., & Lehdonvirta, V. (2018). Online labour index: measuring the online gig economy for policy and research. *Technological Forecasting and Social Change, 137*, 241–248.

Keegan, A., Ringhofer, C., & Huemann, M. (2018). Human resource management and project based organizing: Fertile ground, missed opportunities and prospects for closer connections. *International Journal of Project Management, 36*(1), 121–133.

Kessler, S. (2015). The gig economy won't last because it's being sued to death. *Fast Company*. Retrieved from https://www.fastcompany.com/3042248/the-gig-economy-wont-last-because-its-being-sued-to-death

Kuhn, K. M., & Maleki, A. (2017). Micro-entrepreneurs, Dependent Contractors, and Instaserfs: Understanding Online Labor Platform Workforces. *The Academy of Management Perspectives, 31*(3), 183–200.

Lee, M. K., Kusbit, D., Metsky, E., & Dabbish, L. (2015). *Working With Machines: The impact of Algorithmic and Data-Driven Management On Human Workers*. Paper presented at the Proceedings of the 33rd Annual ACM Conference on Human Factors in Computing Systems, New York.

Meijerink, J. G., & Keegan, A. (2019). Conceptualizing human resource management in the gig economy: Toward a platform ecosystem perspective. *Journal of Managerial Psychology, 34*(4), 214–232.

Meijerink, J. G., Keegan, A., & Bondarouk, T. (2019). *Exploring 'human resource management without employment' in the gig economy: How online labor platforms manage institutional complexity* Paper presented at the 6th International Workshop on the Sharing Economy Utrecht, The Netherlands, June 28–29, 2019.

Nakatsu, R. T., Grossman, E. B., & Iacovou, C. L. (2014). A taxonomy of crowdsourcing based on task complexity. *Journal of Information Science*, *40*(6), 823–834.

Pavlou, P. A., & Gefen, D. (2004). Building effective online marketplaces with institution-based trust. *Information Systems Research*, *15*(1), 37–59.

Rosenblat, A. (2018, October 12). When your boss is an algorithm. *New York Times*. Retrieved from https://www.nytimes.com/2018/10/12/opinion/sunday/uber-driver-life.html

Stanford, J. (2017). The resurgence of gig work: Historical and theoretical perspectives. *The Economic and Labour Relations Review*, *28*(3), 382–401.

Wareham, J., Fox, P. B., & Cano Giner, J. L. (2014). Technology ecosystem governance. *Organization Science*, *25*(4), 1195–1215.

Miguel R. Olivas-Luján, M-Y. Yusliza, and Sergio Madero-Gómez
Emerging Markets and e-HRM

Companies from or working in emerging market economies have a very large potential to benefit from e-HRM. In this entry, we review e-HRM research dealing with such countries; our first challenge was the identification of a practical definition for "emerging market." The International Monetary Fund (IMF), Standard and Poor's (S&P), university research centres, and Morgan Stanley Capital International (MSCI) use this term. The latter has been publishing the "MSCI Emerging Markets Index" since December 1987 (Melas, 2019). In August 2019, this index comprised twenty-six nations, with about 12% of equities around the world: Argentina, Brazil, Chile, China, Colombia, Czech Republic, Egypt, Greece, Hungary, India, Indonesia, Malaysia, Mexico, Pakistan, Peru, Philippines, Poland, Qatar, Russia, Saudi Arabia, South Africa, South Korea, Taiwan, Thailand, Turkey and the United Arab Emirates (https://www.msci.com/market-classification). Their main characteristics are: (1) superior economic growth, (2) low correlation across asset classes, and (3) relative scarcity of information. These are dynamic economies that have not yet achieved "developed" status, but are more stable and industrialised than "frontier markets" (which are less established, with even higher risks and potential for financial returns, like Bangladesh or Nigeria). Universal consensus about which countries belong to which category does not exist, but the above list is widespread.

Multinationals linked to these economies experience needs to automate their HRM functions in culturally and institutionally diverse ways, both within their nations of origin and in other nations. Changing legislation and economic philosophies require a sensibility in the management of people that was not existent even in the recent past. In addition to well-known descriptors of emerging economies, such as lower (but growing) salaries or continuous and fast economic growth, Bondarouk et al. (2016) state that management styles are focused on fast growth and the development of new products and services, and laws and regulations change more rapidly and less predictably vis-à-vis those of developed economies.

Most e-HRM studies are based on research carried out in developed countries (Bondarouk et al., 2016). However, a growing number of publications reflect investigations from outside the well-established countries. We next summarise these studies to uncover a canvass that still needs many painters before we can consider that a state-of-the-art *opus* has been achieved.

https://doi.org/10.1515/9783110633702-037

Comparative Studies Including Emerging Economies

We found two papers using the well-known Cranet database (a multinational comparative HR research effort originally based at Cranfield University; Brewster et al., 2004). Strohmeier and Kabst (2009) compared 23 countries, including "emerging" Czech Republic and Hungary; they were surprised to find that organisations in some of the emerging Central and Eastern European nations of their sample, including the Czech Republic, Slovenia, and Estonia, exhibited e-HRM adoption penetration as high as the richest, developed European economies. They theorised that these nations' recent openness toward the West might have given their organisations an opportunity to adopt e-HRM more rapidly than firms in the more established countries.

More recently, Galanaki et al. (2019) studied 31 countries that include seven considered emerging: Brazil, Hungary, Indonesia, Philippines, Russia, South Africa, and Turkey; they report that e-HRM is operationalised as a combination of the actual degree of technological presence and the degree to which the technology is used to enable HRM activities. They found four types of e-HRM configurations, namely "non-usage", "HR primacy", "Integrated e-HRM", and "IT primacy". The "non-usage" configuration, characterised by a smaller organisational size and a low strategic orientation of the HR function, appeared to be the most frequent configuration in Brazil, Hungary, Russia, and South Africa (most of the "emerging" nations). The "Integrated e-HRM configuration" is typical of large organisation with a strategically oriented HR function; respondents based in Indonesia, Philippines, and Turkey reported this category in larger numbers, as did most companies in the wealthier countries. The "IT primacy" configuration is characterised by medium organisational size and an emphasis on e-HRM outsourcing; no country in the study had a majority of firms reporting this configuration, but the ones that were near 20% were the most developed (e.g., Italy, Sweden, USA). As the number of countries – and the questions measuring e-HRM – increased, the picture became more complex, as did our understanding of how companies in emerging economies differ from the more developed ones in this respect.

The 2000s: China, Malaysia, and Mexico

In addition to comparative studies like the ones above, researchers have been studying e-HRM in emerging countries for over one decade. Zhang and Yuan (2007) described the implementation of an e-HRM system in a large Chinese state-run factory. Hooi (2006) documented that the readiness and feasibility of implementing e-HRM in the SMEs in Malaysia is dependent on the availability of resources and the attitude of the employees; resources covered in this study included expertise, financial and technical resources. Olivas-Luján et al. (2007) described the use and context for four Mexican multi-Latinas in e-learning, employee self-service, e-staffing, and remote collaborations.

Advances in the 2010s: China

During the ongoing decade, more e-HRM studies from emerging countries were published. Interviewing representatives of Western firms in China, Heikkila (2013) found that institutional pressures create both positive transformational and dysfunctional consequences for subsidiaries, and that responses to these pressures can substantially affect the ability of IS to achieve its strategic potential. It is worth mentioning that we did not find more recent e-HRM studies than this one, in spite of the vast dynamism from this economy.

India

Another emerging economy deserving more scholarly attention is India. Rao (2011) offered e-learning implications based on cultural studies for companies interested in India; her untimely death (in 2017) makes it unlikely that those hypotheses will be tested soon. Makkar and Sanjeev (2014) offer an optimistic interpretation of a study with methodological limitations (only 30 responses from one single bank). Finally, Sekhar and Patwardhan (2015) had a sample of 131 employees in service organisations and more sophisticated analyses on a variation of the well-known Technology Acceptance Model (TAM).

Malaysia, More Recently

In Malaysia, Yusliza and Ramayah (2012a) indicated that managing change is positively related to perceived ease of use and perceived usefulness. Yusliza and Ramayah (2012b) also found that clarity of e-HRM goals, user satisfaction with e-HRM, perceived usefulness, perceived ease of use, user support, social influence, and facilitating conditions influenced attitude towards e-HRM. Kassim et al. (2012) also investigated how innovation attributes relate to e-HRM use and its outcomes in companies around Penang. Ibrahim and Yusoff (2015) found evidence that attitude, technology readiness, and readiness for change were related to the components of techno-stress, such as techno-overload, techno-complexity, and techno-insecurity. Yusliza et al. (2017) also tested empirical relations between e-HRM and Green HRM.

Pakistan

Sabir et al. (2015) analysed surveys from 112 employees from three banks; they claim that HRM effectiveness and perceived effectiveness of HR practices are the most important contributors to value creation. Later, Iqbal et al. (2019) surveyed eleven bank branches; responses from operations and managers from 323 branches suggest that e-HRM practices significantly impact HR service quality and employee productivity.

Indonesia

Wahyudi and Park (2014) investigated e-HRM usage in the national Ministry of Finance, a unique and most valuable sample. They found perceived usefulness (PU) to be a strong predictor of e-HRM usage. From an organisational and managerial standpoint, HRM strength has a positive influence on e-HRM usage. In the creation of HRM values, they also found e-HRM usage to be a strong predictor of perceived human resource (HR) service quality, but not a predictor of the creation of a strategic role for the HRM function.

Bondarouk et al. (2016) found that headquarters' influence and the available resources have a strong influence on e-HRM adoption in 11 subsidiaries in Indonesia. Their qualitative approach enabled rich descriptions of organisations in different adoption stages and evidence-based recommendations for managers in emerging economies; to illustrate, talent shortages and legal regulations are major influences for subsidiary e-HRM adoption.

South Africa

We found one publication from this country. Udekwe and de la Harpe (2017) interviewed 21 employees in two South African retailers. They found underutilisation of their HRIS and recommend change management programs that include rigorous training to improve the status quo.

Turkey

In Turkey, Mishra and Akman (2010) documented how different sectors use IT for different HR purposes, noticing a wide variety of applications and uses, often without integration. Erdogmus and Esen (2011) found that technology readiness index contributes significantly to assess perceived usefulness and perceived ease of use. Findikli and Bayarcelik (2015) found that time management, easy acquiring and access to personal data, and reduce administration costs was the primary motivator for e-HRM applications. E-HRM reduced organisational costs, improved better and faster communication between manager and employees, reduced the processing time for e-HRM usage in organisation.

Poland

Here, the focus has been on e-recruiting. Woźniak (2015) described gamification in e-recruitment and used it to compare and understand why Poland lags behind the US in spite of similar levels of employee and business internet usage. Wołodźko and Woźniak (2017) compiled information from 300 e-recruiting, company-specific websites and from 1,054 young Polish professionals; they underscore low use of CSR (Corporate Social Responsibility) as an argument to attract talent.

Taiwan

Suen and Yang (2013) surveyed 501 HR professionals from ten financial companies and probed their findings in 30 interviews. Their analyses suggest that different HR roles, including those mixing IT (Information Technology) and HR are more likely to predict job performance.

Summing Up

The importance of studying e-HRM in emerging markets cannot be overstated, as these are very dynamic nations with a large majority of the world's population and expectations of economic growth. Our overview shows that e-HRM research is still embryonic in these nations, in spite of almost 15 years of published research dealing with them. Many studies show small samples and cross-sectional designs that are susceptible to mono-method and other statistical biases. We believe that more robust research designs (e.g., longitudinal, using more than one data collection method) are needed, as is identifying commonalities and differences within these increasingly important nations.

As the number of studies increases, valuable opportunities to advance the field can be anticipated, for example through systematic reviews uncovering gaps by HR sub-functions and by geographic regions or cultural clusters. These research questions should enable us to compare more precisely e-HRM antecedents, processes, and outcomes, in emerging, developed, and frontier markets.

Great thinkers in this field:

Tanya Bondarouk, Emma Parry, Huub Ruël, Stefan Strohmeier, and Yusliza Mohd.-Yusoff are among the pioneers in this topic. Pramila Rao dedicated her work to HRM research in India and Mexico.

Further Readings

Brewster, C., Mayrhofer, W. & Farndale, E. (2018). *Handbook of Research on Comparative Human Resource Management*. Cheltenham, UK: Elgar.

Melas, D. (2019). The future of emerging markets: 30 years on from the launch of the MSCI emerging markets index. [PDF]. NY: MSCI. Accessed online, https://www.msci.com/documents/10199/239004/Research-Insight-The-Future-of-Emerging-Markets/, July 15, 2019.

References

Bondarouk, T., Schiling, D. & Ruël, H. (2016). eHRM adoption in emerging economies: The case of subsidiaries of multinational corporations in Indonesia, *Canadian Journal of Administrative Sciences, 33*, 124–137.

Brewster, C., Mayrhofer, W. & Morley, M. (2004). *Human Resource Management in Europe: Evidence of Convergence?* London: Butterworth-Heinemann.

Erdogmus, N. & Esen, M. (2011). An investigation of the effects of technology readiness on Technology Acceptance in e-HRM. *Procedia Social and Behavioral Sciences, 24*, 487–495.

Findikli, A. A. & Bayarcelik, E. B. (2015). Exploring the outcomes of Electronic Human Resource Management (E-HRM)? *Procedia – Social and Behavioral Sciences*, 424–431.

Galanaki, E., Lazazzara, A. & Parry, E. (2019). A cross-national analysis of E-HRM configurations: Integrating the information technology and HRM perspectives, in Lazazzara, A., Nacamulli, R. C. D., Rossignoli, C. & Za, S. *Organizing for Digital Innovation: At the Interface Between Social Media, Human Behavior and Inclusion*, Springer, 261–276.

Heikkila, J-P. (2013). An institutional theory perspective on e-HRM's strategic potential in MNC subsidiaries. *Journal of Strategic Information Systems, 22*, 238–251.

Hooi, L. W. (2006) Implementing e-HRM: The readiness of small and medium sized manufacturing companies in Malaysia, *Asia Pacific Business Review, 12* (4), 465–485.

Ibrahim, H. & Yusoff, Y. M. (2015). User characteristics as antecedents of techno stress towards EHRM: From experts' views. *Procedia – Social and Behavioral Sciences, 172*, 134–141.

Iqbal, N., Ahmad, M., Raziq, M.M., & Borini, F.M. (2019). Linking e-HRM practices and organizational outcomes: empirical analysis of line manager's perception. *Revista Brasileira de Gestão de Negócios, 21* (1), 48–69.

Kassim, N.M., Ramayah, T., & Kurnia, S. (2012). Antecedents and outcomes of human resource information system (HRIS) use. *International Journal of Productivity and Performance Management, 61* (6), 603–623.

Makkar, U. & Sanjeev, R. (2014). Determining employees' perception through effective HRIS: An empirical study. *Journal of Strategic Human Resource Management, 3* (3), 26–32.

Mishra, A., & Akman, I. (2010). Information technology in Human Resource Management: An empirical assessment. *Public Personnel Management, 39* (3), 271–290.

Olivas-Luján, M.R., Ramirez, J. & Zapata-Cantu, L. (2007). e-HRM in Mexico: adapting innovations for global competitiveness. *International Journal of Manpower, 28* (5), 418–434.

Rao, P. (2011). E-learning in India: the role of national culture and strategic implications. *Multicultural Education & Technology Journal, 5* (2), 129–150.

Sabir, F., Abrar, M., Bashir, M., Baig, S.A., & Kamran, R. (2015). E-HRM impact towards company's value creation: evidence from banking sector of Pakistan. *International Journal of Information, Business and Management, 7* (2), 123–143.

Sekhar, C., & Patwardhan, M. (2015). Employee's perception towards e-HRM implementation: Indian service sector. *SCMS Journal of Indian Management, 12* (3), 82–93.

Strohmeier, S. & Kabst, R. (2009). Organizational adoption of e-HRM in Europe: An empirical exploration of major adoption factors. *Journal of Managerial Psychology, 24* (6), 482–501.

Suen, H., & Yang, J. (2013). HR professionalism in the computing environment: Predicting job performance within different HR Roles. *International Management Review, 9* (1), 19–31.

Udekwe, E. & de la Harpe, A.C. (2017). The use of human resource information systems in two retail organisations in the Western Cape, South Africa. *SA Journal of Human Resource Management, 15* (0), a827. https://doi.org/10.4102/sajhrm.v15i0.827.

Wahyudi, E. & Park, S. M. (2014). Unveiling the value creation process of electronic human resource management: An Indonesian case. *Public Personnel Management, 43* (1), 83–117.

Wołodźko, K, & Woźniak, J. (2017). The use by large Polish organizations of information about CSR activities in e-recruitment. *Economics & Sociology, 10* (2), 47–60.

Woźniak, J. (2015). The use of gamification at different levels of e-recruitment. *Management Dynamics in the Knowledge Economy, 3* (2), 257–278.

Yusliza, M-Y. & Ramayah, T. (2012a). Electronic Human Resource Management (E-HRM) and Human Resource (HR) Competencies: Some Evidence from an Emerging Market. *International Journal of Information and Communication Technology, 4* (1), 27–39.

Yusliza, M.Y. & Ramayah, T. (2012b). Determinants of attitude towards E-HRM: An empirical study among HR professionals. *Procedia – Social and Behavioral Sciences, 57*, 312–319.

Yusliza, M.Y., Othman, N.Z., Jabbour, C.J.C. (2017). Deciphering the implementation of green human resource management in an emerging economy. *Journal of Management Development, 36* (10), 1230–1246.

Zhang, L. & Yuan, H. (2007). A study of intelligent information processing in human resource management in China. In Xu, L., Tjoa, A., Chaudhry, S. (eds.) *Research and Practical Issues of Enterprise Information Systems II* (1), Boston: Springer, pp. 493–502.

Jeroen Meijerink
HR Shared Services

Shared services are generally referred to as a hybrid organizational model that integrates elements of centralization and decentralization (Maatman, Bondarouk, & Looise, 2010; Maatman & Meijerink, 2017; Richter & Bruehl, 2017). Rather than choosing between establishing staff functions which are centrally controlled by a corporate actor versus delegating full discretion over business activities to individual business units, organizations that implement shared services – at least in theory – combine both options (Bondarouk, 2011; Reilly & Williams, 2003; Strikwerda, 2004; Ulrich, 1995). In so doing, organizations establish a shared service centre (SSC) in which business support activities (e.g. finance, procurement, housing), and the necessary resources (e.g. knowledge, skills, technology) for executing them, are consolidated. Although servicing the line organization, an SSC is often remotely located from the business units that it provides support services to. To service its clients, SSCs rely on information technologies such as self-service portals (Farndale, Paauwe, & Hoeksema, 2009; Meijerink, ten Kattelaar, & Ehrenhard, 2014) and telecommunication technologies for call centre or help desk support (Cooke, 2006). Despite centrally consolidating activities and resources, SSCs are not controlled by a 'central' actor such as the board of directors or the management team. Instead, the activities of the SSC are controlled by those it serves: the decentral business units. Business units jointly exercise control over a SSC through governance mechanisms such as service level agreements, user panels or clients boards, which should align the interests of the SSC with those of the business units (Farndale, Paauwe, & Boselie, 2010; Meijerink & Bondarouk, 2013). Similar to the service delivery, the decentralization of control is also enabled by information technologies as these help to record the performance of the SSC and share performance metrics with the business units (Farndale et al., 2009; Knol, Janssen, & Sol, 2014; Maatman & Bondarouk, 2014). Figure 38.1 shows a visual representation of the ways in which an HR SSC can be positioned vis-à-vis the business units served. The ideal type SSC (Type D in Figure 38.1) is the 'Internal Joint Venture' as it solely reports to the local business units without the direct involvement of a corporate entity. On the other end of the decentralized control spectrum lies the 'Central Service SSC' (Type A in Figure 38.1) as it almost completely controlled by a corporate entity. In the case of the 'Central Service SSC', the business can informally control the SSC by means of user panels and client boards. Albeit being organized differently, the different types of SSC unite as they operate within the spheres of an organization. This makes shared services distinct from outsourcing: in the case of the former, business activities remain within the boundaries of the firm in an SSC, while in the latter, activities are outsourced to an actor outside the organization. Accordingly, shared services have also been referred to as in-sourcing (Farndale et al., 2009).

https://doi.org/10.1515/9783110633702-038

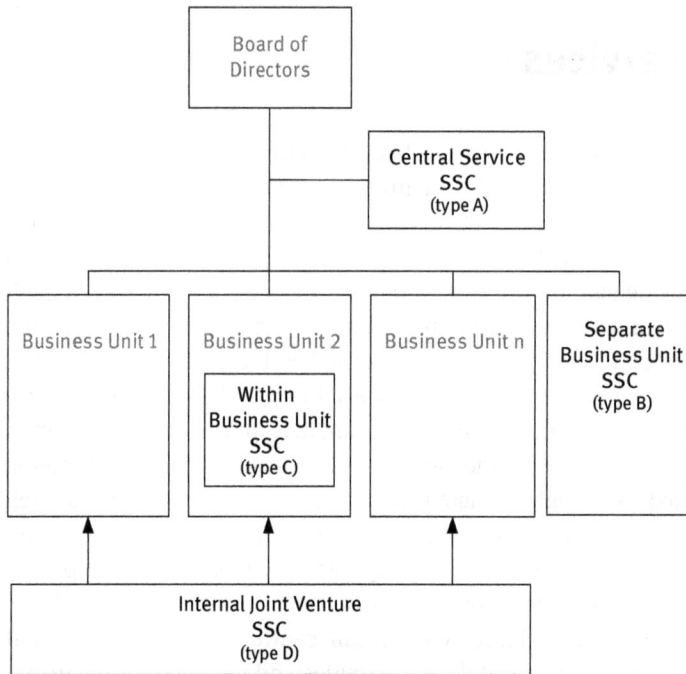

Figure 38.1: Governance structures of HR SSCs.
Source: adapted from Strikwerda (2004).

The notions of shared services and SSC are different, yet nested concepts: while shared services describe the wider organizational model for sourcing business activities, the SSC is an organizational unit that offers performs consolidated business activities for decentral business units. Together with the business units and end-users served, the SSC makes up the shared services model (Maatman et al., 2010).

HRM Activities in Shared Service Centres

Whereas SSCs were initially established for consolidating finance and ICT services, throughout the years, organizations are increasingly relying on the shared service model for implementing human resource management (HRM) activities (Gospel & Sako, 2010; Meijerink, Bondarouk, & Maatman, 2013; Richter & Bruehl, 2017; Strikwerda, 2004). Although HR SSCs are generally associated with execution of transactional HRM activities such as payroll and personnel administration (Boglind, Hällstén, & Thilander, 2011; Ulrich, Younger, & Brockbank, 2008), this is no longer the case. Besides being an administration expert, HR SSCs also offer so-called transformational HRM services related to training and development, employer branding and consultancy (Meijerink et al., 2013). Moreover, due to the sheer amount of transactions processed, and the large amount of data they collect, HR SSCs are in a unique position to engage in HR analytics activities (Marler & Boudreau, 2017; Van den Heuvel & Bondarouk, 2017). Indeed, research shows that transactional HR SSCs develop and leverage capabilities to analyse HR processes and make predictions how to increase process efficiency (Maatman & Bondarouk, 2014).

The Value of HR Shared Services and Its Antecedents

The use of shared services model for the delivery of a wide range of HRM activities is not surprising when considering the promised benefits of the model. Research shows that organizations introduce shared services in hope of reducing costs, improving HR service quality, fostering standardization across business units and enabling HR business partners to focus on their 'core business' (Farndale et al., 2009; Janssen & Joha, 2006; Richter & Bruehl, 2017). To measure whether these outcomes are realized, researchers have studied the value of shared services. Here, shared service value refers to the ratio between benefits (or quality) and costs of HR shared services to their clients (i.e. business units) and end-users (i.e. employees, line managers and HR professionals) (Maatman & Meijerink, 2017; Meijerink, Bondarouk, & Lepak, 2016). Research shows that the value of HR shared services is contingent on the actions and resources of its main stakeholders: the HR SSC, the business units and end-users (Knol et al., 2014; Richter & Bruehl, 2017). According to HR directors, a major success factor for HR SSCs is having the correct competences and experience of HR SSC employees, as well as knowledge exchange within the HR SSC (Cooke, 2006; Farndale et al., 2010). Research indeed shows that HR SSCs create value for their end-users through combine its human capital (i.e. HR SSC staff competences) with social capital (i.e. intra-HR SSC collaboration and knowledge exchange) and organizational capital (i.e. knowledge exchange through codification) (Meijerink & Bondarouk, 2013; Meijerink & Bondarouk, 2018). Furthermore, Maatman and Meijerink (2017) show that both the operational and dynamic capabilities of HR SSCs relate positively to the HR shared services value for business units.

Besides the HR SSC's resources and capabilities, its clients (i.e. the business units) also add to the value of HR shared services through collaborating with the HR SSC and other business units. For instance, Maatman and Meijerink (2017) show that the use of informal control mechanisms (i.e. relationship building and collaboration between the SSC and its clients) by a business unit relates positively with the shared services value to that business unit. Moreover, the use of service level agreements is important for HR SSC success as long as used by the business units for collaboration with, rather than for sanctioning, the HR SSC (Maatman & Meijerink, 2017; Redman, Snape, Wass, & Hamilton, 2007). As such, technology-enabled formal control mechanisms (e.g. assessing service level agreements) primarily adds to the success of the HR shared service model when used to stimulate the use of informal control mechanisms. Finally, business units can best collaborate with one another to ensure HR processes are standardized across business units (Cooke, 2006; Farndale et al., 2009; Meijerink & Bondarouk, 2013) and to avoid competition among the business units for the HR SSC's resources (McIvor, McCracken, & McHugh, 2011; Redman et al., 2007).

Finally, the success of HR shared services is contingent on the contributions of its end-users: the employees, managers and HR professionals. For instance, Cooke (2006) shows that the cost reduction potential of an HR SSC is seriously hampered when end-users engage in 'shadow administration'. Furthermore, research has shown that the value of HR shared services to end-users is contingent on the human capital of these very end-users (Meijerink et al., 2016). As a matter of fact, in some cases, end-users' human capital may substitute for the lack of human capital on the part of the HR SSC (Meijerink & Bondarouk, 2018). To develop the human capital of their end-users, HR SSCs could rely on information technologies. For instance, Meijerink et al. (2013) show that end-user human capital develops primarily through experience. HR SSC's could decide to publish workers' pay slips online to attract them to the HR SSC's self-service portal for gaining more experience with using the HR SSC's services.

To conclude, the bundling of resources in an HR SSC and delegation of control over an HR SSC to the business units serves, may help to improve HR service delivery. Realizing the promised benefits of HR shared services is contingent on the actions and resources of the HR SSC, its clients and end-users.

Future Research Directions

Following available insights on HR shared services, I propose the following questions for future research:
- How does the multitude of relationships among actors (i.e. the HR SSC, business units, end-users, top management) affect the success and value-creating potential of the HR shared services model?
- Chicken or the egg? What is the causal direction in the relationships among end-user's human capital, use of HR shared services and HR shared services value?

Further Readings

Gospel, H., & Sako, M. (2010). The unbundling of corporate functions: the evolution of shared services and outsourcing in human resource management. *Industrial and corporate change*, *19*(5), 1367–1396.

Maatman, M., & Meijerink, J. (2017). Why sharing is synergy: The role of decentralized control mechanisms and centralized HR capabilities in creating HR shared service value. *Personnel Review*, *46*(7), 1297–1317.

McIvor, R., McCracken, M., & McHugh, M. (2011). Creating outsourced shared services arrangements: Lessons from the public sector. *European management journal*, *29*(6), 448–461.

Richter, P. C., & Bruehl, R. (2017). Shared service center research: A review of the past, present, and future. *European management journal*, *35*(1), 26–38.

References

Boglind, A., Hällstén, F., & Thilander, P. (2011). HR transformation and shared services: Adoption and adaptation in Swedish organisations. *Personnel Review*, *40*(5), 570–588.

Bondarouk, T. (2011). Chapter 5 A Framework for the ComparativeAnalysis of HR Shared Services Models. In T. Bondarouk, H. Ruel, & J. K. Looise (Eds.), *Electronic HRM in theory and practice* (pp. 83–104): Emerald Group Publishing Limited.

Cooke, F. L. (2006). Modeling an HR shared services center: Experience of an MNC in the United Kingdom. *Human resource management*, *45*(2), 211–227.

Farndale, E., Paauwe, J., & Boselie, P. (2010). An exploratory study of governance in the intra-firm human resources supply chain. *Human resource management*, *49*(5), 849–868.

Farndale, E., Paauwe, J., & Hoeksema, L. (2009). In-sourcing HR: shared service centres in the Netherlands. *The International Journal of Human Resource Management*, *20*(3), 544–561.

Gospel, H., & Sako, M. (2010). The unbundling of corporate functions: the evolution of shared services and outsourcing in human resource management. *Industrial and corporate change*, *19*(5), 1367–1396.

Janssen, M., & Joha, A. (2006). Motives for establishing shared service centers in public administrations. *International journal of information management*, *26*(2), 102–115.

Knol, A., Janssen, M., & Sol, H. (2014). A taxonomy of management challenges for developing shared services arrangements. *European management journal*, *32*(1), 91–103.

Maatman, M., & Bondarouk, T. (2014). Value creation by transactional shared service centers: mapping capabilities. In T. Bondarouk (Ed.), *Shared Services as a New Organizational Form* (pp. 153–174). Bingley: Emerald Group Publishing Limited.

Maatman, M., Bondarouk, T., & Looise, J. K. (2010). Conceptualising the capabilities and value creation of HRM shared service models. *Human Resource Management Review*, *20*(4), 327–339.

Maatman, M., & Meijerink, J. (2017). Why sharing is synergy: The role of decentralized control mechanisms and centralized HR capabilities in creating HR shared service value. *Personnel Review*, *46*(7), 1297–1317.

Marler, J. H., & Boudreau, J. W. (2017). An evidence-based review of HR Analytics. *The International Journal of Human Resource Management*, *28*(1), 3–26.

McIvor, R., McCracken, M., & McHugh, M. (2011). Creating outsourced shared services arrangements: Lessons from the public sector. *European management journal*, *29*(6), 448–461.

Meijerink, J., Bondarouk, T., & Maatman, M. (2013). Exploring and comparing HR shared services in subsidiaries of multinational corporations and indigenous organisations in the Netherlands: A strategic response analysis. *European journal of international management, 7*(4), 469–492.

Meijerink, J., ten Kattelaar, J., & Ehrenhard, M. (2014). Structuring shared services: Realizing SSC benefits through end-users' usage of an HR portal. In T. Bondarouk (Ed.), *Shared services as a new organizational form* (pp. 105–131): Emerald Group Publishing Limited.

Meijerink, J. G., & Bondarouk, T. (2013). Exploring the central characteristics of HR shared services: Evidence from a critical case study in the Netherlands. *The International Journal of Human Resource Management, 24*(3), 487–513.

Meijerink, J. G., & Bondarouk, T. (2018). Uncovering configurations of HRM service provider intellectual capital and worker human capital for creating high HRM service value using fsQCA. *Journal of Business Research, 82*(1), 31–45.

Meijerink, J. G., Bondarouk, T., & Lepak, D. P. (2016). Employees as active consumers of HRM: linking employees' HRM competences with their perceptions of HRM service value. *Human resource management, 55*(2), 219–240.

Redman, T., Snape, E., Wass, J., & Hamilton, P. (2007). Evaluating the human resource shared services model: evidence from the NHS. *The International Journal of Human Resource Management, 18*(8), 1486–1506.

Reilly, P. A., & Williams, T. (2003). *How To Get Best Value From HR: The Shared Services Option*. Aldershot: Gower Publishing.

Richter, P. C., & Bruehl, R. (2017). Shared service center research: A review of the past, present, and future. *European management journal, 35*(1), 26–38.

Strikwerda, J. (2004). *Shared Service Center: Van Kostenbesparing naar Waarde Creatie*. Assen: Van Gorcum.

Ulrich, D. (1995). Shared services: From vogue to value. *People and Strategy, 18*(3), 12–24.

Ulrich, D., Younger, J., & Brockbank, W. (2008). The twenty-first-century HR organization. *Human resource management, 47*(4), 829–850.

Van den Heuvel, S., & Bondarouk, T. (2017). The rise (and fall?) of HR analytics: A study into the future application, value, structure, and system support. *Journal of Organizational Effectiveness: People and Performance, 4*(2), 157–178.

Part 8: **Technical Issues in e-HRM**

Stefan Strohmeier
Big HR Data

As in many business domains, over half a decade the concept of *big data* is being discussed in HRM, too (e.g., Huselid & Minbaeva, 2019; Campion et al., 2018). Understanding big HR data as an input for HR analyses to provide information and decision support, this discussion relates to and overlaps with the discussion on HR Analytics (Marler & Boudreau, 2017). Beside an application in HR practice, the exploitation of big data in HR research is also considered possible (e.g., McAbee, Landis & Burke, 2017).

State of Research in Big HR Data

Despite of the growing prominence, research on big data is scarce and only few contributions examine big HR data. These few contributions are mostly conceptual in nature; systematic empirical studies do not exist. Consequently, the state of knowledge on big HR data is of nascent nature. As a particularity of the current discussion, there are blatant discrepancies in the assessment of the concept: Proponents of big HR data state that the ongoing digitalization of HRM has generated data of a large volume, various formats and rapid emergence, and that these data contain valuable information, which can systematically improve HR decisions. Big HR data are even understood as a prominent means of improving HRM by changing it from an experience- and intuition-based to a successful evidence- and information-based corporate function (e.g., Huselid & Minbaeva, 2019). Sceptics of big HR data, however, put the concept fundamentally in question. A very basic doubt refers to the actual existence of HR data with a large volume, various formats and rapid emergence (e.g., Capelli, 2017). Further doubts relate to the informativeness and, thus, usefulness of such data, and to the methodical and technical proficiency of the HR profession to exploit them (e.g., Angrave et al., 2016).

Conceptualisation of Big HR Data

For a clarification of the concept, there is a widespread agreement on employing "*Multi-V-Models*" (e.g., Gandomi & Haider, 2015). "V-Models" portray big data as a multi-dimensional concept that can be described based on different dimensions starting with the letter "V". As a broadly accepted base model, the "3-V-model" comprises the dimension of *data volume*, *data variety* and *data velocity* as core dimensions (Laney, 2001). However, further dimensions, such as HR *data veracity* or

https://doi.org/10.1515/9783110633702-039

HR *data value*, are frequently added, and some practitioner publications list ten and even more dimensions of big data (e.g., Firican, 2019). Since such proliferations detract from rather than add to comprehensibility, a parsimonious model that maps the core dimensions seems more adequate. Therefore, in the following a 4-V-Model is employed, that comprises of the base model, which is enriched with "data veracity" since veracity constitutes the core condition of any useful exploitation of big data (e.g., Gandomi & Haider, 2015).

A first dimension refers to the HR *data volume*. Initially, the overall designation of "big" data obviously originates from this dimension, what, however, neglects the multi-dimensional character the concept. Regarding the definition of data volume, there is a simple and common understanding of this dimension that refers to the pure quantity of data available in HRM. There is a technical unit of measurement, which enables an exact measurement and comparison of data volumes in HR ("bytes"). Based on this understanding, big HR data are firstly characterized by a high data volume (e.g., Ryan & Herlemann, 2015). Regarding the operationalization of data volume, it should be noted that a clear-cut threshold to determine high data volumes does not exist. Instead, orders of magnitude such as "terabytes to petabytes" (e.g., McAbee et al., 2017) or even more vague indications such as "too big for conventional databases" are used (e.g., Angrave et al., 2016). Such operationalizations are evidently vague and general, and overlook that data volume in HR must be mandatorily related to the number of employees of a corporation. In very large organizations even terabytes might still stand for rather small data volumes while in small organizations gigabytes might already indicate a large data volume. Evidently, this vague operationalization aggravates an empirical determination of big HR data. Regarding the contribution of data volume, it is – often implicitly – assumed that more HR data would also contain more HR information. However, this assumption has to be assessed for existing HR data stocks since not every datum mandatorily contains decision-relevant information.

A second dimension refers to the *HR data variety*. Regarding the definition of data variety, there is a broad agreement stating that variety refers to the heterogeneity of formats that HR data can show. Based on this understanding, big HR data are, secondly, characterized by a high data variety (e.g., Campion et al., 2018). Regarding an operationalization, the trisection of structured, semi-structured and unstructured HR data is frequently employed as a rough categorization. Structured data are organized in pre-defined data structures (fields and records), unstructured data do not show such pre-defined structures while semi-structured data constitute a hybrid category comprising of both, structured and unstructured data. Since semi- and unstructured data show in particular larger volumes, data variety is related to the volume dimension (Gandomi & Haider, 2015). Based on the categorization, variety is assumed if structured, semi-structured *and* unstructured HR data exist simultaneously (e.g., McAbee et al., 2017). However, variety can also emerge within a data category. For example, different kinds of unstructured data, such as text, audio and video data, also contribute to variety. Currently there is no commonly accepted sub-categorization of structured, semi-structured and unstructured data. Moreover, there is no measurement procedure and measurement unit for data variety. This again aggravates an empirical determination of big HR data. Regarding the contribution of data variety, it is assumed that further data formats such as text or audio data contain further, so far unconsidered valuable information for HR. Again, this assumption must be, however, assessed for individual data stocks since also further data formats, of course, not mandatorily contain decision-relevant information.

A third dimension refers to *HR data velocity*. Regarding the definition of HR data velocity, there are heterogeneous and sometimes unclear understandings of this dimension. A first clarification can be given by distinguishing the velocity of data generation and the velocity of data analyses. The velocity of data generation refers to speed and frequency of data ascertainment ("incoming velocity"). In a narrow understanding, data velocity refers exclusively to incoming velocity. The velocity of data analysis refers to speed and frequency at which generated data are subsequently analyzed ("outgoing velocity"). In a broader understanding, data velocity refers to the combination of incoming and outgoing velocity. It is obvious that both velocities are interrelated since the feasible outgoing velocity depends on the actual incoming velocity. Therewith, data velocity is also related to data volume since an increasing frequency of data generation implies increasing data volumes. Based on this understanding, big HR data thirdly are characterized by a high data velocity (e.g., Lengnick-Hall et al., 2018). Regarding the operationalization of data velocity, the categorization into real-time, near-time and time-lagged data is frequently employed (e.g., Gandomi & Haider, 2015). Real-time implies that data are generated (narrow understanding) and analyzed (broader understanding) simultaneously with HR-relevant changes in the real world. Real-time approaches often require a high frequency of data ascertainment and analysis of the resulting continuous data streams. Near-time implies that data are ascertained and analyzed briefly after an HR-relevant change in the real world. However, a detailed specification of a brief period is missing. Lag-time implies that data are ascertained (and analyzed) with a delay while this delay is not concretized. Again, there is no measurement procedure for data variety, and since being not fully operationalized, this aggravates an empirical determination of big HR data. Regarding the contribution of data velocity, it is assumed that the timely provision of decision-relevant information avoids delays in HRM decisions.

A fourth dimension refers to *HR data veracity*. Regarding the definition of HR data veracity, the dimension largely overlaps with the well-introduced concept of data quality (e.g., Wang & Strong, 1996) which was replaced by veracity mostly because it does not start with the letter "V". Like data quality, veracity comprises of different sub-dimensions such as completeness, correctness or relevance of HR data (e.g., Rubin & Lukoianova, 2014; Wang & Strong, 1996). However, being clearly different from the previous dimensions, big data are not defined by a *high* degree of veracity, but by an *uncertain* degree of veracity (e.g., Rubin & Lukoinova, 2014; McAbee et al., 2017). Uncertainty lies in general data quality problems, such as missing data or wrong entries (e.g., Wang & Strong, 1996), and in particular, in big data-specific data quality problems, such as unclear data sampling or incorrect mapping of data from different sources (e.g., Rubin & Lukoianova, 2014). Regarding the operationalization of HR data veracity, there are different general suggestions of determining data quality that can be employed (e.g., Wang & Strong, 1996). However, since big HR data can show any (high *or* low) degree of veracity, a determination of veracity is not necessary for deciding on the existence of big HR data. Regarding the contribution of HR data veracity, however, it is obvious that only data with high veracity contribute to information and decision quality while low veracity worsens the situation. Thus, a determination of HR data veracity is mandatory for determining the practicability of big HR data.

Definition of Big HR Data

The above discussion offers a parsimonious conceptualization of big HR data that maps the current state of knowledge. Based on the conceptualization, a general definition of big HR data can be provided: *Big HR data refer to data of high volume, high variety, high velocity and uncertain (high or low) veracity.* Further dimensions such as data value or data variability might be added, if instructive against the backdrop of a specific big data project.

Future Directions in Big HR Data

The above conceptualization hints at open research tasks relating to big HR data: A first research task refers to the *operationalization of big HR data*, while this particularly refers to elaborating measures and thresholds of the different data dimensions of big HR data. In doing so, it is crucial to aim at a *domain-specific* operationalization (following a general suggestion of Gandomi & Haider, 2015). For instance, there is little sense in comparing data volumes of HRM with data volumes of video-portals since video-files show *per se* very large volumes, and video-portals often dispose of millions of users uploading their contents. Thus, HR departments will never reach the data volume of a global video portal. Consequently, thresholds for large data volumes must be defined domain-specific. Such domain-specific operationalizations have to be elaborated for all dimensions of big HR data. The resulting domain-specific big HR data concept will actually contribute to a better understanding, and it can be assumed that this already will contribute much to mitigating the current controversy about the existence of big HR data. Based on such an operationalization, a second research task refers to the systematic *assessment of big HR data*. A first step in this is to ascertain, which data stocks actually exist in HRM and whether and how potential future HR data stocks can enrich these. As a subsequent step, the potentials of existing data need a systematic consideration and elaboration. Given some initial and promising attempts to capitalize on the general developments of big data analytics also in HRM (e.g., Campion et al., 2018), this will ensure that existing or potentially obtainable data of HRM are fully exploited and that potentials are not wasted as occasionally feared in current literature (e.g., Angrave et al. 2015). A promising way to elaborate on these potentials is design research to develop and evaluate concrete use cases that identify which concrete decision problems can be supported based on which concrete big HR data using which concrete analysis methods. These further research steps are mandatory to keep pace with the interesting and challenging phenomenon that big data actually constitute for HRM.

Further Readings

Campion, M. C., Campion, M. A., & Campion, E. D. (2018). Big Data techniques and talent management: Recommendations for organizations and a research agenda for IO psychologists. *Industrial and Organizational Psychology, 11*(2), 250–257.

Gandomi, A., & Haider, M. (2015). Beyond the hype: Big data concepts, methods, and analytics. *International Journal of Information Analytics, 35*(2), 137–144.

McAbee, S. T., Landis, R. S., & Burke, M. I. (2017). Inductive reasoning: The promise of big data, *Human Resource Management Review, 27*(2), 277–290.

References

Angrave, D., Charlwood, A., Kirkpatrick, I., Lawrence, M., & Stuart, M. (2016). HR and analytics: Why HR is set to fail the big data challenge. *Human Resource Management Journal, 26*(1), 1–11. https://doi.org/10.1111/1748-8583.12090

Campion, M. C., Campion, M. A., & Campion, E. D. (2018). Big Data techniques and talent management: Recommendations for organizations and a research agenda for IO psychologists. *Industrial and Organizational Psychology, 11*(2), 250–257. https://doi.org/10.1017/iop.2018.14

Capelli, P. (2017). There's no such thing as big data in HR, *Harvard Business Review*, online: https://hbr.org/2017/06/theres-no-such-thing-as-big-data-in-hr

Firican, G. (2019). The 10 Vs of Big Data; online: https://tdwi.org/articles/2017/02/08/10-vs-of-big-data.aspx

Gandomi, A., & Haider, M. (2015). Beyond the hype: Big data concepts, methods, and analytics. *International Journal of Information Analytics, 35*(2), 137–144. https://doi.org/10.1016/j.ijinfomgt.2014.10.007

Huselid, M., & Minbaeva, D. (2019). Big Data and Human Resource Management. *Sage Handbook of Human Resource Management* (2nd edition), Wilkinson, A., Bacon, Lepak L., & Snell, S. (eds.), *in press*.

Laney, D. (2001). *3-D data management: Controlling data volume, velocity, and variety*. META Group Research Note.

Lengnick-Hall, M. L., Neely, A. R., & Stone, C. B. (2018). Human Resource Management in the digital age: Big data, HR analytics and artificial intelligence. In *Management and Technological Challenges in the Digital Age* (pp. 1–30). CRC Press. https://doi.org/10.1201/9781351238922-1

Rubin, V. L. & Lukoianova, T. (2014). Veracity roadmap: Is big data objective, truthful and credible? *Advances In Classification Research Online, 24*(1), 4–15. https://doi.org/10.7152/acro.v24i1.14671

Marler, J. H., & Boudreau, J. W. (2017). An evidence-based review of HR Analytics. *The International Journal of Human Resource Management, 28*(1), 3–26. https://doi.org/10.1080/09585192.2016.1244699

McAbee, S. T., Landis, R. S., & Burke, M. I. (2017). Inductive reasoning: The promise of big data, *Human Resource Management Review, 27*(2), 277–290. https://doi.org/10.1016/j.hrmr.2016.08.005

Ryan, J., & Herleman, H. A. (2015). A big data platform for workforce analytics. In S. Tonidandel, E. B. King, & J. M. Cortina (Eds.), *Big data at work: The data science revolution and organizational psychology.* (pp. 33–56). New York, NY: Routledge.

Wang, R. Y., & Strong, D. M. (1996). Beyond accuracy: What data quality means to data consumers. Journal of Management Information Systems, *12*(4), 5–33.

Christine R. Scheu

General Data Protection Regulation (GDPR), Assessment, and HR Considerations

The General Data Protection Regulation was adopted April 2016 and went into effect May 25, 2018, to replace the 1995 Data Protection Directive ("GDPR FAQs", 2019). In response to increasing concerns about data privacy, data accuracy, and data security, this regulation provides additional rights, security, and transparency to individuals and accountabilities for organisations collecting, using, transferring, and storing personal information at the individual level (Handbook on E.U. Data Protection Law, 2018). GDPR applies to European Union (E.U.) residents, organisations established in the E.U., and all organisations, regardless of location, that process or control the individual level personal data of E.U. residents (Handbook on E.U. Data Protection Law, 2018; "GDPR FAQs", 2019; "GDPR Key Changes", 2019). The implications of GDPR are far reaching and will influence best practices in commerce, research, marketing, and most certainly the activities of human resources (HR) professionals given the vast amount of personal individual level data they interact with on a regular basis (e.g., names, survey data, vitas, performance information, addresses, etc.). It is imperative that HR professionals understand GDPR and how it changes the way they interact with, collect, store, and distribute data.

To be in compliance with GDPR obligations, organisations need to have either a legal or contractual reason to process personal data (e.g., banking details to process payroll) or have acquired informed consent to use, collect, and store personal data (Handbook on E.U. Data Protection Law, 2018). Informed consent needs to clearly address how the data will be used and be easily revocable ("GDPR Key Changes", 2019). Under GDPR, consent needs to be an explicit opt-in activity such as checking a box or signing your name as opposed to some prior approaches which may require individuals to opt-out of activities. Individuals should also be made aware of their rights under GDPR. These include the right to data access, to opt-out of data processing, to withdraw consent, to request data be erased, and the right to data portability or to obtain a copy of their data in a commonly accessible format (Handbook on E.U. Data Protection Law, 2018; "GDPR Key Changes", 2019). To further enhance data security and transparency under GDPR, organisations must also follow data breach notification protocols which include 72-hour notification windows from the time a breach is discovered ("GDPR Key Changes", 2019).

Failure to comply with GDPR can lead to a number of serious consequences including warnings, suspension of data flows, and substantial fines ("GDPR Enforcement and Penalties", 2019). The most severe fines can go as high as 20 million Euros or 4% of annual revenue, whichever is higher ("GDPR Key Changes", 2019). Supervisory authorities will review complaints and determine next steps on a case by case basis ("GDPR

https://doi.org/10.1515/9783110633702-040

Enforcement and Penalties", 2019). Due to the potential for large punitive actions, the complexity of the issues, and the evolving understanding of GDPR, organisations may take more conservative approaches to addressing GDPR policies, protocols, and inquiries and avoid pushing the limits.

GDPR specifically applies to data that contains Personal Identifying Information (PII) at the individual level (Handbook on E.U. Data Protection Law, 2018). PII is any data that can be used to identify a specific individual such as name, email, phone number, computer IP address, photos, assessment results, government identification numbers, system user IDs, and social media posts ("GDPR FAQs", 2019). Organisations are expected to take the necessary steps to safeguard data such as considering ways to store the data in an anonymous or pseudonymous fashion (i.e., removes PII such as names but retains a unique ID or other means to reconnect to PII information) to improve data security. Once data is aggregated and no longer reflects individual level information, it is not subject to GDPR (GDPR, 2018).

Considerations for Assessment and HR Activities

Advancements in technology have dramatically shaped hiring and selection methods leading to a scenario where nearly every aspect of the process including recruitment, application, assessment, and performance reviews might be completed on a phone, personal computer, tablet, or other internet connected device (Dorsey, Martin, Howard, & Coovert, 2017). As a result, PII, data security, and ultimately GDPR and similar pending legislation such as the California Consumer Privacy Act (Gavejian, Lazzarotti, Austin, & Costigan, 2019) can have a significant impact on those using, collecting, and storing HR data. A few of the key considerations, impacts, and questions regarding assessment, HR activities, GDPR, and similar legislation are highlighted below. It is important to note that data protection responsibilities and compliance sit with individual employees, researchers, consultants, HR professionals and other users in addition to their employers. All parties working together are essential to maintaining data security (Dreibelbis, Martin, & Coovert, 2018).

PII is inherently central to HR and assessment scenarios from names and email addresses to culture surveys and test score results, therefore creating increased risks for data security and making GDPR type requirements a critical factor in processes, planning, and protocols. One key question many organisations, researchers, and practitioners may find themselves asking, is what data are required to meet the purpose of the project or assessment process. To reduce risk, the nice to have versus need to have questions may lead to less information being collected at various points along the way. For example, an organization may be interested in knowing the most common learning disabilities leading to requests for timer extensions on a cognitive test available in their assessment catalogue. While this is an interesting research question, it is not central to updating the timer for a specific candidate or to that candidate's assessment process. As a result, the specific disability information should not be collected or stored as part of the candidate's record in the assessment system, both to protect privacy, and to minimize the non-essential information collected. Instead, a separate research project with informed consent for a specific research purpose may be considered outside of the assessment scenario where the goal is to collect test scores for hiring a candidate. Keeping data security and privacy top of mind is becoming an important element of organizational culture and a key part of process, project, and system design (Dreibelbis, Martin, & Coovert, 2018).

Another key element of GDPR is data handling and data security to protect privacy (Handbook on E.U. Data Protection Law, 2018). In an HR scenario, this may mean organisations limiting who has access to individual level candidate data such as survey results and test scores both internally and externally. Mechanisms such as strong passwords, education programs and policies to support GDPR and general data security, as well as, malware detection, monitoring web traffic for signs of breach, and breach response protocols are all essential parts of data handling and security compliance (Dreibelbis, Martin, & Coovert, 2018). Where applicable, organisations may also find value in shifting away from PII and individual level data in favour of aggregate information. In an HR context this may mean creating summary reporting and trend analysis that limits who needs access to reporting containing PII. For example, instead of providing a data set that contains individual names and test times for review, an organization may be able to create an anonymous data set and/or a report that summarizes average test times for a specific time frame, location, or assessment.

The rights granted to individuals by GDPR can also lead to interesting questions in an assessment context. The right to data access and data portability suggest that an individual can know what data are collected, how that data will be used and can ask for a copy of the information in a common and easily accessible format (Handbook on E.U. Data Protection Law, 2018; "GDPR FAQs", 2019; "GDPR Key Changes", 2019). Organisations may find themselves considering what information can be reported out without disclosing intellectual property such as assessment content, scoring protocols, and cut scores or decision criteria. Similarly, organisations may need to consider reporting designed specifically for candidates as opposed to only having reporting for the hiring organization to increase transparency, reduce portability requests, and to better align with GDPR and similar types of legislation.

GDPR also provides for the right to be forgotten which means individuals can request that their data be erased ("GDPR Key Changes", 2019). In an HR context this can lead to considerations beyond the ability to delete data from the testing and survey platforms. In particular, organisations need to consider how this request fits with their test and retest policies, implications for the hiring process of the individual in question, how to balance GDPR with other data retention requirements and regulations, how to manage data already aggregated or anonymized, and how to address reporting or other work products already distributed which may contain the individual's information. Many of these questions will need to be addressed by new organizational policies and procedures developed through partnerships between assessment and survey experts, human resources, and legal departments.

As part of informed consent and various rules for accountability and responsibility under GDPR, individuals have the right to know how their data will be used, how it is being processed, if it will be transferred to third parties, and if any automated or algorithmic decisions are being made using their data (GDPR, 2018; Handbook on E.U. Data Protection Law, 2018). GDPR and other security and privacy rules can yield some interesting policy, ethical, and logistical questions for organisations considering various innovations in recruitment, selection, and assessment (Dorsey, Martin, Howard, & Coovert, 2017). These questions go beyond the standard validity and reliability questions so common for new assessment methods (Dorsey, Martin, Howard, & Coovert, 2017). For example, innovations that utilize or scrape data from social media sites as part of recruiting and hiring decisions, big data algorithms that review resumes to create scoring profiles, video interviewing systems that read and score micro expressions, eye contact and other variables, raise questions regarding how to communicate with applicants about how their data will be used, shared, scored, and contribute to decisions. Similar to the erasure considerations, many of these assessment technology advancements will need to be addressed by new organizational policies and procedures developed through partnerships between assessment experts, human resources, and legal departments.

Organisations and practitioners are still learning to work effectively within the GDPR requirements. As data security, data privacy, information technology, and general understanding of GDPR and similar regulations continue to evolve, it is important to work closely with internal and external legal resources, internal review boards, data protection officers, and other experts to ensure compliance. Similarly, these same resources are critical partners for learning how to flex and maintain the ability to provide quality survey, assessment, hiring, performance reviews, and consulting services in this ever-evolving security, technology, and privacy environment. Finding the balance between data security and conducting business is a challenge that will not be resolved in short order.

Future Research

The many open questions around data protection activities makes it an area primed for additional research. Understanding how or if these new regulations change perceptions of data security, safety procedures, data ethics, and a sense of personal control over PII data could prove fruitful areas of research. Similarly, research focused on understanding how organisations can successfully influence employee behaviour through training and policies to reduce data breaches and risks from within the organization, could have strong practical contributions for improving compliance and security.

Further Readings

EU GDPR.Org. (2019). Retrieved from https://eugdpr.org/

General Data Protection Regulation (GDPR). (2018). *General Data Protection Regulation (GDPR) – Final text neatly arranged*. Retrieved from https://gdpr-info.eu/

Crutzen, R., Peters, G. J. Y., & Mondschein, C. (2019). Why and how we should care about the General Data Protection Regulation, *Psychology & Health*, Retrieved from 10.1080/08870446.2019.1606222/

References

Dorsey, D. W., Martin, J., Howard, D. J., & Coovert, M. D. (2017). Cybersecurity issues in selection. In J. L. Farr & N. T. Tippins (Eds.), *Handbook of employee selection* (pp. 267–290). New York, NY: Routledge.

Dreibelbis, R., Martin, J., Coovert, M., & Dorsey, D. (2018). The Looming Cybersecurity Crisis and What It Means for the Practice of Industrial and Organizational Psychology. *Industrial and Organizational Psychology*, *11*(2), 346–365. Retrieved from 10.1017/iop.2018.3/

EU GDPR.Org. (2019). GDPR FAQs. Retrieved from https://eugdpr.org/

EU GDPR.Org. (2019). GDPR Key Changes. Retrieved from https://eugdpr.org/

General Data Protection Regulation (GDPR). (2018). *General Data Protection Regulation (GDPR) – Final text neatly arranged*. Retrieved from https://gdpr-info.eu/

Gavejian, J. C., Lazzarotti, J. J., Austin, N. W., & Costigan, M. T. (2019). California Consumer Privacy Act: FAQs for Employers. Retrieved from https://www.jacksonlewis.com/publication/california-consumer-privacy-act-faqs-employers/

Giakoumopoulos, C., Buttarelli, G., O'Flaherty, M. (2018). *Handbook on EU Data Protection Law*. European Union Agency for Fundamental Rights and Council of Europe. Retrieved from https://fra.europa.eu/sites/default/files/fra_uploads/fra-coe-edps-2018-handbook-data-protection_en.pdf/

IT Governance. (2019) GDPR Enforcement and Penalties. Retrieved from https://www.itgovernance.co.uk/dpa-and-gdpr-penalties/

Elena M. Auer and Richard N. Landers

Creating Data-Driven HR Insights: Data Science in HRM

In the context of human resource management (HRM), data science is defined as an interdisciplinary area that combines knowledge from statistics, computer science, and the organizational sciences with the goal of extracting meaning from complex employee and organizational data. Data science is not necessarily a new scientific discipline; rather this area borrows and builds upon multiple disciplines to identify the best ways of gleaning insight from data. In the context of HRM, this largely involves creating meaning and insight from employee-relevant data that would be useful to organizational stakeholders. For example, data science approaches may be useful for supporting staffing decisions and talent forecasting, performance appraisal and management, and employee relations and satisfaction measurement (Tonidandel, King, & Cortina, 2015; Huselid, 2018). In doing so, data science makes explicit the practices and procedures of collecting, storing, analyzing, and presenting organizational datasets (Landers, Fink, & Collmus, 2017).

Data Science Approaches and Techniques

Broadly, data science in HRM involves three key areas: (1) *gathering* HRM-relevant data, (2) *storing* and *processing* that data, and (3) *analyzing* and *visualizing* that data to create and share insights. Data scientists can gather HRM-related data using existing organizational databases or by extracting information from the web, oftentimes generating "big data," which refers to data of greater size and complexity than traditionally examined with field-standard practices. As a result, data scientists typically use more technologically sophisticated ways of storing and processing that data than those used by traditional HRM analysts, such as cloud computing systems and statistical programming software. Using such data, data scientists then use analytic techniques including machine learning and natural language processing to glean insights from this data and ultimately use tools such as visualizations, dashboards, and interactive reports to share those insights with stakeholders.

Data Gathering

In the context of HRM, data scientists typically source data from organizational databases or, when relevant, use web-scraping techniques to access information from

https://doi.org/10.1515/9783110633702-041

the internet. Organizational databases containing relevant data typically include 1) human resource information systems (HRIS), 2) applicant tracking systems (ATS), and 3) learning management and performance management systems (LMS/PMS; Putka & Oswald, 2015). Such databases generally contain a wide variety of employee data, including data collected directly from employees or supervisors like satisfaction and performance surveys, structural reporting relationships like supervisory dyads or team memberships, and demographic data, among many others. More non-traditional organizational data, however, may also be useful depending on the goal of the data scientist. For example, trace data from badge access logs or wearables may also be useful in combination with traditional employee data. Accessing data from within the organization typically involves being able to accurately describe the data needed to a data management systems administrator or by accessing these data systems directly using database programming languages such as Structured Query Language (SQL). Additionally, these data are typically located in multiple sources and must be meaningfully combined prior to analysis.

Beyond organizational data, data scientists might use web scraping or application programming interfaces (APIs) to access data from the web. Web scraping is a technique used to automatically identify and code information on webpages (Cooley, Mobasher, & Srivastava, 1997). APIs permit direct communication between a user and a website, making it easier than manual web scraping (e.g., viewing webpages in a web browser and recording what is visible there in a spreadsheeting application) to collect structured information from websites. Much of the data collected using these approaches is behavioral in nature, potentially providing information related to personality or individual differences of users in a naturalistic setting (Landers, Brusso, Cavanaugh, & Collmus, 2016). Web scraping and APIs are commonly used to access data from social media websites such as Twitter, Facebook, or LinkedIn, or to access crowdsourced information from websites such as Glassdoor or Indeed. Twitter posts, for example, can potentially be used to examine job satisfaction (Hernandez, Newman, & Jeon, 2016).

These data collection efforts may or may not result in the creation of big data. Although big data is not a prerequisite for conducting data science, many data science principles and approaches were developed from the special processing requirements created by working with big data. Big data has several different definitions but is commonly described using the Vs of big data, meaning data with high volume (quantity), velocity (pace of data creation and analysis), and variety (forms and sources; Laney, 2001). More broadly, big data can be conceptualized not based on the characteristics of the data and instead the technology needed to handle the data. Under this assumption, data becomes "big" when additional, more sophisticated, storage, processing, and analytic approaches are needed to handle the data (Dumbill, 2013). Big data is often created by combining multiple existing data sources, such as HRIS and data from the web, requiring investment in data merging and cleaning processes. Big data also often incorporate unstructured data, such as text or image data, which needs to be heavily processed to convert it into a useful format for analyses and decision-making.

Data Storage and Processing

Once data are gathered, they need to be stored and processed. The larger, more complex the dataset or analyses, the more computing resources and tools required. Cloud computing can offer the computational power, memory, and storage needed without heavy organizational investment in state-of-the-art computer equipment and software. Cloud computing can be defined as "a model for enabling ubiquitous, convenient, on-demand network access to a shared pool of configurable computing resources (e.g., networks, servers, storage, applications, and services) that can be rapidly provisioned and released with minimal management effort or service provider interaction" (Mell & Grance, 2011, p. 3). In simpler terms, cloud computing offers a remote, virtual computer that allows the user to allocate the computational resources (e.g., memory or processing power) needed for any given project from a much larger pool of available resources. In addition to the increased, customizable computational resources, cloud computing can enable increased collaboration and automation by allowing multiple users to access those resources and data simultaneously and supporting the creation of a system that can automatically pull and analyze data in real time to regenerate reports or update dashboards.

Accessing these computing resources as well as processing and cleaning data typically requires knowledge of one or more programming languages. Data scientists working in HRM typically use the free open source languages Python and R. Both can be used to access, structure, clean, analyze, and visualize data. Whereas R is itself a statistical programming language, Python is a more general-purpose programming language for which open source contributors have developed a rich set of statistical tools. Additionally, both programming languages are well documented, constantly evolving, highly customizable, and have wide community support and resources for learning. Data scientists often leverage these programming languages because they are sufficiently flexible to support the complexity of data manipulation and analyses required in data science. They are also not dependent on paid software licensing, which can hinder collaboration, and should the license expire or software no longer exist, impedes access to current or previous work. Open source programming languages also explicitly encourage fully documented, reproducible data pipelines that track from start to finish all steps in data creation or access, data manipulation, analysis, and visualization.

Data Analytics and Visualization

The third key data science area involves data analytics and visualizations, which are used to create HRM insights and make those insights accessible to a variety of audiences through visualizations. Data scientists may focus on describing, explaining, or predicting phenomena depending on the data they have available and the goal of their analysis. Prediction, however, is usually the primary focus of data science practices in HRM. Data scientists use artificial intelligence methods such as machine learning (ML) and natural language processing (NLP) to create the best possible predictions of future phenomena given existing data. Artificial intelligence refers to computer systems that are designed to achieve some degree of human-like intelligent behavior (Barney, 2019). Machine learning, a subset of the field of artificial intelligence, refers to a computer program that learns from data and makes new predictions with the primary goal of maximizing prediction accuracy in new data (Kotsiantis, Zaharakis, & Pintelas, 2007). These models are in contrast to traditional data modeling methods that focus on explaining how each variable contributes to the unbiased prediction of an outcome given current data, often at the expense of predictive accuracy when applying the model to new samples, especially when complex data are used. Machine learning algorithms iteratively work to identify the model that will best predict outcomes when given new data, maximizing out-of-sample generalizability. Although more research is needed, machine learning has been used to predict outcomes in a variety of areas relevant to HRM. For example, Putka and colleagues (2018) compared machine learning methods with traditional modeling methods in the context of employee selection systems. NLP is another subset of artificial intelligence that refers to a family of approaches used to convert unstructured text sources into structured datasets with the goal of emulating a human-like understanding of the text (Liddy, 2001). NLP offers a variety of tools for creating understanding using HRM text data (Short, McKenny, & Reid, 2018) and has so far been used for scoring of applicant essays in selection systems (Campion, Campion, Campion, & Reider, 2016), performance appraisal (Speer, 2018), and deriving insight from recorded employment interviews (Suen, Chen, & Lu, 2019).

As data and analyses become larger and more complex, there is an even greater need for easy-to-understand visualizations for stakeholders. Visualization is defined as a set of techniques for displaying information graphically for better exploration, explanation, and engagement with data (Sinar, 2015). Visualization and sharing of results is often the final step of data science process although it may also play an important role in initial data exploration. Choosing a visualization method largely depends on the message and the audience, making the visualization design process critical. There are many valid approaches to visualization. Instead of following a single set of rules, creators of visualizations must interpret general design guidelines, such as not overburdening the audience with too many options or information, avoiding inaccurate audience perceptions (e.g., false optical significance), and ensuring that visualizations are accessible to the level of knowledge and abilities of the audience. Dashboards and interactive reports have become increasingly popular ways to share results and visualizations with stakeholders.

Future Research Directions

While many organizations have implemented data science practices into HRM by hiring data scientists and people analytics professionals, research has largely lagged behind in the study of how these approaches affect HRM decision-making and practice. Broadly, researchers should consider examining which types of data traditionally sourced through data science techniques (e.g., accessing HRIS, web scraping, and badge access log data) are meaningful and appropriate in different contexts. For example, can ratings scraped from Glassdoor be used to approximate employee job satisfaction ratings? Additionally, researchers should consider under which conditions modern prediction methods can be used effectively. For example, how do applicant pool size, number of predictors, and diversity of applicant pool affect the appropriateness of using machine learning models in an employee selection system?

Further Readings

Readers interested in more detailed information about data science in the workplace should consider reading the book *Big data at work: The data science revolution and organizational psychology* (Tonidandel, King, & Cortina, 2015) or the *Human Resource Management* journal workforce analytics special issue series (Huselid, 2018). Readers interested in a deeper dive into data science analytic approaches, such as machine learning, should refer to Putka, Beatty, and Reeder's (2018) article on modern prediction methods.

References

Barney, M. (2019). The reciprocal roles of artificial intelligence and industrial-organizational psychology. In R. Landers (Ed.), *The Cambridge handbook of technology and employee behavior* (pp. 38–58). Cambridge, UK: Cambridge University Press.

Campion, M. C., Campion, M. A., Campion, E. D., & Reider, M. H. (2016). Initial investigation into computer scoring of candidate essays for personnel selection. *Journal of Applied Psychology*, *101*(7), 958.

Cooley, R., Mobasher, B., & Srivastava, J. (1997, November). Web Mining: Information and Pattern Discovery on the World Wide Web. In *ictai*, *97*, 558–567).

Dumbill, E. (2013). Making Sense of Big Data. *Big Data*, *1*(1), 1–2.

Guzzo, R. A., Fink, A. A., King, E., Tonidandel, S., & Landis, R. S. (2015). Big data recommendations for industrial–organizational psychology. *Industrial and Organizational Psychology*, *8*(4), 491–508.

Hernandez, I., Newman, D. A., & Jeon, G. (2016). Twitter analysis: Methods for data management and a word count dictionary to measure city-level job satisfaction. In S. Tonidandel, E. King, &

J. Cortina. (2015). *Big data at work: The data science revolution and organizational psychology*. New York: Routledge.

Huselid, M. A. (2018). The science and practice of workforce analytics: Introduction to the HRM special issue. *Human Resource Management, 57*(3), 679–684.

Kotsiantis, S. B., Zaharakis, I., & Pintelas, P. (2007). Supervised machine learning: A review of classification techniques. *Emerging artificial intelligence applications in computer engineering, 160*, 3–24.

Landers, R. N., Brusso, R. C., Cavanaugh, K. J., & Collmus, A. B. (2016). A primer on theory-driven web scraping: Automatic extraction of big data from the Internet for use in psychological research. *Psychological methods, 21*(4), 475.

Landers, R. N., Fink, A. A., & Collmus, A. B. (2017). Using Big Data to Enhance Staffing: Vast Untapped Resources or Tempting Honeypot? 1. In *Handbook of Employee Selection* (pp. 949–966). Routledge.

Laney, D. (2001). 3D data management: Controlling data volume, velocity and variety. *META group research note, 6*(70), 1.

Liddy, E. D. (2001). Natural language processing. *Encyclopedia of Library and Information Science*, 2126–2136. New York, NY: Marcel Dekker.

Mell, P., & Grance, T. (2011). The NIST definition of cloud computing.

Putka, D. J. & Oswald, F. L., (2015). Implications of the big data movement for the advancement of I-O science and practice. In S. Tonidandel, E. King, & J. Cortina. (2015). *Big data at work: The data science revolution and organizational psychology*. New York: Routledge.

Putka, D. J., Beatty, A. S., & Reeder, M. C. (2018). Modern prediction methods: New perspectives on a common problem. *Organizational Research Methods, 21*(3), 689–732.

Short, J. C., McKenny, A. F., & Reid, S. W. (2018). More than words? Computer-aided text analysis in organizational behavior and psychology research. *Annual Review of Organizational Psychology and Organizational Behavior, 5*, 415–435.

Sinar, E. F. (2015). Data visualization. In S. Tonidandel, E. King, & J. Cortina. (2015). *Big data at work: The data science revolution and organizational psychology*. New York: Routledge.

Speer, A. B. (2018). Quantifying with words: An investigation of the validity of narrative-derived performance scores. *Personnel Psychology, 71*(3), 299–333.

Suen, H. Y., Chen, M. Y. C., & Lu, S. H. (2019). Does the use of synchrony and artificial intelligence in video interviews affect interview ratings and applicant attitudes? *Computers in Human Behavior, 98*, 93–101.

Tonidandel, S., King, E. B., & Cortina, J. M. (Eds.). (2015). *Big data at work: The data science revolution and organizational psychology*. Routledge.

Daniel Shore
Cybersecurity Challenges in Protecting Human Resource Information Systems

Cybersecurity refers to the "measures taken to protect a computer or computer system against unauthorized access or attack" ("Cybersecurity", n.d.). Cybersecurity and Human Resource Information Systems (HRIS) are inseparable. First and foremost, those who have access to the HRIS must be properly trained to maintain the security of the system. Additionally, as soon as HR data are loaded onto a database that is internet-connected there simultaneously must be consideration of how to employ cybersecurity professionals to protect these systems. While this entry focuses on HRIS, with HR professionals as the primary user group, there are similar challenges with any e-HRM system that stores employee data and can be accessed through the internet.

The importance of focusing on cybersecurity can be captured through the quantification of damage caused by cybercrimes: smaller data breaches can cost companies nearly $4 million while larger ones can reach up to $350 million in damage. These estimates are based on estimated loss of intellectual property, disruption of operations, recovery costs, etc. (IBM, 2019). An even more terrifying number to contemplate is that cybercrime is estimated to cost companies, collectively, between $445 and $600 *billion* dollars *annually* (Lewis, 2018). One of the most serious HR-related data breaches in US history was a breach of employee records for the US Government's Office of Personal Management (OPM), where hackers gained access to 22 million employee records over the course of two breaches that lasted for a 3-year period (Amerding, 2016). The aftermath includes a contract to provide all of those employees with credit monitoring, which alone may cost OPM upwards of $500 million over time (Townsend, 2017), not to mention the loss of proprietary data, need to increase security of the system, and so forth.

In order to address HRIS-cybersecurity concerns, a comprehensive approach is necessary. The current entry proposes the following "vision" statement (rather than a strict definition) regarding cybersecurity and HRIS: *The development of an organization's capacity to protect an HRIS from internal and external threats requires an understanding of the users, information, and access while ensuring that the appropriate cybersecurity personnel and safeguards are in place.* While the current entry will focus on two primary HR-related cybersecurity challenges – insider threat and the lack of cybersecurity professionals for hire – it is important to note that HR professionals will also face other challenges that are outside the scope of this entry including external threats (e.g., hackers), software vulnerabilities, social engineering, etc.

https://doi.org/10.1515/9783110633702-042

Challenge #1: Inside Access to the System

The primary cybersecurity-related challenge posed by employees of an organization is the sharing of sensitive information. Introducing an HRIS into any organization increases the amount of HR-related information that is accessible via an internal intranet or via an internet-based platform (Stone & Dulebohn, 2013), even if the *intended* audience is strictly HR professionals internal to the organization. In turn, due to the digital nature and access involved with such a system, there becomes an increased need for cybersecurity. Underlying these issues is the fact that organizations already struggle with the challenge of protecting sensitive information internally (Varonis, 2019), and the foray into an HRIS requires extensive attention so that these challenges are not irreparably exacerbated.

While there are external threats and system design vulnerabilities that must be monitored, the issue that falls most directly under the responsibility of an HR department is to protect the HRIS from the threat posed by employees sharing sensitive information, which is known as "insider threat." "Insider" refers to any current employee, while the "threat" refers to an employee's actions "put[ting]an organization's data, processes, or resources at risk" (Pfleeger, Predd, Hunker, & Bulford, 2009, p. 170). Recent research focused on the information security of HRIS emphasized the importance of limiting access to data by internal employees in order to maintain privacy and confidentiality (Zafar, 2012) Making sensitive information accessible via an HRIS naturally exacerbates such a threat, as the more ways that information can be accessed, the more opportunities there are for it be "hacked."

It is critical to point out that not all insider threat behavior is malicious. Employees may also unintentionally share sensitive information or grant access to information (Im & Baskerville, 2005). A prime example is the breach of, ironically, a computer and network security firm, RSA, that took place in 2011, where attackers specifically sought out employees who had access to sensitive information. One of these employees opened a seemingly legitimate email and the Excel attachment in that email deployed a virus that would lead to the pilfering of up to 40 million employee records (costing at least $66 million to remediate the situation (Amerding, 2018; Chabrow, 2011).

Addressing this Challenge

With the potential for such damage, it is clearly important that HR professionals consider ways to stop, or at least limit, insider threat. First, there are traditional HR strategies such as the hiring and training personnel that can be implemented to address this challenge. For example, it is important to adequately invest money and resources into thorough background checks to identify if an employee has previously worked for trusted organizations, and especially those that have their own thorough applicant screening process (Flynn, Huth, Trzeciak, & Buttles, 2013). Similarly, it is important to identify whether an applicant has had issues around insider threat at previous jobs or affiliations with suspect organizations or groups (Colwill, 2009). Once hired, it is important to have non-disclosure agreement put into place as a legal safeguard against insider threat (Flynn et al., 2013). In terms of training, employees should be provided with relevant practice around appropriate use of the HRIS and avoiding errors associated with data access (e.g., simulated scenarios, faux phishing emails; Zafar, 2012).

Second, there are technology-based approaches such as implementing security practices. For example, there should be "data masking, encryption, and . . . [limited] access to data" based on employees' roles and positions (Zielinski, 2019). In particular, it is important to put into place a system for monitoring user activity that allows unusual activity (e.g., large uploads and downloads) to be flagged and investigated (Tetrick et al., 2016). In addition to online user activity, HR professionals could also monitor related psychosocial indicators of insider threat, such as anger, frustration, stress, or personal issues (Greitzer & Frincke, 2010). Should malicious activity be suspected, HR could also team up with cybersecurity experts on a more advanced approach, such as creating what are known as "honeypots" – essentially heavily-monitored, fake databases of information used to lure a perpetrator into inappropriately handling the information in order to catch them. There are, of course, ethical considerations to the aforementioned approaches around employee privacy and disclosure of employee monitoring (Greitzer, Frincke, & Zabriskie, 2011).

Challenge #2: Not Enough Cybersecurity Professionals to Go Around

Cybersecurity is a field with a workforce that is growing at exponential rates yet cannot keep up with the demand and volume of cybercrime. No matter the context for needing to hire cybersecurity professionals, there is a serious imbalance between the supply and demand, with supply being the far lower. Various reports have estimated current number of vacant cybersecurity jobs to be somewhere between 1.5 and 2 million, with some estimates as high as nearly 3 million (ISC[2], 2018a). The cybersecurity employment shortage is fueled by challenges related to key HR functions: attraction of a sufficient pool of applicants, selection of qualified applicants, and attrition of burnt out employees.

On the backend of the cybersecurity employment challenge is a constant threat of turnover for both employees in cybersecurity organizations and cybersecurity positions in non-cybersecurity organizations. One primary cause of high turnover in cybersecurity is the aforementioned shortage itself. The skill set is in high demand and there are plenty of job openings to consider. This lopsided job market leads to what a recent survey found: 70% of cybersecurity professionals are open to considering leaving their current job for another one plus another 14% who indicated they are actively looking to switch jobs (ISC^2, 2018b). A related challenge, according to other survey data, is that almost half of cybersecurity professionals are courted by other organizations on a *weekly* basis (Oltsik, 2016).

Addressing this Challenge

HR professionals must work diligently to recruit and hire analysts to protect their information systems – a monumental task considering the severely limited pool of qualified applicants to fill a wide variety of specific needs and roles within cybersecurity teams. Beginning in the early 2000's, the government recognized that there was and would continue to be a critical need to educate, recruit, train, develop, and retain a highly-qualified workforce (Newhouse, Keith, Scribner, & Witte, 2017). In turn, the government created the National Initiative for Cybersecurity Education (NICE) Framework. The goal of the NICE Framework is to create a national standard and common language around building a cybersecurity workforce. As part of this effort, the government's National Institute of Standards and Technology (NIST) proposed 7 broad categories of cybersecurity functions that should be considered when hiring cybersecurity employees. Additionally, the Framework provides specific roles within cybersecurity teams or departments along with the relevant knowledge, skills, and abilities that an applicant should have for such a role. Most pertinent to HR professionals, this framework can be used to guide the recruitment, hiring, and training of cybersecurity professionals to protect HRISs.

In some cases, companies have been getting creative in their efforts to address the dearth of recruits and applicants. For example, IBM has created a category of jobs that they label as "new collar" jobs – jobs that "prioritize skills, knowledge, and willingness to learn over degrees" and over previous work experience (van Zadelhoff, 2017). This fits a growing trend of talent mobility – the capacity to identify talent internally that could be more easily moved to a new job, project, or team compared to the effort needed for full-on talent acquisition. Talent mobility has been posited as a key strategy to combat applicant and employee shortages (Volini et al., 2019; Vorhauser-Smith, 2015), and plays a particularly important role for emerging positions such as those in cybersecurity.

Outsourcing cybersecurity functions is an increasingly common trend as well. Cybersecurity is complex, with many layers, and organizations differ on which functions they handle in-house and which are provided by third parties. The range of functions include the following: security operations, vulnerability management, physical security, training and awareness, insider threat detection, application security, identity and access management. In a recent survey, 65% of CISOs indicated that they outsource 21–30% of their organization's cybersecurity functions. Security operations and insider threat detection were the top two functions in terms of money being spent on outsourced services (Deloitte, 2019). It is important, of course, for HR professionals to properly vet third-party service providers in order to mitigate the external threats to the HRIS (Flynn et al., 2013).

Future Research Directions

There are myriad possibilities for future research directions in such a nascent area of HR, though there should be a limited number of priorities set in order to build the foundation of this line of research. One priority for research at the intersection of cybersecurity and HRISs is to identify effective strategies for motivating individuals to be diligent when working with sensitive information in order to reduce the risks associated with access via an intranet or internet platform; this type of motivation would likely stem from the ways in which employees are empowered and entrusted to handle sensitive information (e.g., Thomas, 2018). A second priority, in an effort to begin addressing the limited applicant pool for cybersecurity positions, is to examine effective methods for training employees with non-cybersecurity backgrounds on cybersecurity skills so that they can take on such responsibilities for an organization (e.g., Adams & Makramalla, 2015). A third priority that must be addressed in this research is the predictors of a strong cybersecurity culture, which, in addition to recruiting and placing employees in appropriate roles, includes setting clear policies that tie together the technology with data protection, organizational goals, and employee trust. In the modern era where cybersecurity is an inherent part of organizational operation, every company is part of the cybersecurity industry. In order to succeed in this modern era of HR, companies and HR professionals must take into consideration the challenges associated with cybersecurity at a holistic level in order to be competitive and sustainable (e.g., Huang & Pearlson, 2019).

Further Readings

Ponemon Institute Library, available at https://www.ponemon.org/library
Tetrick, L. E., Zaccaro, S. J., Dalal, R. S., Steinke, J. A., Repchick, K. M., Hargrove, A. K., . . . Niu, Q. (2016). *Improving social maturity of cybersecurity incident response teams*. Fairfax, VA: George Mason University. Available at: http://calctraining2015.weebly.com/the-handbook.html
SHRM Blogs related to cybersecurity, available at https://blog.shrm.org/tags/cybersecurity
Verizon Enterprise (2019). Data breach investigations report. Available at: https://enterprise.verizon.com/resources/reports/dbir/

References

Adams, M., & Makramalla, M. (2015). Cybersecurity skills training: an attacker-centric gamified approach. *Technology Innovation Management Review*, *5*, 5–14.

Amerding, T. (2016). *The OPM breach report: A long time coming*. Retrieved from the CSO website: https://www.csoonline.com/article/3130682/the-opm-breach-report-a-long-time-coming.html

Amerding, T. (2018). *The 18 biggest data breaches of the 21st century*. Retrieved from the CSO website: https://www.csoonline.com/article/2130877/the-biggest-data-breaches-of-the-21st-century.html

Chabrow, E. (2011). *"Tricked" RSA worker opened backdoor to APT attack*. Retrieved from the Bank Info Security website: https://www.bankinfosecurity.com/tricked-rsa-worker-opened-backdoor-to-apt-attack-a-3504

Colwill, C. (2009). Human factors in information security: The insider threa – who can you trust these days? *Information Security Technical Report*, *14*, 186–196.

Cybersecurity [Def. 1]. (n.d.) In *Merriam-Webster Online Dictionary*. Retrieved from https://www.merriam-webster.com/dictionary/cybersecurity.

Deloitte (2019). *The future of cyber survey 2019*. Retrieved from https://www2.deloitte.com/content/dam/Deloitte/us/Documents/finance/us-the-future-of-cyber-survey.pdf.

Flynn, L., Huth, C., Trzeciak, R., Buttles, P. (2013). *Best practices against insider threats in all nations* (Technical Note CMU/SEI-2013-TN-023). Pittsburgh, PA: Carnegie-Mellon University, Software Engineering Institute, CERT Division.

Greitzer, F. L., & Frincke, D. A. (2010). Combining traditional cyber security audit data with psychosocial data: towards predictive modeling for insider threat mitigation. In *Insider threats in cyber security* (pp. 85–113). Springer, Boston, MA.

Greitzer, F. L., Frincke, D., & Zabriskie, M. (2011). Social/ethical issues in predictive insider threat monitoring. In *Information Assurance and Security Ethics in Complex Systems: Interdisciplinary Perspectives* (pp. 132–161). IGI Global.

Huang, K., & Pearlson, K. (2019, January). For what technology can't fix: Building a model of organizational cybersecurity culture. In *Proceedings of the 52nd Hawaii International Conference on System Sciences*.

IBM Security (2019). *Cost of a data breach report*. Retrieved from https://www.ibm.com/security/data-breach

Im, G. P., & Baskerville, R. L. (2005). A longitudinal study of information system threat categories: the enduring problem of human error. *ACM SIGMIS Database: the Database for Advances in Information Systems*, *36*, 68–79.

ISC[2] (2018a). *Cybersecurity workforce study*. Retrieved from https://www.isc2.org/-/media/ISC2/Research/2018-ISC2-Cybersecurity-Workforce-Study.ashx?la=en&hash=4E09681D0FB51698D9BA6BF13EEABFA48BD17DB0

ISC[2] (2018b). *Hiring and retaining top cybersecurity talent*. Retrieved from https://www.isc2.org/-/media/Files/Research/ISC2-Hiring-and-Retaining-Top-Cybersecurity-Talent.ashx

Lewis, J. A., (2018). *Economic impact of cybercrime*. Retrieved from the Center for Strategic and International Studies website: https://www.csis.org/analysis/economic-impact-cybercrime

Newhouse, W., Keith, S., Scribner, B., & Witte, G. (2017). *National initiative for cybersecurity education (NICE) cybersecurity workforce framework*. Retrieved from the NIST website: https://nvlpubs.nist.gov/nistpubs/SpecialPublications/NIST.SP.800-181.pdf

Oltsik, J. (2016). *The state of cybersecurity professional careers: An annual research report (Part 1)*. Retrieved from the ESG Global website: https://www.esg-global.com/hubfs/issa/ESG-ISSA-Research-Report-State-of-Cybersecurity-Professional-Careers-Oct-2016.pdf

Pfleeger, S. L., Predd, J. B., Hunker, J., & Bulford, C. (2009). Insiders behaving badly: Addressing bad actors and their actions. *IEEE Transactions on Information Forensics and Security*, *5*, 169–179.

Stone, D. L., & Dulebohn, J. H. (2013). Emerging issues in theory and research on electronic human resource management (eHRM). *Human Resource Management Review*, *23*, 1–5.

Tetrick, L. E., Zaccaro, S. J., Dalal, R. S., Steinke, J. A., Repchick, K. M., Hargrove, A. K., . . . Niu, Q. (2016). *Improving social maturity of cybersecurity incident response teams*. Fairfax, VA: George Mason University. Available at: http://calctraining2015.weebly.com/the-handbook.html

Thomas, J. (2018). Individual cyber security: Empowering employees to resist spear phishing to prevent identity theft and ransomware attacks. *International Journal of Business Management*, *12*, 1–23.

Townsend, C. (2017). *OPM breach costs could exceed $1 billion*. Retrieved from the Symantec website: https://www.symantec.com/connect/blogs/opm-breach-costs-could-exceed-1-billion

van Zadelhoff, M. (2017). *Cybersecurity has a serious talent shortage. Here's how to fix it*. Retrieved from the Harvard Business Review website: https://hbr.org/2017/05/cybersecurity-has-a-serious-talent-shortage-heres-how-to-fix-it

Varonis (2019). *2019 Global data risk report* from the Varonis Data Lab. Retrieved from https://info.varonis.com/hubfs/Varonis%202019%20Global%20Data%20Risk%20Report.pdf

Violini, E., Schwartz, J., Roy, I., Hauptmann, M., Van Durme, Y., Denny, B., & Bersin, J., (2019). *Talent mobility: Winning the war on the home front*. Retrieved from the Deloitte website: https://www2.deloitte.com/us/en/insights/focus/human-capital-trends/2019/internal-talent-mobility.html

Vorhauser-Smith, S. (2015). *Is HR disconnected? Here's how HR can reconnect and embrace the future*. Retrieved from the Forbes website: https://www.forbes.com/sites/sylviavorhausersmith/2015/10/15/is-hr-disconnected-heres-how-hr-can-reconnect-and-embrace-the-future/#3d954f73cda6

Zafar, H. (2013). Human resource information systems: Information security concerns for organizations. *Human Resource Management Review*, *23*, 105–113.

Zielinski, D. (2019). *5 top cybersecurity concerns for HR in 2019*. Retrieved from Society for Human Resource Management website: https://www.shrm.org/resourcesandtools/hr-topics/technology/pages/top-cybersecurity-concerns-hr-2019.aspx

Janet H. Marler
HR/People Analytics

With the emergence of big data, data analytics, and notions of the digital economy, HR/People analytics has grown in popularity. Along with this increasing interest, are a proliferation of terms used for this new technological innovation. The earliest label appearing in popular literature was Workforce Analytics, followed by HR Analytics, Talent Analytics, Predictive HR Analytics and People Analytics, the latter having emerged as the most frequently used term (Edwards & Edwards, 2019; Marler & Boudreau, 2017; Tursunbayeva, Di Lauro, & Pagliari, 2018). Along with different terms, there are many, albeit overlapping, definitions. These definitions and labels have several things in common (Marler, Cronemberger & Tao, 2017). First, HR Analytics does not focus exclusively on human resource management (HRM) functional data, rather involves linking data from other internal functions as well as data external to the firm. Second, HR Analytics involves using information technology to digitize, store, manipulate and report data. Third, HR Analytics is about supporting people-related decisions. Finally, HR Analytics is about linking HRM decisions to employee, operational and organizational outcomes. Bringing various definitions together, Marler and Boudreau (2017) define HR Analytics as *an HRM practice enabled by information technology that uses descriptive, visual, and statistical analyses of data related to HR processes, human capital, organizational performance, and external economic benchmarks to establish business impact and support data-driven decision-making.*

History

Analyses of data in human resource management has been around for many years. In fact, the notion of measurement and analysis of HRM data can be traced back to the early 1900s (Kaufman, 2014). The first book on "How to Measure Human Resources Management" was published in 1984 by a pioneer in the modern era of HRM measurement, Jac Fitz-enz (Fitz-enz, 1995). However, the current notion of analytics in HRM can be traced back to the early 21st century. In 2004, in one of the first published studies to introduce the notion of HR Analytics, Lawler, Levenson & Boudreau (2004) distinguish HR Analytics from HR metrics in terms of strategic impact in organizations. HR metrics focuses on measuring HR efficiency and effectiveness. HR Analytics, on the other hand, focuses on linking HRM processes to broader organizational impact. Thus while HR metrics such as headcount, and ratios such as administrative cost per employee and percent participation in employee training programs, along with descriptive satisfaction survey data, are useful, they do not provide insights into the real impact of HR programs and practices on organizational and employee outcomes (Lawler,

https://doi.org/10.1515/9783110633702-043

Levenson & Boudreau, 2004). HR Analytics therefore goes beyond HR metrics and significantly expands on the more functionally narrow descriptive insights HR metrics provides decision-makers.

Theory and Evidence

Explanations about how HR Analytics links HRM processes and human capital to operational and financial outcomes are rooted in three theoretical models. The first model, known as the LAMP model (Boudreau and Ramstad, 2007) stands for the interrelationship of logic, analytics, measures, and processes, that are key to developing a cause-effect model that predicts the relationship between HRM processes and business outcomes. In addition to the LAMP model, the HR Scorecard is another model that establishes how HRM processes and people are linked to business outcomes (Becker, Huselid & Ulrich, 2001b). Both these models are derived from strategic management theories and in particular, the Resource-Based View, which focuses on developing internal value producing and unique capabilities and resources (Marler & Boudreau, 2017). A third model in the literature on HR Analytics adopts agency theory as the primary theoretical lens. Aral and colleagues (2012) argue that companies which use a combination of pay for performance compensation, Human Capital Management (HCM) software, and HR Analytics are more productive because this combination allows managers to both align incentives and monitor employee behavior. Using a panel sample of 189 firm-level data collected over 5 years from 1995–2006, they show that HR Analytics only in combination with HCM software or in combination with HCM software and pay for performance predicts higher employee productivity. Although Aral et. al (2012) use agency theory as their explanatory framework, their results are also consistent with strategic HRM Ability Motivation and Opportunity theory (Delery & Shaw, 2001; Jiang, Lepak, Hu, & Baer, 2012). Companies that hire individuals that have ability to perform a job and provide motivation and opportunity will perform better than those without this combination.

Technology

Laying the foundation for HR Analytics' and fueling its adoption is the increasing availability of technological innovations such as business intelligence tools and reporting tools including dashboards and scorecards. Beginning in the late 1990s, a major software provider, Oracle (at the time it was PeopleSoft), announced the availability of "a line of analytic applications for managing human-resource issues" (InfoWorld Media Group, 1999, p. 5). Competitors soon followed with related HR Analytics software products. By 2014, CedarCrestone's 17th Annual HR Systems

Survey reported 16% of respondents reported adoption of HR Analytics. Although this level of diffusion appears to be low given HR Analytics software was first introduced in 1999 (InfoWorld, 1999), innovation theorists would predict that adoption of HR Analytics will continue to accelerate as information about its effectiveness spreads and greater learning about how to use it effectively is developed, (Rogers, 2003). In fact, over the last 5 years the number of specialized conferences such Wharton's People Analytics Conference, People Analytics & Future of Work and HCI Workforce Planning and People Analytics Conference and HR Analytics blogs and pundits on Twitter has exploded (Edwards & Edwards, 2019).

To meet predicted demand for HR Analytics software solutions, software suppliers developed solutions they called Corporate Performance Management (CPM) or Enterprise Performance Management (EPM)(Ohata & Kumar, 2012). These software solutions integrate differing sources of data such as transactional data from financial, supply chain, customer, and human resources with unstructured data (e.g. written text in social media or employee surveys), with data from external suppliers (e.g. salary survey data, benefits data). These data are stored in data cubes in data warehouses or data marts, which make it easier to retrieve relevant data to create reports (electronic or printed), "dashboards", and "scorecards".

A key challenge in most organizations is learning what are the key drivers of their business success so that critical data can be collected and tracked in reports, dashboards or scorecards. To figure this out, managers need to develop hypotheses that link operational activities of the organization to financial outcomes. For example, Coco, Jamison & Black (2011) provide a detailed case study of how the home improvement retail chain was able to establish that increasing store management training aligned with increasing employee engagement, which predicted increased higher average customer ticket sales per store. In this example the first hypothesis is that better trained managers are positively linked to better employee engagement. The second hypothesis is that better store level employee engagement is linked to higher store sales. Pulling all these hypothesized relationships together results in a causal value chain in which a human resource outcome is the initial cause, or a leading indicator that indirectly *over time* and through intervening operational outcomes results in a financial effect.

Of course, in order to create useful and relevant causal models, managers must know what the strategic goals of the company are. For companies whose shares are traded on a stock exchange, critical goals are achieving strong financial performance as measured by such as increasing share price, sales growth, earnings per share (EPS), and profit margin (net income divided by sales). There are also more company specific strategic goals such as customer focused outcomes like increasing market share, customer satisfaction, or operational outcomes such as improved product quality, inventory turnover, or reduced product shrinkage.

The key to transforming such electronically collected and stored data into information for decision making is in integrating the capabilities of the information technology with the capabilities of the company's managers who will be using the technology to access information to make decisions(Marler & Fisher, (2017). To create a working model of cause and effect relationships requires managers knowledgeable about the business. To apply this knowledge to the creation of useful information requires information technology that collects, stores, combines, and reports relevant electronic data. In sum HR analytics is about providing relevant information for managers to diagnose and solve business problems and to execute strategic HRM practices effectively.

Further Readings

Edwards, M. R., & Edwards, K. (2019). *Predictive HR analytics: mastering the HR metric* (2nd Edition). New York: Kogan Page Ltd.

Marler, J. H., & Boudreau, J. W. (2017). An Evidence-based Review of HR Analytics. *The International Journal of Human Resource Management, 28*(1), 3–26. https://doi.org/10.1080/09585192.2016.1244699

Marler, J. H., & Fisher, S. L. (2017). *Making HR technology decisions: A strategic perspective.* New York: Business Expert Press.

References

Aral, S., Brynjolfsson, E., & Wu, L. (2012). Three-Way Complementarities: Performance Pay, Human Resource Analytics, and Information Technology. *Management Science, 58*(5), 913–931. Retrieved from bth.

Becker, B. E., Ulrich, D., & Huselid, M. A. (2001). *The HR Scorecard: Linking People, Strategy, and Performance* (1 edition). Harvard Business Review Press.

Boudreau, J. W., & Ramstad, P. M. (2007). *Beyond HR: the new science of human capital.* Boston, Mass: Harvard Business School Pub.

Coco, C. T., Jamison, F., & Black, H. (2011). Connecting People Investments and Business Outcomes at Lowe's: Using Value Linkage Analytics to Link Employee Engagement to Business Performance. *People & Strategy, 34*(2), 28–33.

Delery, J. E., & Shaw, J. D. (2001). The strategic management of people in work organizations: Review, synthesis, and extension. In *Research in Personnel and Human Resources Management. Research in personnel and human resources management, Vol 20* (pp. 165–197). US: Elsevier Science/JAI Press.

Edwards, M. R., & Edwards, K. (2019). *Predictive HR analytics: mastering the HR metric* (2nd Edition). New York: Kogan Page Ltd.

Fitz-enz, J. (1995). *How to Measure Human Resources Management* (2nd ed.). New York: McGraw-Hill.

InfoWorld Media Group, I. (1999). *InfoWorld.* InfoWorld Media Group, Inc.

Jiang, K., Lepak, D. P., Hu, J., & Baer, J. C. (2012). How Does Human Resource Management Influence Organizational Outcomes? A Meta-Analytic Investigation of Mediating Mechanisms. *Academy of Management Journal, 55*(6), 1264–1294. https://doi.org/10.5465/amj.2011.0088

Kaufman, B. E. (2014). The historical development of American HRM broadly viewed. *Human Resource Management Review, 24*(3), 196–218. https://doi.org/10.1016/j.hrmr.2014.03.003

Lawler III, E. E., Levenson, A., & Boudreau, J. W. (2004). HR Metrics and Analytics: Use and Impact. *Human Resource Planning, 27*(4), 27–35.

Marler, J. H., & Boudreau, J. W. (2017). An Evidence-based Review of HR Analytics. *The International Journal of Human Resource Management, 28*(1), 3–26. https://doi.org/10.1080/09585192.2016.1244699

Marler, J. H., & Fisher, S. L. (2017). *Making HR technology decisions: A strategic perspective.* New York: Business Expert Press.

Marler, J., Cronemberger, F. and Tao, M. (2017). HR Analytics: The Influence of eHRM in Talent Management). Here to stay or short-lived management fashion?(pp59-86), In Bondarouk, T, Parry, E. and Ruel, H. (Eds.), EHRM in the Smart Era. London: Emerald Press.

Ohata, M., & Kumar, A. (2012). Big Data: A Boon to Business Intelligence. *Financial Executive, 28*(7), 63–64.

Rogers, E. M. (2003). *Diffusion of Innovations* (5th ed). New York: Free Press.

Tursunbayeva, A., Di Lauro, S., & Pagliari, C. (2018). People analytics-A scoping review of conceptual boundaries and value propositions. *International Journal of Information Management, 43*, 224–247. https://doi.org/10.1016/j.ijinfomgt.2018.08.002

Eleanna Galanaki and Alessandra Lazazzara
HR Metrics

Technology has allowed to perform tasks that were not possible in the past. HR metrics are an example of how technology enables HRM to develop and deliver more than in the past. HR metrics are the measurements that are used to determine (1) *what* HRM does, (2) how *efficiently* and (3) how *effectively* this is done, and (4) *how it relates* to organizational performance. For example, "total hours of training" or "internal to external recruitment ratio" describe how HRM is applied. "HR to employees ratio", "Cost per hire" and "successful appointments over total employment offers ratio" are HRM efficiency indicators. "Return on investment (ROI) of training", "employee morale" and "employee advocacy level" are measures of HRM effectiveness. Metrics such as "employment over operational cost", "employee productivity", "quality of customer service" are business level indicators of how well HRM contributes to business outcomes. HR Metrics are therefore tools that can add value to organizations by reducing uncertainty in managerial decision- making through information availability and evidence.

Relevant related terms are "HR analytics" and "KPIs". HR Analytics has been used interchangeably with HR Metrics, but HR Metrics put more emphasis on the measurement (i.e., what is measured, how often, how it relates to HR and business strategy and how it informs decision making, what the measure means, and how it compares with other measurements (benchmarking)), while HR Analytics – which is a more recent term – puts the emphasis on how data are managed and analyzed in order to bear useful results for business strategy. The latter also puts more emphasis on predictive rather than predictive statistic analysis. Key Performance Indicators (KPIs) are the metrics used to communicate numerically and set S.M.A.R.T.[1] goals in business strategy. They may refer to any function of the business (finance, operations, supply chain, customers, marketing, CSR and employees) (Marr, 2012), therefore they do not focus only on HRM like HR Metrics do. However, the employee- related KPIs are basically a form of HR Metrics.

The discussion over HR metrics, measuring HRM and its outcomes, and HR data (either big or small) has attracted increased interest lately and "the search for meaningful generic HR metrics is like HRM's Holy Grail" (Tootell, Blackler, Toulson, & Dewe, 2009:375). Indicatively, in a recent systematic literature review report commissioned by CIPD and realized by the University of Leeds and the University of Loughborough, the authors decided to review only papers published after 2005, as "this period saw a considerable growth in the number of publications within the

---

[1] S.M.A.R.T. is an acronym and it stands for Specific, Measurable, Acheivable, Realistic and Time-bound. It is used to describe goals.

https://doi.org/10.1515/9783110633702-044

analytics domain" (CIPD, 2017). Human Resource Metrics are currently considered as a key formative aspect of the HRM profession, according to the proposition of major international HRM professional and accrediting associations (indicatively, the Society of HRM in the US- www.shrm.org, the Chartered Institute of Personnel and Development in the UK- www.cipd.co.uk, the ANSI- the American National Standards Institute- https://www.ansi.org/). For example, SHRM includes HR Metrics in the Required Content Areas for Graduate programs' accreditation, like it does for Compensation and Benefits, Job Analysis and Design, Training and Development, and Workforce Planning and Talent Management (SHRM & AACSB, 2018).

HR Metrics has emerged as a topic first in books and management practitioners' publications and later in academic journals. For example, the now classic "HR Scorecard" (Becker, Huselid, & Ulrich, 2001), the books of Fitz- Entz (Fitz-Entz, 1995, 2009, 2010; Pease, Byerly, & Fitz-Entz, 2013) and later the books and articles of Bassi (Bassi, 2012; Bassi & McMurrer, 2007) have set the ground. At the same period, articles in practitioners- oriented journals, like the Harvard Business Review have been focusing on HR Metrics- related issues (for example Barber & Strack, 2005; T. Davenport, Harris, & Shapiro, 2010; Fleming, Coffman, & Harter, 2005; Pfeffer & Sutton, 2006). After 2010, the number and variety of books on HR Metrics increased (for example Bassi, 2012; Cascio & Boudreau, 2011; T. H. Davenport, Harris, & Morison, 2010; Phillips & Phillips, 2012; Smith, 2016). Lately, there has been a sharp increase of purely academic publications on HR Metrics. Indicatively, during a search (May 2019) at Web of Science for articles containing either HR Metrics or HR Analytics, the database returned 52 items. From these, only 13 were published before 2014 and 39 were published from 2014 till 2019. To this have notably assisted the recent Special Issues of Journals such as Human Resource Management (Huselid, 2018) and the inauguration of academic journals that bear an HR Metrics-oriented title, such as: Evidence-based HRM: a Global Forum for Empirical Scholarship and Journal of Organizational Effectiveness-People and Performance (both from Emerald).

Finally, it should be noted that the work on HR Metrics is conducted by scientists and is presented in outputs from several management and business disciplines. The largest one is obviously HRM, but a considerable body of research is presented in and focuses on other disciplines. This is most evident in the earliest works on HR Metrics, that drew on Finance (Barber & Strack, 2005), Communication (Smith, 2016) and most notably on Management Information Systems (Mehra, Langer, Bapna, & Gopal, 2014; Tursunbayeva, Di Lauro, & Pagliari, 2018).

SHRM and CIPD currently provide lists of HR Metrics, directions for their computation and benchmarks by sector and job category. However, some metrics dominate the relevant literature. For example, best-known HR metrics are absenteeism (Nandialath, David, Das, & Mohan, 2018), turnover (Diestel, Wegge, & Schmidt, 2014; Schiemann, Seibert, & Blankenship, 2018), gender diversity metrics, such as female- male manager ratio (CIPD, 2017) and ROI on training, for which there has been intense interest since the early 1990's (see for example Davidove & Schroeder, 1992; Purcell, 2000) . Some of the HR metrics have been linked to what is called HR efficiency, and they measure how well the HRM function operates. Examples of HR efficiency metrics are the "cost-per-hire" and the "HR-to-employee ratio". Effectiveness metrics show how effective HRM is in terms of business output. "Sales or innovation per full-time- employee equivalence" are examples of HRM effectiveness metrics. Companies may decide to adopt HR metrics for different purposes, such as evaluating HR strategy's strengths and weaknesses, comparing two or more treatment factors, and highlighting the heterogeneity across segments of the workforce. Moreover, HR metrics may be the input for HR decisions and help HR managers to set target goals for the HR function, measuring their performance and making them accountable.

HR Metrics and e-HRM

The fields of HR Metrics and e-HRM converge in the sense that the provision of HR metrics data, analysis and presentation can only be applied through information systems. In fact, many have attributed the development of the HR metrics field to the advancements of technology in HRIS, e-HRM and ERP systems which have allowed the application of HR metrics in practice. The current challenge in HR Metrics is to move from a purely descriptive function that allows historical and benchmarking comparisons, to a predictive function that will assist in formulating and applying business strategy, allowing HRM to realize the "strategic partner" role (Lawler & Boudreau, 2009). The emerging term "HR Analytics" that in practice currently tends to replace "HR Metrics", puts the emphasis on prediction, while the more traditional, "HR Metrics" encompass both descriptive and predictive data processes. Indeed, evidence from the Sierra-Cedar 2018–2019 HR Systems Survey shows that 40% of large organizations are adopting Enterprise resource planning (ERP) systems and that those systems mainly integrate specific analytical tools for benchmarking (38%), statistical analysis (33%), predictive analytics (26%), sentiment analysis (16%), and machine learning (14%). Therefore, the enhancement of the strategic role of the HR function through ICT can only become reality with effective e-HRM systems and practices. The same source also indicates that data-driven and performance- driven organizations rely on e-HRM to achieve their strategic objectives (Harris & Spencer, 2018). In 2018, almost 58% of organizations in Sierra-Cedar 2018–2019 HR Systems Survey had declared to use their HR Technology to influence workforce business decisions, while 38% use them to inform the business strategy.

If we were to predict how the two fields are going to be connected in the future, the current practice of e-HRM seems to set the tone: lately the large ERP and e-HRM developers and providers, such as SAP and Oracle, have incorporated in their services, especially the cloud- based ones, the possibility for their clients to download aggregate measures and reports for their sector, country, region etc. Traditionally consultants have been providing benchmarking data and reports (a key HR metrics pursuit). Currently, the cloud technology allows for organizations that use the same ERP, to have HR benchmarking data from all other users of the same service. The challenge is for the right metrics to be chosen and the correct calculations to be applied. Therefore e-HRM will need to integrate HR metrics' methodologies. On the other hand, the field e-HRM will also need to document its own performance with the right metrics, so new metrics will need to be developed to assess e-HR's practice, efficiency, effectiveness and effect on business outcomes. Therefore, we predict that the connection between the two functions will become even closer.

Further Readings

Cascio, W., & Boudreau, J. (2011). *Investing in People: Financial Impact of Human Resource Initiatives*. Upper Saddle River, NJ: Pearson Education.

Huselid, M. A. (2018). The science and practice of workforce analytics: Introduction to the HRM special issue. *Human Resource Management*, 57(3),679–684. doi: doi:10.1002/hrm.21916

Phillips, J. J., & Phillips, P. P. (2012). *Proving the Value of HR: How and Why to Measure ROI* (2nd ed.): Society for Human Resource Management.

References

Barber, F., & Strack, R. (2005). The Surprising Economics of a "People Business". *Harvard Business Review, 83*(6), 80–90.

Bassi, L. (2012). *HR Analytics Handbook*. Amsterdam: Reed Business.

Bassi, L., & McMurrer, D. (2007). Maximizing Your Return on People. *Harvard Business Review, 85*(3), 115–123.

Becker, B. E., Huselid, M. A., & Ulrich, D. (2001). *The HR Scorecard: Linking People, Strategy and Performance*. Boston: Harvard Business Review Press.

Cascio, W., & Boudreau, J. (2011). *Investing in People: Financial Impact of Human Resource Initiatives*. Upper Saddle River, NJ: Pearson Education.

CIPD. (2017). Human capital metrics and analytics: assessingthe evidence of the value and impact of people data-Technical Report Retrieved from https://www.cipd.co.uk/Images/human-capital-metrics-and-analytics-assessing-the-evidence_tcm18-22291.pdf

Davenport, T., Harris, J., & Shapiro, J. (2010). Competing on talent analytics. *Harvard Business Review, 88*(10), 52–58.

Davenport, T. H., Harris, J., & Morison, R. (2010). *Analytics at Work: Smarter Decisions, Better Results*: Harvard Business School Publishing.

Davidove, E. A., & Schroeder, P. A. (1992). DEMONSTRATING ROI OF TRAINING. *Training & Development, 46*(8), 70–71.

Diestel, S., Wegge, J., & Schmidt, K.-H. (2014). THE IMPACT OF SOCIAL CONTEXT ON THE RELATIONSHIP BETWEEN INDIVIDUAL JOB SATISFACTION AND ABSENTEEISM: THE ROLES OF DIFFERENT FOCI OF JOB SATISFACTION AND WORK-UNIT ABSENTEEISM. *Academy of Management Journal, 57*(2), 353–382. doi: 10.5465/amj.2010.1087

Fitz-Entz, J. (1995). *How to Measure Human Resources Management*. NY: McGraw-Hill,Inc.

Fitz-Entz, J. (2009). *The ROI of Human Capital: Measuring the economic value of employee performance* (2nd ed.). New York: AMACOM.

Fitz-Entz, J. (2010). *The New HR Analytics: Predicting the Economic Value of your Company's Human Capital Investments*. NY: AMACOM.

Fleming, J. H., Coffman, C., & Harter, J. K. (2005). Manage your human sigma. *Harvard Business Review, 83*(7/8), 106–114.

Harris, S., & Spencer, E. (2018). The Sierra-Cedar 2018–2019 HR Systems Survey White Paper Sierra-Cedar (Ed.) Retrieved from https://www.sierra-cedar.com/wp-content/uploads/sites/12/2019/02/Sierra-Cedar_2018-2019_HRSS_WhitePaper.pdf

Huselid, M. A. (2018). The science and practice of workforce analytics: Introduction to the HRM special issue. *Human Resource Management, 57*(3), 679–684. doi: doi:10.1002/hrm.21916

Lawler, E. E., & Boudreau, J. W. (2009). What makes HR a strategic partner. *People & Strategy, 32*(1), 14–22.

Marr, B. (2012). *Key Performance Indicators: The 75 measures every manager needs to know.* Harlow, UK: Pearson Education.

Mehra, A., Langer, N., Bapna, R., & Gopal, R. (2014). ESTIMATING RETURNS TO TRAINING IN THE KNOWLEDGE ECONOMY: A FIRM-LEVEL ANALYSIS OF SMALL AND MEDIUM ENTERPRISES. *Mis Quarterly, 38*(3), 757–771.

Nandialath, A. M., David, E., Das, D., & Mohan, R. (2018). Modeling the determinants of turnover intentions: a Bayesian approach. *Evidence-Based Hrm-a Global Forum for Empirical Scholarship, 6*(1), 2–24. doi: 10.1108/ebhrm-10-2016-0025

Pease, G., Byerly, B., & Fitz-Entz, J. (2013). *Human Capital Analytics: How to harness the potential of your organization's greatest asset*. Hoboken, NJ: John Wiley & Sons Inc.

Pfeffer, J., & Sutton, R. I. (2006). Evidence-based management. *Harvard Business Review, 84*(1), 62–74.

Phillips, J. J., & Phillips, P. P. (2012). *Proving the Value of HR: How and Why to Measure ROI* (2nd ed.): Society for Human Resource Management.

Purcell, A. (2000). 20/20 ROI. *Training & Development, 54* (7),28-+.

Schiemann, W. A., Seibert, J. H., & Blankenship, M. H. (2018). Putting human capital analytics to work: Predicting and driving business success. *Human Resource Management, 57*(3), 795–807. doi: doi:10.1002/hrm.21843

SHRM, & AACSB. (2018). SHRM Human Resource Curiculum. Retrieved from https://www.shrm.org/certification/for-organizations/academic-alignment/Documents/2019%20Curriculum%20Guidebook%20Update_FNL.pdf

Smith, K. (2016). How to Measure Share of Voice: PPC, SEO and Social Media. Retrieved from https://www.brandwatch.com/blog/ website: https://www.brandwatch.com/blog/how-to-measure-share-of-voice/

Tootell, B., Blackler, M., Toulson, P., & Dewe, P. (2009). Metrics: HRM's Holy Grail? A New Zealand case study. *Human Resource Management Journal, 19*(4), 375–392. doi: 10.1111/j.1748-8583.2009.00108.x

Tursunbayeva, A., Di Lauro, S., & Pagliari, C. (2018). People analytics-A scoping review of conceptual boundaries and value propositions. *International Journal of Information Management, 43*, 224–247. doi: 10.1016/j.ijinfomgt.2018.08.002

Miguel R. Olivas-Luján
Blockchains in HRM

Blockchains, also known as "distributed ledger technologies" (DLTs) are an innovation that many expect will transform the business environment in the decade of the 2020s. Blockchains are a specific type of database, with functionality and properties that made it the ideal application for cryptocurrencies (e.g., Bitcoin, Ethereum, Dash, etc.) but is now being used in supply chains, cross-border payments and other applications (cfr., https://www.ibm.com/blockchain/solutions). For e-HRM, there is a tangible possibility of improving Human Resource Management (HRM) processes that include, but are not limited to educational and credential verification, employment screening, worker payments, and automated contracts. The need for HRM and information technology professionals and researchers to understand the main properties, advantages, and limitations of blockchains is increasingly apparent; this may help companies allocate resources (e.g., managerial time, personnel, budgets) in an evidence-informed manner. Their stakeholders, including employees, suppliers, stockholders, and others, might also benefit from an early adoption of this technology, if done adequately.

Nevertheless, at the time of this writing, very few blockchain applications seem to have a strong potential for adoption; credential verification, incident filing, and identity registries are among the ones that might be able to reach the proverbial "tipping point." This entry's focus is on this emerging, digital technology's HRM applications.

Background

Blockchains will remain linked to cryptocurrencies like Bitcoin, Ethereum, and hundreds of other electronic or "crypto" currencies. The notion of a currency that was not issued by a central government, but by a consensus of stakeholders was a thought experiment that was not implemented until 2009, inspired by "Satoshi Nakamoto's" white paper (2008). Many believe that Nakamoto is not an actual person, but a pseudonym for the inventors of Bitcoin (Cheah & Fry, 2015). The white paper proposed a procedure to automate a consensus-driven electronic ledger that would eventually become known as a "blockchain". From a technical perspective, the emergence of cryptocurrencies brought along possibilities that resemble the early days of "creative destruction" of the Internet, but within financial and other trust-based industries like banking, certified supply chains, or land registries.

The early days of the Internet (mid- to late 1990s) saw the emergence of free email (e.g., Hotmail, Yahoo! Mail), e-retailers (e.g., amazon, e-bay), Internet news outlets

https://doi.org/10.1515/9783110633702-045

(e.g., the Drudge Report, HuffPost), and many other services that successfully did away with or drastically disrupted traditional intermediaries like postal services, bookstores, and newspapers, but banks, insurers, and other organisations that manage money largely remained undisrupted; it could be argued that they even gained efficiencies. Many predicted that, in the 2010s, cryptocurrencies and other blockchain applications would similarly do away with intermediaries such as banks and other institutions (e.g., land or property registers) whose main value proposition is to legitimise service trans-actions, but those predictions have not become a reality.

Blockchains

At the end of the day, a blockchain is a particular type of database, more similar to a matrix or a spreadsheet than to a relational database (which is a more efficient type of database in which tables or matrices are stored and retrieved based upon relations among the items stored). What makes a blockchain different is that it can-not be altered retroactively; once a record is added, it will not be deleted or changed, because multiple copies exist in a network of computers that works through cryptographically-secured consensus. Technical and other details on the specific way blockchains realise these properties, as well as associated limitations can be found in Olivas-Luján (2020). For example, the benefit that records recog-nised by a blockchain cannot be modified is qualified by the fact that transactions in the Bitcoin blockchain might take thirty to sixty minutes to be confirmed. The Bitcoin Wiki (https://en.bitcoin.it) is another useful source of technical and histori-cal information that can help readers interested in more information about this emerging and evolving technology.

Blockchains in Human Resource Management

In this entry, the central issue is whether and how might blockchains be used in e-HRM. Databases are a core component of most technologies used within each and every sub-function of e-HRM. Job descriptions, analyses and designs are stored both for internal, organisational use (e.g., to advertise or evaluate jobs) and for ex-ternal use (e.g., to justify pay differentials to applicants or to regulating agencies). In e-recruiting, applicants' information needs to be collected to identify candidates and assess their potential fit with the company needs. In e-training, employees' competencies and developmental activities are gathered to increase the likelihood that the tasks are performed at desired performance levels. For e-performance, eval-uations on each employee's accomplishments and progress stages have to be re-corded periodically, in order to affect e-compensation and e-benefit decisions. Even international HR processes, such as management of expatriates or of non-native employees demand the use of databases to store and utilise legal and other important information with reliability, accuracy, and in a timely fashion.

Credential Verification

Reliability is the characteristic that blockchains excel at; as stated above, once a record is added, it cannot be changed or deleted. For this reason, authentication of educational (or other) credentials seems to be one type of applications that could be successfully adopted within e-recruiting. As early as 2017, the Massachusetts Institute of Technology (MIT) began using DLTs as an option for some of its graduates to receive their diplomas (Levine, 2017). Other institutions of higher learning, including the University of Melbourne, EM Lyon Business School, IAE Nantes Économie & Management, Université Paris Descartes, and Financial University in Moscow, Russia are offering blockchained diplomas too (Olivas-Luján, 2020). It is not a stretch to anticipate that other qualifications (e.g., HR certifications, diplomas or competencies in financial, accounting, medical, and other areas) at any educational levels may benefit individuals and organizations through the immutability offered by blockchains.

Incident Filing

Incident logging or filing is another potential HRM application that might benefit from such immutability. HRM and other departments in many organizations already use online logging or filing of incidents with potential liability. For example, the states of California and New York, in addition to many universities and even private firms, have whistle-blowing web forms enabled with the aim of documenting harassment or other illegal behaviours. Biron (2019) reports that Chinese users of social media apps like Weibo and WeChat have reported incidents of censorship anonymously on the Ethereum blockchain. She also described two blockchain-based applications where users can log sexual harassment reports, Vaultplatform.com and Ciaspora, which was designed to log sexual harassment in university campuses.

The sensitive nature of these reports creates implementation challenges for such applications, however. While immutability may be a desirable property of a report, as it would increase a victim's or a whistle-blower's credibility, privacy was not a high priority in the original blockchain design; transparency was, with the aim of keeping cryptocurrency balances easily computable. Filing a blockchained report that identifies a suspect could unfairly damage an individual's reputation even if the author could remain anonymous. Cryptographic techniques can be used to ensure that the content of the report is legible only to the parties that need to see its content, but this requires levels of complexity that were not part of the original DLT design, and might violate privacy regulations like the General Data Protection Regulation (GDPR) or the right to erasure or be forgotten (ICO, n.d.).

Identity Registries

Identity registries have also been highlighted as a high potential blockchain-based application with implications for HRM, though their use might be even more important in the least developed countries or areas of the world where civil registration systems do not cover all (or even most) of their citizens. UNICEF (2017) estimates that about 25% of the global population of children under five have never been registered; without a birth certificate, they might have a hard time entering the labour market, secure recognition before the law, vote, obtain a passport, etc. Blockchain-based Tykn (https://tykn.tech) is a supplier of identity and access management systems that is addressing this problem, as well as those related to records destroyed by wars or other hazards of paper-based civil registries. This organization was in fact cofounded by Tey Al-Rjula, a Kuwait émigré and blockchain specialist whom, lacking documents to prove his identity to the Dutch government, was forced to move between five refugee camps for two years (https://tykn.tech/about/).

Another e-HRM application sample or "proof of concept" is sponsored by IBM. Among its blockchain initiatives, IBM offers identity management solutions, including a demo (https://youtu.be/cz-6BldajiA) that credits work on "verifiable organisations" performed by the government of British Columbia in Canada). Both job applications and employment verification are central parts of this demo.

Into the Future

Only a few blockchain applications of e-HRM have so far been identified as promising. The advantages of an immutable database might be insufficient to justify the costs of a slower and less efficient database than a conventional one, simply housed by a well-designed organization. Still, e-HRM researchers should be able to address knowledge gaps in sub-function applications and their implications for all important stakeholders, such as employees, employers, and others. To illustrate, in the nascent field of macro talent management which deals with country-level programs and actions intended to attract, develop, retain, and mobilise top talent to nurture competitive advantage (Sparrow, Vaiman, Schuler, & Collings, 2019), might well-coordinated identity registries be a way for governments and non-governmental organizations to benefit their societies by attracting and retaining the best talent?

Great Thinkers in this Field

As DLTs are a technology that was used in the field of finance, cryptocurrency to be more precise, more than great "thinkers" we should probably identify great "implementers." The most notorious is probably Satoshi Nakamoto, referred to above. Vitaly (Vitalik) Buterin is another well-known name for blockchain enthusiasts, as he is one of the most vocal designers and co-founders of Ethereum, the blockchain for "smart contracts" and similar enhancements. Finally, Don Tapscott, a well-known author of technology trade books and Adjunct Professor of the University of Toronto, has been using his considerable intellectual and social capital to galvanise interest in blockchain applications through the Blockchain Research Institute (BRI; https://www.blockchainresearchinstitute.org/).

Further Readings

Landers, R.N., & Collmus, A.B. (2018). Crash Course in I-O Technology: A Crash Course in Blockchain. *TIP: The Industrial-Organizational Psychologist*, *55*(4), 1–7.

Nakamoto, S. (2008). Bitcoin: A Peer-To-Peer Electronic Cash System. Accessed online, https://bitcoin.org/bitcoin.pdf, July 15, 2019.

Olivas-Luján, M.R. (2020). Blockchains 2019 in e-HRM: Hit or Hype? In Bissola, R. & Imperatori, B. (Eds.), *HRM 4.0 for Human-Centered Organizations*. Bingley, UK: Emerald Group Publishing, Ltd.

References

Biron, B. (2019). How Blockchain Can Help Fight Harassment in the Workplace. *Breaker Magazine*. Accessed online, https://breakermag.com/how-blockchain-can-help-fight-harassment-in-the-workplace/, July 23, 2019.

Cheah, E-T. & Fry, J. (2015). Speculative Bubbles in Bitcoin Markets? An empirical investigation into the Fundamental Value of Bitcoin. *Economic Letters*, *130*, 32–36.

ICO (Information Commissioner's Office). (n.d.). Right to Erasure. Accessed online: https://ico.org.uk/for-organisations/guide-to-data-protection/guide-to-the-general-data-protection-regulation-gdpr/individual-rights/right-to-erasure/, July 24, 2019.

Levine, M. (2017). Are Blockchain Diplomas the Real Deal? *Bloomberg.com*. Accessed online: https://www.bloomberg.com/view/articles/2017-10-22/are-blockchain-diplomas-the-real-deal, July 20, 2019.

Nakamoto, S. (2008). Bitcoin: A Peer-To-Peer Electronic Cash System. Accessed online, https://bit coin.org/bitcoin.pdf, June 15, 2019.

Smith + Crown (2019). Blockchain Tech Series: Ethereum, EOS, and Hyperledger. Accessed online, https://www.smithandcrown.com/blockchain-technology-memo/, May 17, 2019.

Sparrow, P., Vaiman, V., Schuler, R.S., & Collings, D.G. (2019). Introduction: Macro Talent Management in Developed Markets: Foundations for a Developing Field. In *Macro Talent Management: A Global Perspective on Managing Talent in Developed Markets* (1st ed., Vol. 1, pp. 1–16). NY: Routledge.

UNICEF (2017). Birth Registration. Accessed online, https://data.unicef.org/topic/child-protection /birth-registration/, July 20, 2019.

Authors

Elena Auer (MS, I-O Psychology, Old Dominion Univ.) is an Industrial-Organizational Psychology doctoral student at the University of Minnesota. Her research interests include the use of innovative technology in employee selection and methodology.
Email: auer0027@umn.edu

Valentina Battista is Lecturer in Human Resource Management at Cranfield School of Management, UK. Valentina's research focuses on the impact of emerging technologies on people management and organisational performance.
Email: v.battista@cranfield.ac.uk

Rita Bissola is associate professor of Organization Design and Organizational Behavior at the Department of Economic and Business Management Sciences, Università Cattolica del Sacro Cuore, Milan, Italy. Her research interests focus on innovation and HRM challenges, individual and team creativity, and employee engagement.
Email: rita.bissola@unicatt.it
Web page: https://docenti.unicatt.it

Tanya Bondarouk is Professor of HRM and technology at the University of Twente, Netherlands. She is the head of the HRM department.
Email: t.bondarouk@utwente.n
Web page: https://www.utwente.nl/en/bms/hrm/staf/bondarouk/l

Anthony S. Boyce, PhD, is principal research scientist at Amazon.com where he helps set and execute global talent assessment strategy to support the continued growth of Amazon's workforce.
Email: anthonyboyce@gmail.com
Web page: https://www.linkedin.com/in/anthonyboyce/

https://doi.org/10.1515/9783110633702-046

Christine E. Boyce is Vice President and Principal Consultant for Right Management, and Director of the ManpowerGroup Global Assessment Center of Excellence. She has over 15 years of experience as a talent assessment expert.
Email: christine.boyce@right.com
Web page: https://www.linkedin.com/in/christinecorbetboyce/

Thomas Calvard is Senior Lecturer in Organisation Studies at the University of Edinburgh Business School. His research focuses on how organisations and actors make sense of social perspectives, viewpoints, limits and boundaries, with an emphasis on identity, diversity, technology and ethics.
Email: Thomas.calvard@ed.ac.uk
Web page: https://www.business-school.ed.ac.uk/staff/thomas-calvard

Julio C. Canedo (Ph.D., University of Texas, San Antonio) is Assistant Professor at the Marilyn Davies College of Business of the University of Houston Downtown. He is certified in coaching, human resource management (HRM), and ethics. His research interests include HRM, e-HRM, strategic HRM, leadership, and cross-cultural issues at work.
Email: canedosotoj@uhd.edu
Web page: https://www.uhd.edu/academics/business/faculty/Pages/bio-Julio-Canedo.aspx

John L. Cotton is Professor and Faculty Director of the EMBA Program at Marquette University. He received his Ph.D. from the University of Iowa, and has taught there, Iowa State University, Purdue University, and Marquette.
Email: John.cotton@marquette.edu
Web page: https://www.marquette.edu/business/directory/john-cotton.php

Stefan V. Dumlao is a doctoral student studying industrial-organizational psychology at Texas A&M University, College Station. His primary research interests are employee reactions to wearable monitors and occupational safety.
Email: sdumlao@tamu.edu
Web page: http://people.tamu.edu/~sdumlao/

Regan Eggli is a first-year Master of Human Resources (MHR) student at USU, where she previously graduated with a B.A. in Psychology. She was awarded the 2019 USU Robins Awards Woman of the Year.
Email: reggli96@gmail.com
Web page: www.linkedin.com/in/regan-eggli/

Sandra L. Fisher recently joined the School of Business at FH Münster in Münster, Germany as a senior research fellow and lecturer. She was formerly an Associate Professor at Clarkson University, Potsdam NY, USA. Her research interests include the use of technology in HR practices, contingent and non-standard forms of work, and learner control.
Email: sandy.fisher@fh-muenster.de

Eleanna Galanaki is Assistant Professor of Organizational Behavior at the Athens University of Economics & Business. Her current research interests include management information systems, organizational culture and HR Metrics.
Email: eleanna@aueb.gr
Web page: https://www.aueb.gr/en/faculty_page/galanaki-anna-eleni

Jamie A. Gruman is Full Professor and Senior Research Fellow in the Gordon S. Lang School of Business and Economics at the University of Guelph, in Canada. His current research interests include organizational socialization, and positive organizational psychology.
Email: jgruman@uoguelph.ca
Web page: https://www.uoguelph.ca/lang/people/jamie-gruman

Christopher J. Hartwell is Assistant Professor in the Management Department at Utah State University (USU) and a human resource management consultant. He received his Ph.D. from Purdue University.
Email: chris.hartwell@usu.edu
Web page: www.chrishartwell.com

Guido Hertel is Professor of Organizational and Business Psychology at the University of Münster, Germany. In his research, he addresses emerging trends and challenges in work organizations, among them digitization of work, demographic changes and migration, and synergy effects in cooperation and negotiations.
Email: ghertel@wwu.de
Web page: ttps://www.uni-muenster.de/OWMS/ueber-uns/mitarbeiter/guido-hertel.html

Miriam Höddinghaus is a doctoral student in the department for Organizational and Business Psychology at the University of Münster, Germany. Her research deals with collaboration and leadership in the digital age.
Email: Miriam.hoeddinghaus@uni-muenster.de
Web page: https://www.uni-muenster.de/OWMS/ueber-uns/mitarbeiter/miriam-hoeddinghaus.html

Anna B. Holm, PhD, is Associate Professor of Management at Aarhus University, and has conducted and published research on e-HRM, employment relations, e-recruitment, e-selection and virtual organizing.
Email: annah@mgmt.au.dk
Web page: http://pure.au.dk/portal/en/annah@mgmt.au.dk.dk/portal/en/annah@mgmt.au.dk

Barbara Imperatori is full professor of Organization Design and HR Management at the Department of Economic and Business Management Sciences, Università Cattolica del Sacro Cuore, Milan, Italy where she is the director of the Master programme in International Human Resource Management. She received her Ph.D. Degree in Management and Business Administration at Bocconi University. Her research interests are innovation and work arrangements; e-HRM systems and employees' perceptions; team creativity, organizational learning and design; employee engagement.
Email: barbara.imperatori@unicatt.it
Web page: https://docenti.unicatt.it/ppd2/it/#/it/docenti/17012/bar bara-imperatori/profilo

Debora Jeske is a work psychologist in Berlin, Germany. She has a PhD in Industrial-Organizational Psychology (USA, 2011) and worked as a researcher and lecturer in work and organisational psychology, computer security and HRM in the UK and Republic of Ireland. Her research focuses on how technology is implemented at work.
Email: adminapsych@ucc.ie
Web page: https://www.ucc.ie/en/apsych/

Richard D. Johnson, PhD, University of Maryland, is Associate Professor at the University at Albany, SUNY. His research focuses on information technology, human resources, and e-learning.
Email: rjohnson@albany.edu

Surinder Kahai is Associate Professor and a Fellow at the Center for Leadership Studies at Binghamton University, State University of New York (SUNY). He has a program of research that spans over 25 years and attempts to understand how information and communication technologies mediate leadership, collaborative work, and learning.
Email: kahai@binghamton.edu
Web page: https://www.binghamton.edu/som/research/profile.html?id=kahai

Richard Landers is Associate Professor of Psychology at the University of Minnesota and holds the John P. Campbell Distinguished Professorship of Industrial-Organizational Psychology.
Email: rlanders@umn.edu
Web page: https://rlanders.net/

Alessandra Lazazzara is Assistant Professor of Organization and Human Resource Management at the University of Milan. Her research interests focus on job crafting, e-HRM, and diversity and inclusion.
Email: alessandra.lazazzara@unimi.it
Web page: https://www.researchgate.net/profile/Alessandra_Lazazzara

Sergio Madero-Gómez is Research Professor in School of Business at Tecnologico de Monterrey, campus Monterrey (México) who deals with Human Resources Management, Rewards systems, Workplace environment, Latin American studies.
Email: smadero@tec.mx

Sebastian Marin is a doctoral student in the Industrial-Organizational Psychology program at the University of Minnesota. He researches employee motivation, gamification, modern prediction methods, and research methods.
Email: marin343@umn.edu
Web page: https://rlanders.net/researchers/sebastian-marin/

Janet H. Marler, PhD., is Professor of Management at the School of Business at University at Albany-State University of New York. Her research focuses on the strategic use of HR technology and HR analytics, strategic compensation, and alternative employment arrangements.
Email: jmarler@albany.edu
Web page: https://www.albany.edu/business/Janet_H_Marler.php

Sarah M. Meeßen is a doctoral candidate in the department for Organizational and Business Psychology at the University of Münster, Germany. Her research deals with trust in information systems and technology at work.
Email: sarah.meessen@uni-muenster.de
Web page: https://www.uni-muenster.de/OWMS/ueber-uns/mitarbeiter/sarah-meessen.html

Jeroen Meijerink, PhD, is Assistant Professor of Human Resource Management (HRM) at the University of Twente (The Netherlands). His research activities focus on HRM and value creation in the digital economy.
Email: j.g.meijerink@utwente.nl
Web page: https://people.utwente.nl/j.g.meijerink

Anjelica M. Mendoza is a Texas A&M University Industrial-Organizational Psychology doctoral student. She is interested in examining the interactions between technology, law, and performance management.
Email: amm19@tamu.edu
Web page: https://liberalarts.tamu.edu/psychology/profile/anjelica-mendoza/

Andrea R. Neely is Assistant Professor at the Gary W. Rollins College of Business at the University of Tennessee at Chattanooga. She received her Ph.D. from the University of Texas at San Antonio. Her current research interests include social exchange (including e-mentoring), workplace deviance, and management education.
Email: Andrea-neely@utc.edu
Web page: https://www.utc.edu/college-business/profiles/management/hdj717.php

Sladjana Nørskov, PhD, is Associate Professor at Aarhus University, Denmark. Her research focuses on organizational behaviour, innovation management and social robotics.
Email: norskov@btech.au.dk
Web page: https://pure.au.dk/portal/en/norskov@btech.au.dk

Miguel R. Olivas-Luján is Professor at Clarion U. of Pennsylvania. Past Chair for MED of the AOM, his research includes ITCs, Diversity, and related. Senior editor for *Advanced Series in Management*, serves in various editorial boards.
Email: molivas@clarion.edu
Web page: www.drolivas.org

Emma Parry is Professor of Human Resource Management and Head of the Changing World of Work Group at Cranfield School of Management. Her interests focus on the impact of the changing external context on managing people.
Email: emma.parry@cranfield.ac.uk
Web page: https://www.cranfield.ac.uk/som/people/professor-emma-parry-1335315

Stephanie C. Payne is Professor of Psychology at Texas A&M University. In addition to her research interests in performance evaluation and management, she also studies individual differences and workplace safety.
Email: scp@tamu.edu
Web page: https://liberalarts.tamu.edu/psychology/profile/stephanie-c-payne/

Hilla Peretz is a senior faculty member in ORT Braude College, Israel. Her research concerns international human resource management, particularly comparative study and cross culture aspects.
Email: hillap@braude.ac.il
Web page: http://www.braude.ac.il/faculty/hilla_peretz.aspx

Huub Ruël is professor of global talent management and international business at Hotelschool The Hague (The Netherlands). His research focuses on technology-enabled global talent management and international business diplomacy in the hospitality industry.
Email: h.ruel@hotelschool.nl

Alan M. Saks is Professor of Human Resources Management and Organizational Behavior in the Centre of Industrial Relations and Human Resources at the University of Toronto. His main areas of research include recruitment, job search, transfer of training, employee engagement, and the socialization and on-boarding of new employees.
Email: saks@utsc.utoronto.ca
Web page: https://www.cirhr.utoronto.ca/people/directories/all-faculty/alan-saks

Christine Scheu is U.S. Assessment Practice Leader at Lee Hecht Harrison. Christine has over 18 years of consulting experience in the areas of selection, training, leadership, competency modelling, and survey design.
Email: christine.scheu@lhh.com
Web page: https://www.linkedin.com/in/christinescheu/

Daniel Shore is an organizational researcher/consultant who specializes in cybersecurity team effectiveness and founded Strategies for Effective Teamwork LLC, a teamwork training company.
Email: Daniel@EffectiveTeam.work
Website: www.EffectiveTeam.work

Stefan Strohmeier is Professor for Management Information Systems and Head of the Chair of Management Information Systems at Saarland University, Germany. He researches, teaches and consults in the area of digital HR technologies and digital HRM, where he is one of the pioneers and well-recognized researchers of the field.
Email: s.strohmeier@mis.uni-saarland.de
Web page: www.mis.uni-saarland.de

John P. Ulhøi is Professor of OMT at Aarhus University. His areas of expertise include: organization and management theory, organization behaviour, strategy and business development, technology and innovation management.
Email: jpu@mgmt.au.dk
Web page: http://pure.au.dk/portal/en/jpu@mgmt.au.dk

Michael Wasserman, PhD, is Professor of International Management at FH Münster in Münster, Germany. His research interests include the integration of technology and human capital into business strategy and the linkages among managerial thinking, technology, and firm performance.
Email: wasserman@fh-muenster.de

Sharna Wiblen is Lecturer (Assistant Professor) in Management at the Sydney Business School, University of Wollongong, working at the intersection of Talent Management, Information Technologies and HR Analytics.
Email: swiblen@uow.edu.au
Web page: www.talkabouttalent.com

Yusliza Mohd Yusoff is Associate Professor of Organisational Behaviour and Human Resource Management at Universiti Malaysia Terengganu.
Email: yusliza@umt.edu.my
Web page: https://yuslizamohdyusoff.wordpress.com

List of Tables

https://doi.org/10.1515/9783110633702-047

List of Figures

https://doi.org/10.1515/9783110633702-048

Index

https://doi.org/10.1515/9783110633702-049

www.ingramcontent.com/pod-product-compliance
Lightning Source LLC
Chambersburg PA
CBHW061801210326
41599CB00034B/6841